Volume One: To 1877

A HISTORY OF THE
AMERICAN PEOPLE

Volume One: To 1877

A HISTORY OF THE AMERICAN PEOPLE

STEPHAN THERNSTROM
Harvard University

HARCOURT BRACE JOVANOVICH, PUBLISHERS

San Diego   New York   Chicago   Atlanta   Washington, D.C.
London   Sydney   Toronto

Illustration Credits

Cover: The National Archives

Maps and graphs: Evanell Towne

Pictures: Part One, 3, 37, 61 (top), 107, 127, 331, Library of Congress; 18, Colonial Williamsburg Photograph; 61 (bottom), National Maritime Museum, London; 81, Quaker Collection, Haverford College Library, Haverford, PA 19041; 148, 151, Courtesy of the New-York Historical Society; 181, Brown Brothers; 205, 233, 257, 359, HBJ Collection; 279, White House Collection; 303 Culver Pictures.

ISBN: 0-15-536530-4
Library of Congress Catalog Number: 83-081524
Printed in the United States of America

To Melanie and Sam

Preface

After taking an examination in American colonial history as a graduate student at Johns Hopkins University in 1884, Woodrow Wilson wrote in disgust that he went into it "crammed with one or two hundred dates and one or two thousand minute particulars of the quarrels of nobody knows who with an obscure governor for nobody knows what. Just think of all that energy wasted! The only comfort is that this mass of information won't long burden me. I shall forget it with great ease." History presented as an endless string of names and dates, battles and treaties, can be excruciatingly boring, and it is natural to wonder about the point of studying it.

In writing this book, I have been mindful of Wilson's complaint. Inevitably this book includes a good many names, dates, and descriptions of key historical actors and events—but only those details I consider truly important to the beginning student. An American history without George Washington, Abraham Lincoln, or Woodrow Wilson would be like a *Hamlet* without the Prince of Denmark. Chester A. Arthur, though, can safely be left out of the main story, although he occupied the White House from 1881 to 1885. So too can chief executives whose administrations were uneventful, obscure bills, treaties, battles, and scandals that authors of textbooks customarily feel obliged to cover because all the other texts include them.

Too many details overwhelm the reader. A textbook can also be boring not just from an excess of facts but from a lack of a strong connective tissue of *ideas* to give those facts meaning. History is not "one damned thing after another"—X happened, then Y happened, then Z happened. History examines the relationship between X, Y, and Z, and explores how one led to the next. A description of five acts passed by Congress in 1863 will not interest anyone unless he or she is prodded to think about why the measures passed when they did and what their consequences were. The historian must be analytical, asking not only what happened but how and why it happened in that sequence and what difference it made. The descriptive passages in this volume serve a purpose too. They provide the necessary raw material to make the "how" and "why" questions comprehensible. Asking why things turned out as they did and not some other way is always central to this book's purpose.

Like most historians today, I believe that history is more than past politics. Therefore, the central focus of this book is not on political life, although major political developments are indeed treated. I think the central question to ask about American history is: Who are the American people and how did they come to be that way in the nearly four centuries that have elapsed since the first British settlement at Jamestown in 1607? Scholarly inquiry in such new fields as urban, ethnic, family, and women's history has shed much new light on that overarching issue in recent years. Studies of life at the "grassroots" now tell us far more about the millions of anonymous Americans in the past than we knew before. I have drawn upon this recent literature, as well as upon still valuable older studies, to fashion a fresh overview of the contours of American history.

I hope then that readers will take from this book something more meaningful than what Woodrow Wilson claimed from his study of colonial history. If I have succeeded in my aim, readers will gain a greater measure of self-understanding and a stronger sense of connection with their ancestors, a new feeling for what Abraham Lincoln called "the mystic chords of memory" that tie successive generations of Americans together. Another of our greatest presidents, Franklin D. Roosevelt, spoke of why our history matters:

> A nation must believe in three things. It must believe in the past. It must believe in the future. It must, above all, believe in the capacity of its people so to learn from the past that they can gain in judgment for the creation of the future.

I am grateful to the following historians who reviewed portions of the manuscript in its various drafts: Barton J. Berstein, Stanford University; John Morton Blum, Yale University; A.M. Burns, University of Florida; Maurice A. Crouse, Memphis State University; Jack Diggins, University of California at Irvine; Michael Frisch, State University of New York at Buffalo; Sheldon Hackney, Princeton University; Donald W. Hensel, California Polytechnic State University; Stanley N. Katz, Princeton University; Dr. Myron A. Marty, formerly at Florissant Valley Community College, now with the National Endowment for the Humanities; John M. Murrin, Princeton University; Nell Irvin Painter, University of North Carolina, Chapel Hill; James T. Patterson, Brown University; Raymond Robinson, Northeastern University; Laurence Veysey, University of California at Santa Cruz; and Daniel J. Walkowitz, New York University.

Contents

Index   I-1

Volume One: To 1877

A HISTORY OF THE
AMERICAN PEOPLE

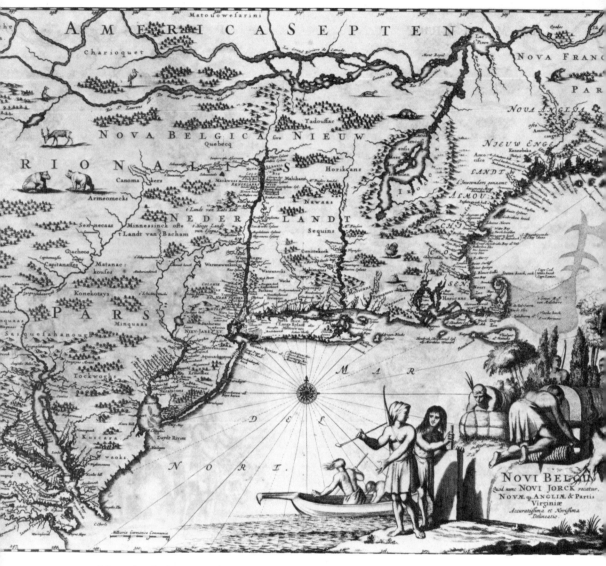

Mapmaker Ogilby's 1671 depiction of "Novi Belgii" revealed the east coast of America from Maine to just south of Chesapeake Bay, including areas inhabited by various Indian tribes along with more standard topographical features.

Part One

*The Peopling of America:
Founding the Colonies*

Chapter One

The European Invasion

Half an hour before sunrise on August 3, 1492, the *Pinta*, the *Nina*, and the *Santa Maria* slipped their moorings in the harbor at Palos, Spain and headed out into the open Atlantic. Christopher Columbus, their commander, had begun his daring quest to reach the Orient by a new route—by sailing westward around the globe. On October 12, with the fearful crew on the verge of mutiny, he spied land. It was not Asia, though, but the Bahamas. Columbus had not discovered a new route to the Orient; he had discovered a "new world."

Most of us learned the tale in childhood. The factual details are correct, but the new world myth is a European invention that obscures a crucial truth. Columbus did not really find a new world, only a world new to Europeans. The Western Hemisphere was not virgin soil 500 years ago. Many millions of people already lived there—the native peoples Columbus called "Indians" out of the delusion that he had reached Asia. Columbus established contact between two worlds already old, thereby opening the way for a great invasion that transplanted Western European civilization on new territory. To exploit the rich resources of the western hemisphere, aggressive European newcomers conquered the original inhabitants and lived off their labor. Late in the fifteenth century, Europe gained mastery over the oceans of the world and created a new Europe-centered global economy. The invasion of America, a key step in the process, was made possible because inventive and ambitious Europeans had no scruples about using their newly developed sources of power to impose their will upon others.

With the aid of an interpreter, Pizarro and DeSoto interrogate South American Indians in this engraving from Debry's America *(1590).*

EUROPE LOOKS OUTWARD

A visitor from another planet touring the world in 1400 to determine which of its societies was most highly developed would have had little reason to single out Western Europe. The civilization of western Christendom in the late Middle Ages was rich and vibrant in certain respects. A visit to the great cathedral of Notre Dame in Paris, or a look at an intricate illuminated manuscript, would doubtless have impressed him. But the Chinese, Persian, and Byzantine empires had made comparable cultural achievements. Nor did Europe enjoy a clear advantage in any other important realm—levels of agricultural and commercial development, scientific and technological know-how, the capacity of the government to preserve order, or the like. A hundred years later, Europe had become distinctly more advanced than other parts of the world in some basic respects, but its superior dynamism was not evident in 1400.

Indeed, western Christendom had previously undergone three centuries of expansion. Between 1000 and 1300, the population more than doubled and the economy flourished. Living standards improved, trade increased, and agriculture became more efficient because of technological advances. New iron ploughs replaced wooden implements, enabling farmers to penetrate the heavy soils of previously unarable land. The introduction of the three-field system of crop rotation increased output per acre. Better harnesses and nailed horseshoes allowed the substitution of more efficient horses for oxen. At the same time, an "urban revolution" was occurring. Cities that had been stagnant since the fall of Rome in the fifth century began to grow in size and wealth and many new towns were established.

Symptomatic of the expansive vitality of Western Europe in this era were the Crusades (1095–1270), great holy wars launched to recapture the holy places of Palestine from the Muslims. Although the crusaders were eventually beaten back, they returned to Europe with new tastes that had important historical consequences. In the Middle East, Europeans first encountered the silks, jewels, and spices of Asia. The most significant of these luxuries—spice—soon was regarded as a necessity in wealthy households. Meat cooked in smoky fireplaces, often in an advanced state of decay, was almost inedible without an ample dose of pepper to disguise the taste. Spices, furthermore, were thought to have aphrodisiac effects. To satisfy the growing European appetite for Asian goods, Middle Eastern merchants organized overland trading routes to the East, using their monopoly to extract enormous profits from their customers. To a great extent, the discovery of the new world was sparked by the high price of spices. It stimulated European adventurers to search for sea routes to China and India and open up direct trade with them.

Contraction

The first outthrust of Western Europe was not sustained. The failure of the last crusade in 1270 marked the beginnings of a period of decline. Territorial expansion ceased, and soon the frontiers of Christendom began to contract under pressure from Turks on the east and Moors on the west. Three centuries of rapid growth had expanded the population beyond the land's capacity to sustain it. In a rural society like that of medieval Europe, the population can continue to grow only if more land can be brought under cultivation or if existing land can be worked more efficiently. By 1300 neither was happening. All the arable land was already under the plough, and there were no new breakthroughs in agricultural technology to increase yields per acre. A "Malthusian crisis" began. As food prices rose to a level the poorest could not afford, their diets deteriorated; the death rate edged upward.

Then came a crisis of another kind—the Black Death. In 1347, trading caravans from Mongolia reached Europe, bringing in their wake packs of rats infested with fleas carrying the microparasite that causes bubonic plague (now recognized as *Pasteurella pesta*). The plague cut through Europe like a great scythe, killing a third of the population, 25 million people, in a mere six years. Because diseases pass easily from person to person in dense urban quarters, cities, the focal points of social, economic, and cultural development, were much the hardest hit. Many cities lost at least half of their inhabitants; 60 percent of the people of Venice died within 18 months. And the plague did not disappear after its first horrifying outburst. Smaller epidemics recurred for the rest of the century.

The onset of the Black Death initiated a period of general economic and social decline. Production fell and villages were abandoned. A profound pessimism and fatalism appeared in literature and art. "Oh miserable and very sad life," sighed a French poet. "We suffer from warfare, death, and famine; cold and heat, day and night, sap our strength; fleas, scabmites, and so much other vermin make war on us. In short, have mercy, Lord, upon our wicked persons, whose life is very short." It was a time of widespread violence and internal disorder, manifested in the savage Hundred Years War between France and England (1337–1453) and in bloody peasant uprisings like the Jacquerie in France (1357) and Wat Tyler's Revolt in England (1381). Europe was retreating steadily before the advancing Ottoman

---

THE IMPACT OF THE BLACK DEATH

Many men and women abandoned their own city, their houses and their homes, their relatives and belongings as if the wrath of God could not pursue them, but would only oppress them within city walls. They were apparently convinced that no one should remain in the city, and that its last hour had struck. The calamity had instilled such terror in the hearts of men and women that fathers and mothers shunned their children. It had come to pass that men who died were shown no more concern than dead goats today.

—Boccaccio, *The Decameron*

Turks. The Turks blocked the trading routes to the Far East and menaced the European heartland itself. In 1453, Constantinople (Istanbul) fell to the Ottomans, whose armies then penetrated deeply into Greece and the Balkans. Europeans were terrified at the encroachment of these "most inhuman barbarians, the most savage enemies of the Christian faith, the fiercest of wild beasts."

Technological Foundations of European Supremacy

Europe's fears of domination by Islamic invaders proved unfounded. In the latter half of the fifteenth century, Europe made a great leap forward. Its armies developed the strength to push the Turks back. And its navies won supremacy over the oceans, opening a new European-dominated epoch in world history. Portugal and Spain, the leaders, made a remarkable end run around the Turkish blockade by discovering sea routes to the Far East. In the process, they stumbled on the previously unknown lands they came to call "the New World."

After two centuries of regression, Europe entered the period of intellectual, artistic, and scientific flowering we know as the Renaissance. Among the achievements of the Renaissance were revolutionary advances in marine technology and weaponry that made possible the great voyages of discovery and conquest. Mastery of the science of navigation was part of the revolution. Ships capable of sailing across thousands of miles of open ocean had been available long before this. Leif Ericson's Norsemen had crossed the Atlantic around 1000, and the Irish who settled Iceland had probably visited North America before that. It has even been argued, inconclusively, that the feat was accomplished much earlier by the Phoenicians or the Hebrews. But to venture so far from shore without chart or compass took remarkable daring; returning to tell the tale was a matter of luck. The development of astronomical instruments and trigonometrical tables to plot the location of the sun and the stars, charts drawn to scale, and better understanding of wind patterns and ocean currents in fifteenth-century Europe eliminated much of the uncertainty of setting far out to sea.

Dramatic improvements in weaponry and shipbuilding were being made at the same time. Although the Chinese had invented gunpowder centuries earlier, they had failed to put it to effective military use, developing cannons of only the lightest and most ineffectual variety. Chinese society was profoundly conservative, and particularly hostile to military innovation because military pursuits were held in very low esteem. Europeans, by contrast, worked ceaselessly to build ever larger and more powerful guns. By the end of the fifteenth century, they had enormous weapons that could hurl various projectiles through city walls and the hulls of ships.

Such heavy artillery was of somewhat limited use in land warfare, because it was difficult to transport from place to place. That was not a problem at sea, though, and Europeans soon succeeded in building larger and faster sailing ships that could carry dozens of large guns. The naval vessels then in use elsewhere in the world—galleys powered by oars pulled by slaves, which waged war by ramming enemy ships and dispatching boarding parties to engage in hand-to-hand combat—were no match at all for these. The great three-masted European sailing ships that were developed by 1450 had the speed and firepower to destroy a dozen galleys before any of them could come close enough to board.

This was the technological foundation of European military supremacy on the high seas. Replacing oarsmen with sails and providing warriors with guns supplemented limited human energies with inanimate power. The gun-carrying sailing ship represented a new concentration of power against which peoples lacking the new technology had little defense.

The pioneer maritime nation was tiny Portugal. It had no internal frontier for expansion, and faced the open Atlantic. The men of the dynamic trading and shipping community of Lisbon had entrepreneurial vision and the capital to invest in risky ventures. After 1385 Portugal was a united kingdom, largely free of civil strife while most of the rest of Europe was embroiled in war or internal disorders. The son of John I, Prince Henry the Navigator (1394–1460), launched what we would call today a research and development program to find a sea route to the East. He combed Europe for some of its best mathematicians, astronomers, shipbuilders, and navigators and brought them to work at his court. As the Portuguese learned to build better ships and to navigate by the stars, their vessels steadily edged farther into the uncharted waters of the Atlantic. Bartholomew Dias rounded the Cape of Good Hope in 1488, and might have gone on toward India had not a mutinous crew forced him to turn back. Ten years later, Vasco de Gama led the first Portuguese ship to India via the African route.

Columbus

By then, of course, the adventurous son of a Genoese weaver had tested his theory that the Far East could be reached more easily by sailing in the opposite direction and circling the globe. Christopher Columbus (1451–1506) was a zealous visionary with awesome self-confidence. After more than a decade spent searching for a royal sponsor for his expedition, he at last persuaded King Ferdinand and Queen Isabella of Spain to back him. In 1492, he set sail with 90 men, including one who knew Arabic, which was assumed to be very similar to Chinese! Contrary to legend, Columbus was not unique in his belief that the world was round—that was well understood long before. On two other points, his views were more distinctive—and quite mistaken. He underestimated the circumference of the earth by two-sevenths, and he believed that the Asian land mass extended several thousand miles farther to the east than it actually did. These twin errors were responsible for his delusion that he could reach Japan by sailing 2,400 miles west from the Canary Islands.

Until his death in 1506, Columbus continued to insist that he had reached Asia. Other Spanish explorers who followed his route soon realized that they had encountered another continent altogether. In their determination to reach India, they viewed this new land merely as an annoying obstacle to be surmounted, and for a time searched for a water route through which they could sail on to the Far East. Before long, however, it became clear that the New World offered riches of its own—precious resources, and people who could be forced to extract those resources and hand them over.

THE CHRONOLOGY OF DISCOVERY AND CONQUEST

1420	Portuguese occupation of Madeira Islands
1432	Portuguese colonization of the Azores
1462	Portuguese settlement on Cape Verde Islands
1488	Bartholomew Dias (Portugal) rounds Cape of Good Hope
1492	Christopher Columbus (Spain) reaches America
1497	John Cabot (England) explores North American coast
1498	Vasco da Gama (Portugal) reaches India by sea
1500	Pedro Cabral (Portugal) explores Brazil
1513	Vasco Balboa (Spain) crosses Panama to discover the Pacific Ocean
1519–21	Hernando Cortez (Spain) conquers Mexico
1519–22	Ferdinand Magellan (Spain) circumnavigates the globe
1530–32	Francisco Pizarro (Spain) conquers Peru

THE NATIVE PEOPLES

No one knows even approximately how many people were living in the Western Hemisphere when Columbus' ships appeared on the horizon. Some recent scholarly estimates place the figure as high as 100 million, about a third more than the entire population of Europe at the time! That estimate, based on a number of questionable assumptions, is hard to credit.[1] But the most conservative researchers agree on a minimum figure of 14 million, twice the population of Spain and Portugal. America was in no sense an empty land, a trackless forest waiting to be "discovered."

People have been living in the Western Hemisphere for 30,000 to 40,000 years. In a sense, the Indians were immigrants too. There are competing theories as to when and how they came, and little hard evidence on which to choose among them. The most common view is that the first Indians were Asians from the cold and barren plains of Siberia. Some may have crossed the Bering Straits, only 56 miles wide, by raft. Others could have come on foot toward the end of the Ice Age, around 10,000 B.C., when enough ocean water had piled up in mile high glaciers to put the bottom of the Bering Straits above water. These migrants slowly drifted southward through North, Central and South America in search of a hospitable environment. As groups settled in different habitats, many radically different tribal cultures evolved. Overexposure to the stereotypes in Hollywood Westerns makes it difficult for us to grasp the elemental fact that there was no one Indian people, no

---

[1]Colin McEvedy and Richard Jones, *Atlas of World Population History* (1978), Part 4, judiciously review the wildly conflicting estimates. Their skepticism about recent high figures finds further support in Rudolph A. Zambardino, "Mexico's Population in the 16th Century: Demographic Anomaly or Mathematical Illusion?", *The Journal of Interdisciplinary History,* Summer, 1980.

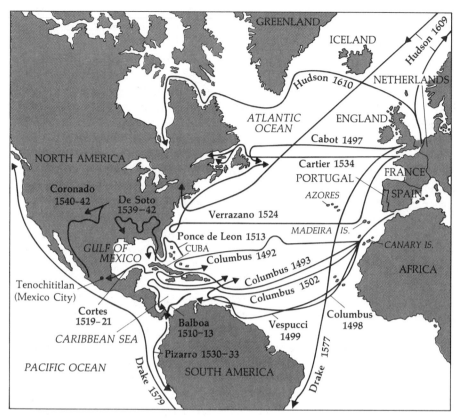

MAP 1-1
Europeans Explore the Americas, 1492–1610

one Indian language, no single Indian way of life. At least 2,000 quite distinct languages were spoken in America when Columbus landed, many as different from each other as Norwegian is from Sanskrit. Cultural differences were equally marked. Some Indians belonged to small roving bands who lived by hunting and gathering wild plants; a few subsisted largely on acorns. The Hopis and Zunis of the Southwest, by contrast, lived in large villages, in gigantic apartmentlike structures, and practiced sophisticated irrigated agriculture. The Iroquois were a confederation of five tribes with 10,000 members, skilled farmers and aggressive warriors who dominated most of the tribes from New York and Pennsylvania to the Great Lakes. The Aztecs in Mexico and the Incas in Peru ruled over empires numbering in the millions; their great capital cities were resplendent with huge temples, pyramids, and elaborate statues. The peoples we lump together as "Indians" differed from each other far more than the Spaniards, Portuguese, English, French, and other European colonists.

The native peoples did have some basic things in common. All lived in organized societies with political structures, moral codes, religious beliefs, and modes of dealing with outsiders. All had made intricate adaptations to the particular environment in which they lived. Mother Earth, the source of their sustenance, had deep religious significance for them. The idea of private ownership of land was foreign; land was held communally and worked collectively.

Two other generalizations may be made about Indian societies on the eve of the European invasion: They lacked advanced technology and immunity to disease.

Even the largest and most complex of the Indian cultures was technologically backward by Western European standards. Aztec and Inca agriculture were at about the level that had developed in the Near East by 2000 B.C., and they supported similar population densities of one to three persons per square kilometer (if the conservative population estimates are correct). They had no ploughs to break the soil, and their largest domesticated animal (except for the Incas' llamas) was the dog. The wheel had been invented, but it was used only as a toy, not as a tool. The Indians lagged particularly far behind Europeans in those forms of technology that may be used to dominate other peoples. None approached European levels of sophistication in the shaping of metal into guns, swords, or tools, and none had gunpowder, sailing ships, or mounted warriors. Their lack of guns, swords, ships, and horses obviously put them at a disadvantage when the Indians encountered invading Europeans.

A second handicap was less obvious, but even more important: Whenever they first encountered Europeans, the native peoples frequently fell ill and died. The invaders regarded this as a sign that God looked favorably upon their cause. The true explanation only became clear centuries later, when modern science developed a sound understanding of the sources of infectious disease. The Indians of America lacked the biological defenses that Europeans possessed. Medieval Europe was disease-ridden, and its population had gradually built up resistances to the most common illnesses. (The Black Death was so devastating because bubonic plague had been unknown in Europe for several hundred years.) But before Columbus, the native American peoples were remarkably free of the major diseases that infected Europeans. Smallpox, typhus, diphtheria, plague, cholera, measles, and influenza all seem to have been unknown. Syphilis may have been indigenous to the Western Hemisphere—scholars are still debating that question—but in other respects the environment was astonishingly healthful. "There was then no sickness," an Indian told a priest after the conquest. "They had no aching bones; they had then no high fever; they had then no consumption; they had then no headache."

This enviable condition, however, became a perilous liability once the germs of the Old World were imported with the first voyages of exploration. It takes several decades for a virgin population to develop natural immunities against new diseases. Until then, even such maladies as measles, mumps, and whooping cough—mild childhood afflictions among peoples accustomed to them—appear in death-dealing epidemic form, and are particularly virulent to young adults. The invisible killers European whites unknowingly introduced into the New World in 1492 were a far more potent weapon than their horses, cannons, and swords.

Other forms of life in the New World, indeed, were vulnerable in the face of competition from the hardier products of the complex European environment. Kentucky bluegrass, dandelions, daisies, and a surprisingly large number of other plants and grasses we think of as characteristically American are not indigenous to the hemisphere but imports—green immigrants. In fact, most of our cultivated flowers, vegetables, fruits, grains, and grasses today, and 70 percent of our weeds, originated from abroad. Part of the explanation, of course, is that invading Europeans introduced and cultivated plants they were accustomed to. But that does not explain why they spread into the wild and displaced native American species. The answer is that forms of plant life were more highly evolved in the more varied European environment, and thus better equipped to come out on top in the struggle for survival.

The Pattern of Conquest

Columbus and his men were warmly welcomed by the first Indian people they met, the Arawaks of San Salvador. In his journal Columbus described them as "generally tall, good looking and well proportioned." After the Spaniards gave the Arawaks presents of red caps and glass beads, Columbus reported, "they were greatly pleased and became so entirely our friends that it was a wonder to see. Afterwards they came swimming to the ship's boats and brought us parrots and cotton threads in balls, and we exchanged them for other things."

The friendly and innocent Arawaks had no idea what was in store for them. Columbus was not there to open up trade on a peaceful and equitable basis, but to conquer and rule over them. It was his right and sacred duty, for he saw them as savage pagans who "had no religion." A few months before the voyage, Pope Alexander VI had granted Spain sovereignty over all parts of the world not already in Christian hands,[2] so that the heathen might "embrace the Catholic faith and be trained in good morals." Ferdinand and Isabella had delegated that authority to Columbus by naming him "High Admiral of the Ocean Seas, and Viceroy and Governor of all the islands and continents" that he might discover. In exchange for receiving the blessings of Christian civilization, Columbus expected the natives to work for their conquerors. He believed the Arawaks would make "good servants"; they seemed to him "fit to be ordered about, made to sow and do aught else that may be needed." He hoped that they could be "delivered and converted to our holy faith rather by love than by force." But he was acutely aware of the power realities. The Arawaks, he observed, "do not bear arms or know them, for I showed them swords and they took them by the blades and cut themselves through ignorance. They are unprotected and so very cowardly that a thousand" would not be a match for three of his men.

The conquest of the Arawaks and other tribes of the Caribbean islands was easy but profitless. Simple societies of the West Indies had no treasures to be looted. The invaders set the natives to work, but they quickly died off. The small and completely isolated island populations were even more vulnerable to the new European diseases than the people of the mainland. Within three quarters of a century, 90 percent of the population had died; before much longer, the Arawak people were extinct.

---

[2] Two years later, in the Treaty of Tordesillas (1494), the Pope modified the grant to do justice to Portugal for its pioneering explorations. The new arrangement gave Spain rights to newly discovered lands west of an imaginary line 370 leagues west of the Cape Verde Islands. Portugal was given everything east of that. This was the basis for the Portuguese seizure of Brazil.

The Aztec and Inca Empires

Not all the peoples of the Western Hemisphere were as defenseless as the Arawaks, the Spanish soon learned. The Aztecs in Mexico and the Incas in Peru ruled over extended empires with formidable armies. They also had something of far more interest to the invaders than anything the poor Arawaks could provide—abundant gold and silver, which they used for ornamental and ceremonial purposes. After Spanish explorations revealed their existence, the great *conquistadores* Hernando Cortez and Francisco Pizarro laid plans to subdue them. Both Cortez and Pizarro had risen in the military from extremely humble origins, and both were driven by the same religious zeal, greed, and lust for fame that moved Columbus. They aimed, said Cortez, to "serve God and his Majesty, to give light to those who were in darkness, and to grow rich as all men desire to do." In 1519 Cortez audaciously led an invading force of only 600 men into Mexico, and in two years routed the troops of the emperor Montezuma and captured his empire. A decade later Pizarro invaded Peru and toppled the Inca empire with an even smaller army.

The numerical odds against the Spanish in these campaigns stagger the imagination. How could they possibly have won? Their military technology was superior, but not that superior. The Spanish swords and primitive muskets were not dramatically more lethal than the bows and arrows and spears of tens of thousands of defending warriors.

The hidden biological advantage of the invaders played a decisive role. The mere arrival of the conquistadores immediately triggered deadly epidemics among the natives and depleted their fighting forces. Early in the war with the Aztecs, Cortez and his men were driven from the Aztec capital of Tenochtitlan, but Montezuma was unable to pursue and wipe them out because smallpox had felled so many of his troops. The conquest of Peru was similarly eased by a raging smallpox epidemic.

Even more important than sheer depletion of the native armies was the profoundly demoralizing appearance that the invaders were magically immune from these maladies. The traditional native gods offered no protection against the afflictions, it seemed, while the god of the Spaniards was powerful enough to leave them untouched. It appeared that the conquerors themselves were gods rather than men. If Europe in 1350, staggering under the impact of the Black Death, had been invaded by Hindus or Muslims who were utterly unaffected by the plague, the emotional effects on the Christian population might have been equally dramatic.

The Imperial System

European diseases continued to take a heavy toll of the native population until almost a century after the conquest, when enough resistances had been built up to arrest the decline. How large the pre-conquest population was and how rapidly it fell thereafter is still under debate, but at least a third died off, as large a proportion as Europe lost to the Black Death, and possibly more. But the peoples of the core areas of advanced agriculture, in the Aztec and Inca empires, did not suffer extinction like the Arawaks and some North American tribes later encountered by the British. They survived, as "servants" to their new rulers.

AN AZTEC VIEW OF THE CONQUISTADORES

They went out to meet the Spaniards . . . in the Eagle Pass. They gave [them] ensigns of gold, and ensigns of quetzel feathers, and golden necklaces. And when they were given these presents, the Spaniards burst into smiles; their eyes shone with pleasure; they were delighted by them. They picked up the gold and fingered it like monkeys; they seemed to be transported by joy, as if their hearts were illumined and made new. The truth is that they longed and lusted for gold. Their bodies swelled with greed, and their hunger was ravenous; they hungered like pigs for that gold.

—A native report collected by a Spanish missionary
[quoted by Miguel Leon-Portilla, *The Broken Spears, p. 511*]

The Spanish government organized its possessions in the Western Hemisphere in two units, the Vice-Royalty of New Spain and the Vice-Royalty of Peru. New Spain had essentially the same boundaries as the Aztec empire, with the capital city of Tenochtitlan renamed Mexico City; Peru was a reorganization of the Inca empire. Outside the two vice-royalties, which included about 80 percent of the Indians of the Americas, the population was too thin and the level of economic development too low to make colonial administration worthwhile. The Church, however, built missions to carry on its religious work over a much wider area, including lands as far north as Florida, Texas, and California.

Unlike the English who came to North America a century later, the Spaniards who crossed the oceans to seek their fortunes did not intend to settle and work the land. Their aim was to become feudal lords, extracting labor from a native peasantry. The first conquerors established the *encomienda* system, a trusteeship which gave them the right to demand taxes and labor from the natives of a specific area. Important leaders claimed holdings embracing dozens and dozens of villages; their lesser followers were given smaller grants.

New Spain and Peru were suitable for the production of many valuable commodities—wool and leather, tobacco, sugar, indigo and cochineal dyes. The conquerors, however, had little interest in such mundane products as long as they could find precious metals. With abundant deposits of gold and silver available, the invaders set natives to work in the mines, driving them with a merciless disregard for health and safety. It was a form of slavery.

The conquistadores were not allowed an absolutely free hand in their dealings with the Indians for long. Both the Crown and the Church (effectively controlled by the monarch, though ultimately responsible to the Pope in Rome) had a strong interest in the empire. On the heels of the conquerors came royal officials and priests. In 1524 the Spanish monarch established the powerful Council of the Indies, which was given full control over every aspect of colonial policy. The council shipped out governors and a host of lesser officials, and exercised continuing close supervision over their activities. All trade between Spain and the New World was restricted to merchants licensed by the Council. The Crown was to receive a one-fifth share of all gold and silver that was found, as well as duties on other imports and exports, and an elaborate bureaucracy was developed to ensure compliance. All important issues were decided at the center, and orders came down from on high. In sharp contrast to the pattern in the later British North American colonies, Spanish colonists were not allowed to establish assemblies or other representative institutions to defend the interests of settlers when they clashed with dictates from Madrid.

An important conflict developed over the treatment of native labor. The conquistadores saw the Indians as little more than beasts of burden, and tried to squeeze as much work as possible from them. The priests, by contrast, viewed them as heathens whose souls could be saved. The Roman Catholic position, as stated by Pope Paul III in 1537, was that "all are capable of receiving the doctrines of the faith," and that "the Indians are truly men." Priests from Spain built mission churches across the land, and won over millions to the new faith. Although they were not uniformly successful, it was one of the most dramatic examples of wholesale cultural change in history. The priesthoods, ceremonies, and ways of life of preconquest times had been crushed by the invaders and the germs they brought with them, and Catholicism filled the void.

Although the missionary priests were primarily concerned with the spiritual rather than the physical well-being of the native peoples, the brutally exploitative *encomienda* system dismayed many of them. Bartoleme de Las Casas and others launched a campaign to persuade the Crown to intervene. Moved by their arguments, and by a practical desire to keep the conquistadores from becoming an entrenched hereditary aristocracy independent of royal control, Emperor Charles V proclaimed the New Laws of the Indies in 1542. The New Laws declared that Indians were "free persons and vassals of the Crown," and could not be enslaved. They barred further *encomienda* grants, and dissolved all existing ones upon the death of the recipient, guaranteeing that the system would die out within a generation. Severe punishments for mistreatment of natives were provided.

The freedom of the Indians, however, was severely circumscribed by the system that was introduced to replace the *encomiendas—repartimiento*. Natives could no longer be forced to work by individual settlers, but colonial magistrates were authorized to require each village to supply a certain proportion of its male population for a certain number of weeks, in rotation throughout the year. They were allocated to public service jobs or to private employers, and were paid a token wage. They wage was much too low to live on, so that natives were compelled to devote the time they were not drafted by the government to scratching out a subsistence on their farms.

The Fruits of Conquest

The great hordes of gold and silver that her treasure ships carried back from America made Spain the richest country in the world, and excited the envy of other European monarchs. In the long run, however, the easy money created more problems than it solved. Its impact on the Spanish economy proved more stultifying than stimulating. The inflow of bullion created runaway inflation, to which the rigid and tradition-bound Spanish economy could not adjust. The soaring prices attracted a flood of manufactured imports, overwhelming home industry. The generous share of the treasure earmarked for the royal coffers had another unfortunate effect: It encouraged the king's grandiose ambition to dominate the affairs of Europe and led him into a series of foreign wars that ended in defeat and national impoverishment.

Spain doggedly held on to its empire until the nineteenth century independence movements, and established a chain of new mission settlements in California in the eighteenth century. But its waning economic and military power made it impossible for it to enforce its exclusive claim to the Western Hemisphere by repelling the efforts of other powers to establish overseas outposts there. By the end of the sixteenth century, the way was open for the establishment of the British settlements out of which the United States of America would eventually grow.

SUGGESTED READINGS

J.M. Huizinga's *The Waning of the Middle Ages* (1924) is a poignant psychological portrait of European society in the late Middle Ages. On the Black Death and the role of disease in history in general, see William H. McNeill's fascinating *Plagues and Peoples* (1976). The fullest analysis of why Europe achieved world dominance is E.L. Jones, *The European Miracle: Environments, Economics, and Geopolitics in the History of Europe and Asia* (1981). Carlos Cipolla, *Guns, Sails, and Empires: Technological Innovation and the Early Phase of European Expansion, 1400–1700* (1965) is brief and penetrating. The voyages of discovery are lucidly described in J.H. Parry, *Europe and a Wider World, 1415–1715* (1949) and *The Age of Reconnaissance* (1963), Samuel Eliot Morison, *Christopher Columbus, Mariner* (1956), and David Quinn, *America from Earliest Discovery to First Settlement* (1977).

On the natives of New Spain, see Alfred W. Crosby, *The Columbian Exchange: Biological and Cultural Consequences of 1492* (1972), Eric Wolf, *Sons of the Shaking Earth* (1959), and Charles Gibson, *The Aztecs under Spanish Rule* (1964). William H. Prescott, *History of the Conquest of Mexico* (1843) and *Conquest of Peru* (1847) are classics that still stir the imagination. Norman Wachtel, *The Vision of the Vanquished* (1977) describes the conquest from the Indian point of view. Charles Gibson, *Spain in America* (1966) and J.H. Parry, *The Spanish Seaborne Empire* (1966) clarify the Spanish system of governance. James Lang, *Conquest and Commerce: Spain and England in the Americas* (1975) is a useful comparative study. For contrasting views of the economic consequences of European expansion into the Western Hemisphere, see Ralph Davis, *The Rise of the Atlantic Economies* (1973) and Immanuel Wallerstein, *The Modern World System: Capitalist Agriculture and the Origins of the European World Economy in the Sixteenth Century* (1974), a sometimes murky and overly schematic but stimulating study.

Chapter Two

Tobacco and Servants: The Founding of Virginia

T he Spanish claimed title to all of North America, and established the oldest city in the United States, St. Augustine, Florida, in 1565. However, they made no effort to settle the areas British colonists moved into during the seventeenth century. They thought there was nothing of value there. The tragic beginnings of the first permanent British settlement in North America, the colony at Jamestown, Virginia, suggested that the Spanish were right. Virginia, the first English explorers claimed extravagantly, was "earth's only paradise." It was better than a land of milk and honey; "instead of milk we find pearls, and gold instead of honey." That delusion led thousands of English investors to help finance the Virginia company, and induced thousands more to cross the ocean in hope of making their fortunes. The hapless investors lost their capital, and most of the first settlers lost their lives. The Jamestown colony eventually flourished, but only after the settlers received a painful education concerning the nature of the American environment.

SOURCES OF THE ENGLISH COLONIZATION DRIVE

England had a very early claim on portions of the Western Hemisphere. Only four years after Columbus's first voyage, King Henry VII denied Spain and Portugal's exclusive right to rule over the non-Christian peoples of the world. He commissioned John Cabot, an Italian navigator living in Britain, to explore, "conquer, occupy, and possess" the lands of "heathen and infidels" across the Atlantic. Cabot and his son Sebastian ranged along the North American coast from Newfoundland

In 1751, mathematics professor Joshua Fry and surveyor Peter Jefferson produced a map of Virginia. In 1775, Jefferson's son, Thomas, sent the British Comissioners for Trade and Plantations a copy of that map emblazoned with a cartouche bearing this detail of a tobacco wharf on the shores of Chesapeake Bay.

to the Chesapeake Bay, giving England a basis for asserting "dominion, title, and jurisdiction" over much of North America.

For a long time to come, however, no attempt was made to establish an English presence in America. Until the 1550s England was allied with Spain against France, and unwilling to strain the alliance by challenging Spain's hegemony in the Western Hemisphere. The high point of this alliance came during the brief reign of Queen Mary, 1553–58, who was married to Philip II of Spain and a blood relative of the Spanish ruling dynasty. The accession to the throne of Queen Elizabeth in 1558 ended the harmony and produced tensions that eventually brought full scale war. Unlike Mary, Elizabeth was a Protestant and she had no blood ties to the Spanish monarchy. Elizabeth rightly suspected Spain of designs to reimpose Catholicism on Britain and to replace Elizabeth with her second cousin, Mary, Queen of Scots.

When Protestants in the Netherlands began a war for independence from Spain in 1567, Elizabeth sent them aid. And she tacitly condoned raids on Spanish treasure ships and Spanish outposts in the Western Hemisphere by English pirates like Sir Francis Drake and John Hawkins. The idea of establishing English settlements in North America to serve as bases from which to conduct such raids began to be considered in official circles in the 1560s. Advocates argued that enlightened English settlers would treat the "natural people" there with such "humanity, courtesy, and freedom" that the Indians would "revolt clean from the Spaniard." That would bring England "the treasures of the mines of gold and silver and the whole trade of merchandise that now passeth hither by the Spaniard's only hand."

At about the time Elizabeth took the throne, a major shift in England's economic position made the prospect of such new treasure and trade especially attractive. England's boom industry in the first half of the sixteenth century was woolen cloth and raw wool, the bulk of which it shipped to Antwerp (then part of the Netherlands) for distribution on the Continent. In the mid-1550s that market became saturated and collapsed. After 1567, the Netherlands' war with Spain prevented the trade from reopening. The mercantile community was forced to look for new markets and trading routes. The result was the formation of a number of new companies to organize trade with other areas of the world—in 1555 the Guinea Company to deal with Africa and the Muscovy Company for Russia, in 1579 the Eastland Company for the Baltic lands, in 1581 the Levant Company for the Middle East, in 1600 the East India Company for India and Southeast Asia. The Jamestown settlement was the work of a commercial organization like these, the London-based Virginia Company.

Another force behind the developing English interest in overseas expansion was population pressure. The people of Elizabethan England were living through what they regarded as an alarming population explosion. Between 1500 and 1650 the population grew from less than three million to more than five million. The sheer growth in numbers was not itself the problem. England's American colonies would later see their populations double each quarter of a century without anyone worrying about overpopulation. The problem was that the English population was growing more rapidly than the capacity of the economy to provide employment. Throughout the sixteenth century landlords were enclosing their fields by building hedges around them, adopting forms of cultivation that required less labor, and expelling the peasants who had previously worked for them. To meet the demands of the burgeoning woolen industry, land that once had been cultivated by dozens of tenants was turned over to flocks of sheep tended by single shepherds. "Sheep ate men," the saying went—they deprived them of their accustomed means of subsistence.

Of course the growth of woolen manufactures created some new jobs—in weaving, for example. But there was no industrial revolution on a scale to absorb the full surplus. Uprooted peasants drifted into London and other cities and towns; the population of London soared from about 60,000 in the early sixteenth century to six times that by 1650. Most of these impoverished migrants found no regular work in the cities, and consequently faced terrible hardships. The flood of hungry job seekers forced the average wage down by two-thirds over the course of the sixteenth century. The well-to-do complained of "the great number of idle vagabonds" and the "plague of beggars." Brutally repressive laws were applied to no avail. Elizabethan legislation provided that beggars were to be punished by burning through the gristle of their ears for a first offense; two-time losers were put to death. If new colonies could be developed overseas, they would serve as a safety valve to release these dangerous population pressures. "If England cry out that there is so many in all trades that one cannot live for another, as in all places they do," imperial expansion would provide new employment opportunities. The children of "the wandering beggars of England" could people "waste countries, to the home and foreign benefit and to their own more happy state."

Population pressures were stimulating a new interest in colonization in the upper ranks of society as well. English noble families, for reasons not yet understood, were producing many more children in the century after 1550 than before or since, and it is probable that this was the case for the landed gentry as well, the class of large landholders just below the nobility. The children of elite families would never be reduced to begging, needless to say, but they were experiencing strain because of the custom of primogeniture. When a landowner died, his entire real estate holding went to the eldest male child. His daughters could be married off, but what was to happen to the younger sons? The traditional solution had been to place them in a profession, as clergymen or military officers, for example. But by the end of the sixteenth century there were more younger sons than the professions could absorb. The country, wrote a leading publicist of the colonization movement in 1584, was "swarming at this day with valiant youths rusting and hurtful by lack of employment." The development of a new England across the seas would offer an opportunity to escape from their cramped circumstances at home and a chance to acquire the wealth denied by accident of birth.

The gradual buildup of these expansionist pressures during the long reign of Elizabeth (1558–1603) led to some efforts to plant colonies in North America, but all were ill-fated. While searching for a northwest passage to the Orient northeast of Hudson Bay in the late 1570s, Martin Frobisher found a glittering substance he took to be gold. He returned with a fleet of eleven ships to establish a gold mining colony in Baffin Land, but the substance turned out to be fool's gold (iron pyrites). In 1583 Sir Humphrey Gilbert set out to plant an English settlement in Newfoundland, with the equally misguided conviction that it was rich in gold; his ship went down in a storm. Sir Walter Raleigh, sponsor of the "lost colony" on Roanoke Island off the North Carolina coast, had no better luck. The 118 men, women, and children landed there in 1587 had disappeared without a trace by the time supply ships, delayed by war with Spain, returned in 1590.

THE JAMESTOWN FIASCO

In November of 1606 three small ships belonging to the Virginia Company left London. The beginning of the voyage was frustrating. Contrary winds at the mouth of the English Channel pinned them within sight of land for a full six weeks. By the time they were truly underway, provisions were running low, the preacher was dangerously ill, and the passengers were quarreling bitterly. It was an omen of the troubles that would wrack the colony for two decades to come.

The Virginia Company was a joint stock company; many investors pooled their resources and shared the profits in proportion to their investment. Other joint stock companies of the time were paying off handsomely; the Muscovy Company turned a 90 percent profit in 1611, and the East India Company a glittering 500 percent in 1607. The merchants, landowners, and tradesmen who backed the Virginia Company, most of them investors in other such enterprises as well, had similar hopes. They were the "adventurers." Those who actually went to America (a much greater and far from pleasant adventure, as it turned out) were the "planters," the residents of the new "plantation" abroad. They were employees of the firm for a term of years, who received food, clothing, tools and weapons from the company warehouse during their service and would be given a share of the profits at the end.

The Virginia Company was a private enterprise without financial support from the Crown. But it was a creature of government; James I issued the charter under which it operated, and retained the right to modify or cancel it at his pleasure. In 1606 James claimed dominion over two million square miles of North America, from North Carolina to Newfoundland, and authorized two groups of his "loving subjects" to establish settlements there. Each was allowed to pick out an area 100 miles long and 100 deep in which to dig for precious metals and plant crops. In return, they were to give one-fifth of all the treasure they found to the Crown. One of these two companies came to nothing and collapsed; the other launched the Jamestown settlement.

Hard Times

The early history of Jamestown was a nightmare for all concerned. The hoped-for profits failed to materialize, and few of the planters who went there to better themselves lived long enough to have claimed a share had there been any. Europe at the time of the Black Death was a considerably safer place to live than Virginia at its beginnings. Only 38 of 104 settlers survived the first year. Replacements were sent, but almost half of them died off during the notorious "starving time" of the

So lamentable was our scarcity that we were constrained to eat dogs, cats, rats, snakes, toadstools, horsehides, and what not. One man, out of the misery he endured, killing his wife, powdered her up to eat her, for which he was burned. Many besides fed on the corpses of dead men, and one who had gotten insatiable out of custom to that food could not be restrained until such time as he was executed for it. And indeed, so miserable was our estate that the happiest day that ever some of them hoped to see was when the Indians had killed a mare, they wishing while she was boiling that Sir Thomas Smith [Treasurer of the Virginia Company] was upon her back in the kettle.

— *Journals of the Virginia House of Burgesses*, 1624

winter of 1609–10.[1] Murderously high mortality rates continued into the 1620s—37 percent in 1623–24, for example.

Why was Virginia such a death trap? Bad luck and medical ignorance, for one thing. Jamestown was located on a narrow peninsula 57 miles up the James River from the ocean. The river's deep channel at that point made it possible to directly unload ocean-going vessels, and the site was easily defended against Indian or Spanish attack. But it had grave disadvantages in the summer. The level of the James, the source of the colony's water supply, fell sharply then, and salty ocean water invaded the river, trapping human waste carrying organisms that breed typhoid and amoebic dysentery. Even uncontaminated salt water is hazardous to health. Salt poisoning produces painful swellings, extreme lassitude and irritability, and can cause death. Each summer at flood tide, Jamestown residents were drinking water with a salinity concentration five times higher than the maximum safe levels calculated by public health officials today (see map). The returning ebb tide, though less salty, seethed with typhoid and dysentery pathogens. As the settlers complained, water from the James was "verie salt" and "full of slime and filth." Some of them suspected that bad water was the source of the epidemics, and urged relocation of the settlement at a place where pure fresh water was available. The directors back in London, regrettably, were skeptical, and opposed to spending the money and labor time that would be needed to begin anew at another site. The graveyard thus continued to do a very active business.

---

[1]The "starving time" was indeed horrible—see box—but the traditional estimate that only 60 of 500 men in the colony survived it has recently been shown to be grossly exaggerated. There were only 220 colonists in the fall of 1609, and 100 survived the winter, a better record than the first year. Furthermore, starvation was not the primary killer but disease; see Carville Earle's essay on "Environment, Disease, and Mortality in Early Virginia," in Thad W. Tate and David L. Ammerman, *The Chesapeake in the Seventeenth Century* (1979).

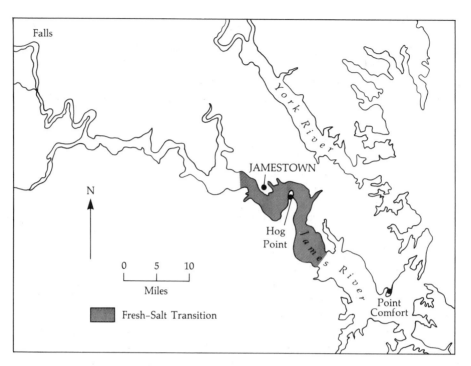

MAP 2-1
The James River

An inadequate diet weakens the body's normal resistances to disease, and that was another problem that plagued the unfortunates at Jamestown. Famine threatened the colony's existence not only during the "starving time" of 1609–10 but for another dozen years. It would have taken little effort to grow enough food for survival in Virginia's rich soil. The native peoples in the area had no difficulty doing so. But the colonists did not make the effort. Part of the reason was that the company did not grasp its importance. The investors hungered for quick profits, and had hopelessly unrealistic ideas about how to obtain them. They directed the planters to hunt for gold and silver like the Spanish had found, and to search for a great river through which vessels could sail into the Pacific and the Far East. Hoeing a corn field seemed an unnecessary distraction from such great tasks. Food could be imported while the search for treasure went on. But when immediate profits failed to materialize, the investors were stingy about providing the supplies necessary to keep the colonists alive. Their parsimony was understandable, because they were personally liable for the company's debts; it was not a limited liability investment like corporate stocks today. The settlers, though, paid the price by enduring terribly lean winters.

When the company did begin to see the folly of depending so heavily on imported food and urged the planters to cultivate gardens, the results were disappointing, because the kind of men who had been attracted to the venture lacked the skills and motivation to farm successfully. It is hard to imagine a group of people less well-suited to that mundane task. Most of the pioneers fell into one of three categories. First, there were aristocratic gentlemen who looked with contempt upon manual labor. There were their personal servants to take care of them. Finally, there were highly specialized artisans like goldsmiths, jewelers, and perfumers, who were there either to process the gold and silver thought to be present or to supply the gentlemen with the luxuries they desired. There were no farmers, and few settlers accustomed to any form of hard labor. The tough and practical soldier of fortune, Captain John Smith, saw the problem clearly. "In Virginia," he remarked, "a plaine Souldier that can use a pickaxe and spade is better than five Knights." Jamestown had a great excess of "Knights," and all too few "plaine Souldiers."

Dale's Police State

After three years of no profits and requests for still more supplies, the Virginia Company took drastic action. In 1610 a new governor, Sir Thomas Dale, was appointed and authorized to put the colony under martial law. Every settler was given a military rank, and was placed under officers to be "trained up in Martial manner and war-like Discipline." All were to work fixed hours on the company's business. Slackers were dealt with by means extraordinarily harsh even by the standards of that brutal age. For example, the penalty for stealing two pints of oatmeal from the storehouse was to have a needle driven through your tongue and to be chained to a tree until you starved to death. Except for the handful of married couples, the company's men lived in barracks with superior officers to watch over them. They were marched to church in orderly ranks each morning and evening to be instructed in the need for industry and subordination to the established author-ities. Colonists were forbidden to leave Virginia without the governor's permis-sion, and their letters home had to pass the scrutiny of the company censor. A number of men found this life unendurable and fled to live with the Indians. When they were recaptured, the fortunate ones were shot or hanged; Governor Dale had the others burned at the stake or broken on the wheel.

Running the colony like a labor camp reduced the extent of petty pilfering, but did not transform the settlement into an economically viable enterprise. New settlers were hard to recruit. As John Smith observed, few men would leave England for Virginia "to have less liberty there than here." The terrorized, mal-nourished, disease-ridden residents of Jamestown were unable either to feed themselves or to produce anything worth exporting.

White Over Red

The aims of the Virginia Company would have been more easily attained if the English had been able to put the local Indians to work as the Spaniards had. They tried, but were unsuccessful. The English knew something of the unhappy fate of the native peoples under Spanish rule, and claimed that they would be far more kind and benevolent. Their basic objectives, however, were no less exploitative. They assumed that the natives of North America would hand over their gold and silver, as well as food, and could doubtless be induced to produce more in exchange for the blessings of Christianity. As an anonymous poet of the day put it:

> The land full rich, the people easilie wonne,
> Whose gaines shalbe the knoweledge of our faith
> And ours such ritches as the country hath.

Although English aims were not fundamentally different from those of the Spanish, Virginia was not Mexico or Peru. There were no precious metals there, and the native peoples were not "easily won" and made into dutiful servants. For one thing, there were very few of them—perhaps 30,000 in the entire Chesapeake region—and their numbers quickly began to fall under the impact of new European diseases. They were not rooted in ancient villages and accustomed to external domination as had been the peoples of the Aztec and Inca empires. Most of the two dozen tribes of the area were part of a loose alliance under the chief Powhatan, but conquering Powhatan was not at all comparable to overcoming and replacing Montezuma. The Chesapeake Indians traveled light, and could resist subjection and exploitation by slipping away into the interior and resettling beyond the reach of the white man.

What could not be gained through compulsion might have been obtained through inducement. The English had things the Indians wanted and vice versa. Iron pots, knives, and fishhooks could be traded for corn, meat, fish, and fur. Some friendly trade did take place in the early years. John Rolfe's famous 1614 marriage to Powhatan's daughter, Pocahontas, symbolized the possibility of peaceful coexistence and eventual blending of the races. Very few Englishmen followed Rolfe's example, however. The fact that Pocahontas died two years later of a white man's disease contracted while on a trip to England was a better symbol of what was to happen. The Spanish, on the other hand, although not without prejudice, frequently intermarried with the natives, producing a large racially mixed *mestizo* element in the population. The English, by contrast, kept their distance despite the acute shortage of white women in the colony. They were aloof and imperious. Convinced of their moral as well as military superiority, they were unable to treat the natives with respect and understanding. Instead of asking, they demanded; if refused, they took anyway. When Powhatan sent them a message that struck them as "prowde and disdayneful," they launched a punitive expedition against a small tribe nearby, killing a dozen warriors and burning the village to the ground. After bringing the queen and her children back as captives, they thought better of it. The queen was put to the sword; the children they threw into the river, "shoteinge owtt their Braynes in the water."

Although company officials back in London still dreamed of converting the natives to Christianity and chided the settlers for their brutal behavior, the men on the scene were soon convinced that the Indians must be expelled from all land near the settlement. There was a profound difference, they believed, between "a bloody invasion and the planting of a peaceable Colony in a waste country, where the people doe live but like Deere in heards, and have not as yet attained unto the first modestie that was in Adam." The natives naturally failed to see the distinction and resisted the encroachment. By 1622, they could take no more. Powhatan's successor, Opechancanough, led a surprise attack that killed 347 settlers, more than a quarter of the total. More than 20 years of intermittent fighting followed. The English raided villages and destroyed grain supplies to force the Indians to flee into the interior or starve. On one occasion they poisoned 200 with wine they brought to celebrate the conclusion of a fake peace treaty. With the aid of such tactics, Virginians finally crushed the resisting natives in 1644. Opechancanough was killed and the confederacy was dissolved. The survivors were placed under direct English rule, and ordered into the interior beyond the line of white settlement.

New Inducements

After several years of Governor Dale's draconian rule had failed to yield profits, the company introduced reforms designed to improve conditions in Virginia enough to attract a flood of new settlers. In 1616 Dale was removed and the most punitive features of martial law were eliminated. In deference to England's long tradition of representative government, the company decided to allow the creation of a new representative assembly, on the grounds that "every man will more willingly obey lawes to which he hath yielded his consent." It was not to be a Parliament in miniature, with strong law-making power; its decisions had to be approved by the London Company, and were subject to veto by the governor. The company declared that it would not impose new regulations without the assent of the assembly, but there was nothing to prevent it from changing its mind and imposing its orders unilaterally once again. The assembly consisted of the governor, his council, and 22 "burgesses" elected by a vote of the free adult males of the colony. (In seventeenth century England a "burgess" was a member of Parliament from a borough or incorporated town.) Later in the century the elected representatives became a separate body, the House of Burgesses.

The first assembly met at Jamestown in July, 1619. In six days of frantic activity, it agreed on a series of new statutes. Although it acknowledged that company officials in London had the right to review them, it took the significant step of declaring that its decisions took effect immediately, "for otherwise this people would in short time grow so insolent as they would shake off all government." It was a historic assertion of the right of self-government. July in Jamestown, though, was an unfortunate time and place for the meeting of America's first representative assembly. The session had to break up in unseemly haste because of the "intemperature" of the weather and "the falling sick of diverse of the Burgesses" from drinking the slimy, salty water of the James.

A second important reform introduced by the company was the importation of women so that normal family life could develop in the colony. Beginning in 1619, the company offered passage to Virginia to "young," "handsome," and "uncorrupt" maids, to be paid for by "those that takes them to wife." The object was to "make the men there more setled," tied to the community by "the bondes of Wyves and Children." Ninety women went in the first shipment, another 100 in a second, women whose willingness to take the gamble testifies to the lack of opportunities available to them at home. Whether their appearance and morality met the standard is uncertain, but there is no doubt of their popularity. They were snapped up at the auctions at Jamestown—one of the very few investments of the Virginia Company that ever returned a profit. The number sent was not nearly enough to produce an even balance of the sexes in Virginia; the colony would have a large surplus of single male servants and slaves for the rest of the century. But it was the beginning of the transformation of Virginia from a military camp to a family-based society.

The most important inducement to new settlers was an innovative scheme to give them land—the headright system. The planters who arrived in the colony under Governor Dale's rule were required to toil for seven years before they were eligible to receive a share of the profits and 100 acres of land for themselves. In 1616 the company made a far more attractive offer—50 acres of free land immediately for any man, woman, or child over 15 who made the trip at their own expense.

The cost of the journey was too great for the common people of England, however. Other arrangements were made to attract them. Some were brought to work as tenants on the land retained by the company, in which case they kept half of the profits from their labor and then received title to 50 acres. Another much larger group was composed of indentured servants, bound into service to settlers who paid the cost of their passage. In 1617 the company added to the incentive to do that by giving masters 50 acres for each servant they transported. In addition to the land, the colonial masters had the right to the servants' labor for the term specified in the indenture agreement, usually four to seven years, and were free to sell them to another employer at any time. The streets of London, Bristol, Liverpool, and other English ports were crowded with hungry young people who had come there in search of work and failed to find it. The indentured servant trade offered a mechanism for transferring them to a place where their labor was needed. All that was needed was for Virginians to discover the right product on which to concentrate their efforts.

The Tobacco Boom

They did find the right product—tobacco. A craze for tobacco, first introduced by the Spanish, was sweeping Europe when the Jamestown colony began. The plant was native to Virginia and was used by the Indians. Some tobacco was exported with the first returning ships, but European tastes judged the local variety much inferior to Spanish leaf. However, the enterprising John Rolfe was not deterred. He experimented with seeds from Trinidad, which yielded tobacco of a quality to rival the Spanish type, and found them suitable to Virginia's soil and climate. The first substantial crop was exported in 1617; ten years later the colony shipped out half a million pounds of the leaf, by 1635 a million pounds, by the late 1660s 15 million. The faltering colony boomed at last. Virginia was built on smoke; it owed its prosperous future to the contagious spread of nicotine addiction in the western world.

The surge in tobacco production was not the result of efforts by the Virginia Company; it came about despite company efforts to discourage it. Ill-fated to the end, the company let the wealth generated by the flow of brown gold slip through its fingers. It failed to see the potential of what King James I called "that stinking weed," and forbade planters from growing it except in small amounts. Instead, they were ordered to devote themselves to the production of goods that were thought to offer greater prospect of profit—iron, silk, wine, and glass. But the company had no means of enforcing more than lackadaisical pro forma efforts on these projects, all of which failed. The settlers devoted every spare moment and every empty acre they could find to tobacco, and scraped together the cash to bring over as many indentured servants as possible to work in the tobacco fields. While they prospered the company languished. The calamitous losses from the Indian uprising of 1622 and the news of continuing high mortality from disease and famine led to an investigation of the company's misgovernment and a 1624 decision by the King to dissolve the company and make Virginia a royal colony with a governor appointed by the Crown.

THE EVOLUTION OF CHESAPEAKE SOCIETY

When the Virginia Company was dissolved and the colony put under royal administration, the assembly had been meeting annually for six years, and had grown accustomed to having a voice in the way the colony was governed. The demise of the company threatened to silence that voice. James I and his son Charles I, who succeeded him in 1625, were suspicious of representative assemblies and fervent believers in "the divine right of kings." (Their heavy-handed attempts to undermine the authority of Parliament would before long lead to the English civil war.) The assemblymen greeted the news that Virginia had been placed under the King's thumb with dismay. They immediately petitioned for royal recognition of their legitimacy, and asserted that appointed governors had no power to tax Virginians without the consent of the assembly. James and Charles refused to grant recognition, and insisted that the governors they appointed had full power, including the power to levy taxes without consulting anyone.

The King's edict, as it turned out, had little impact on what actually happened on the other side of the ocean. The governors who arrived from London quickly found that they could accomplish nothing without the cooperation of the most influential planters. Some of the planters were appointed by the King to the governor's council, which he did recognize. But successive governors felt it necessary to have a broader basis of support and convened unauthorized meetings of an elected assembly on a fairly regular basis. The governor's council became, in effect, the upper house of the Virginia legislature; the House of Burgesses became the lower house. The assembly continued to claim the exclusive right to approve taxes, and governors found it politic to concede it. The King showed no concern that his orders were being ignored, as long as duties on the ever-increasing flow of tobacco imports continued to pour into the royal coffers. He had considerably more pressing things to worry about than affairs in that remote place—the struggle with Parliament that ended in civil war and his own execution by Parliamentary forces in 1649. The settlers of Virginia—and of the other English colonies established in these years—therefore had breathing space, the freedom to shape their lives with minimal interference from central authorities in the mother country.

Population Growth and Family Patterns

After limping along painfully for almost two decades, Virginia at last took off when company rule ended. Only 1,200 people lived there in 1625. A decade later, the population had risen to 5,000, 18,000 by 1650, 30,000 by 1670. The colony ceased to be a death trap; the mortality rate dropped 50 percent between 1625 and 1634. Company policy had been responsible for the concentration of settlement around Jamestown and its deadly water. With no one to enforce continued concentration, and every incentive to move out to tobacco plantations in the interior, the population dispersed into a healthier environment. (The term "plantation" was first used to mean an estate on which cotton, tobacco, sugar, or other crops are grown with servile labor in 1706, but the institution itself appeared at the beginning of the tobacco boom.) They were more likely to find safe drinking water, and the lower density of settlement was itself conducive to health. When disease did strike, it was less likely to spread—a principal reason why through most of history city dwellers have died younger than country folk. Those who remained in the tidewater area had to depend on shallow wells that were easily contaminated—deeper ones would have produced salt water. But the planting of apple orchards eased the problem. An apple a day didn't quite keep the doctor away, but consuming several crushed into cider did; it was a much healthier beverage than impure water.

Virginia remained a pretty hazardous place in which to live, though, despite the marked improvement after 1624. A twenty-year-old could expect to live only 20 more years, on the average, less than half as long as a contemporary in New England (see Chapter 3). Just what caused this striking difference in life expectancy is still debated. The warm, moist climate of the Chesapeake region certainly was partially responsible; it provided a congenial breeding ground for the anopheles mosquito, the carrier of malaria. Malaria, unknown in New England, was chronic in Virginia.

Another reason that the average lifespan was so short in Virginia is that—unlike New England—the colony included a large indentured servant class who were worked so hard by exploitative masters that it sent them to an early grave. About 40 percent of those who immigrated to Virginia under indentures around the middle of the seventeenth century died before they had completed their four-year terms. Their masters were determined to get rich quick, and could see that driving servants mercilessly was the way to wealth. Back in England, centuries of tradition placed restraints on the length of the work week and the intensity of labor that could be demanded from a bound servant, and selling servants against their will was forbidden. Traditional constraints did not operate on the other side of the ocean. On the isolated tobacco plantations there was no one to whom an over-worked and abused young bondsman or bondswoman could appeal, and nothing to prevent them from being bought and sold like cattle. Masters pinched for other resources sometimes put up their servants as stakes in card games.

The high death rate and the very large numbers of immigrant servants in the colony made it difficult to establish orderly family life along familiar English lines.[2] Because planters preferred male to female servants, men who were fortunate enough to live long enough to claim their freedom frequently could not find a wife. In the 1630s men outnumbered women by six to one among new arrivals; as late as 1704 there were three adult males for every two adult females in the colony. Bachelors were very common, and spinsters exceedingly rare.

A second distinctive feature of family life in the Chesapeake region was that families tended to be small. The typical woman had two or three children who

---

[2]Much of our evidence about social patterns, it should be noted, comes not from Virginia but from its neighbor, Maryland, which has been studied more intensively. Maryland was established as a result of a 1632 royal grant to Lord Baltimore. Its climate and geography closely resemble those of Virginia, and it had a similar tobacco economy and indentured labor force. It seems reasonable to assume that findings from Maryland may be generalized to apply to Virginia as well.

lived beyond infancy, as contrasted with seven or eight in New England. Servants were not free to marry until they completed service, but by then many of a woman's fertile years were already past. Many wives died early in their marriages, because malaria is especially virulent for pregnant women. And many of the children died young. The net effect was that the population failed to grow at all by natural increase—the excess of births over deaths. In most years, deaths outnumbered births. The only source of population growth until late in the century was continued immigration. Long after the initial settlement, Virginia was a land of newcomers, a pioneer society with few residents who could claim deep roots there.

High mortality had a profoundly unsettling effect on family life. The average marriage did not last as long as those in our present divorce-ridden society. "Till death do us part" had an immediacy it lacks now. Half of all marriages broke up within seven years due to the death of one of the partners. Two out of three children in the colony lost at least one parent before they reached eighteen; almost a third lost both. The Chesapeake colonies had to develop a new legal institution—the Orphans' Courts—to deal with the problem. The shock of early bereavement was compounded by the bewilderingly complex family situations children experienced when the surviving partner remarried. Before the eldest child of the original marriage came of age, he or she was sometimes living with a stepfather, a stepmother, and younger children to whom they had no blood ties at all. In one case, a chain of six different marriages on the part of seven adults produced twenty-five children, whose relationship to each other and to the adults in the household only a skilled genealogist could keep straight.

Family ties in the early Chesapeake were fleeting and transitory. The clear generational lines that appear in most societies—children, parent, grandparent— and the stable structure of authority associated with it failed to develop. Hardly anyone lived long enough to lay eyes on his or her grandchildren; mothers and fathers were not usually present to shape the development of their offspring until they reached full maturity. Opportunities for transmitting tradition from the elderly to the young were severely limited. About all that was passed on in the chaotic homes in which young Virginians were reared, we may suspect, was the fiercely competitive, individualistic, "looking out for number one" spirit that so many of the first settlers brought with them. In such circumstances, it was easy to believe that it was a Hobbesian world, in which life was "nasty, brutish, and short."

Settlement Patterns and Social Structure

Seventeenth-century Englishmen were accustomed to living in densely populated communities, whether great cities like London or small farming villages. Jamestown followed that pattern, but after the collapse of the Virginia Company it was abandoned and settlers fanned out into the interior, along the banks of the James and York rivers. Clustering in villages would have made it much easier to defend themselves against Indian attacks, such as had claimed the lives of about a quarter of the entire colony in 1622. But the lure of the land, and of the wealth the planters

THE SERVANT'S LOT—
A LETTER FROM VIRGINIA, 1623

Loving and kind father and mother my most humble duty remembered to you hoping in God of your good heatlh, as I myself am at the making hereof, this is to let you understand that I your child am in a most heavy case by reason of the nature of the country is such that it causeth much sickness, as the scurvy and the bloody flux, and diverse other diseases, which maketh the body very poor, and weak, and when we are sick there is nothing to comfort us; for since I came out of the ship, I never ate anything but peas, and loblollie (that is water gruel) as for deer or venison I never saw any since I came into this land, there is indeed some fowl, but we are not allowed to go, and get it, but must work hard both early, and later for a mess of water gruel, and a mouthful of bread, and beef, a mouthfull of bread for a penny loaf must serve for 4 men which is most pitiful if you did not know as much as I, when people cry out day, and night,....

But I am not half a quarter so strong as I was in England, and all is for want of victuals, for I do protest unto you, that I have eaten more in [a] day at home then I have allowed me here for a week. Goodman Jackson pitied me and made me a cabin to lie in always when I come up, and he would give me some...home...which comforted me more than peas, or water gruel. He much marveled that you would send me a servant to the Company, he saith I had been better knocked on the head, and indeed so I find it now to my great grief and misery, and saith, that if you love me you will redeem me suddenly, for which I do entreat and beg, and if you cannot get the merchants to redeem me for some little money then for God's sake get a gathering or entreat some good folks to lay out some little sum of money, in meal, and cheese and butter, and beef.... [I]f I die before it come I have entreated Goodman Jackson to send you the worth of it, who has promised that he will. Good father do not forget me, but have mercy and pity my miserable case. I know if you did but see me you would weep to see me.

—Kingsbury, *Records of the Virginia Company,* 1935

hoped to gain by growing tobacco, was stronger than their fear of hostile natives. The land was free, the labor scarce, so they farmed in a quick and dirty way. The woods were taken down by girdling the trees. The stumps would be left, and tobacco plants set in between them. After three or four years, the yield would diminish and tobacco would be planted in another cleared area, leaving the land planted earlier to revert to forest and recover its fertility. It took a great deal of land, but the land was there in abundance. Dispersion meant isolation and an absence of community, but planters were willing to pay that price.

Tobacco invited a dispersed settlement pattern; the special geography of the Chesapeake region made it economically feasible. The complex coastline of the area was broken by many bays, inlets, and rivers accessible to ocean-going vessels. Planters did not need to haul their bulky crop to towns to sell it, buy supplies, and obtain credit. Instead, they could deal directly with English traders on shipboard, without the assistance of local middlemen. The result was an absence of towns and of an urban merchant class. "The ambition each man had of being lord of a vast, though unimproved, territory," and "the advantage of the many rivers which afforded a commodious road of shipping at every man's door," said one of the colony's earliest historians, led Virginians to spread across the land in a manner that was, by European standards, "without any Rule or Order."

One of the most important sources of order and cohesion in seventeenth-century European communities was the church. Everywhere there was an established state church, to which all citizens were expected to belong. Virginia had a state church, a branch of the Church of England, and was divided into parishes just as the mother country was. But the parishes were empty boxes on an organizational chart, not vital functioning realities. In the days of company rule, ministers from the Church of England were sent to Jamestown. During Sir Thomas Dale's Spartan regime, the clergy dutifully assured their captive audiences that deference to authority was divinely ordained. Thereafter, though, church influence in the colony rapidly waned. The population grew much more rapidly than the number of ministers the English hierarchy made available for overseas service; in 1662 the colony had four dozen parishes but only ten clergymen to man their churches.

The rare parishes that did have a minister bore little resemblance to their English counterparts; some were as much as 60 miles long, with the inhabitants scattered too thinly to be accessible before the days of automobiles and super-highways. Nor did the few clergymen receive the deference they expected as the ordained representatives of a hierarchical state church. There was no Anglican bishop in Virginia (or any other of the American colonies), and effective control over the selection of ministers fell to the settlers, who refused to vote funds for ministerial salaries to anyone not to their liking. It was in fact, though not in theory, a form of church organization much like Congregationalism in New England (see Chapter 3). The resemblance to New England ended there, however. In Virginia religious indifference was far more common than religious zeal, and the church was not a major force binding the society together.

The Englishmen who braved the ocean to settle in Virginia were the products of an aristocratic society dominated by a nobility and a landed gentry. Inherited social rank, wealth, and power, they believed, naturally went hand in hand. The wellborn would dominate in every sphere; the middling and lower sorts would defer to those above them. Conditions in Virginia, however, precluded the transplantation of the familiar social hierarchy. A good many gentlemen did arrive during the dismal years of company rule, but they either died off or returned home disillusioned. The

RELIGION IN A FRONTIER TOWN

There may be 40 or 50 houses, most of them small and built without expense. A citizen here is counted extravagant if he has ambition enough to aspire to a brick chimney. Justice herself is but indifferently lodged, the courthouse having much of the air of a common tobacco house. I believe this is the only metropolis in the Christian or Muhammadan world where there is neither church, chapel, mosque, synagogue, or any other place of public worship of any sect or religion whatever. What little devotion there may happen to be is much more private than their vices. The people seem easy without a minister, as long as they are exempted from paying for him.

—William Byrd, II, *The Dividing Line*, 1729

immigrants who arrived after 1624 included very few from the upper ranks of British society. They were people from the middle and lower classes. The top of the English social pyramid was missing in Virginia.

Furthermore, blood and breeding did not count for nearly as much as in the mother country. Connections based on family ties, the key to success in business or politics in England, had little influence upon who acquired a prosperous tobacco plantation and who went bankrupt. It was a fluid, mobile society of grasping men scrambling to make a buck. Of course it helped to have a head start in the race; a number of the most successful planters arrived with significant capital assets. But a great many did not. Four out of five seventeenth century immigrants to the Chesapeake region arrived as indentured servants. Close to half of them did not live to claim their "freedom dues" at the end of their service—some clothing, an axe and hoe, and a few barrels of corn. But those hardy or lucky enough to survive had very good prospects of becoming masters themselves. A study of bondsmen who completed their service before 1674 in one Chesapeake county shows that over a third (37 percent) of them who could be traced in later records became large or middling planters; another quarter acquired small farms of their own. Less than four in ten lived out their lives as landless tenants or laborers. (A majority of freed servants, however, disappeared altogether from the documents; what happened to them is unknown.)

Opportunities for servants to rise in the world would decline sharply in the closing decades of the century when a hereditary ruling elite—the "first families of Virginia"—emerged and black slaves replaced white servants (see Chapter 4). But in this early period, the distance between the top and bottom rungs of the social ladder was not great; many men made the ascent. Most planters had been servants themselves. Few had large numbers of bondsmen working for them; the estates classified as "large" in the study previously mentioned averaged only 3.4 per household. Servants worked side by side with their masters in the fields, took meals in common with them, and lived under the same roof. The work was hard and the danger of an early death was great. But for the survivors it was a poor man's paradise compared to England.

Early Virginia was a good place for ambitious men who could shoulder their way to the top. Staying there over the generations, like the English country gentry, was another matter. Death usually frustrated those who hoped to perpetuate the family line. With few exceptions, the most prominent planting families in the first decades of the colony's history faded from the scene because the head of the family died before he produced a male heir who would live long enough to marry and have a son himself. A stable elite whose status and power derived from genteel birth would not develop until late in the century when death rates fell and families began to have more children who survived to maturity (see Chapter 5).

SUGGESTED READINGS

G.R. Elton, *England under the Tudors* (1955), reveals the forces behind Elizabethan expansionism. English exploration of the Western Hemisphere is vividly described in Samuel Eliot Morison, *The European Discovery of America: The Northern Voyages, A.D. 500-1600* (1971). Wallace Notestein, *The English People on the Eve of Colonization, 1603-1630* (1954), and Carl Bridenbaugh, *Vexed and Troubled Englishmen, 1590-1642* (1968) are traditional accounts based on literary sources. A deeper understanding of the economic and demographic factors that underlay the colonization drive may be gained from Peter Laslett, *The World We Have Lost* (1965), Peter Clark and Paul Slack, eds., *Crisis and Order in English Towns* (1972), and John Patten, *English Towns, 1500-1700* (1978).

Alden Vaughan, *American Genesis: Captain John Smith and the Founding of Virginia* (1975) is a good brief account of the Jamestown experience. Carl Bridenbaugh, *Jamestown: 1544-1699* (1982) offers more detail. Edmund Morgan, *American Slavery, American Freedom* (1975), is rich in insight. The hazards of the environment are analyzed in Carville Earle's fine essay in Thad W. Tate and David Ammerman, eds., *The Chesapeake in the Seventeenth Century: Essays on Anglo-American Society and Politics* (1979). Wesley F. Craven, *The Southern Colonies in the Seventeenth Century, 1607-1689* (1949), and Carl Bridenbaugh, *Myths and Realities: Societies of the Colonial South* (1952) remain useful. T.H. Breen, ed., *Shaping Southern Society: The Colonial Experience* (1976), and Aubrey C. Land, *et al.*, eds., *Law, Society, and Politics in Early Maryland* (1977) are valuable collections of recent essays. Carville V. Earle, *The Evolution of a Tidewater Settlement System* (1978), analyzes settlement patterns.

For contrasting views of the encounter between English settlers and the native peoples, see Wesley F. Craven, *White, Red, and Black: The Seventeenth Century Vir-*

ginian (1971), Gary B. Nash, *Red, White, and Black: The Peoples of Early America* (2nd ed., 1982), Wilcomb E. Washburn, *The Indian in America* (1975), Robert Berkhofer, Jr., *The White Man's Image: Images of the American Indian from the Colonial Times to the Present* (1979), and James T. Axtell, *The European and the Indian: Essays in the Ethnohistory of Colonial North America* (1981).

Chapter Three

The Puritans of New England

The tiny band of Pilgrims who sailed on the *Mayflower* and landed at Plymouth in 1620 found New England a strange and forbidding place. The new land, said Governor William Bradford, was "full of wild beasts and wild men." One of the first settlers of the Puritan colony established along Massachusetts Bay a decade later reported glumly that "the air of the country is sharp, the rocks many, the trees innumerable, the grass little, the winter cold, the summer hot, the gnats in summer biting, the wolves at midnight howling."

Why did almost 20,000 English men and women leave their homeland in the 1620s and 1630s, make a long and dangerous ocean crossing, and begin their lives anew in such an inhospitable spot? Their motives were varied and often mixed. Some sought economic betterment, some adventure, some escape from painful personal entanglements. But the dominant impulse behind the Great Migration to New England was religious. The leaders of the move and the bulk of their followers were dissenters from the established state church. They were Puritans, who accepted the hardships and uncertainties of the new land to escape religious persecution at home. Enduring the frigid winters, the blazing summers, and the wolf howls at midnight were to them a small price to pay for the freedom to worship as they pleased. Englishmen went to Virginia to make money. They went to Plymouth, Massachusetts Bay, and their later offshoots to create religious utopias, societies based upon Puritan principles. The communities they established evolved in directions their founders could not foresee. But they long continued to have distinctive features that reflected their Puritan origins.

The Mayflower Compact was signed on board ship, November 11, 1620. This nineteenth century engraving of the event by Gauthier is after an original painting by Matteson.

THE RISE OF ENGLISH PURITANISM

The Puritan settlement of New England was one of the last acts in the drama that had begun a century before with the great European religious upheaval we call the Reformation. In 1517, in Wittenberg, Germany, a young divinity professor nailed a revolutionary document to the church door. Martin Luther's 95 theses did not deny the supreme authority of the Pope or challenge any other fundamental Roman Catholic doctrine. But Luther's sharp criticisms of church practices he considered corrupt started a quarrel that soon led him to take a far more extreme position. Stung by charges that his views were heretical, he began to denounce "the tyranny of Rome" and to advance radical new doctrines. He proclaimed "a priesthood of all believers," giving the individual conscience primacy over any church organization. Salvation was attainable by faith alone, without the intercession of priests, confessions, and other Catholic rituals. The religious individualism at the core of Luther's message was anathema to the Roman hierarchy, and the Pope not surprisingly branded Luther "a wild boar in the vineyard" and excommunicated him. Instead of submitting docilely, Luther took advantage of the newly developed printing press and carried his message to the people in a series of eloquent religious tracts. They opened a period of fierce ideological warfare that led to the formation of Lutheran state churches in much of northern and central Europe and permanently shattered the religious unity of western Christendom.

Although it convulsed much of continental Europe, the Protestant Reformation at first passed England by. Henry VII remained loyal to the Pope, and wrote a book denouncing Lutheranism. His son Henry VIII broke with Rome a generation later, in the 1530s, after the Pope refused to annul his marriage (to Katherine of Aragon) to allow him to marry another woman (Anne Boleyn) who might bear a son to succeed him on the throne. After the Pope excommunicated him for remarrying, Henry declared himself supreme head of an independent Church of England, and confiscated all the land held by Catholic monasteries in his country. England was now formally a Protestant nation. England's defection from the Catholic fold, however, was the result of the monarch's determination to perpetuate the Tudor line, and did not entail a basic rejection of Catholic doctrine or church organization. The priests and bishops of the Church of England acknowledged the King rather than the Pope as the ultimate source of authority, but little else was changed. Anglican priests dressed in Roman vestments, heard confessions, used the cross in baptisms, and continued to employ other Catholic rituals. Judged by strict Protestant standards, the Church of England had retained many "papish remnants."

Calvinism

A growing number of English men and women came to that conclusion over the course of the century between England's formal break with Rome and the Puritan Revolution of the 1640s. They drew their inspiration not from Luther but from John Calvin in Geneva. Born in France, Calvin had fled to Switzerland in 1535 to be free to preach his special brand of Protestantism. He found support among the elite who ruled the independent city of Geneva, and made the community a Protestant Rome, the international center of the Protestant movement. Calvin's God was stern, angry, and utterly implacable; he could see the corruption in every human heart. "In Adam's Fall," the Calvinist believed, "we sinned all." Calvin had nothing but scorn for the Catholic view that lighting candles, saying rosaries, or performing other rituals could help to rescue one from eternal damnation. Whether you were saved or damned for eternity was up to God alone, and it was predestined, decided at the moment of creation. Doing good works could not assure salvation, although leading an undisciplined, overtly sinful life was a sure sign of nonelection or damnation.

And yet there was hope for man. Despite the crushing burden of original sin, God had sent his only son to earth as the Redeemer, and had revealed his purposes in a holy book—the Bible. God had called some to salvation through Christ, and those who were called would have a mystical experience of regeneration in Christ's church. These saints would read the Word regularly, attend church faithfully, work diligently at their "calling" in this world, and exercise ruthless self-discipline. They would refuse to indulge in sinful worldly pleasures like dancing, gambling, the theater, and luxurious clothing. They were in the world but not of the world, ever wary of pleasures that would distract them from their holy mission. Their aim, as one young convert confided in his diary, was to make their "whole life a meditation of a better life, and godliness in every part." He resolved to "follow my calling; lose no time at home or abroad, but be doing some good; mind my going homeward; let my life never be pleasant unto me when I am not fruitful and fit to be employed in doing good, one way or another."

Calvinism exerted a magnetic appeal to Europeans living through the unsettling social changes that accompanied the disintegration of the medieval order and the genesis of the modern world. It was an age of anxiety, and the traditional rituals of the Church of Rome had lost their consoling power for many. Calvinism offered a new world view and a new prescription for living that channeled their anxieties into a crusade to purify themselves and the societies in which they lived.

The English Puritans

In England the followers of Calvin became known as "Puritans." It was initially a term of abuse used by their opponents; they called themselves simply "God's people," and only much later accepted the label bestowed on them in history. English Puritanism was not a cohesive, tightly organized movement with a sharply defined membership. It represented an intellectual tendency and a temperament shared by people who disagreed about many specifics. What they all had in common was the feeling, held with varying degrees of intensity, that the Church of England was impure and should be purged of surviving Roman Catholic customs. Church organization, they insisted, had to be based squarely on the Bible, the Word, which provided no sanction for the elaborate bureaucratic institution that had grown up in the 1,500 years since the death of Christ. "Every plant which my heavenly father hath not planted" had to be "rooted up." Church services, in their view, should offer less ritual and more intellectual content; their centerpiece should be the sermon, a searching examination of the meaning of a biblical text as applied to contemporary life. Inspired preaching of the Word, said one Puritan, was the chariot on which salvation came riding into the hearts of men. Active lay participation in church affairs was a Puritan tenet; Puritan leaders organized prayer meetings at which ordinary people testified about their religious experiences. And of course they held to the strict Calvinist moral code and sought to make their whole life "a meditation of a better life," constantly scrutinizing their souls to check sinful impulses.

Although there were people with Puritan leanings in every social class, some elements of the population were more responsive to the new faith than others. More than half of the people in Elizabethan England—almost all of the common laborers, servants, and small farmers—were illiterate. A religion that so emphasized individual reading of the Word could have held little appeal for them. At the other end of the social scale, the rich and wellborn tended to be content with their lot and suspicious of anyone who wanted to disturb the status quo. People who loved the pomp of court life and maintained their social position by displays of conspicuous consumption found the Puritan's righteous disdain for worldly pleasure insufferable. Puritan recruits therefore tended to be educated people from the middle ranks of society—professionals, merchants, skilled tradesmen, farmers with moderate holdings. They were neither established enough to be complacent about their situation nor poor enough to have abandoned hope of personal and societal betterment.

Although all Puritans hoped to see major changes in the Church of England, their opinions differed radically concerning how drastic the surgery should be. Presbyterians, who had the largest following, took the more moderate line. They wanted to reshape the Church of England without sacrificing two of its central principles—the conception of centralized, hierarchical church organization, and the tenet that church membership should be open to all, sinners as well as saints. Congregationalists, who played the critical role in the settling of New England, were a more radical minority. Because the Bible did not explicitly provide for an elaborate religious bureaucracy governed from the top down, they claimed that each individual congregation should have the right to choose its own ministers without interference from higher authorities like bishops or presbyters (the Presbyterian hierarchy of ministers and lay elders). Besides making church government more responsive to the wishes of the congregation, Congregationalists wanted to purify the church by restricting membership to "the godly"—those who knew the correct doctrine and made a suitable profession of faith.

Repression

The spread of Puritan sentiment during the forty-five-year reign of Queen Elizabeth (1558–1603) dismayed the monarch and her advisors. Throughout Europe in that era, religion was regarded as a necessary prop to the state. Religious unity was necessary to promote obedience to duly constituted authority; religious dissent seemed tantamount to treason. "People are governed more by the pulpit than the sword," it was thought. "The dependency of the Church upon the crown is the chiefest source of royal authority." In Elizabeth's view, the Church of England—a blend of mildly Protestant and diluted Catholic conceptions—was the only viable middle way between two dangerous extremes of Puritanism and Romanism. Adherents of either extreme should be stamped out.

Catholics received more attention and more brutal treatment during her administration because they posed a greater political threat and could be regarded as agents of a foreign power. Catholic Spain was England's great rival, and there were grounds for believing that the Pope and King Philip were plotting an uprising by English Catholics to put a Catholic heir to the English throne—Mary, Queen of Scots—in power and bring England back into allegiance to Rome. Hundreds of Catholic priests and laymen were executed for their involvement, real or fancied, in such plots. In 1587 Elizabeth had Mary beheaded for alleged involvement in a planned *coup d'état.*

Puritans had a much easier time of it than Catholics under Elizabeth, but those who were indiscreet enough to make public stands deemed too radical were persecuted. Many lost church or university posts in the 1580s and 1590s for giving voice to dissenting views, and one Archbishop was forced out of office for being too soft on Puritans under his charge. A solid core of Puritan supporters or sympathizers remained, however, within the church, in Parliament, at Cambridge University, and at the Inns of Court, London's chief institution for legal education.

English Puritans had reason to be concerned when Elizabeth died in 1603 and was replaced by Mary's son James I, the first of the Stuart kings. James was already King of Scotland—then independent from England—and had alienated Puritans by attempting to subvert the Presbyterian system that was in force there. He believed in "the divine right of kings," and regarded lay participation in church government as a menace to monarchical supremacy. At a meeting with leading ministers at Hampton Court in 1604, he exploded upon hearing of a moderate Puritan proposal for reform along those lines. It was a step towards Presbyterianism, he declared, and "as well agreeth with monarchy as God and the devil. Then Jack and Tom and Will and Dick shall meet, and at their pleasure censure me and my council and all our proceedings."

Presbyterianism was not as radically democratic as James claimed, but it was indeed inconsistent with the kind of unrestrained and absolute power James hoped to establish. Calvin had insisted that God did not give absolute power to any earthly creature, and argued that elective government like that in Geneva was superior to hereditary kingship. John Knox, his leading follower in Scotland, made this doctrine a potent political weapon in his successful campaign to end the rule of Mary, Queen of Scots. Likewise, it was Puritan members of Parliament who led the resistance to James' demands. It was no wonder that James threatened dissenters that he would "harry them out of the land."

James' rhetoric was harsher than his actual policies. Not much was done to impede Puritan activity, and the King was careful not to press his claim to absolute power to the point at which Parliament would refuse to cooperate. However,

James' son Charles, who succeeded him in 1625, was much more zealous and imperious. He dissolved his first Parliament for challenging his actions and refusing to levy a tax he sought, and told the new one that "Parliaments are altogether in my power for their calling, sitting and dissolution." When denied a tax he wanted, he raised the money he needed through illegal forced loans. Charles was married to a Catholic and personally sympathetic to Catholicism, and he attempted to remodel the Church of England along more Roman lines. His Archbishop, William Laud, held views that were outrageously "papish" in Puritan eyes. He preached Arminianism, the doctrine that salvation can be attained through good works, and promoted only those churchmen who agreed with him. In 1629 Parliament passed a resolution condemning Arminianism and popery, but to no avail. Charles disbanded Parliament and proceeded to govern England without any popular assembly for the next eleven years.

The eventual result of the Stuart assaults on the Puritan and parliamentary forces was the civil war of the 1640s, during which both Charles and Laud died at the block. A more immediate result was the migratory wave that peopled the Puritan colonies of New England.

THE PILGRIM EXODUS

The first Puritans to flee across the ocean were a tiny group, quite unrepresentative of the Puritan mainstream. The 101 Pilgrims who arrived at Plymouth in 1620 were radical Congregationalists, "separatists" who had renounced all allegiance to the Church of England. In their view, it was corrupt beyond all redemption, little better than "the harlot of Rome." The nucleus of the group came from a Puritan congre-

---

A PURITAN VIEW OF THE CONTENDING FORCES

The one side laboured to have the right worship of God and discipline of Christ established in the church, according to the simplicity of the gospel, without the mixture of men's inventions; and to have and to be ruled by the laws of God's Word according to the Scriptures. The other party endeavoured to have the episcopal dignity (after the popish manner) with their large power and jurisdiction still retained, with such means as formerly upheld their antichristian greatness and enabled them with lordly and tyrannous power to persecute the poor servants of God.

—William Bradford, *Of Plymouth Plantation*, 1650

gation in the small town of Scrooby, 150 miles north of London. To escape harrassment from state authorities early in the reign of James I, the Scrooby parishioners had fled to Holland. They were allowed to worship as they pleased there—a remarkable condition in the Europe of the seventeenth century—but were able to make only the barest of livings. After a decade, furthermore, they noticed that their children were losing their English identity and assimilating into Dutch society. Consequently, they began to consider another move, this time to a distant land that was nominally English, yet without an administrative apparatus to enforce conformity to the state religion. There they could construct a holy community in which they could retain their national identity and religious purity and prosper as well.

It was not the sheer distance from London that gave them that freedom. More than 3,000 miles separated Spain from its holdings in the Western Hemisphere, yet royal and church authorities enforced strict obedience to dictates from the center. Fortunately for the Pilgrims, the English colonization pattern was quite different. The Crown delegated authority to form overseas settlements to corporations like the Virginia Company, whose operators were unconcerned about heretical religious ideas if cooperating with those who held them would turn a profit. Thus it was that in 1619 the Virginia Company agreed to let these "pilgrims" settle in the northern part of their New World domain, which extended all the way up the coast to the mouth of the Hudson River. The would-be settlers were advanced funds for transportation and supplies on much the same terms as those given to the planters of Jamestown.

Freedom from the authorities at home was a blessing, but it entailed certain dangers as well. A good many of the people aboard the Mayflower were not dedicated Pilgrims but "strangers," servants, soldiers, and artisans whose services were needed. When the ship lowered its anchor in Provincetown harbor, some of these men threatened to "use their own liberty" when they reached shore, on the grounds that the proposed settlement was more than a hundred miles north of the area over which the Virginia Company of London had legal jurisdiction. The Pilgrims were convinced that God had led them to Plymouth and were unwilling to move south. But they needed a new foundation of government that would ensure the subordination of these "discontented and mutinous" elements of the population.

As the party prepared to go ashore, therefore, the leaders of the party composed the Mayflower Compact, which pledged "all due submission and obedience" to the laws they thought necessary "for the general good of the colony." All male settlers, except for servants already bound by indenture agreements, were required to sign the document before going ashore. Although the Mayflower Compact has often been described as a great contribution to the tradition of representative government, its immediate purpose and effect was to ensure the political dominance of the Pilgrim elite. It provided the legal basis by which Governor William Bradford, whose magnificent history *Of Plymouth Plantation* is a classic of American literature, was to rule over the affairs of the colony for more than three decades to come.

The Mayflower's voyage had been a long one—fully eight weeks—and the passengers staggered ashore weakened by confinement and short rations to face a cruel Massachusetts winter. They had "no friends to welcome them," recalled Bradford, "nor inns to entertain or refresh their weather-beaten bodies; no houses to repair to." Before them was a wilderness of "a wild and savage hue"; behind them was "the mighty ocean," a "main bar and gulf to separate them from all the civil parts of the world." The first winter was a repeat of the "starving times" at Jamestown, with only half of the settlers surviving to see the spring. Bradford's wife fell victim not to disease but to the crushing depression many must have felt; her death by drowning, historians suspect, was suicide.

Of course there were some possible friends on hand—the local Indians. The corn, fish, venison, and fowl the Pilgrims obtained from them with the aid of Squanto, their interpreter and go-between, have been enshrined in our national Thanksgiving folklore. The honeymoon period of peaceful cooperation between the races was exceedingly brief, however. By the time the Pilgrims celebrated their second Thanksgiving, in the fall of 1622, the stockade at Plymouth was decorated with the severed head of a local chief slain by Captain Miles Standish's men. From then on, the natives called the Pilgrims "wotowquenange," which meant "cutthroats." There was less fighting between natives and settlers at Plymouth than at Jamestown, but not because the Pilgrims were notably more restrained and considerate of Indian interests. It was because by 1620 a large fraction of the native population of New England had already died off from diseases triggered by earlier contacts with English fishermen, undermining their capacity to put up military resistance. The Pilgrims believed they had a right to whatever land they wanted because they held a charter from a Christian king, and they interpreted the epidemics as evidence that God smiled on their enterprise. As Englishmen, they were the products of a complex, hierarchical society with a highly developed sense of private property, and they could not begin to understand or respect a culture so radically different from their own. As the Pilgrim population grew and its need for land increased, the colonists shouldered the Indians aside without scruple.

The Pilgrim Fathers came to Plymouth to sever all contact with what they regarded as a hopelessly corrupt world. In that, they succeeded. By hard work at farming, supplemented by fishing and fur trading, they scraped up enough money to repay the London investors in 1648, thereby ending financial ties to any external authority. In their self-imposed isolation they created a community that was pious and disciplined but parochial. Their religion was more of the heart than the head. The great issues that agitated Puritan intellectuals in England were not a source of intellectual ferment in Plymouth. Few of the Pilgrims had more than an elementary education; fewer than 20 university graduates immigrated there and only three remained long. The colony had no public schools until it was absorbed into Massachusetts at the end of the century; none of its youths went to college, although Harvard was less than 50 miles away. Although the legend of the Pilgrims lives on, the colony they established was an intellectual and cultural backwater that had very little impact on the subsequent development of English civilization in North America.

THE GREAT MIGRATION TO MASSACHUSETTS

Eleven English ships with 1,000 passengers set sail for Massachusetts in 1630. It was the first wave of the Great Migration that brought approximately 20,000 men and women there over the next dozen years. Like the Pilgrims, most of them fled to escape religious repression and to find the freedom to worship in unorthodox ways. But they were not separatists who believed the Church of England was irredeemable. They were "nonseparating" Congregationalists who regarded the Church of England as their "deare Mother," and believed that it could be reformed. Carrying on the struggle for reform at home was too difficult and dangerous while Charles I and Archbishop Laud were stifling dissent. Thus they resolved to create a new godly community across the ocean to serve as "a city upon a hill." Theirs was "an errand into the wilderness," with a grand mission of creating a working model that would demonstrate to the people of England how their "sinfull lande" could be transformed and purified.

The new settlement was the work of the Massachusetts Bay Company, a commercial enterprise like the Virginia Company—like it, yet profoundly different, for its prime investors were devoted Puritans whose objectives rose above mere profit. Unlike the "adventurers" of the Virginia Company, who ventured their money but remained safely in England, the key figures in the Massachusetts Bay Company were prepared to journey into the wilderness themselves, to be "planters" as well as "adventurers."

They were willing to make the journey, however, only on one condition—that they could govern the new colony without external interference. The typical trading company of the day could not allow such freedom to colonists, for royal charters normally specified where company meetings were to be held—London, Bristol, or Liverpool, for example. Basic decisions thus had to be made in the mother country, under the watchful eyes of the King's men. But for reasons that are still uncertain, the charter granted to the Massachusetts Bay Company in 1629 failed to include this customary requirement. Taking advantage of the omission, John Winthrop and eleven other leading Puritans met in Cambridge and pledged to move to New England if the company stockholders would permit the charter and the company headquarters to be transferred to Massachusetts. The stockholders accepted the terms of the Cambridge Agreement, Winthrop was named governor, and the organizers set to work at recruiting settlers.

Winthrop, a wealthy attorney and landholder, and other Puritan leaders spread the news of the venture among friends and neighbors. Many of the first volunteers were from the East Anglian countryside near Puritan Cambridge, but the recruiting network soon penetrated into communities in the North, West, and South of

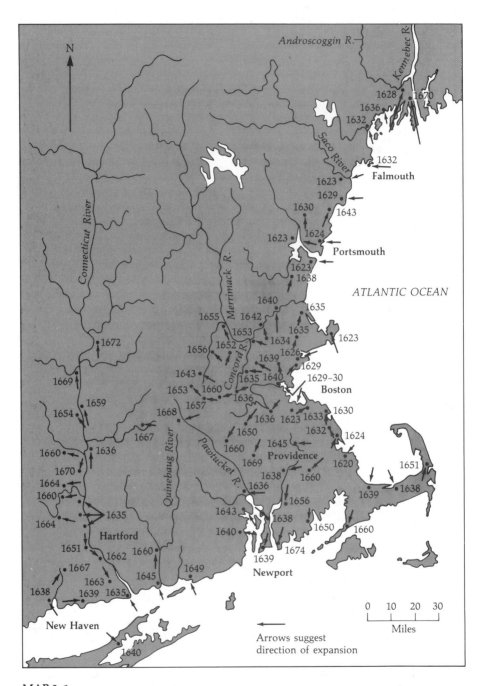

MAP 3-1

The Spread of Settlement in New England, 1620–75

Source: Douglas Edward Leach, *The Northern Colonial Frontier, 1607–1763* (New York, 1966), 34.

England. In glaring contrast to the Jamestown experience, careful efforts were made to ensure that people with necessary skills would be attracted in sufficient numbers. Perhaps for that reason, no specific religious test was imposed. Settlers had only to demonstrate that they believed in the godliness of the enterprise and had a record of working diligently at their callings. The screening was applied to those arriving after Winthrop reached Boston as well; late in the first year, for example, a ship bearing 60 prospective settlers was turned away for "having no testimony" as to their good character. Very few footloose, adventure-seeking single males were accepted; the great majority were sober married couples. Migrants were drawn from a wide range of occupations but were disproportionately from the middle ranks of English society. Few were extremely rich, few were desperately poor. It was a strikingly homogeneous population in economic and social as well as religious background.

The Rule of the Saints

In the free air of Massachusetts, the Puritans were at last free to organize churches along the lines they believed God had intended. Some simple statistics demonstrate the strength of their commitment to that end. By 1650 there were 37 clergymen in the Bible Commonwealth, one for every 415 residents. Virginia, with a somewhat larger population, had only seven ministers then, one for every 3,329 residents. Virginians begged the Church of England to send out more ministers to serve them, but did nothing when their requests were ignored. Massachusetts Puritans escaped a similarly dependent position by promptly creating a college to train their own clergy. Harvard College was founded only six years after the first settlement at Boston. Virginia would not create and support an institution of higher learning for more than a half century to come; William and Mary College was not established until 1693.

The church was the foundation of the Puritan social order, and everyone in the colony was legally required to attend services. Full membership in the congregation, and therefore a voice in such decisions as the election of a minister, was not open to all, however. Membership was not a right but a privilege, and it had to be earned. A proper church, in the Puritan view, was not an "inn" that indiscriminately welcomed everyone. Instead, it was a "household" for the demonstrably godly, run by the "visible saints." The tests imposed to discriminate between saints and sinners were elaborate and arduous. Applicants had to persuade the minister and the members of their "knowledge in the principles of religion, and of their experience in the ways of grace, and of their godly conversation among men," and were subject to close grilling about the state of their soul. Those found "ignorant," "graceless," or "scandalous" were barred. The process of winning admission could take years, but a majority of the first generation settlers succeeded.[1] The intense psychological bonds formed in this public soul-searching were crucial to the

---

[1]The proportion varied over time and also from community to community, but this rough generalization holds for the first generation in most Massachusetts towns.

solidarity of the community. The core families who comprised the membership developed intense tribal loyalties to each other. Those who did not gain entry into the charmed circle were outsiders whose voices counted for little in any aspect of community life.

Membership in a church was a prerequisite for participating in the colony's politics. By the terms of the royal charter, all political authority in the colony was lodged in the hands of the "freemen"—that is, the company shareholders. But Governor Winthrop and a dozen of his friends were the only freemen to make the journey to Massachusetts. To stick by the letter of the law would give a handful of men a monopoly of political power in a community whose population would soon number in the thousands. It would make the political system considerably more oligarchical than that of the old country they were fleeing, where the owners of moderate amounts of property had a voice in political decisions. Winthrop recognized the anomaly and dealt with it before the end of the first year by offering freeman status to all "honest and good men"—all adult male church members. Since a large fraction of the colony's men did gain admission to a congregation, this decision broadened the electorate dramatically.

Accepting freeman status meant agreeing to the terms of the civil covenant. The concept of a covenant was crucial to Puritan thought. The Puritans believed they had a covenant, a contract, with God; if they abided by the terms of the contract, He would grant them saving grace. (This is a crude formulation of a conception too complex for adequate exposition in a textbook.) Parallel to the covenant with God was the church covenant, which bound members of the congregation together in holy fellowship. It followed naturally that civil government should also stem from a voluntary agreement by all responsible members of the community—that is, the adult male church members.

The extension of political rights to a wide segment of the population was not undertaken out of any faith in the equality of man and the wisdom of the common people. Winthrop and his friends believed in rule by an elite. "The best part of the community," he said bluntly, "is always the least, and of that least part the better is always the lesser." Once chosen, rulers had divine sanction to carry out the law without consulting "the voice of the people." Voters were expected to show proper deference to "the best part of the community" by returning men like Winthrop to office. Anyone who passed the searching scrutiny of the minister and the congregation could be trusted to do so. The government of the Bible Commonwealth was "democratic" in the limited sense that fairly large numbers of its inhabitants participated in the framing of the laws and the election of officials. In every other respect, it was far removed from anything later Americans would consider democratic.

Winthrop initially intended to establish a single centralized community at Boston. Arriving settlers, however, refused to be confined within its cramped confines. The borders of the colony were enormous, and newcomers pressed into the interior to obtain large plots of land. Many arrived in parties with others from the same area of England, and they scouted the country to find places where the landscape most resembled the one they had left behind. By 1631 there were six new communities outside of Boston, extending from Saugus in the north to Dorchester

THE PERILS OF VIOLATING THE PURITAN SABBATH

This puts me in mind of another child very strangely drowned a little before winter. The father had undertaken to maintain the mill-dam, and being at work upon it in the afternoon of the last day of the week, night came upon them before they had finished what they intended, and his conscience began to put him in mind of the Lord's day, and he was troubled, yet went on and wrought an hour within night. The next day, after evening exercise, and after they had supped, the mother put two children to bed in the room where they themselves did lie and they went out to visit a neighbor. When they returned, they continued about an hour in the room and missed not the child, but then the mother going to the bed, and not finding her youngest child (a daughter about five years of age), after much search she found it drowned in a well in her cellar. Which was very observable, as by a special hand of God, that the child should go out of that room in another in the dark, and then fall down a trap door or go down the stairs, and so into the well in the farther end of the cellar, the top of the well and the water being even with the ground. But the father, freely in the open congregation did acknowledge it the righteous hand of God for his profaning his holy day against the checks of his own conscience.

—John Winthrop, *Journal*

in the south and Watertown in the west. Twenty years later, the people of the Bay Colony were scattered among two dozen towns, and former residents of the colony had fanned out into Rhode Island and Connecticut as well. Only one-fifth of the Massachusetts population lived in Boston.

These new towns enjoyed greater political autonomy than units of local government in England, then under heavy pressures from Stuart efforts to impose stronger centralized administration. They were ruled by local officials elected in town meetings. Practices varied considerably, but in many communities the town meetings were open even to residents who did not qualify as freemen by colony-wide standards—that is, those outside the church. As the population grew and scattered, it became impossible for all the freemen of the colony to attend meetings of the Massachusetts General Court in Boston, and the General Court was transformed into a representative body composed of two delegates elected from each town. Local communities were legally subordinate to the governor and the General Court, but in practice the central government intruded very little in local affairs. The autonomy of the Puritan town matched that of the self-governing Puritan congregation.

The thrust of settlement into the interior naturally provoked conflict with the local Indians, who regarded the land as theirs. The charter of the Massachusetts Bay Company stated that the "principal ende" of the venture was to "wynn the natives of the country to the knowledge and obedience of the onlie true God," and the official company seal bore the figure of an Indian and the words "come over and help us." Few of the Puritans who came to Massachusetts, however, acted in accord with these pronouncements. The major exception was Reverend John Eliot, who translated the Bible into a local dialect and established four settlements of "praying Indians." But these settlements attracted no more than 1,100 Indians, and only a tenth of them actually converted to Christianity. The natives did not find the white man's religion attractive, and the Puritans were far more concerned with perfecting their "city upon a hill" than with carrying their message to the unreceptive heathen.

The pattern of red–white relations in Massachusetts followed the lines laid down in Virginia and Plymouth. The Puritans sought to obtain the land they wanted peacefully. They engaged in trade and negotiated to purchase land from the tribes. But they were quick to draw their swords when they encountered resistance. In 1637, after Puritan settlers moving into Connecticut River Valley were harassed by the Pequot Indians, a Puritan war party burned down the main Pequot fort and killed not only all the braves, but many women and children, something the "barbaric" Indians were not in the habit of doing in their own intertribal wars.[2] "It was a fearful sight to see them thus frying in the fire and the streams of blood quenching the same," said one English observer, "and horrible was the stink and scent thereof; but the victory seemed a sweet sacrifice, and they gave the praise thereof to God, who had wrought so wonderfully for them."

Structure of the Puritan Community

The line of settlement in Massachusetts pushed ahead about as rapidly as in Virginia after the dissolution of the company. The settlement pattern in the two colonies, however, differed radically. Instead of scattering on isolated farmsteads, the Puritans formed tight-knit, strongly centralized communities. At their center was the meeting house, surrounded by the village green or commons. Clustered tightly around were the residences of the inhabitants. A 1635 law forbade the building of any dwelling more than half a mile from the meeting house. Although the law was repealed a few years later, the custom of centralized residence remained strong in many places long after.

Beyond the dense inner circle of houses were the parcels of farm land. Despite the strong communal elements in Puritan doctrine, communal rather than individ-

---

[2]Some of their righteous fury may have been inspired by such Indian military customs as the taking of scalps. Some recent popular accounts flatly deny that scalping was indigenous to North America. Vine Deloria's best-selling *Custer Died for Your Sins* claims that scalping was "introduced by the English." For a review of the overwhelming evidence to the contrary, see James T. Axtell and William C. Sturtevant, "The Unkindest Cut, or Who Invented Scalping," *William and Mary Quarterly*, July, 1980, pp. 451–72. It is true that the English presence stimulated scalping, because colonial governments paid bounties for the scalps of members of tribes with which they were at war, but that is another matter altogether.

ual ownership of land was never contemplated. Like other Englishmen of their day, they assumed without question that private property was the proper basis of civilization. Two different systems of land holding were followed, depending on the practices followed in the regions of England the migrants came from. Some communities employed the ancient European open field pattern, in which individual holdings were scattered about and many tasks were performed cooperatively. One person might hold ten acres of pasture in one area, twenty acres of woodlot in another direction, and a cornfield somewhere else. In other towns, individual holdings were consolidated and enclosed with fences from the beginning. Whatever system of ownership prevailed, everyone lived together near the center. No "outlivers" were allowed to reside on the outskirts, where they would be free of the scrutiny of the saints.

Like other Englishmen of the day, the Puritan leaders who came to Massachusetts believed that men were innately unequal, and that social stratification was divinely ordained. "At all times," declared Winthrop, "some must be rich, some poor, some high and eminent in power and dignity, others mean and in subjection." Nevertheless, the most basic economic resource in the Puritan community—land—was distributed in a manner that precluded extremes of wealth and poverty. The Massachusetts General Court held title to all unsettled land in the colony. To establish a new town, a group of families petitioned for a land grant, promising to lay out farms, build a church and hire a minister as quickly as possible. If their petition was approved, they proceeded to divide up the land, setting a stock aside for future settlers. They employed three quite different criteria in deciding who was to receive how much land.

One criterion was egalitarian—the principle of need. Anyone who was accepted into the community was thought to deserve a share of its resources, regardless of ability to pay. A minimum plot was therefore assigned to every adult male, except those bound in service to another. Men with larger than average families were given extra acreage on the basis of need. The second consideration in allocating land was the community's need to attract people with valued skills. Ministers, for example, were offered larger plots as an inducement to settle. The third principle was aristocratic: "to him that hath it shall be given." Men of wealth and social standing in England were assigned more land than their social inferiors.

The precise weight given to these three criteria varied from place to place; accordingly, so did the degree of inequality in land ownership. But in the early years of settlement, the overall pattern was strikingly egalitarian by comparison with seventeenth-century England or Virginia, or with the America of a later day. Property was widely, though unequally, diffused; very few families had to depend on others for their livelihood.

Economic Development

Unlike their unhappy countrymen at Jamestown and Plymouth, the first immigrants to Massachusetts Bay came with an ample stock of provisions to support them until native crops could be grown and harvested. Over the decade of the

Great Migration, they developed a thriving agricultural economy. They had an assured market for any surplus they could produce. The newcomers who followed them brought capital from the sale of their property in the mother country and used it to buy food, cattle, lumber for houses, and other necessities from earlier arrivals. These funds were used in turn to pay for English products that the colonists could not make for themselves. When the outbreak of civil war in England cut off the flow of newcomers in 1641, the economy plunged into depression.

To restore prosperity in the Bay Colony, residents had either to reduce their need for imported goods by manufacturing substitutes at home or to find new foreign markets for local products. Both strategies were tried. Through subsidies, tax incentives, and other devices, the governor and the General Court promoted the production of clothing, ironware, and shoes in the 1640s. Domestic cloth and iron could not withstand the competition of superior English brands for long, but the shoe industry prospered. The quest for markets abroad was more successful. Nothing produced in New England was of much value in the mother country. England's farms and fisheries produced enough to feed her population without colonial imports. Fur obtained by trade with the Indians was salable, but the supply quickly dried up as the advance of the frontier drove fur-bearing animals back into

WHAT TO BRING ON THE VOYAGE TO MASSACHUSETTS, JOHN WINTHROP TO HIS WIFE

Be sure to be warm clothed, and to have store of fresh provisions, meal, eggs put up in salt or ground malt, butter, oat meal, pease, and fruits, and a large strong chest or 2: well locked, to keep these provisions in; and be sure they be bestowed in the ship where they may be readily come by, (which the boatswain will see to and the quarter masters, if they be rewarded beforehand), but for these things my son will take care. Be sure to have ready at sea 2 or 3 skillets of several sizes, a large frying pan, a small stewing pan, and a case to boil a pudding in; store of linen for use at sea, and sack to bestow among the sailors; some drinking vessels, and peuter and other vessels: and for physic you shall need no other but a pound of Doctor Wright's Electuariu lenitivu, and his direction to use it, a gallon of scurvy grass to drink a little 5 or 6 mornings together, with some saltpeter dissolved in it, and a little grated or sliced nutmeg.

Thou must be sure to bring no more company than so many as shall have full provision for a year and half, for though the earth here be very fertile yet there must be time and means to raise it; if we have corn enough we may live plentifully.

—John Winthrop, *Letters*, 1630

lands occupied by tribes tied to Dutch traders in New Netherlands and French traders in Canada. Lumber, shingles, staves, turpentine, pitch and other wood products from New England forests could not penetrate a British market flooded with cheap imports from Scandinavia. However, enterprising Massachusetts merchants found that their surplus fish, grain, and timber could be sold at good prices in Spain, Portugal, the wine islands of the Eastern Atlantic, and the sugar islands of the Caribbean. This flourishing trade generated the earnings to finance needed imports from Britain. It had another beneficial economic effect as well; the need for ocean-going vessels to carry on the trade stimulated the shipbuilding industry in Boston and other ports.

Farming, fishing, shipbuilding, and foreign trade together set the Massachusetts economy on a firm foundation. Settlers in remote towns of the interior, however, remained outside the commercial network. Bulky farm products could not be moved to port cities at a reasonable cost with the primitive means of transportation available. It was hard to produce a marketable surplus in much of the area in any event, for the New England growing season was short and much of the soil was poor. The fields were strewn with boulders, whose usefulness for building stone fences was inadequate compensation for the toil required to pry them out of the ground. The heavily wooded hills offered little forage for livestock. Farmers there engaged in subsistence agriculture, growing enough to feed their families but little more. For them, farming was a way of life, not a means of making money on which to live.

Population and Family Patterns

Immigration from England halted with the English Civil War, and the flow never resumed thereafter. Yet the population of Massachusetts and the other New England colonies that spun off from it continued to grow very rapidly, from about 14,000 in 1640 to 33,000 in 1670 and 93,000 by the end of the century. Some 130,000 English men and women immigrated to the Chesapeake colonies in the seventeenth century, seven times as many as came to New England. Remarkably, however, the population of Virginia and Maryland in 1700 was somewhat smaller (88,000) than that of New England. New England, in short, had a very high rate of natural increase, a great many more births than deaths. For much of the century, the Chesapeake population failed to reproduce itself, much less to increase naturally.

One reason for this glaring difference is that the death rate in New England was extremely low. It was not because Puritan conceptions of medicine were advanced (see box). The brisk New England climate was fortunately inhospitable to many of the deadly organisms that flourished in the Chesapeake region, and safe drinking water was readily available. Few women died before their child-bearing years were over, and not as many babies died of disease before reaching maturity. The more favorable disease environment kept the death rate low; the special character of the Puritan migration stimulated a high birth rate. Most Puritans came in family groups, so the sex ratio was fairly balanced from the beginning. There were no tobacco fields to employ a large class of indentured servants, who would marry late in life or not at all. Marriage was almost universal, and the average woman lived long enough to give birth to eight or nine children.

The Puritans saw the family as "a little church," a "little commonwealth," and "a school wherein the first principles and grounds of government and subjection are learned." The patriarch at its head played an active and continuing role in child rearing. Calvinists believed children were innately rebellious, and felt it was essential to break their stubborn will when it first began to manifest itself. "Children should not know, if it could be kept from them, that they have a will of their own." The repression of willfulness began remarkably early. "When turned a year old (and some before) they were taught to fear the rod and to cry softly." And it continued, with daily Bible meeting and prayer sessions at which the necessity of obedience to God and one's parents was the central theme. The chains of dependence forged by such methods remained strong even after children reached maturity, and they were reinforced by economic pressures. Massachusetts fathers allowed their grown sons to farm land they themselves were not using, but kept title over it until their death. The stability and order of the communities of early New England owed much to the stability and order of the Puritan family.

RELIGIOUS DISSENT AND SOCIAL CHANGE

Massachusetts was not literally a theocracy, a state ruled by religious authorities. Puritan thought was modern in its conception that the church and the civil government were quite distinct and in barring ministers from holding public office. Puritan leaders, however, did not adhere to modern notions about the liberty of conscience in religious affairs. They were supremely confident that their views were correct, and ready to use the power of the state to enforce religious uniformity and to suppress heretical beliefs. The first true exponent of religious freedom in American history, Roger Williams, learned that to his regret. Williams was an outspoken and unbending young minister who used his pulpit at Salem to advance incendiary ideas. He took the Calvinist doctrine of the depravity of men so seriously that he denied the possibility of identifying who was elect and who damned. That meant that the colony's leaders were no purer than other citizens, and thus had no right to silence dissenters. Williams even questioned the validity of the Massachusetts Bay Charter, on the grounds that it ignored the rights of the Indians to the land. The General Court tried Williams for advocating these heretical ideas in 1635, convicted him, and ordered him banished from the colony. He moved on with a small band of followers to establish Rhode Island, where religious dissenters of every stripe were tolerated.

Another rebel against Puritan orthodoxy soon joined him there. Anne Hutchinson was an intelligent, forceful, and exceedingly strong-willed woman who attracted the attention of Winthrop and the clerical establishment by holding popular prayer meetings at her home each week. There she accused most of the colony's ministers of not being truly saved. Mrs. Hutchinson was an "Antinomian," a believer that elect Christians need not abide by the codes governing ordinary people, and she made the breathtaking assertion that the source of her radical ideas was direct, personal revelation from on high. Her position threatened not only the religious unity but the social stability of the Bible Commonwealth. If Mrs. Hutchinson could claim a direct pipeline to God, so too could anyone else, and all authority would be undermined. Her sex rendered her challenge all the more unsettling to the males who controlled church and civil affairs. After an assembly at Cambridge condemned 80 of her beliefs or alleged beliefs as "blasphemous, erroneous, and unsafe" in 1637, Anne Hutchinson was banished by the General Court and fled to Rhode Island.

The punishments meted out to Roger Williams and Mrs. Hutchinson were relatively mild. In the years following the Antinomian crisis, considerably harsher steps were taken to repress religious dissent. Quakers who insisted on making public witness of their faith were whipped, branded, and had their ears cut off. Four were hanged when they defied an earlier banishment and returned to the colony, and another had his children taken away from him and sold as slaves in the West Indies. The only liberty allowed to heretics, said a leading minister grimly, was "free liberty to keep away from us."

Such repressive policies, however, could not resolve all religious difficulties. One was the dismaying fact that the triumph of the Puritans in the English Civil War did not lead to a reshaping of England in accord with the Massachusetts model, as Winthrop and the others had anticipated. The split within the English Puritan movement proved to be unbridgeable, and no agreement could be reached on which system of church organization—Presbyterian or Congregational—should be imposed on the country. To the horror of the Bay Colony Puritans, when Oliver Cromwell seized power he extended a pragmatic tolerance to all Protestant sects. English Puritans made a hero of Roger Williams and condemned the Bay Colony for its intolerance of religious dissent! By the time of Winthrop's death in 1649, it was plain that the "city upon a hill" would never play the grand historical role its creators had assigned to it.

The bad news from England was all the more unsettling because of religious developments in the colonies. Church membership began to fall off around mid-century, as the first generation began to die off and their American-born children came of age. The founders' success in imposing religious orthodoxy had a paradoxical result. The younger generation never went through the religious contention and persecution their parents had known in England, anxiety-producing experiences that had prepared their parents' hearts for the transforming conversion experience that was required to win church membership. As a result, they found it difficult to follow in their parents' footsteps upon reaching maturity. Despite earnest prayer, church attendance, and Bible study, their hearts remained cold to God. Their inability to qualify for church membership had troubling implications. When they married and began to raise a family, their children would not be eligible for baptism. Baptism was no guarantee of salvation for a Calvinist, of course, but it was regarded as a vital part of "preparation" for salvation; a child who died unbaptized ran a greater risk of eternal damnation.

Faced with a shrinking constituency and diminishing influence in the affairs of the colony, the ministry proposed a major reform in 1662. The "Half-Way Covenant" authorized the baptism of children whose grandparents were members, even if their parents were not. It had little effect at first, because the clergy as a group did not have the authority to compel compliance. It was up to the individual congregation to decide such matters, and the great majority of the colony's churches held firmly to the old ways. After 1675, however, most began to accept "half-way" members. It seemed a necessary expedient to prevent further attrition, but it diminished the significance of church membership, and was a step towards the nonexclusive Anglican conception of the church that the first generation had found repugnant.

Individualism Unleashed

The good Puritan, according to John Winthrop, was *in* the world but not *of* the world. He was enjoined to labor diligently at his calling not for material reward but for the welfare of the community and the glory of God. Winthrop had no intention of fostering a competitive, materialistic community of people with their hungry eyes on the main chance. All residents were to be "knit together as one man in brotherly affection," always ready to deny themselves "superfluities for the supply of others' necessities." It was a delicately balanced, intensely communal vision.

In practice, however, the line between energetically pursuing one's calling and pursuing wealth for its own sake was difficult to draw. As economic development brought individual and communal interests into conflict, the balance tilted increasingly towards the individual. In 1639 one of Boston's leading merchants, Robert Keayne, violated the custom that traders charge no more than the traditional "just price" for their wares. The market for supplies was tight and Keayne decided to charge what the market would bear, boosting his prices well above the customary level. Keayne was convicted of "extortion," fined heavily, and required to make a "penetentiall acknowledgement" of his sin before his congregation. His prosecution for evading traditional communal constraints, however, was one of the last of its kind. The rapid growth of trade, and the prosperity it brought, weakened the bonds of "brotherly affection" and unleashed the competitive, self-aggrandizing instincts that Winthrop hoped to keep in check. By mid-century a leading minister could complain that "an over-eager desire after the world hath so seized on the spirits of many, as if the Lord had no further work for his people to do but every bird to feather his own nest." He exaggerated, doubtless, to persuade his audience of the need to repent. But there is no question that, at least in Boston and other commercial centers linked to it, "an over-eager desire" for individual gain was more in evidence than the first builders of the "city upon a hill" would have wished.

SUGGESTED READINGS

The best brief account of the Puritan settlement of New England is Edmund Morgan, *The Puritan Dilemma: The Story of John Winthrop* (1958). Samuel Eliot Morison's *The Builders of the Bay Colony* (1930) is a fuller and highly readable account. Concerning the Pilgrims, see George Langdon, *Pilgrim Colony: A History of Plymouth, 1620–1691* (1966). Perry Miller's *The New England Mind: The Seventeenth Century* (1939) and *The New England Mind: From Colony to Province* (1953) are masterpieces. Students who are intimidated by those dauntingly large and complex books can gain access to many of Miller's key ideas in his collections of essays, *Errand into the Wilderness* (1956) and *Nature's Nation* (1967). Michael Walzer, *The Revolution of the Saints* (1965) is excellent on the rise of Puritanism in England. Edmund Morgan, *Visible Saints: The History of a Puritan Idea* (1963), and David D. Hall, *The Faithful Shepherd: A History of the New England Ministry in the Seventeenth Century* (1972) discuss its transplantation in New England. Sacvan Bercovitch, *The Puritan Origins of the American Self* (1975) treats the impact of Puritanism on later American thought.

Everything that is known of the Indian tribes of the region is reviewed in the Smithsonian Institution's *Handbook of North American Indians: The Northeast* (1978). Alden T. Vaughan, *New England Frontier: Puritans and Indians, 1620–1675* (1965) and Francis Jennings, *The Invasion of America: Indians, Colonialism, and the Cant of Conquest* (1975) offer radically contrasting judgments of Puritan–Indian relations. Charles M. Segal and David Stineback, ed., *Puritans, Indians, and Manifest Destiny* (1977) is an excellent collection of primary sources.

New insights into the structure of the Puritan community and the character of family life may be gleaned from a series of close studies of local communities. These include Sumner C. Powell, *Puritan Village: The Formation of a New England Town* (1963), Darret B. Rutman, *Winthrop's Boston: A Portrait of a Puritan Town* (1965), John Demos, *A Little Commonwealth: Family Life in Plymouth Colony* (1970), Philip Greven, Jr., *Four Generations: Population, Land, and Family in Colonial Andover, Massachusetts* (1970), and Kenneth A. Lockridge, *A New England Town: The First Hundred Years* (1970). David G. Allen, *In English Ways: The Movement of Societies and the Transferal of English Local Law and Custom to Massachusetts Bay in the Seventeenth Century* (1981) emphasizes persisting cultural continuities.

The course of economic and social change may be followed in Bernard Bailyn, *New England Merchants in the Seventeenth Century* (1955), James F. Shepherd and Gary M. Walton, *The Economic Rise of Early America* (1979), T.H. Breen, *Puritans and Adventurers: Change and Persistence in Early America* (1980), Paul Boyer and Stephen Nissenbaum, *Salem Possessed: The Social Origins of Witchcraft* (1974), and John Demos, *Entertaining Satan: Witchcraft and the Culture of Early New England* (1982).

Chapter Four

Slavery and the Colonial Economy

I n the fierce political struggle that culminated in the Revolutionary War and the winning of independence for the American colonies, patriots charged that the British sought to deprive them of their liberty and reduce them to slaves: "Those who are taxed without their own consent are slaves. We are taxed without our consent. We are therefore slaves." They saw no incongruity in denouncing slavery while living in a society which held almost half a million black people, a fifth of the entire population, in permanent bondage. In the southern colonies from Maryland to Georgia, slave labor was the foundation of the economy. Slaves were to be found in every northern colony as well, and many merchants there owed their wealth to the profits they derived from the slave trade and the exchange of products made by slave labor. In Boston, the "cradle of liberty," three out of four families in the upper quarter income bracket had slave servants in their homes. Slavery was an integral and vital part of Britain's flourishing imperial economy. Close to 40 percent of all goods imported into Britain in the late eighteenth century were the products of slave labor; more than half of Britain's exports went to slave colonies. How and why slavery developed into such a central institution in British North America is one of the central problems of early American history.

THE BEGINNINGS OF SLAVERY IN THE WESTERN HEMISPHERE

The European invasion of the Western Hemisphere had tragic consequences not only for the native peoples already there but for Africans as well. The potential of the land was rich, but labor was scarce. Only the Spanish found large numbers

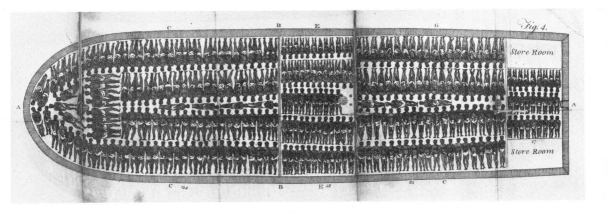

The dual nature of slaves—cargo and passengers—is suggested by this diagram and the only known drawing executed aboard a slave ship.

of Indians who could be compelled to work for them; and even New Spain experienced labor shortages as the Indians succumbed to new diseases and over-work. It was impossible to attract enough immigrants from Europe to perform the lowly and backbreaking tasks that had to be done. To fill the vacuum, Spanish, Portuguese, Dutch, English, and French colonizers developed an enormous inter-national slave trade. The sailing ships that carried riches back to the mother country on the eastward run returned with their holds crammed with black people in chains. Africans outnumbered Europeans in the New World as early as 1650. From 1492 to 1776 the forced migration of helpless Africans contributed far more to the growth of the population of the hemisphere than the voluntary migration of European whites. About a million whites chose to come to the Americas in those years; almost five million blacks were so forced, and another five million followed between 1776 and the closing of the trade in the nineteenth century.

Evolution of the Slave Trade

Slavery was not invented by European whites. It has a very long history and has existed in many cultures around the globe. By the fifteenth century it had died out in most of Christian Europe, but was still recognized in Spain and Portugal. It existed in most of Africa and in the Arab world. Soldiers defeated in battle saved their lives by accepting servitude to their conquerors; people were enslaved for committing serious crimes; others were sold when unable to discharge their debts. The institution of slavery differed in crucial respects from what developed later, however. Slavery was not necessarily a lifetime condition; it was sometimes for a limited period. It was not confined to any one racial group. Slaves had some legal rights, such as the right to marry. Most important, the children of a slave did not always inherit the status of their parents.

A long-distance trade in African slaves also long predates the first European contacts with Africa. After the Arab conquest of North Africa in the eighth century, Arab traders moved south into the heart of Africa to purchase bondsmen. They marched them back across the Sahara, leaving a trail of skeletons bleaching in the sands. This trade was quite small, however—about 1,000 people a year at most.

When the Portuguese first reached the coast of sub-Saharan Africa in the middle of the fifteenth century and began to trade with African chiefs, they were offered not only gold, ivory, and pepper, but slaves as well. They saw nothing repugnant in the trade in human merchandise. By 1492 they had brought about 25,000 black people back to the Iberian Peninsula or the islands off the African Coast—the Canaries, the Azores, and Madeira. Some were employed as personal servants, but most were used in an innovative way that foreshadowed what would become the dominant pattern in the New World—in large-scale plantation agri-culture. In response to Europe's rapidly growing sweet tooth, the Portuguese established sugar plantations and set Africans to work at gang labor in the cane fields.

If the Western Hemisphere had not been opened up for European exploitation at the end of the fifteenth century, the slave trade would probably not have

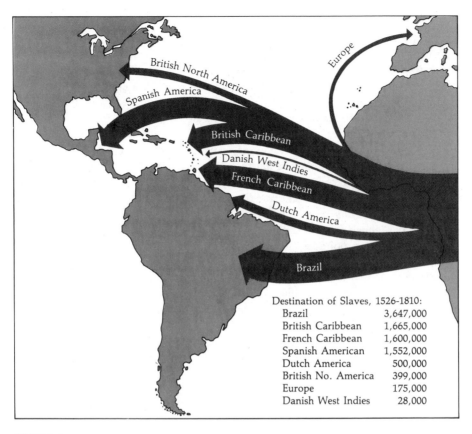

Destination of Slaves, 1526-1810:

Brazil	3,647,000
British Caribbean	1,665,000
French Caribbean	1,600,000
Spanish American	1,552,000
Dutch America	500,000
British No. America	399,000
Europe	175,000
Danish West Indies	28,000

MAP 4-1
The Slave Trade to the Americas, 1526–1810

extended beyond these modest dimensions. But the acute labor shortage that developed in the European colonies in the New World transformed the trickle into a flood. By 1600, 5,000 Africans were crossing the ocean each year, 30,000 by 1700, and 75,000 annually in the peak years of 1750–1800. Africans were a better source of labor than Indians in a crucial respect; when exposed to European diseases they did not sicken and die with such appalling frequency. The disease environments of Africa and Europe were quite similar, and Africans therefore possessed inherited immunities Indians lacked. Indeed, they had better biological defenses for surviving in the tropical parts of America than European whites did, coming from cultures that had long known malaria and yellow fever.[1] In tropical zones, the death rate of European newcomers was triple that for blacks. Slaves were a costly

---

[1] The sickle-cell trait still to be found among some American blacks is an example. It is an inherited blood characteristic found in many populations that inhabit malarial environments. It can lead to a dangerous form of anemia, but heightens resistance to malaria, and was more of an asset than a liability in the areas where it originated.

long-term investment. Ironically, it was the special biological hardiness of the African that made it profitable to enslave him.

European slave traders did not physically capture their victims, as suggested in Alex Haley's fanciful novel and television program *Roots*. The rulers of African coastal states did not allow European kidnapping parties to conduct raids in the interior of the continent. (The Europeans wouldn't have survived long if they had; before the medical breakthroughs of the late nineteenth century, no less than half of the Europeans who arrived in Africa for duty in the colonial service died within a year.) Slaves were captured by fellow Africans, brought to West African ports by forced march, and sold to Europeans by native chieftains and merchants in exchange for guns, iron, copper, and rum. It was a flourishing business, in which some powerful Africans grew fat upon the misery of others. In 1695 a slave in good health brought 8 guns or 600 bars of iron on the African coast; prices rose considerably higher over the next century.

Africa's extreme political and cultural fragmentation made this grim trade possible. The continent contained countless tribes, speaking more than 800 different languages. Africans had no sense of a common national identity that might have made them reluctant to sell their fellow countrymen. Strong tribes had always preyed on weaker ones. The intrusion of Europeans greatly intensified the competition, setting in motion a "gun/slave cycle." Tribes used the guns they obtained from slave traders to raid their neighbors to obtain slaves who could be sold for still more guns; their neighbors in turn felt compelled to conduct slaving raids to be able to purchase guns for their own protection.

Almost ten million Africans landed and were sold in the ports of the New World before the slave trade was cut off in the nineteenth century, and an unknown but large number died resisting capture, were killed trying to escape, or committed suicide (see box). And then there were the hazards of spending several weeks in cramped quarters below the decks, with inadequate provisions for sanitation and insufficient food. About 15 percent of the unwilling passengers, it is estimated, never saw land again. Those who fell sick were tossed overboard to keep disease from spreading to their fellows. Many of the survivors must have envied the dead. Inextricably ripped from their communities, bound for an unknown destination for an unknown purpose, they must have felt deep despair and numbing disorientation.

New Spain and Brazil

The Spanish imported black slaves purchased from Portuguese traders into New Spain as early as 1502; by 1570 there were as many slaves as Spaniards there. The form of slavery was milder and more flexible than elsewhere in the hemisphere. The Spanish did not develop large plantations which employed slaves in agricultural work. Africans clustered in cities, where they served as soldiers or learned various European skills and crafts. They identified with many aspects of Spanish culture, and were considered by the Indians to be part of the dominant

THE TERROR OF ENSLAVEMENT

Many of these slaves we transport from Guinea to America are prepossessed with the opinion that they are carried like sheep to the slaughter, and that Europeans are fond of their flesh; which notion so far prevails with some as to make them fall into a deep melancholy and despair, and to refuse all sustenance, tho' never so much compelled or even beaten to oblige them to take some nourishment: notwithstanding all which, they will starve to death; whereof I have had several instances in my own slaves both abroad and at Guadalupe. I have been necessitated sometimes to cause the teeth of these wretches to be broken, because they would not open their mouths, or be prevailed upon by any entreaties to feed themselves; and thus have forced some sustenance into their throats.

—John Barbot, *Description of Guinea*, 1682

group. Pressures from the church and royal officials gave them a number of basic freedoms. Slaves could marry freely, even against the wishes of their masters, and own property. They had a right to purchase their freedom at a price fixed by a court; by 1600 a quarter of the blacks of New Spain were in fact free. There was no sharp color line. Blacks mingled freely with Indians and whites to form a new intermediate racially mixed social grouping.

The Portuguese pioneered in introducing a far more brutal and oppressive type of slavery into the New World. Having successfully used slave labor to cultivate sugar in their Atlantic islands, they began to import massive numbers of blacks to toil in the large sugar plantations they established in northeast Brazil after 1550. This model soon would be copied by other colonizing powers elsewhere in the Americas. The plantation produced staples that were prized by Europeans and were not well-suited for cultivation in the European climate—sugar, rice, coffee, tobacco, or cotton. High profits could be reaped, even at relatively low prices, because using slaves kept labor costs low. An African bondsman purchased for a few hundred pounds of sugar could produce that much sugar in a single year. After that everything he turned out represented pure profit for the owner, except for the expense involved in providing him the minimal food, shelter, and clothing necessary for subsistence. Slaves worked in large gangs under the surveillance of drivers who whipped them freely if they gave less than their all. The pace of work was so draining that many died young; but replacements could be had so cheaply that masters did little to reduce these losses. Society was sharply polarized; a large black servile class devoid of rights was ruled by a small white master class.

THE EVOLUTION OF THE PLANTATION ECONOMY
IN THE SOUTHERN COLONIES

The first Africans in Virginia were landed within a dozen years of the founding of Jamestown. A Dutch slave ship brought 20 of them in 1619. It is striking, however, that very few other blacks were imported for a long time to come. A census in 1640 counted only 150, and there were fewer than 1,000 as late as 1670, less than 4 percent of the colony's population. After 1670 the numbers soared, so that by 1700 enslaved blacks composed half of the Virginia work force, and the same transformation had taken place in the neighboring tobacco colony, Maryland.

In these early decades, when the black minority was so small, it is uncertain what their status was. In many respects they were initially treated much like the white servants they worked, ate, and slept beside. If a slave is someone who owes a lifetime of labor to his master, and whose children inherit that condition, the first Africans in Virginia were not clearly slaves. The fact that they were sold when they first landed does not establish that they were slaves, because white indentured servants were also sold. The scanty records that survive from this early period do not reveal how long these Africans worked for their masters, or what happened to any children they might have had. There were as yet no laws specifying that their servitude was for life. Perhaps it was simply assumed, and the numbers involved were too small to require legislative attention. It is clear, however, that as late as 1660 some blacks in the colony were not listed as having masters and were apparently free. One African freedman, Anthony Johnson, was even the master of another black. Some evidence suggests that conversion to Christianity was ground for release from life servitude.

After 1660 the Virginia legislature and courts moved forcefully to eliminate any ambiguity in the status of blacks and to establish their permanent bondage. A 1662 statute provided that children born in the colony were bound or free "according to the condition of the mother." Subsequent laws declared that conversion did not bring free status, forbade interracial marriages, and denied blacks the right to own property, to testify in court, to participate in politics, to congregate in public places, and to travel freely. A 1691 act barred masters from freeing slaves unless they paid for their immediate transportation out of the colony. Every effort was made to ensure their separation and subordination. Legally they were property, and their owner had virtually unlimited power to treat them as he saw fit. The last will and testament of a Virginia gentleman casually expressed his wish that "all my negroes, horses, and other property be sold."

Causes of the Changeover

Why weren't more Africans brought to Virginia in the early years, as soon as the potential of its tobacco fields became clear? And why did their numbers grow so rapidly and their position deteriorate so drastically late in the seventeenth century? Much of the answer lies in changing labor market conditions. In the first half of the century, England's population was growing more rapidly than the capacity of its economy to absorb them. Wages were falling, and there was an abundant pool of

HUMAN RIGHTS IN VIRGINIA (1705)
WHITE SERVANTS

All masters and owners of servants, shall find and provide for their servants, wholesome and competent diet, clothing, and lodging, by the discretion of the county court; and shall not, at any time, give immoderate correction; neither shall, at any time, whip a christian white servant naked, without an order from a justice of the peace: And if any, notwithstanding this act shall presume to whip a christian white servant naked, without such order, the person so offending, shall forfeit and pay for the same, forty shillings sterling, to the party injured: To be recovered, with costs, upon petition, without the formal process of an action....

BLACKS AND INDIANS

And if any slave resist his master, or owner, or other person, by his or her order, correcting such slave, and shall happen to be killed in such correction, it shall not be accounted felony; but the master, owner, and every such other person so giving correction, shall be free and acquit of all punishment and accusation for the same, as if such accident had never happened; And also, if any negro, mulatto, or Indian, bond or free, shall at any time, lift his or her hand, in opposition against any christian, not being negro, mulatto, or Indian, he or she so offending, shall, for every such offence, proved by the oath of the party, receive on his or her bare back, thirty lashes, well laid on, cognizable by a justice of the peace for that county wherein such offence shall be committed.

—Hening, *Laws of Virginia*, 1823

footloose, jobless men available for service in the colonies. It was cheaper for a planter to pay their passage than to buy an African.

Around the middle of the century, England's population began to level off, and wages began to rise. Consequently, the number of people desperate enough to accept indentured servitude in Virginia fell. Planters experiencing greater difficulty recruiting new servants first responded by attempting to tighten the screws on those they already had on hand. In the 1660s the planter-dominated assembly added three years to the term of servants who had come to the colony without a prearranged indenture contract, and further raised the already stiff penalty of additional years of service for runaways. This was counterproductive, however. Virginia was no longer a police state with mail censorship. As the news of these changes filtered back across the Atlantic, the number of volunteers for indentured service there fell off even more. Soon planters were forced to face up to the reality and to embark upon the opposite course—increasing the "freedom dues" paid to servants at the end of their terms and softening the penalties for such crimes as running away, drunkenness, and carrying arms.

These efforts to make voluntary servitude more attractive were not sufficient to restore the flow of newcomers to its old levels. Planters had either to accept a shrinking income or to turn to the only other available alternative—slave labor. By the 1660s evidence that it could be profitable was near at hand, in the British West Indian islands in the Caribbean. Barbados, Jamaica, and the Leeward islands, which Britain had seized from Spain earlier in the century, had begun much like Virginia. They were settled by English whites who worked as farmers or indentured servants in the tobacco fields. They failed to prosper, however, and an economic slump that hit the West Indies in the late 1630s brought a sudden economic and social transformation in the next quarter of a century. White servants fled, and men of wealth acquired large estates and proceeded to buy African slaves to grow and process sugar. The "sugar revolution" brought tremendous wealth to West Indian planters, and Virginians were well aware of it.

The other factor that promoted the switch from white servants to black slaves was Britain's new involvement in the slave trade. The small numbers of Africans in Virginia before 1660 had been purchased from Dutch traders, who had replaced the Portuguese as world leader in the slave traffic. In 1660 Parliament cut off that source by forbidding colonists to trade with the merchants of other nations. At about the same time, Britain entered the slave trade in a major way. The chartering of the Royal Adventurers to Africa in 1662, reorganized as the Royal African Company in 1672, marked the beginnings, but the great spurt came after the company's monopoly was dissolved by Parliament in 1698. Free competition brought a dramatic rise in the number of British and American vessels plying African waters in search of slaves. Britain quickly surpassed Holland as the world's largest slave trader, and held the lead throughout the eighteenth century.

The dwindling supply of white servants and the increasing availability of African slaves inevitably changed the cost of each. The price of servants edged upward as the price of slaves fell. In 1674 a slave who would serve for life sold for 2.9 times as much as a temporary indentured servant; by the end of the century slaves sold for only twice as much as servants. Since slaves could be expected to live much more than twice as long as the span of the normal indenture, planters had a strong new incentive to turn to bound African labor. Once the key element in the Chesapeake labor force, indentured servants were only a seventh of the population in 1700. Africans were half the labor force, and considerably more in plantation areas near the coast. There was no reason to fear that the increasingly harsh slave codes that relegated blacks to a distinct and subordinate place would keep other Africans from coming to Virginia and Maryland, since they had no choice in the matter.

Tobacco is not necessarily a plantation crop. It can be grown efficiently on small farms, and was in the Chesapeake throughout the colonial years and later. But it was well suited to cultivation by slave labor. Slavery, it has been said, "requires that all hands be occupied at all times," because unfree workers must be fed, clothed, and provided other necessities the full year round. They cannot be laid off and left to fend for themselves during slack times like free men. Tobacco has a long growing season, and requires intensive labor over much of the year. During the mild southern winters after the crop was in, slaves could do the repair, construction, and land clearance work they were too busy for during the growing season.

Colonization of the Lower South

The political turmoil generated by the Puritan Revolution drew attention away from opportunities in England's fledgling empire overseas. When it came to an end with the restoration of the monarchy in 1660, a new colonizing thrust began. One of its chief targets was the 600 miles of unsettled coastline from the southern border of Virginia to Spanish Florida. In the colonization of "Carolina"—eventually split into North Carolina, South Carolina, and Georgia—slavery was introduced more rapidly and deliberately than along the Chesapeake.

Some of the most powerful members of King Charles II's court were committed to the establishment of English settlements in Carolina. In 1663, eight of them persuaded Charles to issue a charter naming them proprietors of the entire area, with exclusive rights to rent or sell land to settlers. Few colonists came at first; the proprietors' assumption that they need not invest any funds to launch new communities was unrealistic. Carolina was reorganized in 1669, under the Fundamental Constitutions written by the great English political philosopher John Locke. Locke's constitution was a bizarre attempt to recreate a vanished feudal order, a rigid hierarchical society with great lords of the manor and a permanent class of tenants. It neglected the elemental fact that no one could be induced to accept lifelong subordinate status as a tenant in a country in which land ownership was so easily accessible. The Fundamental Constitutions did point to the future clearly in one respect, however—it bluntly provided that "every free man in Carolina shall have absolute power and authority over his negro slaves."

The reorganization of Carolina committed the proprietors to provide financial backing for the first time. The first permanent settlement was established in 1670, and the colony grew rapidly thereafter. The time was ripe, because the great transformation then taking place in the British West Indies provided both potential settlers and a strong market for Carolina products. The sugar revolution was squeezing out indentured servants and many small planters, forcing them to look elsewhere. Thousands of them moved on to Carolina in the 1670s. The shift to sugar production in Barbados and the other islands opened new economic opportunities in Carolina. Sugar was so profitable that all available land was given over to it; the product of a single acre of cane would purchase more corn than could be raised on five acres, with enough left over to pay shipping charges to import the corn. Likewise with lumber; all of the trees were felled to make room for more cane, so that wood for fuel, building, and barrels had to be imported. Carolina, the closest English colony in North America, was the prime source of those imports. Settlers there prospered by shipping meat, corn, and wood products to the West Indies, in exchange for sugar, slaves and credits on London mercantile houses.

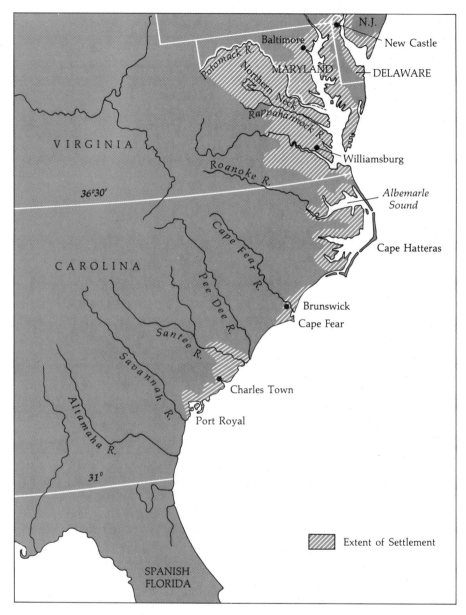

MAP 4–2
Southern Settlements by 1700

Although slaves were present in substantial numbers from the beginning, particularly in what became South Carolina, slavery did not immediately force out free labor. Growing cattle and corn and cutting lumber did not require large capital investments, and they offered no "economies of scale"—large plantations could not produce these commodities at a lower average cost per unit than small farms.

Yeoman farmers prospered in the first phase of Carolina's economic development. This initial stage came to an end in the 1680s, however, when the West Indian sugar industry stagnated and demand for Carolina products decreased abruptly. The faltering market forced Carolinians to search for a staple that could be sold in European markets. They tried sugar, tobacco, cotton, silk, ginger, and wine—all without success—before discovering that the climate and terrain were well suited to rice. It is probably more than coincidental that they discovered how to cultivate and process rice shortly after the number of African slaves in the colony began to increase dramatically. Englishmen knew nothing about the many complexities of rice cultivation, but Africans did. Rice was a major crop in West Africa; slave traders bought it to provision their ships in the port cities. We can never know for sure, because of the paucity of surviving documents, but it seems likely that the experience and skills the slaves brought with them were what made the experiment succeed.

Rice was to the economy of the lower South what tobacco was to the Chesapeake economy. At least 1.5 million pounds of it were shipped out of Carolina in 1710, 18 million by 1730, 76 million by 1770. The spread of rice culture wrought a social transformation as thorough as the sugar revolution in the Caribbean islands. Rice was not a crop for the small farmer. It was most efficiently grown on large estates, with gangs of workers toiling on their knees in the muck. White men could not be enticed to do such work, but slaves could be compelled. White small farmers fled the low-lying, swampy areas suitable for rice cultivation, and the soaring slave trade brought black bondsmen to replace them.

Sullivan's Island in Charlestown harbor, where arriving slaves were briefly quarantined, has been called "the Ellis Island of the Afro-American people." In the eighteenth century it was the entry point for over 40 percent of all slaves arriving in North America, a much larger share than at any other port. South Carolina had a black majority as early as 1708, and Africans outnumbered whites by two to one by 1740. Figures for the colony as a whole understate the magnitude of change, because they include many white farmers living outside the coastal rice belt. In the tidewater area around Charlestown there were eight or nine black slaves for every white, a ratio as high as in the West Indies. Savagely repressive slave laws modeled on those of Barbados were quickly enacted to keep the large black majority under the thumbs of their masters.

Wealth and Its Distribution

The spectacular rise in output of rice and tobacco cultivated by slave labor provided the dynamism behind the growth of the southern economy in the colonial years. Of course there were other economic activities. In the lower South, indigo for blue dye, also produced on slave plantations, was an important staple, and trade in deerskins with local Indians yielded significant earnings. In the Chesapeake colonies in the eighteenth century a growing number of planters reduced their vulnerability to fluctuating tobacco prices by growing more foodstuffs, especially wheat. And there were always a good many subsistence farms without slaves in the backcountry and in scattered pockets of poor land elsewhere. But tobacco and rice dominated the southern economy, just as cotton was to do in the nineteenth century.

Slavery made the southern colonies rich—more precisely, it made some southern whites rich. Evidence is spotty for much of the colonial period, which economic historians call a "statistical Dark Age." However, a pioneering study of the wealth of the citizens of the various colonies in 1774 shows the South to have been strikingly prosperous. The total value of the land, tools, livestock, furnishings, financial assets, and slaves per free person in New England was £33 sterling. In the commercially more developed mid-Atlantic colonies—New York, New Jersey, and Pennsylvania—the figure was £51. The average for the South was £132, more than two and a half times the mid-Atlantic level and quadruple that for New England!

But we may wonder if wealth *per free person* is a proper measure of the prosperity of the South, since 40 percent of its population was not free. Is it appropriate to count the more than £33 million in human property held by southern whites in assessing the region's economic development? Is it appropriate to exclude slaves, who did so much of the wealth-generating work, from the population base used to calculate the per capita wealth figures? If we eliminate the value of slave property from the calculation, and recompute an average figure for all residents of the South rather than just for free persons, the picture looks very different. In this hypothetical South without slavery, the average estate would have been only £43, only moderately above the New England level and actually below that for the mid-Atlantic colonies.

Of course this alternative calculation is unhistorical. Slaves *were* treated as property, and the vast sums invested in them were as real and remunerative as the money sunk in land, farm houses, or anything else. And they were *not* potential wealth holders like southern whites; they were denied the right to own property.

WORK ON A CAROLINA RICE PLANTATION, 1755

Our staple commodity for some years has been rice, and tilling, planting, hoeing, reaping, threshing, pounding have all been done merely by the poor slaves here. Labor and the loss of many of their lives testified the fatigue they underwent in satiating the inexpressible avarice of their masters. You may easily guess what tedious, laborious and slow method it is of cultivating lands to till it all by hand, and then to plant 100, 120 acres of land by the hand, but the worst comes last for after the rice is threshed they beat it all in large wooden mortars to clean it from the husk, which is a very hard and severe operation.

—G.C. Rogers, ed., *The Papers of Henry Laurens*, 1968

TABLE 4-1
Wealth per Free Person by Region, 1774,
and in a Hypothetical South Without Slavery
(in pounds sterling)

	New England	Mid-Atlantic Colonies	Actual South	Hypothetical South*
Total wealth	33	51	132	43
Slaves	†	2	58	0
Land	28	27	55	32
Other§	5	22	19	11

*This assumes complete uncompensated emancipation of all southern slaves before 1774. Slave property no longer exists, and former slaves are considered potential wealth holders and included in the base population from which per capita figures are derived.

† Less than half of a pound—actually .02.

§ Crops, livestock, tools, furnishings, financial assets, and so on.

However, the exercise glaringly exposes the extent to which the seemingly great prosperity of the South was reserved for whites only, and the degree to which it depended on the unpaid forced labor of the black underclass.

Slavery in the North

Slavery took root in the northern as well as the southern colonies, but it never became vital to their economies. Slaves formed 4 percent of the northern population at most. Except for humanitarian Quakers, northerners had no more moral scruples against depriving men of their natural liberty than their southern counterparts. Slave servants and artisans made up a fifth of the population of New York City in 1750, and there were about 1,000 in Boston. Their presence in the families of such respected Puritan divines as Cotton Mather and Jonathan Edwards suggests how thoroughly respectable it was. Northern newspapers routinely carried advertisements offering rewards for the return of runaways and announcements of forthcoming slave auctions. And Yankee merchants and captains were the colonists most active in the trade that carried Africans to bondage in the land of liberty.

Slavery remained economically peripheral in the northern colonies—and hence vulnerable to attack when sensibilities began to change in the revolutionary era—because it was ill-suited to the kind of agriculture that was economically dominant there. The growing season was too short for tropical staples like rice, sugar, or tobacco. A short growing season, furthermore, meant that idle slaves would have to be maintained over the long winter months. The main products of northern farms—grain and meat—were not plantation crops that offered "economies of scale." They could be grown efficiently on family farms. Consequently, northern slaves remained a luxury for the urban rich, a badge of gentility. Because city dwellers were only a small fraction of the population of the northern colonies, relatively few slaves were to be found there.

THE EXPERIENCE OF BONDAGE

Uprooted Africans transplanted in New World soil had to make a painful accommodation to a bewilderingly different world. What it meant for the men and women forced to endure it can never be fully recreated; virtually no direct testimony from slaves in colonial America has survived in the historical record. It is clear, however, that the history of slavery is more than the history of what all-powerful whites did to the blacks they owned. Masters indeed wielded awesome powers, including the power to whip recalcitrant slaves to death. However, slaves were not robots who would do precisely what was called for when the right button was pushed. They were reasoning human beings with traditions and values of their own, and they tenaciously struggled to preserve their sense of self-worth within the confines of a brutally exploitative system. They managed to find some breathing space, some room for maneuver, to make that possible. Slavery denied their humanity, but never succeeded in extinguishing it.

The most important institution that made their endurance possible was the family, and the extended and complex kin network that radiated from it. Although American slaves had no legal right to marry, they did in fact pair off and raise children. These unions, frequently long-enduring, provided the emotional support that sustained slave men and women in the draining round of labor from sunup to sundown. The Afro-American family was not a recreation of the traditional African family, but neither was it a carbon copy of the families of the white master class. Marriages between first cousins, common in the planter group, were taboo among slaves, and slaves had their own special customs governing the naming of children and fixing the obligations of other relatives like aunts and uncles. Slave children were socialized to the norms of the slave community within their families, more often than not living with both father and mother.

The slave family, of course, was not secure from disruption. The master had the legal right to sell husband, wife, or child to anyone he pleased. How commonly he exercised that right in the colonial years has not been systematically investigated, but it was probably not usual to break up families by sale. Some planters felt moral scruples against it; those without such scruples hesitated to do so out of fear that slaves whose kin were taken from them would be too demoralized to work effectively. A study of the domestic slave trade in the years just before the Civil War reveals that most sales were of young single men and women of about the age at which it would have been normal to leave home if they had been free. Quite possibly this was also true in the earlier period.

The first blacks to arrive in the colonies had only limited opportunities for family life. In the early decades most lived alone with their masters, or with small groups of their fellow countrymen, spread thinly over a vast territory. Their chances of finding a mate were poor. For slave men the problem was compounded by the fact that the slave trade brought in two males for every female. Even if every woman found a spouse, many surplus males were left without a partner, doomed to bachelorhood. Over time, however, the development of large plantations produced larger concentrations of slaves and a larger pool of potential mates. And as slave women gave birth to an increasing number of children, the sex ratio (the number of males per 100 females) began to even out; the native-born generation naturally included as many females as males.[2] As they came of age and mated, the slave population began to grow very rapidly from natural increase. Over the eighteenth century, slave births exceeded slave deaths by 18 percent per decade. Between 1700 and 1780, a quarter of a million Africans were imported into North America by slave traders, but the black population increased by almost twice that (by 488,000).

This may seem unremarkable, but in fact it was very remarkable. No other slave society in the Western Hemisphere had anything like this record. In most, slave deaths exceeded slave births, and planters had to keep purchasing new ones to make up for the losses. In the colonial period, the British Caribbean islands imported five times as many slaves as went to North America. Yet in 1770 the Afro-American population in the mainland colonies was larger than that of the British West Indies! Brutal and oppressive though it was in many ways, the slave system of the American colonies was notably less destructive of life itself.

The cause of this dramatic difference is not altogether clear. It was at least partly the result of differences in the disease environment. The tropical diseases that were such killers on the islands could not endure the temperate climate of North America. South Carolina is an exception to this generalization, perhaps the exception that proves the rule. Its hot and humid climate resembled that of the West Indies, and tropical diseases did decimate many of its inhabitants, white and black.[3] For a good part of the eighteenth century, South Carolina's slave population did not grow from natural increase, consistent with the environmental interpretation. The expanding rice plantations obtained new workers from the slave trade, like their counterparts in the Caribbean. The excess of slave births over slave deaths occurred mainly in the Chesapeake colonies.

The favorable disease environment in North America kept the death rate low. But it cannot explain why the slave birth rate was so high—the other part of the puzzle. The key to the distinctively high fertility of American slaves, recent writers argue, was their own decisions about sexual conduct and living arrangements. That they chose to marry young and rear large numbers of children suggests that they found parenthood profoundly gratifying. It was a means of affirming life while enmeshed in a cruel system that denied them most other sources of personal satisfaction. The rarity of abortions and infanticide, common in other slave societies, lends some support to this view.

---

[2]Not quite, actually. Human populations do not have even sex ratios at birth. Approximately 105 males are born for every 100 females. Males, however, are less hardy and have higher death rates at every age. This brings the sex ratio into balance among young adults, and unbalances it in the opposite direction among the elderly. In the United States in 1950 there were only 78 males for every 100 females who were 75 or more; among the tiny group aged 100 or more the sex ratio was a mere 39. There were two and a half times as many female as male centenarians.

[3]This might seem to contradict the earlier point that Africans brought immunities to tropical diseases with them to the New World (p. 63). It does not. They did indeed weather outbreaks of malaria and yellow fever better than South Carolina whites. But their immunity was relative, not absolute, and the South Carolina lowlands were so unhealthy that neither race could flourish there.

Slave preferences in this instance meshed well with those of their owners. American planters could easily grasp, as Thomas Jefferson callously explained, that "a woman who brings a child every two years is more profit than the best man on the farm, for what she produces is an addition to capital, while his labor disappears in mere consumption." That is why female slaves sold for about as much, on the average, as males, despite the fact that males were stronger and more productive (see box). The proprietors of West Indian sugar estates, by contrast, were not as eager to see their work force perpetuate and enlarge itself. They treated slave women with a harshness that was foolhardy—working them excessively long hours in the late stages of pregnancy, underfeeding them, grudging them the time to nurse infants. Stillbirths, infant deaths, and women too worn down to be able to conceive again were the inevitable results. Although such abuses sometimes happened in North America as well, they were uncommon. Instructions planters gave their overseers reveal great concern about the welfare of prospective mothers. American slave owners understood that their long-run interests would best be served by treating their chattels in a manner that would not impair their capacity or willingness to reproduce.

Acculturation, Work, and Resistance

Although the causes of the distinctive demographic pattern of American slaves are debatable, they had one undeniable result. The rapid growth of the population through natural increase made the colonies less dependent on the slave trade to obtain new laborers and speeded slave acculturation. American participation in the international slave trade continued until 1808, but as early as 1720 a majority of the country's blacks had been born in the New World. As slaves who had never seen Africa became increasingly dominant, a new Afro-American cultural type emerged. Fluent in English, accustomed to eating American food and working with American tools, the new generation assimilated in a variety of ways. Some elements of African culture were retained in modified form. Slave music had a distinct

---

A VIRGINIA PLANTER'S ORDER FOR SLAVES, 1683

I will give 3,000 lbs. of tobacco for every youth or girl between the age of 7 and 11 years old, 4,000 lbs. of tobacco for every youth or girl that shall be between the age of 11 to 15, and 5,000 lbs. of tobacco for every young man or woman that shall be above 15 years of age and not exceed 24. Upon your delivery and my receipt of the Negroes according to the ages above mentioned and that they be sound and healthful at their delivery, I will give payment of the tobacco by the 20th of December.

—William Fitzhugh, to Mr. Jackson

African stamp; the Christianity of the slave quarters was infused with beliefs from African folk religion; the Gullah dialect of South Carolina slaves was a creative blend of English and African tongues; slave parents named children in accord with African customs. But African survivals in the mainland were far less apparent than among the slave population of the West Indies, which was fed by a continuing heavy flow of African newcomers and had a much smaller fraction of natives.

The great majority of colonial slaves worked in gangs as field hands in tobacco fields or rice paddies. The work was heavy, especially so on rice plantations, and long—from dawn till dusk. A fortunate minority escaped the stoop labor in the fields to work as house servants or at various skilled tasks. The South lacked a native white class of blacksmiths, carpenters, shoemakers, and the like, and plantation slaves were consequently trained to be artisans. Slave craftsmen were hired out to other employers in the neighborhood when their services were not needed on the plantation, and thereby obtained knowledge of the larger world. There was a shortage of whites to supervise the field work as well, so that slaves often worked as drivers and sometimes as plantation overseers. The less arduous jobs in the planter's household and those involving special skill or responsibility were rarely given to newly arrived Africans. They tended to go to those more adjusted to American ways.

Although slavery was a system of forced labor, it did not depend on mere force. Masters employed the carrot as well as the stick to induce their bondsmen to work diligently. Although practices varied widely, and studies treating the colonial period are rare, many planters apparently provided positive incentives in the form of released time from work, extra allowances of food and clothing, and sometimes even cash payments for work well done. The possibility of being advanced to a less exhausting and monotonous job was another incentive. Nevertheless, the master's unrestricted right to inflict physical violence upon his chattels was the cornerstone of the system. Strict labor discipline was the absolute prerequisite to profit making. Even the kindest of masters—and there were kind ones—had to be prepared to order the whipping of an unruly or laggard slave, lest all the others emulate him. Fear of the lash was the strongest single incentive the slave had to do his master's bidding.

The slaves resisted as best they could with the limited means at their disposal. They shirked their tasks when unobserved, and were willfully "stupid," misusing and breaking valuable tools and "mistaking" young corn seedlings for weeds. Many stole food, clothing, and drink whenever they could. George Washington estimated ruefully that his slaves drank two bottles of his wine for every one consumed by his guests; a not uncharacteristic entry in the diary of another Virginia planter reads: "Ankara was whipped yesterday for stealing the rum and filling the bottles with water." Such instances of "day-to-day" passive resistance to slavery were merely a headache for most planters; they did not occur on a large enough scale to cut deeply into profits. Vigilant supervision and stern punishment were adequate to contain them.

Slaves who "stole themselves" by running away were a more serious threat. The unacculturated Africans who attempted escape were usually apprehended easily; their broken English and strange appearance gave them away. Natives, particularly those trained in a craft, were both more likely to flee and to succeed in the attempt. If they reached a town where they could find shelter in the small free black community, they often found work with employers who were too desperate for help to ask awkward questions. To deal with this mounting difficulty, patrols were strengthened, passes were required for blacks who left their owner's plantation, and stricter punishments were meted out. Most important, owners offered rewards not only to fellow whites who captured runaways but also to slaves who provided information that led to a capture. Fugitives could no longer count on the support of their fellow blacks; they could never be sure who might sell them out to better their own position. The new repressive apparatus did not stamp out the runaway problem altogether, but it did keep it from reaching critical proportions.

The ultimate fear in the mind of any slave-owner was that his exploited bondsmen would rise up in rebellion against him. The odds against a successful slave revolt in colonial North America were prohibitively high, and such uprisings were rare, much rarer than in the British West Indies. In the Chesapeake colonies, where most slaves lived, whites outnumbered blacks. The average plantation was relatively small, with about 20 slaves; opportunities for much larger groups of blacks to communicate with each other and plan resistance were nonexistent. The number of men newly arrived from Africa—who played a key role in most slave conspiracies in the New World—was not enormous because the American-born population grew so rapidly. Africans, furthermore, were typically dispersed in the interior. Because tobacco exhausted the soil within a few years, planters had to keep opening up new plots of virgin land well away from the home plantation. Africans in parties of a dozen or so were sent there to clear the land and begin cultivation. Although those who resisted their enslavement more fiercely might run away toward Indian country, there was little prospect that they could seize arms and organize military resistance.

The rice belt of the Lower South was quite different, and it is not surprising that the largest slave uprising in British North America occurred there—at Stono, South Carolina in 1739. Rice plantations were much larger than tobacco plantations, and whites were a small and shrinking minority because a flood of Africans had been imported by the slave trade in the 1720s and 1730s. By 1740 at least half of all the slaves in the colony had lived in the New World less than ten years. The planters who dominated the colony's government were well aware of the rebellious potential of the unwilling newcomers, but could not agree on a program to enhance their security. Lightning struck one Sunday morning in September, 1739, when a band of 20 Angolan slaves at Stono, 20 miles from Charlestown, broke into a store, killed its owner, and seized guns and powder. They slaughtered two dozen whites in the area and burned their farms, then marched south toward Spanish Florida, known as a haven for runaways. Before the day was out their numbers had grown to several dozen; some slaves along their route gladly joined in, while others came at gunpoint. A party of armed planters on horseback overtook and killed or captured the main body at the end of the day, but about 30 managed to elude capture for a week and a few hid out in the woods for years. Approximately 100 blacks perished in this abortive bid for freedom.

To avert a repetition, the South Carolina assembly passed a Negro Act that represented a far more intensive effort to control and divide the slaves. The militia was expanded to provide stricter surveillance of slaves, and fines for masters who failed to keep their chattels in line were increased. Larger rewards were provided for "loyal" slaves who informed on their disaffected brethren. Finally a stiff export duty on the importation of slaves from abroad was imposed, cutting the flow of newcomers by 90 percent. It was lowered within a decade, when the scarcity of new hands became too painful, but never again would South Carolina have such an imbalance between the number of fresh Africans and the number of whites available to control them. There would be other smaller slave conspiracies or alleged conspiracies in the future, the most famous being Nat Turner's uprising in Virginia in 1831, but nothing that rivalled the Stono Rebellion. Although southern planters liked to claim that their bondsmen were happy under the rule of benevolent masters, their vigilant and unceasing efforts to secure black subordination and white supremacy indicate clearly that they knew better.

SUGGESTED READINGS

Excellent brief reviews of the African background and the origins of the Atlantic slave trade are provided in the essays by Marian Kilson, Basil Davidson, and Philip D. Curtin in Nathan Huggins, ed., *Key Issues in the Afro-American Experience*, Vol. I (1971). Philip D. Curtin, *The Atlantic Slave Trade: A Census* (1969) lucidly sketches the dimensions of the trade from its beginnings to the nineteenth century.

Debate over the reasons for the comparatively late introduction of slavery into Virginia was initiated by a probing essay by Oscar and Mary Handlin, "The Origins of the Southern Labor System," in *Race and Nationality in American Life* (1957). Different views are presented in Winthrop Jordan, *Black Over White: American Attitudes towards the Negro, 1550–1812* (1968), abridged as *The White Man's Burden: Historical Origins of Racism in the United States* (1974), and Edmund Morgan, *American Slavery, American Freedom* (1975). David B. Davis, *The Problem of Slavery in Western Culture* (1966) traces the evolution of the concept of slavery in Western thought. Richard S. Dunn, *Sugar and Slaves: The Rise of the Planter Class in the English West Indies, 1624–1713* (1972) describes the model that would later be adopted in the Carolinas. Peter Wood, *Black Majority: Negroes in Colonial South Carolina from 1670 through the Stono Rebellion* (1975) shows that race relations were surprisingly fluid until large rice plantations developed in the eighteenth century. Other useful accounts of slave life are T.H. Breen and Stephen Innes, *"Myne Own Ground": Race and Freedom on Virginia's Eastern Shore, 1640–1676* (1980), the essays by Russell Menard and Allen Kulikoff in Aubrey C. Land, *et al.*, eds., *Law, Society, and Politics in Early Maryland* (1977), Herbert G. Gutman, *The Black Family in Slavery and Freedom, 1750–1925* (1979), Gerald Mullin, *Flight and Rebellion: Slave Resistance in Eighteenth Century Virginia* (1972), and the April, 1978, issue of the *William and Mary Quarterly*.

For illuminating comparisons between the American South and other slave societies, see Marvin Harris, *Patterns of Race in the Americas* (1974), Laura Foner and Eugene Genovese, eds., *Slavery in the New World: A Reader in Comparative History* (1969), Carl Degler, *Neither Black Nor White: Slavery and Race Relations in Brazil and the United States* (1971), and Herbert S. Klein, *Slavery in the Americas* (1967). Although it does not treat British North America, Magnus Morner, *Race Mixture in the History of Latin America* (1967) is extremely suggestive.

Chapter Five

"A Very Mixed Company": The Peopling of Colonial America

A traveler who visited Philadelphia in 1744 reported that he dined at a tavern with "a very mixed company of different nations and religions." The 25 men at the table included "Scots, English, Dutch, Germans, and Irish; there were Roman Catholics, Presbyterians, Quakers, Methodists, Seventh day men, Moravians, Anabaptists, and one Jew." The political and legal institutions of the North American colonies were cut from English cloth, but well before the Revolution the people had become "a very mixed company" indeed.

THE MIDDLE COLONIES AND THE NEW IMMIGRATION

It was no accident that this comment about the striking ethnic and religious diversity of the colonial population was made in Philadelphia. Pennsylvania and the other "Middle Colonies"—New York, New Jersey, and Delaware—were the least English of all the colonies, and the ones most tolerant of religious variety. From their beginnings, they exhibited features that would later characterize American society as a whole.

The Middle Colonies filled the yawning gap in the British North American Empire that was occupied by England's most powerful commercial rival, Holland, until after the Restoration. On the basis of Henry Hudson's 1609 exploration of the river that bears his name, the Dutch laid claim to the territory between Connecticut and Maryland. Holland was a great power, and it was by no means inevitable that

"The Quaker Meeting" by Heemskerk (1645–1704) is a contemporary depiction of such gatherings.

the British would be able to remove the Dutch presence and establish an unbroken chain of settlements along the Atlantic. In 1624, when the only Englishmen living in North America were the handful of Pilgrims at Plymouth and the hapless wretches at Jamestown, the Dutch West India Company dispatched settlers to posts along the Hudson and Delaware rivers and planted a village on Manhattan Island—New Amsterdam. (Sweden also sent over a small band of Swedes and Finns to live at the mouth of the Delaware in 1638; New Sweden was taken over by the Dutch in 1655.) New Netherlands was not to be an agricultural colony like Virginia, of whose precarious condition West India Company officials were well aware. It was to be a cluster of trading forts to obtain fur from the Indians, much like the company's other forts in Brazil and Africa.

The Dutch later attempted to stimulate agricultural development along the Hudson by creating great feudal estates—"patroonships"—whose proprietors would import supplies and tenants. However, only one patroonship actually came into being—the million-acre estate of Rensselaerswyck around Fort Orange. With a population only one-third that of England, Holland lacked a surplus of adventurers who could be recruited into colonial service overseas. New Netherlands languished, with less than 5,000 discontented inhabitants in 1660. Neither company investors nor the masses of settlers reaped much profit from the thriving fur trade; the riches were siphoned off by a few sharp operators in New Amsterdam. By then the burgeoning English colonies nearby were filling up. Land-hungry Englishmen filtered into the area from Connecticut. They squatted on unoccupied land and refused to recognize Dutch authorities. The feeble defenses of New Netherlands and the evident unhappiness of most of its original settlers made it a plum ripe for the taking. In 1664, four British ships landed soldiers in New Amsterdam and the Dutch governor, Peter Stuyvesant, surrendered. King Charles' brother, the Duke of York, was made proprietor and the colony was renamed New York.

At the time of its conquest and absorption into the British empire, New Netherlands had not only Dutch and English settlers but a medley of other peoples—Swedes, Finns, Germans, Belgian Walloons, Portuguese, and French. The West India Company had welcomed aliens because it could not attract enough Hollanders to come. Instead of attempting to force this polyglot population into a single mold, the new English government grudgingly tolerated ethnic and religious differences. With its fertile soil, abundant water resources, and acceptance of religious and cultural variety, New York became a magnet for dissatisfied people from the other colonies and abroad. It would have been a more powerful magnet, however, if it had developed a more liberal land distribution policy. Although Rensselaerswyck was the only patroonship that survived from the period of Dutch rule, other great estates along the Hudson like Livingston Manor were handed out to powerful political insiders after the English took over. In the 1690s Governor Benjamin Fletcher made fortunes for himself and his friends by confirming earlier grants and making several more huge gifts. More than two dozen manors occupied over two million acres of choice land. One result was that New York had more of an aristocracy than any other northern colony. Another result was that immigrants who hoped to own their own farms rather than serve as tenants of a large landlord went elsewhere.

The most important elsewhere was Pennsylvania. Like Massachusetts, it began as a haven for a persecuted religious sect—the Quakers. Unlike the Puritans, however, the Quakers were willing to offer other groups something more than "free liberty to keep away from us." The Society of Friends, a religious body that rejected ritual and hierarchy and celebrated the "inner light" within each person, had been founded by George Fox during the English Civil War. The nickname "Quaker" was suggested by their excited trembling when gripped by religious ecstasy. The Quakers had the intense evangelical zeal of Mormons and Jehovah's Witnesses today, and they made many converts, despite strenuous repressive efforts by English church and government officials. The campaign to silence the Quakers mounted in intensity in the late 1670s, when hundreds of them were jailed and fined heavily for attending their own religious meetings rather than Church of England services. Fortunately for them, one of the most ardent Friends in the land had close ties to King Charles II. William Penn, the son of a distinguished admiral, was a religious radical with shrewd political instincts. He first used his considerable influence in court circles in an effort to win freedom of worship for Quakers and other dissenters in the western part of New Jersey in the mid-1670s, but the political situation there was hopelessly chaotic. In 1681 he persuaded the King to make him an extraordinary gift. To pay off a Crown debt to Penn's father, and perhaps to rid England of pesky Quakers, Charles granted him ownership of the entire area west of New Jersey from New York to Maryland. (Delaware was part of the original grant, but Penn conceded Lower Pennsylvania independent status and the right to an assembly of its own in 1701.)

Pennsylvania was an instant success story. It had 4,000 settlers by the time Penn first visited it in 1682, 21,000 by the end of the century, 120,000 by 1750. Pennsylvania offered rich land on generous terms. Any man who brought a family with him was given 500 acres free, if he agreed to pay Penn a modest annual "quitrent"; another 50 acres could be claimed for each servant he brought with him. An acre of land could be bought, furthermore, with the wage a carpenter could earn in one day. It offered full religious freedom as well. That was a matter of principle for Penn, as for any good Quaker, but there were pragmatic reasons for tolerance as well. "This unpeopled country," Penn remarked, "can never be peopled if there be not due encouragement given to sober people of all sorts to plant." His first Frame of Government for the colony gave that encouragement to "people of all sorts"— or almost all sorts. Officeholding was granted to Christians, and liberty of conscience only to those who believed in God, but neither qualification was of practical importance at the time. Penn ensured that pamphlets advertising the freedoms and opportunities available in his colony were widely distributed, not only in the British Isles but on the Continent as well.

The Middle Colonies were better suited to commercial agriculture than New England. The soil was more fertile, the growing season was longer, and the penetration of major rivers like the Hudson, Delaware, and Susquehanna made it possible to transport bulky farm products cheaply. Philadelphia and New York were superb natural harbors, and they quickly outpaced Boston to become North America's first and second largest cities. Quaker merchants in Philadelphia and their English and Dutch counterparts in New York commanded a thriving trade with the rapidly expanding agricultural hinterland. The Middle Colonies became America's breadbasket, the prime source of vast quantities of wheat shipped to the ports for export to the West Indies and Europe. Wheat and flour comprised almost 20 percent of North America's exports in 1770, ahead of rice and second only to tobacco—and almost all of it passed through Philadelphia or New York. The soaring grain harvest provided the profits to finance a rising living standard. The value of English imports into the Middle Colonies increased 400 percent between 1745 and 1760, while the population grew only 70 percent. By 1776, the average resident of New York, New Jersey and Pennsylvania owned £51 worth of property, well above the £33 New Englanders had.

The New Non-English Immigrants

From the late seventeenth century onward, the Middle Colonies in general, and Pennsylvania in particular, appeared a promised land to an increasing number of discontented people across the ocean. Some Englishmen were among them, including about 35,000 criminals who were given the choice of seven years of hard labor in America or the gallows. (Benjamin Franklin suggested that the colonies should return the favor by exporting a few shiploads of rattlesnakes to England.) The major immigration waves, however, were those of Celtic people from the British Isles—the "Scotch-Irish," Scots, and Welsh—and the Germans. Their coming drastically altered the ethnic composition of the American population.

The largest of these groups was the Scotch-Irish, descendants of the Presbyterians who left impoverished Scotland for northern Ireland (Ulster) early in the seventeenth century at the urging of the Crown. They drove the native "wild Irish" from Ulster, establishing Britain's first overseas colony (and creating ethnic antag-

---

A EUROPEAN TRAVELLER ON FARMING IN THE MIDDLE COLONIES

The Europeans coming to America found a rich, fine soil before them, lying as loose between the trees as the best bed in a garden. They had nothing to do but cut down the wood, put it up in heaps, and to clear the dead leaves away. They could then immediately proceed to plowing, which in such loose ground is very easy; and having sown their grain, they got a most plentiful harvest.

—Peter Kalm, *Travels in North America*, 1753

---

onisms that still divide Ulster today). In Ulster the Scots had the gratification of looking down on the Catholic Irish with disdain, but they were second class citizens in many respects. They resented paying taxes to support the Anglican establishment, rents that went to absentee English lords, and laws barring Irish products from English markets. They were more unhappy still after a 1704 law kept non-Anglicans from political office and invalidated marriages conducted in Presbyterian churches. A small group organized by ministers left for America in 1717, but mass movement began as a result of deteriorating economic conditions in the 1720s—steep rent increases and a series of failed harvests. About 100,000 Scotch-Irish came to North America over the next half century. Pennsylvania was their favored destination, both because of its well-advertised attractions and because Ulster's shipping connections to the colonies centered on the port of Philadelphia. A smaller but quite substantial number of other Celtic peoples also moved to colonial America—Scots, chiefly from the depressed Highlands, and Welshmen.

The other major immigrant stream to the colonies consisted of Germans from the upper Rhine valley, especially the Rhenish Palatinate west of the river. Germany was divided into many small states and principalities—unification came only in 1870—and it was a hotbed of militant religious dissent. Hounded by the authorities in both Catholic and Lutheran states, groups like the Mennonites, Amish, and Dunkers were accustomed to frequent migration in search of religious toleration. Unpredictable economic conditions compelled Catholics and Lutherans to move as well. Overpopulation in the wine-growing region, heavy taxes, and a devastatingly severe winter in 1708–09 triggered the first large-scale movement of Germans to North America. About 100,000 had come by the time of the Revolution. Again, Philadelphia was their favored destination, but New York and New Jersey also received many.

The long journey across the ocean was usually trying, sometimes horrifying. In 1731, to cite an extreme case, a ship that left Rotterdam with 150 Palatines was buffeted about for a full year before reaching land. Its avaricious captain *sold* the passengers water, rats, and mice; only 34 survived. Conditions were worst for those whose only means of paying for their passage was to sell themselves into indentured service. The £6–£10 cost of the voyage amounted to at least four years' savings for European laborers. The passage money could be had, however, in return for an agreement to work as a servant for a few years. From half to two-thirds of the immigrants to the colonies came on that basis. Temporary servitude was the mechanism that financed the movement of poor people from Europe into the labor-starved colonies. Servants were crammed in unventilated holds on wooden beds only two feet wide, and fed the barest of rations. When the vessel landed and the regular passengers went joyfully down the gangplank, they were confined on board until they could be sold to an employer.

Immigrants who had the resources to pay part of their fares, as many Germans did, could strike a better bargain. They could become "redemptioners," borrowing the balance they needed from a shipping merchant. They had a fixed period after landing, usually two weeks, to find a "redeemer" to discharge their debt. Otherwise they could be sold into service for a term proportional to the amount.

Redemptioners could negotiate with a number of prospective employers and settle for the most attractive terms; indentured servants had to go with whoever bought them.

After the Puritan migration of the 1630s, few immigrants to America went to New England. The New England economy was not hungry for labor, and the oppressive weight of its religious establishment repelled non-Congregationalists. The common belief that most colonists were of English origin, however, is true only of New England. In all of the colonies to the south, the heavy migration of non-English peoples soon made the English a minority. A recent study reveals that by 1790, the earliest date for which estimates are available, men and women of Celtic origins made up 43 percent of the white population of Pennsylvania, and Germans accounted for one-third. Only one in five were English. Some 44 percent of the population of New York was English, 27 percent Celtic, 18 percent Dutch, and 8 percent German. By 1790 the supply of cheap land in the Middle Colonies had long been exhausted, and immigrants had pushed southward through the Virginia and Maryland backcountry all the way down to South Carolina and Georgia. Not one of the southern colonies was as much as 50 percent English; Celtics were a majority (of the whites) in both North and South Carolina.[1]

Colonial officials did what they could to stimulate immigration, because it increased the labor supply and drove up land values. But they found the newcomers a mixed blessing. The Scotch–Irish burned with resentment at the English establishment and were anything but deferential to authority. The Germans had no love for English ways, and were eager to preserve their own culture and language. Both groups gravitated toward the frontier, where the grasp of government was weak or nonexistent. They settled in clusters with their fellow countrymen, often arriving before any government agent and squatting on the land. "Both these sorts sit frequently down on any sort of vacant land they can find," complained the governor of Pennsylvania in 1727, "without leave or paying anything." When challenged, he reported, they said "it was against the laws of God and Nature that so much Land should lie idle while so many Christians wanted it to labor on and make their Bread." The Scotch–Irish were long accustomed to dealing roughly with the Catholic natives in Ulster, and they showed the same pugnacity and brutality when they encountered North American natives occupying lands they coveted. Their aggressive behavior was a particular trial for the Quaker pacifists who controlled the Pennsylvania government. Most of the colonies were troubled by recurrent political conflict between long-settled eastern areas and newly developed western ones, over such issues as reapportionment of assemblies in accord with population shifts and expenditures for Indian warfare. Much of the bitterness of these struggles stemmed from ethnic antagonisms between English and non-English elements of the population.

---

[1]These estimates are based on an analysis of the surnames of the household heads enumerated in the U.S. Census of 1790. They indicate more Celts and fewer English than the figures given in the standard reference work, *Historical Statistics of the United States*, and repeated in many books. For a convincing critique of the methods by which the older figures were derived and a defense of these new estimates, see Forrest and Ellen McDonald, "The Ethnic Origins of the American People, 1790," *William and Mary Quarterly*, April, 1980, pp. 179-99.

THE POPULATION EXPLOSION IN BRITISH NORTH AMERICA

When the Puritan migration to New England came to an end in 1641, the number of Europeans in the British colonies in North America barely exceeded 25,000, not enough to fiill the football stadium in many American universities today. By 1700 the figure had increased a remarkable tenfold, to about 250,000. Over the next 75 years, it grew ten times more, to almost 2.5 million, and the frontier had advanced from the ocean to the Appalachian mountains 400 miles into the interior. In the middle of the seventeenth century, the people of England outnumbered their brethren in North America by 100 to 1; in 1700 the ratio was down to 20 to 1, and by 1775 it was only 3 to 1. As the father of demography, Scotsman Thomas Malthus, observed in 1793, it was "a rapidity of increase without parallel in history."

Some part of that remarkable growth, of course, was due to immigration. Reliable figures on colonial immigration are not available, but the highest estimate for the years from 1640 to 1775 is about 400,000. And yet over that span the white population of the colonies increased by 1.6 million, four times as much. Natural increase—more births than deaths—was therefore the most important source of the population explosion.

The English who crossed the ocean to the colonies in the seventeenth century, and the Germans and Celts who followed in their footsteps, had much larger families than those who remained at home. In the late seventeenth century the typical woman in the English village of Coylton gave birth to an average of 4.2 children; in Andover, Massachusetts the figure was 8.3. The mother of William Phips, a leading Boston merchant and first governor of the colony, had 26 sons and daughters—exceptional, to be sure, but not unique. Families in the Chesapeake colonies in the seventeenth century were much less fruitful, for reasons given in Chapter 2, but their birth rate approached the New England norm thereafter. Patrick Henry, born in Virginia in 1736, had 18 brothers and sisters.

TABLE 5-1
The Growth of the Colonial Population*

	Estimated Total	White	Black
1640	26,634	26,037	596
1670	111,935	107,400	4,535
1700	250,888	223,071	27,817
1740	905,563	755,539	150,024
1770	2,148,076	1,688,254	459,822

*Historical statistics, indeed all statistics, must be approached with caution. All too often, as Oskar Morgenstern demonstrates brilliantly in *On the Accuracy of Economic Observations,* the sense of exactitude they convey is specious. The numbers above are not based on a uniform census of the population of the British colonies at these dates. Nothing like that was conducted until the first U.S Census in 1790. They are estimates based on a few censuses in the various colonies and partial counts like tax and militia lists. The broad pattern they reveal is undoubtedly correct, but new work in the flourishing field of demographic history may revise them substantially some day.

MAP 5-1
The Rush of Settlers into the Interior, 1650–1770

The root cause of this striking difference was early and almost universal marriage in the colonies. New England women were usually married by their early twenties, and southern women even earlier, whereas in Britain the average was almost 30. Because a woman's fertile years usually do not extend beyond her early forties, to wed at 20 rather than 30 almost doubled her child-bearing years. Furthermore, a substantial minority of English women remained childless spinsters for life, a rare occurrence in the colonies. Because all adult women are included in calculations of average fertility, the spinster population lowered the English average.[2]

English women married much later, and some failed to marry at all, for basically economic reasons. A young couple could not establish a household and begin to raise a family without means of support—savings, a well-paid job, or a productive plot of land. But these were hard for the young to find in an overcrowded preindustrial society. Most youths began their careers as servants or apprentices, and depended on their masters for sustenance. Approximately a third of English families were sufficiently wealthy to employ servants; most people in the lower two-thirds worked in service in their early years. They could not marry without the consent of their masters, which was rarely given. There was no frontier, no wilderness to settle, and only eldest sons had any prospect of inheriting land, thanks to the custom of primogeniture.

These checks on family formation were absent, or much weaker, in America. Land was abundant and labor was in short supply. Even an indentured servant who arrived without any capital had a good chance to acquire a farm of his own after a few years if he survived.[3] With so much land available, primogeniture made little sense; the colonists adopted a more egalitarian system of "partible inheritance"—equal shares for all the children. The high rate of marriage, the low average marriage age, and the very high fertility of the colonial population were natural results.

The Low Death Rate

Even a very high birth rate will not make a population increase naturally if it is accompanied by an equally high death rate. The colonial mortality rate, however, was low. In New England, deaths averaged 25 per 1,000 people annually, as compared with about 40 per 1,000 in England and France. The South, of course, was a distinctly less healthy place for much of the seventeenth century, but conditions improved considerably thereafter. By the eighteenth century the population of the southern colonies was increasing naturally almost as rapidly as in the North.

---

[2]One other factor may have contributed to the high fertility pattern in the colonies, though convincing proof of its importance is hard to find. There are at least a few scraps of evidence suggesting that American infants were breast fed for only the first year and then weaned. Since lactation inhibits conception, early weaning would mean more frequent pregnancies—a shorter interval between births—than in a population that practiced more prolonged breast feeding. We know that the average interval between births for women in seventeenth century Plymouth was only two years, as contrasted with two and a half years in the French village of Crulai. Not a very dramatic difference, it might seem. But it means that a mother bearing children over a span of 20 years would have ten offspring in Plymouth and eight in Crulai (20/2 versus 20/2.5).

[3]Opportunities to obtain land in long-settled seaboard communities diminished with time, a point considered later in this chapter. But the glaring contrast between American and European conditions remained.

Just what made life in the colonies less hazardous than life in the Old World is not yet fully understood, but it is clear that the low density of settlement of a scattered, overwhelmingly rural population limited the spread of infectious disease. Even more important, perhaps, was the abundance of cheap food. In preindustrial Europe there were periodic "crises of subsistence," years in which crop failures produced such acute food shortages that large numbers of people starved to death or succumbed to diseases because of their weakened condition. The famine of 1696–97, for example, wiped out 28 percent of the population in the hardest hit area of Finland. The entire population of Denmark dropped by a fifth during the ghastly crisis years of 1650–60. Poor harvests in 1740–43 sent death rates soaring in much of Western Europe. After the "starving times" of the initial years of settlement, by contrast, the British colonies in North America never experienced food shortages severe enough to kill off a significant fraction of the population. Even in New England, where the climate, soil, and topography limited the production of a surplus for export, there was always plenty to eat.

And plenty to drink as well, perhaps rather more than was good for the health. Many writers have marveled at how the Puritans sat through long Sabbath sermons in unheated meeting houses during bitter New England winters. Few have pointed out that churchgoers customarily warmed their insides with a stiff jolt of rum at the village tavern beforehand, and often had an encore afterward. One of the best kept secrets about colonial America is that its people were extraordinarily hard drinkers. In 1710, the earliest year for which statistical evidence is available, the average colonist aged 15 or more consumed the alcoholic equivalent of 13 gallons of 80-proof whisky each year, a full quart a week. By 1770 consumption had risen to over 16 gallons a year—*two and a half* times as much as in a recent year in which Americans did not seem conspicuously abstemious, 1975! Because women tended to drink less than men and slaves had less access to alcohol than free people, the true average for free males would be even higher than that. In colonial America spirits were almost universally regarded as nutritious and healthful, and people in every region and every walk of life indulged in them. "Drink," said the eminent Reverend Increase Mather, "is in itself a creature of God, and to be received with thankfulness." In Danvers, Massachusetts, licenses to sell liquor were held not only by two deacons of the Congregational church but by the minister as well. Fermented cider was normally served at every meal in the apple country from Virginia northward; John Adams, the second President of the United States, was accustomed to starting his day with a 16-ounce tankard of it that contained as much alcohol as a double martini. Rum distilled from West Indian sugar was plentiful and incredibly cheap; at a price of two shillings per gallon in 1738, a laborer's wages for a day would buy a week of inebriation.

This is not to suggest that most colonists stumbled through life in an alcoholic haze. Most drink was consumed in small quantities spread over the day, and it was often taken with food. Actual inebriation was less frequent than the figures might suggest. But drunkenness did become increasingly common in the eighteenth century, and some Americans began to view it as a serious problem. Some critics linked alcohol with social disorder and political chicanery (see box, page 92). Physicians argued that it was poison. Quakers and Methodists, a new sect that was spreading like wildfire in the mid-eighteenth century, called for abstention on religious grounds. Their exhortations had very little effect on the masses, however. The formation of an effective national temperance movement and a decline in alcohol consumption would not occur until the second quarter of the next century.[4]

THE BEST POOR MAN'S COUNTRY

Curious Europeans who visited colonial America believed that it was "the best poor man's country in the world." Those who chose to stay did not change their view upon closer acquaintance. Hector St. Jean de Crèvecoeur, a young Frenchman who bought a farm in upstate New York in the late 1760s, made it the central theme of his eloquent *Letters from an American Farmer* (1782). American society, he said, was "not composed, as in Europe, of great lords who possess everything, and of a herd of people who have nothing. A pleasing uniformity of decent competence appears throughout our habitations. We have no princes for whom we toil, starve, and bleed: we are the most perfect society now existing in the world."

Crèvecoeur was somewhat extravagant. The colonies had some people with less

---

[4]After that popular historians ignored and obscured the embarrassing facts about their ancestors. Patrick Henry kept a tavern for his father-in-law. One nineteenth century biographer left out the fact and referred only to his occasional visits to the tavern; another biography a little later failed to mention the tavern at all. The respected *Encyclopedia of American History* (1953) refers vaguely to Henry's "early career as a storekeeper and farmer."

than a "decent competence" and some with a good deal more. And they had a large
group that was cruelly compelled to "toil, starve, and bleed" to enrich others—half
a million black slaves. America was anything but a perfect society for them. With
that major exception, however, the basic contrast that struck these observers was
real. Throughout early modern Europe hereditary landed aristocracies lived off the
labor of masses of peasants who paid them a large share of their harvests for the
right to work the soil. A few hundred families owned *half* of all the land in England
in 1750; more than 80 percent of the fields were tilled by tenants. The vast majority
of colonists, by comparison, were independent farmers working on land they
owned. It was at least "the best poor white man's country," prosperous, fluid, and
relatively egalitarian.

Easy access to land was the key to the difference. Of course it took some capital
to launch even the most primitive farm. But the presence of an inexhaustible
supply of land in the west kept wages two to three times as high as in England,
making it possible for freed servants to steadily add to their freedom dues and save
up enough to move west after a few years of working as a farm laborer for someone
else. Another route to farm ownership was serving as a tenant, for tenancy in North
America was not the permanent dependent relationship it was in Europe. The basis
for a permanent tenant class was seemingly present in several colonies. Awe-
somely large tracts of land had been granted to Crown favorites, not only in New
York. The Earl of Granville owned most of the northern half of North Carolina;
Lord Fairfax held title to five million acres on the Northern Neck of Virginia. The
proprietors of these great estates, however, found they were unable to reap enor-

mous profits by following the English strategy of charging heavy rents to a permanent tenant class. They were forced to keep rents low to attract tenants at all, to credit tenants for the improvements they made in clearing the land for cultivation, and to sell them the land when they saved enough to purchase it. The great estates, with some exceptions, consequently self-destructed over time. Landlords acquired large fortunes this way, but it steadily enlarged the class of independent yeoman farmers. Some landlords behaved more like English gentlemen, charging high rents and denying tenants secure leases. When they did, as on some New York and New Jersey estates in the 1750s and 1760s, it caused them headaches. Tenants refused to pay and engaged in a series of riots known as the "land wars." Landlords who were too unbending saw their tenants pick up stakes and head for Vermont, which was just opening up for settlement.

A Trend Toward "Europeanization"?

While conceding that colonial American society differed from that of Europe in basic respects, some historians have argued recently that it was *becoming* more Europeanized with the passage of time. The *trend*, they assert, was toward greater economic and social stratification and diminished opportunity for the common man. A wealthy elite group did indeed develop as colonial society matured, as they suggest. But the claim that opportunities were closing down for ordinary people is open to question.

The great planters of the South, owners of dozens and even hundreds of slaves and huge tracts of land, ranked among the richest and most powerful men in America. Elegant estates like Mt. Vernon and Monticello were American versions of the English gentleman's country house, monuments to the social superiority of the patriarchs who ruled over them. Of course they lacked the formal titles and special privileges of European aristocrats; the basis of their eminence was property rather than inherited status. On the other hand, opportunities to acquire fortunes and break into the group diminished over time, and the American elite assumed a hereditary character. The spread of slavery made it increasingly difficult for men without capital to scramble to the top of the social ladder. The price of slaves tripled between 1660 and 1750, and land values also soared as population increased and the best land was occupied. A pioneer planter in North Carolina bought 1,500 acres for £30; at his death it was valued at £3,000 (over $200,000 today). Inherited capital gave a decisive advantage to the offspring of the already affluent. An inbred landed elite—the "First Families of Virginia" and their counterparts in the other slave colonies—emerged at the top of the social pyramid.[5] No less than 80 of the richest 100 Virginians at the time of the Revolution had inherited all of their wealth; ten had added to substantial inheritances; only ten could be considered "self-made." The list included nine members of the Cocke family; eight Fitzhughs, Lees, and Washingtons; and seven Harrisons, Randolphs, and Carters.

A wealthy class developed in the northern colonies as well. The flow of exports

---

[5]The very high death rate in early Virginia had kept most estates from accumulating over the generations, as noted in Chapter 2. By the late seventeenth century, improved longevity removed that barrier.

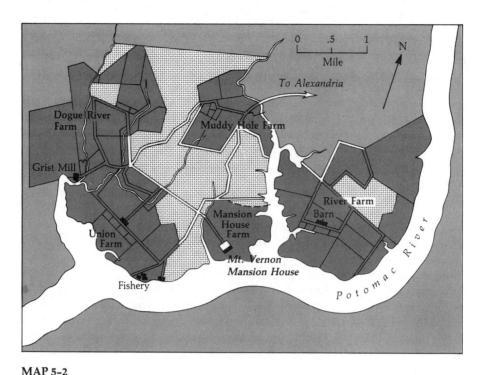

MAP 5-2
Mount Vernon Plantation
Shortly after the Revolution, George Washington's estate included approximately 10,000 acres worked by more than 200 slaves. It was almost an independent small village, with a spinning house, a smokehouse, and carpenter's, tailor's, shoemaker's, and blacksmith's shops.

and imports through Philadelphia, New York, and Boston brought healthy profits to the merchants who organized the trade. Politics was another avenue to riches. Royal officials and men in professions dependent on government favor exploited their political connections to great advantage. Britain's wars with France for ascendancy in North America from 1689 to 1713, 1744 to 1748, and 1756 to 1763 provided glittering prizes to merchant princes like Boston's Peter Faneuil and John Hancock, and New York's Stephan De Lancey and the Schuyler brothers, who won the contracts to provide the needed supplies and equipment. They traveled from their fine homes to the counting house in carriages imported from England. The commercial elite of the northern colonies differed from the planter elite in two important respects. It was considerably less wealthy. The richest 100 families in Philadelphia in 1765 had an average estate of £4,000, as compared to £10,000 for the top Virginia planters. And it was more fluid and open to penetration from below. Only 66 percent of the most affluent Philadelphians and 57 percent of the comparable group in Boston had inherited all their wealth, much below the 80 percent figure for Virginia.

Most colonial city dwellers were artisans and craftsmen who were in business for themselves, or apprentices who would strike out on their own after their training was completed. Few were proletarians in the modern sense—people without capital or skills, solely dependent on wages. Only 7 percent of the men employed in Philadelphia in 1771 were casual laborers. Artisans were vulnerable to economic fluctuations and could suffer severe financial setbacks during slack periods. About 1,000 of Boston's 15,000 inhabitants were either in the poor house or receiving charitable aid at home in 1757; throughout the late 1750s and early 1760s over 100 strangers per year were "warned out" of that city, told that if they remained they were ineligible for poor relief. Almost a tenth of Philadelphia's population was classified as impoverished on the eve of the Revolution. Most, however, were very recent immigrants who had arrived with nothing. In light of the very heavy influx of newcomers, the figure is surprisingly low rather than surprisingly high. The propertyless at any one time tended to be young people who would manage to accumulate something in the future. Almost half (45 percent) of the artisans with no property on Philadelphia's 1769 tax lists had acquired some wealth by 1774. Half of the most affluent craftsmen and small manufacturers had risen from more humble origins.

Prospects for men of humble origins were also excellent in the countryside, where more than 90 percent of the population lived. It is true that with the passing of time, higher population density and rising land values brought increased economic differentiation. When all the land within the originally spacious boundaries of the New England town had been distributed, the fathers of adolescent sons could no longer count on their acquiring a farm in town when they came of age. Land would have to be bought for them, and only the prosperous could afford that. As market production increased, especially in the Middle Colonies, some farmers proved to be more aggressive, more ambitious, or luckier than their neighbors, and others fell behind in the race. In the first generation of settlers in Chester County, Pennsylvania in the 1680s, the richest 10 percent of taxpayers owned 24 percent of the total wealth, whereas the poorest 30 percent had 17 percent. By 1760 the top 10 percent had increased its share to 30 percent, and the holdings of the bottom 30 percent had shrunk to a mere 6 percent of the total.

This increase in wealth concentration, however, did not mean that the rich were getting richer and the poor poorer. Commercial development made everyone's property more valuable. The well-to-do simply captured a larger slice of the growing pie. Nor did it mean that the sons of smaller farmers no longer would have a chance to become farm owners themselves. Their prospects of obtaining a plot of the increasingly valuable land in Chester County were slim, to be sure. But Chester County was not all of America. There was always an open frontier to the west, and it advanced as rapidly as the population grew. Land was much cheaper there, and those whose parents couldn't afford to give them a boost could climb the "agricultural ladder" to ownership by working for a while as hired hands or tenants. Of the landless families living in the Connecticut frontier town of Goshen in 1771, 86 percent of those still residing there a decade later had acquired farms of their own. Of the whites in Lunenberg County, Virginia who were landless in 1764, 80 percent were owners 18 years later. Their children would find it harder to obtain local land when they reached maturity, but they too would move on to new frontiers.

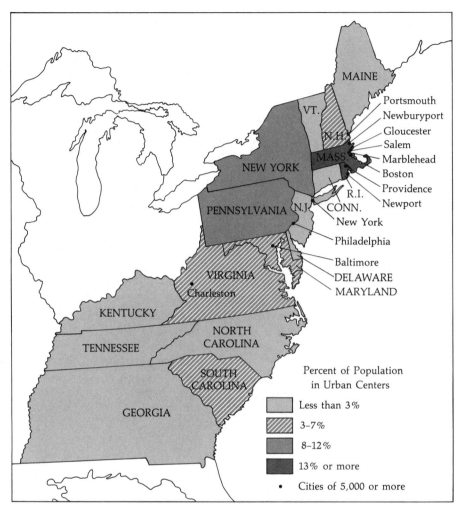

MAP 5-3
Levels of Urbanization by State, 1790

A look at population changes in 88 New Hampshire communities a few years before the Revolution reveals how land availability determined migration patterns (see Table 5-2). New Hampshire in general was still only lightly settled, but the newest towns with the lowest density of occupancy were growing most rapidly by attracting newcomers. The oldest and most densely settled—with 60 or more persons per square mile—were stagnating. A 60-acre farm was the maximum optimal size for a family, given the climate, soil, and available technology, which made the maximum optimal density 60 people per square mile. The closer a town approached that level, the fewer the migrants who chose to move into it. There was

BENJAMIN FRANKLIN
(1706–1790)

$\mathbb{B}$ enjamin Franklin was an extraordinary American, not a representative one. But the fascination his rise to fame and fortune held for his fellow countrymen reflected their confidence that their society offered abundant opportunities to men of humble origins. Franklin was born in Boston in 1706, the tenth son of a candlemaker. After only two years of school, he began an apprenticeship with his father at the age of ten. Restless in that, he went to work for his brother, a printer. (In colonial America, printers were not mere typesetters; they were writers and editors as well, and important opinion-makers.) After learning the trade, Franklin moved to Philadelphia, North America's fastest growing city. He worked for another printer for a time and then set up his own shop with the assistance of his friend, the governor of the colony. In 1730 he became publisher of the *Pennsylvania Gazette* and made it a lively and an influential newspaper. After angling his way into the lucrative post of public printer for the colony, he became rich enough to retire from business altogether in his early forties and devoted his time to science and public affairs. He went on to become postmaster general for the colonies, a drafter of the Declaration of Independence, negotiator of the peace treaty with Britain after the Revolution, and a key member of the Constitutional Convention at Philadelphia.

Franklin is too often remembered for the self-righteous platitudes of his *Autobiography* and *Poor Richard's Almanack*—"Waste not, want not;" "Early to bed, early to rise;" and "Time is money." Closer acquaintance reveals a rich and complex personality. He had great intelligence, insatiable curiosity, and unflagging energy. He taught himself Latin, French, Italian, and Spanish, made pioneering experiments with electricity, invented a stove that heated many an American home, and wrote thoughtfully on a wide range of subjects. A partial list of the institutions he founded or helped to found includes the American Academy of Arts and Sciences, the first circulating library in America, Philadelphia's first fire company, its city hospital, and the University of Pennsylvania. He was a master politician in the best sense of the word, a cunning manipulator of his fellow men and a genius at organizing people for collective action for the common good.

TABLE 5-2
Population Change and Density of Settlement of New Hampshire Towns, 1767–73

Population Density per Square Mile	Mean Population Change per Year
2.0 and under	17.1
2.01–5.0	11.2
5.01–8.0	9.7
8.01–11.0	7.5
11.01–15.0	6.1
15.01–35.0	2.7
35.01–60.0	.8
60.01 and above	-.2

a perfect inverse relationship between density and population growth. The open frontier was a critical safety valve that kept American society from evolving along Enropean lines by assuring opportunities for migration and social mobility.

FROM STATE CHURCH TO RELIGIOUS PLURALISM

A Lutheran priest from Sweden visited Pennsylvania in the middle of the eighteenth century and registered his bewilderment at the religious scene there. "Here are fanatics almost without number," he wrote. "Because there is freedom of conscience, here they have gathered together, of every opinion and belief. Even in the same family or house four or five may be found each professing a different religion: parents and children, owners and servants, yes even man and wife may each have his religion." The diversity of faiths he found so unsettling was most pronounced in Pennsylvania. But by then every one of the colonies had abandoned the traditional conception of "one state, one church" and moved toward religious pluralism. In the short run, John Winthrop triumphed over Anne Hutchinson and Roger Williams. But in the long run, the American environment proved more congenial to headstrong individualists who distrusted authority and asserted their right to worship God just as they pleased.

A chart of the religious landscape in 1750 reveals the drift away from orthodoxy (see Table 5-3). The New England colonies, except for Williams' Rhode Island, were still heavily Congregationalist. But not uniformly so. Massachusetts and Connecticut together had 36 Anglican, 28 Baptist, and 9 Presbyterian churches. The Anglican church was legally established throughout the southern colonies. But south of Virginia there were almost twice as many dissenting as Anglican churches; Virginia and Maryland too had dozens of Baptist, Lutheran, Presbyterian, German Reformed, and Roman Catholic congregations competing with the Church of

TABLE 5-3
Churches by Denomination, 1750*

	Anglican	Baptist	Congregational	Lutheran	Presbyterian	Dutch Reformed	French Reformed	German Reformed	Roman Catholic
New England									
New Hampshire	1		40		5				
Massachusetts	17	16	231		8				
Connecticut	19	12	155		1				
Rhode Island	7	30	12						
Middle Colonies									
New York	20	4	5	26	35	48	4	7	1
New Jersey	18	14	2	19	51	24		4	2
Pennsylvania	19	29		73	56	7		64	11
Delaware	14	2		3	27				1
South									
Maryland	50	4		3	18			4	15
Virginia	96	3		5	17			5	
North Carolina	9	13		1				2	
South Carolina	16	5	4	5	9		2	4	
Georgia	3			2	1				
TOTAL	289	132	465	138	233	79	6	90	30

*In addition there were over 100 Quaker meetings, principally located in Pennsylvania, North Carolina, New Jersey, and New York.

England. The Middle Colonies, of course, had all of these denominations in abundance, as well as Quaker meetings and Dutch Reformed and French Reformed churches.

The weakness of the Anglican establishment was in part due to its inability to find enough ministers to keep pace with the surging population. Without the huge endowments that financed its activities at home, the Church of England had to depend on local taxes to pay ministerial salaries. That dependence, and the unwillingness of local lay leaders to recommend their clergy for lifetime appointments, undermined the authority of the minister and made him dependent on pleasing his local constituents. Anglicanism became Congregationalism in fact, though not in theory. This made it difficult to attract well-trained English clergy for service in the American wilderness. It would have been very difficult in the best of circumstances to obtain enough ministers, because the English universities that trained them were in a period of stagnation, whereas the colonial population was doubling every quarter of a century. The appointment of an American bishop with powers of ordination might have lessened the crippling dependence on an imported clergy, but that was never done. One branch of the Church of England, its missionary Society for the Propagation of the Gospel in Foreign Parts, did what it could to strengthen the Anglican church in the American colonies. Its resources, however, were too slender to meet the need.

The New England Puritans had Harvard College (and, after 1701, Yale as well) to stock its pulpits with men of proper views. By the end of the seventeenth century, the New England ministry had moved away from the pure Congregational insistence on the absolute autonomy of the self-governing congregation and established more centralized structures controlled by the clergy. The tendency went farthest in Connecticut, where the Saybrook Platform of 1708 created a colony-wide general association of ministers with disciplinary powers. A similar informal strengthening of ministerial authority occurred in Massachusetts. The circumstances made strict control difficult to maintain, however. The population was thinly scattered across a large terrain, with very primitive means of transportation and communication. Congregations retained the power to hire and fire their minister, and he had to be responsive to their desires. If a significant element of the population was seriously disaffected, there was always the option of splitting off and moving on to form another community, as Roger Williams had done.

The most important force that compelled toleration of religious deviants was the eagerness of the colonists to attract more settlers. Many people owned more land than they could ever cultivate themselves; its value would appreciate with the arrival of newcomers. (New England farmers were less oriented to the market, and consequently less welcoming to strangers.) Because immigrants of the proper religious persuasion were not available in large numbers, it was necessary to open the door to English Quakers, Scotch–Irish Presbyterians, German pietists, and others. They naturally would not immigrate unless assured the right to worship as they pleased. Instructions given by the Dutch West India Company in 1663 to the New Netherlands governor Peter Stuyvesant show this motive clearly at work. The company ordered Stuyvesant to admit Quakers and Jews to New Netherlands. "Although we heartily desire that these and other sectarians remained away from there," it said grudgingly, "we doubt very much whether we can proceed rigorously against them without diminishing the population and stopping immigration. You may therefore shut your eyes and allow everyone to have his own belief."

The Great Awakening

The trend toward religious pluralism, already well advanced, was accelerated by a remarkable religious upheaval that shook the colonies in the second quarter of the eighteenth century—the Great Awakening. By the 1720s most American churches were stagnant, and religious indifference was spreading. Aging ministers went through the motions, putting their audiences to sleep with sermons that stressed arid points of dogma. "The generality of preachers," a critic claimed, spoke of "an unknown, unfelt Christ. The reason why congregations have been so dead is because they had dead men preaching to them." In Puritan New England the dilution of the meaning of church membership that had begun with the Half-Way Covenant had proceeded to the point at which membership in many churches was open to all "with a knowledge of the principles of religion and not scandalous by open sinful living." The old insistence on the necessity of a transforming conversion experience had been abandoned. Everywhere colonists seemed "cold and careless as to the concerns of their souls and eternity," and "overheated and deeply engaged towards the profits, pleasures, and preferments of the world."

The Great Awakening was an emotional earthquake that overturned the old order. Its first tremors were felt in the Middle Colonies in the 1720s. William Tennent of the Presbyterian church and Theodorus Frelinghuysen, a Dutch Reformed minister, began to attract wide followings by vivid hellfire and damnation preaching designed to terrify listeners into opening their hearts to God. In the 1730s Jonathan Edwards, a Yale graduate and the most powerful thinker and writer of the Awakening, provoked a wave of conversions in Northampton, Massachusetts and surrounding towns of the Connecticut River Valley with images of "Sinners in the Hands of an Angry God" who held them "over the pit of Hell, much as one holds a spider, or some loathesome insect, over the fire." At any moment He might let you drop into eternal damnation. Edwards consciously sought to terrorize his congregation; he thought it "a reasonable thing to fright a person out of a house on fire." Two of his followers were so frightened that they fell into unshakable depression and slit their throats in despair. But a great many experienced the spiritual rebirth, the sense of saving grace, that Edwards promised.

The Great Awakening became a national movement with the arrival of the English evangelist, George Whitefield, in the colonies in 1739. Although only 23, Whitefield had already played a leading role in the creation of the English Methodist movement. He was an amazing orator, and took the colonies by storm. It was said that he could reduce his audiences to tears merely by pronouncing the word "Mesopotamia." Even Benjamin Franklin, who was both a religious skeptic and a penny pincher, was overwhelmed. He attended a sermon "resolved to give nothing" but carrying "a handful of copper money, three or four silver dollars, and five pistoles in gold. As he proceeded I began to soften, and concluded to give

SINNERS IN THE HANDS OF AN ANGRY GOD

The God that holds you over the pit of Hell, much as one holds a spider, or some loathsome insect, over the fire abhors you, and is dreadfully provoked; his wrath towards you burns like fire; he looks upon you as worthy of nothing else, but to be cast into the fire; he is of purer eyes than to bear to have you in his sight; you are ten thousand times so abominable in his eyes as the most hateful and venomous serpent is in ours. You have offended him infinitely more than ever a stubborn rebel did his prince: and yet 'tis nothing but his hand that holds you from falling into the fire every moment: 'tis ascribed to nothing else, that you did not go to Hell the last night; that you were suffered to awake again in this world, after you closed your eyes to sleep: and there is no other reason to be given why you have not dropped into Hell since you arose in the morning, but that God's hand has held you up.... How dreadful is the state of those that are daily and hourly in danger of this great wrath and infinite misery! But this is the dismal case of every soul in this congregation that has not been born again, however moral and strict, sober and religious, that they may otherwise be.... And it would be a wonder, if some that are now present should not be in Hell in a very short time, before this year is out. And it would be no wonder if some person, that now sits here in some seats of this meeting-house in health, and quiet and secure, should be there before tomorrow morning....

—Jonathan Edwards, 1741

the copper. Another stroke of his oratory determined me to give the silver; and he finished so admirably that I emptied my pocket into the collector's dish, gold and all."

Over the next few years, Whitefield and numerous American imitators traveled from town to town bearing their message. Many of the itinerant preachers of the revival were ordinary laymen who felt the call and were not inhibited by their lack of education. Their basic message was much like Anne Hutchinson's a century before: Follow the dictates of your heart, even when they clash with the views of supposedly learned authorities. The essence of religion was not correct doctrine and proper ceremonies but experience, the experience of being born again. Conservative ministers might know Latin and Greek, but if they "did not experimentally know Christ" they were as "blind as moles," as "dead as stones," "hypocritical varlets" who had no right to lead their flocks. To the shocked targets of these attacks, the revivalists were people who "speak and act after a wild manner as is adapted to affrighten people out of their wits, rather than possess their minds of such a conviction of truth as is proper to men who are endowed with reason and understanding." Instead of encouraging the people to "fall greatly in love with them," they said, Awakeners should insist that their listeners "love God, love your neighbor, and obey them that have rule over you." "Good order" was "the strength and beauty of the world."

Appeals to "good order"—what revivalists scornfully called the "doctrine of blind obedience"—could not calm the storm. The young were particularly receptive to its anti-authoritarian message. The converts who joined churches during the Awakening were six years younger, on the average, than had been customary. The tumult it created at Yale, a bastion of orthodoxy, is revealing. Itinerant preachers arrived in New Haven to argue that what the college provided was merely "natural knowledge" which "puffs up the mind and raises the natural vanity of man." What they needed instead was "saving knowledge" that "renders you a child of God." Many students were persuaded, with results as disruptive as the campus revolts of the late 1960s. In 1742 Yale had to close its doors a month early because "the students would neither mind their studies nor obey the rules of the college. Almost all of them pretended to an inward teacher which they ought to follow, and several of them made excursions into the country and exhorted people from town to town." It was as if college students today were to announce their mass conversion to astrology, and to declare that the books and lectures that made up the regular curriculum were worthless. The Connecticut assembly attempted to suppress the unorthodoxy by outlawing itinerant preaching. The framers of a new charter for Yale found it necessary to explicitly forbid students from calling the President or the tutors "hypocrites, carnal, or unconverted"!

The flames of the revival began to die down after 1745. Reliable statistics on the number of converts it brought into the churches are not available, and it is even less certain how many who claimed to have experienced a conversion resisted the temptation to lapse into their former ways for the rest of their lives. The Awakening changed America in major ways, though. It provoked fierce battles between pro- and antirevival forces that split every major denomination except the Quakers and Anglicans into warring camps. By 1750 the colonial religious scene was even more varied than is apparent in Table 5-3 (page 99). The 465 Congregational churches listed there no longer represented a unified denomination. Many small towns that once had only one church now had two—New Light Congregational or Old Light Congregational, or New Side and Old Side Presbyterian in affiliation. The clear territorial boundaries of earlier churches and the identification of the church with the community were eroded, because itinerants regarded everyone as a potential soul to be harvested for Jesus. The separation of the church from the state was sharpened. Although some churches continued to hold a privileged position in certain colonies for a long time to come—Congregationalism was formally the established religion in Massachusetts until 1833—a giant step had been taken towards a society whose churches competed freely with each other and acquired members by persuasion.

The Awakening undermined the traditional authority of the educated clergy. Although it won converts from all classes, it was fundamentally a revolt of the masses, said one preacher, "against the mighty, of whatever rank, age, or station they be." It was an assertion that God was no respecter of social or economic status, and that all people were equally capable of finding salvation. It brought a new form of mass communication to the colonies, with ordinary people addressing each other with an authority derived not from formal credentials and titles but from their powers of persuasion. It fed a rebellious and self-righteous spirit that could, in the right circumstances, lead to a questioning of other forms of established authority.

If the Awakening was an expression of radical individualism, it was at the same time a unifying and nationalizing influence for the 13 separate and diverse colonies. It was the first American social movement, in a sense, posing the first great ideological issue that cut across the boundaries of the colonies from New Hampshire to Georgia. It stimulated a new collective national consciousness that provided a base for common action in future years.

SUGGESTED READINGS

Brief introductions to the history of the peoples of British North America with bibliographical suggestions are provided in the entries on Afro-Americans, Dutch, English, French, Germans, Pennsylvania Germans, Scots, and Scots-Irish in Stephan Thernstrom, ed., *The Harvard Encyclopedia of American Ethnic Groups* (1980). The legal incorporation of foreign peoples into British America is described in an essay on "Naturalization and Citizenship," in the same volume, and in James H. Kettner, *The Development of American Citizenship, 1608–1870* (1978). The servant trade that brought most of them across the ocean is analyzed in Abbot E. Smith, *Colonists in Bondage: White Servitude and Convict Labor in America, 1607–1776* (1947) and David Galenson, *White Servitude in Colonial America: An Economic Analysis* (1981). The opening chapters of Walter S. Nugent, *Structures of American Social History* (1981) and Part I of Robert V. Wells, *Revolutions in Americans' Lives: A Demographic Perspective on the History of Americans, Their Families, and Their Society* (1982) summarize what is presently known about colonial demographic history. Further insight into family life may be gained from Philip J. Greven, Jr., *The Protestant Temperament: Patterns of Child-Rearing, Religious Experience, and the Self in Early America* (1977), and Daniel Black Smith, *Inside the Great House: Planter Family Life in Eighteenth-Century Chesapeake Society* (1980).

Richard Hofstadter, *America at 1750: A Social Portrait* (1971), and James Henretta, *The Evolution of American Society, 1700–1815* (1973) are outstanding syntheses, although the latter's stress on growing economic inequality has been undermined by recent research. See in particular Jeffrey G. Williamson and Peter H. Lindert, *American Inequality: A Macroeconomic History* (1978). Jackson Turner Main, *The Social Structure of Revolutionary America* (1965) contains much valuable material. Stuart Bruchey, *The Roots of American Economic Growth, 1607–1861* (1965), James F. Shepherd and Gary M. Walton, *The Economic Rise of Early America* (1979) and Alice Hanson Jones, *Wealth of a Nation To Be: The American Colonies on the Eve of the Revolution* (1980) cover economic development.

Richard L. Bushman, *From Puritan to Yankee: Character and the Social Order in Connecticut, 1690–1765* (1967), Douglas L. Jones, *Village and Seaport: Migration and Society in Eighteenth-Century Massachusetts* (1981), Charles S. Grant, *Democracy in the Connecticut Frontier Town of Kent* (1961), and the community studies cited at the end of Chapter 3 illuminate the development of New England society. Sung Bok Kim, *Landlord and Tenant in Colonial New York: Manorial Society, 1664–1775* (1978) casts new light on an important subject. Economic and social change in Pennsylvania are examined in James T. Lemon, *"The Best Poor Man's Country": A Geographical Study of Early Southeastern Pennsylvania* (1972), Stephanie G. Wolf, *Urban Village: Population, Community, and Family Structure in Germantown, Pennsylvania, 1683–1800* (1976), and Frederick B. Tolles, *Meeting House and Counting House: The Quaker Merchants of Philadelphia, 1682–1783* (1948). Verner W. Crane, *Benjamin Franklin and a Rising People* (1954) is the best brief biography of the colony's most famous resident. Franklin's *Autobiography*, available in many editions, is a classic, but it must be read with an understanding that its author was a more complex character than he let on. The best introduction to the large literature on the Great Awakening is J.M. Bumsted and John W. Van de Wetering, eds., *What Must I Do To Be Saved? The Great Awakening in Colonial America* (1976).

Chapter Six

Governing the Empire

F rom the viewpoint of British officials concerned with imperial affairs, the function of England's colonies overseas was quite simple: They were to add to the wealth of England and thereby enhance her power and glory. Each colony had its own governing institutions to deal with matters of local concern, but the effect of "every act of a dependent provincial government" was supposed to be to "the advantage of the mother state unto whom it owes its being and protection." The parent-child relation was the most common metaphor used to describe the imperial connection; the colonies were infants who required the firm guidance of a wise adult. Varying the metaphor, the Governor of New York in 1705 described the colonies as mere "twigs belonging to the main tree, entirely dependent upon and subservient to England."

These bold pronouncements may seem to imply that British North America, like New Spain, was dominated by a vast imperial bureaucracy with arms extending into every community. That was not the case at all. The British government carefully regulated the flow of trade into and out of the colonies, but it did not intrude strongly in their internal politics. Thriving institutions of local and colony-wide government were allowed to develop, and an indigenous leadership class that was skilled at political combat soon emerged. American political institutions were modeled on those of the mother country, but they operated in unexpected ways in a very different environment. There was a wide gap between the theory of colonial subordination and the reality of effective self-government. When the British government finally made a concerted and sustained effort to close the gap by expanding and tightening its imperial administration in the 1760s, it was too late. By

Statues of George III were demolished all over the Colonies, as demonstrated in this John C. McRay engraving of a New York City mob in 1776.

then most colonists did not see themselves as mere "twigs belonging to the main tree." A prosperous, diverse, and dynamic society of headstrong individualists resisted and rebelled.

THE MERCANTILIST SYSTEM

Seventeenth and eighteenth century British statesmen, like their counterparts in rival European countries, believed in an economic theory that came to be known as "mercantilism." It assumed that the key to national strength was a favorable balance of foreign trade. Countries that sold more abroad than they imported from other countries would accumulate gold reserves from nations who did the opposite, and gold was all-important as the "sinews of war." Colonies were crucial to mercantilist thinkers. Possessions like New Spain were ideal, because they produced precious metals that directly swelled the national treasury. Though lacking in gold, the North American colonies helped England's balance of trade in two ways: They supplied staple crops that she had previously purchased from other nations, stopping the outflow of bullion that had gone to pay for sugar, tobacco, oranges, and other desired items that could not be grown efficiently in the British Isles. At the same time, such colonies were a valuable market for British exports, stimulating industrial development and creating more jobs at home. These happy results would not occur, however, if colonists sold their tobacco to and bought their tea from the Dutch, or if they manufactured goods that competed with British products in the colonial market. Laws governing colonial trade and manufacturing were needed to prevent those possibilities.

Regulation of colonial economic activity began shortly after the first successful cultivation of tobacco in Virginia. James I issued an edict forbidding the direct shipment of Virginia leaf to continental markets. First it had to go to England, where the shipper had to pay a substantial duty before it could be sent on for sale in Europe. In compensation, James banned the growing of tobacco in England. Enforcement of these orders was quite lax at first, because of the political turmoil caused by the English Civil War, and Virginians continued to do a thriving business with Dutch traders. Between 1651 and 1673, however, Parliament passed a series of Navigation Acts with real teeth in them. They provided that all goods entering or leaving England had to be carried on English ships. No sugar, tobacco, cotton, or indigo—the most valuable colonial products—could be shipped anywhere but to England, and a stiff duty had to be paid before they could be reexported. Subsequent laws extended the list of these "enumerated commodities" to rice, molasses, furs, copper ore, turpentine, and a variety of wood products. Only non-enumerated items—the most important of them fish, rum, and grain—could be directly sold in foreign ports. Similar restraints were placed on various enumerated imports into the colonies from other countries. They had to pass through England, travel on English ships, and have high duties levied on them.

The political influence of England's rising manufacturing interests increased greatly during the seventeenth century, and by its end they won legislative pro-

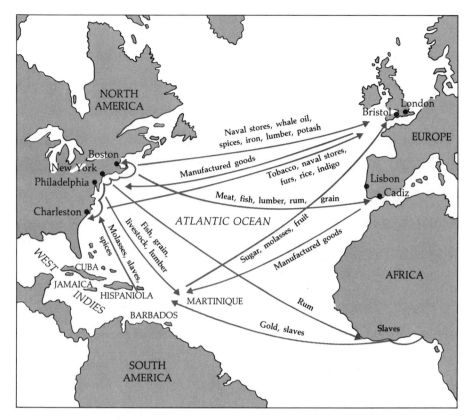

MAP 6-1
Eighteenth-Century Atlantic Trade

tection to keep colonial markets for their products open. A series of "restraining acts" regulated colonial manufacturing to the benefit of English producers. Most colonial manufacturing was carried out in tens of thousands of small shops and private homes, making effective regulation administratively impossible. But two key industries that were at the cutting edge of Britain's incipient Industrial Revolution—woolen goods and iron—were given meaningful protection from American competition. In 1699 Parliament banned the export of woolens from the colonies, even from one colony to another. The Hat Act of 1732 gave similar protection to English hatmakers, whose customers had been buying cheap beaver hats made in New York or New England. The Iron Act of 1750 helped English producers of finished iron products by forbidding colonists from building mills for rolling or slitting iron or steel furnaces. Colonists could smelt raw iron, but would have to ship it to Britain for final processing.

In order to enforce these regulations throughout England's far-flung empire, the customs service was enlarged. Officers under the direct control of Crown officials in London were dispatched to the colonies to monitor shipping and collect duties. The Lords of Trade, a special committee to advise the King and his Privy Council on matters of enforcement, was created in 1675. In 1696 it was reorganized as a permanent supervisory body, the Board of Trade and Plantations, with broad responsibility for colonial affairs.

Costs and Benefits

In the tense years just before the Revolution, angry patriots charged that recent British trade regulations were stifling the colonial economy. Some historians have portrayed the entire mercantilist system embodied in the Navigation Acts in similar terms—as an exploitative and tyrannical system that unfairly taxed American producers and prevented them from grasping economic opportunities that were rightfully theirs. This indictment is overdrawn. If it had been true, it is difficult to understand how the colonists could have achieved by 1774 a standard of living that the leading authority, Alice Hanson Jones, calls "probably the highest achieved for the great bulk of the population in any country up to that time."[1] It is equally difficult to understand why there was so little sustained American opposition to the Navigation Acts in the century preceding the turbulent 1760s.

Mercantile restraints did impose costs on the colonists, of course. Producers of enumerated commodities that had to pass through England en route to European markets were stung with extra shipping and handling charges and with duties. Colonial consumers who wanted to buy enumerated imports from non-British sources had to pay higher prices for the same reason, as did colonists denied the opportunity to purchase woolens, beaver hats, and finished iron produced cheaply elsewhere in America.

If there were costs to the colonists, however, there were benefits as well, and the benefits probably outweighed the costs. Perhaps most important, the Navigation Acts sheltered colonial traders, and those who produced the grain, fish, meat and other goods they traded, from Dutch competition. The seacoast trade among the colonies themselves and trade between the mainland and the West Indies flourished mightily once the formidable Dutch were out of the picture. Another benefit was that the British government paid special subsidies or "bounties" to encourage colonists to grow indigo and to supply forest products useful to the British Navy—"naval stores" such as timber for masts, pitch, and turpentine. No less than £1.7 billion was paid out in such bounties to Americans between 1706 and 1774. Colonial producers of enumerated commodities were granted a monopoly of the English market, which in most cases was large enough to absorb the crop at a decent price. Tobacco and rice were major exceptions; a large share of both crops had to be reexported to continental markets. Planters, however, were given rebates to offset the export duties; these rebates amounted to the full cost in the case of tobacco and half of it in the case of rice. They also had the benefit of the

---

[1]This statement may seem surprising, since Britain's position as the world's first industrial nation made her distinctly wealthier than the colonies on the eve of the Revolution. Wealth in Britain, however, was not broadly distributed among "the great bulk of the population," as it was in America.

superior marketing facilities available in London. Another major advantage of the regulatory system for Americans was the stimulus it gave to colonial shipbuilders, since vessels made in the colonies were counted as "British." With an inexhaustible supply of timber so readily available, New England naval yards could turn out vessels 30 to 50 percent cheaper than in Europe. By the middle of the eighteenth century, a third of all merchant ships flying the Union Jack were American made.

Restraint on colonial manufacturing might seem to have been a major cost the system inflicted on Americans, but in fact it was not. The eagerness of the British to keep the American market open for British-made goods was of slight practical significance. In America the high ratio of land to labor made it impossible to recruit industrial workers except at prohibitively high prices. The only branches of manufacturing in which Americans could compete effectively were those in which easy access to raw materials was important enough to compensate for inflated labor costs. Shipbuilding, ironmaking, and the manufacture of beaver hats were the major examples. Iron and hatmakers did indeed suffer from the restrictions imposed on them. But they were exceptional. The capital and the labor supply necessary for an American industrial revolution would not become available until the nineteenth century, long after Britain's imperial yoke had been thrown off.

Being part of the empire, in short, offered advantages that offset—and perhaps more than offset—the disadvantages. All groups did not share equally in the gains and losses, of course, and some found the restrictions onerous. The most important potential clash between imperial and colonial interests involved the New England and Middle Colony merchants engaged in the triangular trade with the sugar islands of the West Indies.[2] They took grain, meat, fish, and lumber to the islands, traded them for sugar to carry to England, and returned from England laden with British manufactures. It was all perfectly legal. The difficulty was that many of the Caribbean islands were not in English but in French, Dutch, or Spanish hands. These were very attractive markets, and French sugar in particular was available at bargain prices. The English government tolerated this trade during peacetime, because it did not involve enumerated exports or imports, and because it provided the earnings that allowed the northern colonies to pay for the manufactures they bought in England. But during the recurrent wars that pitted Britain against foreign powers, British officials attempted to cut off trade with them. Colonists were largely successful in evading these efforts (as were English traders as well), but it was clear that England either did not comprehend that the prosperity of the colonies depended on the trade with the other sugar islands or cared very little about their interests.

The extent of British disregard for the economic well-being of the colonies became clearer still after Parliament, responding to pressures from the powerful group of absentee landlords with holdings in the British sugar islands, passed the

---

[2]This was but one of several triangular routes Yankee captains followed. A second took northern foodstuffs to southern Europe, wines and fruits from there to England, and manufactures back on the westward journey. A third took northern rum to Africa, returned slaves to the West Indies, and brought molasses back to New England's rum distilleries.

Molasses Act in 1733. It was an attempt to revive the sagging economy of the British islands by imposing a high duty on sugar and molasses imported into the mainland colonies from the foreign islands. Had it been enforced, the Molasses Act would have sent the economy of the northern colonies into a tailspin. American traders believed the law was grossly unfair, and so too did English merchants who were most deeply involved in trade with the northern colonies. A complex political struggle unfolded, ending in a bizarre compromise. The law remained on the books, but the customs officers responsible for enforcing it looked the other way and allowed American ships to smuggle in as much foreign molasses as they wished. At the time it must have seemed the best way to "muddle through" a very messy situation. But the effect was to make an important sector of the colonial merchant elite feel they were justified in operating outside the law. The experience invited broader critical reflections concerning their obligations to established authority. When British officials launched a vigorous new program to enforce the mercantilist system, one of its principal provisions was a crackdown on foreign molasses. After a third of a century of ignoring a parliamentary dictate, they found many Americans had grown unaccustomed to automatically deferring to imperial commands. It was not mere coincidence that in the crisis of the 1760s and 1770s, the most militantly patriotic members of the colonial mercantile community were those who had specialized in the West Indian trade.

GOVERNORS AND ASSEMBLIES

Nine of the thirteen colonies that eventually rebelled against British authority were by then under direct royal rule; the Crown appointed both their governors and the upper house of their legislatures, the councils (see Table 6–1). Not one *began* that way, however—a fact of crucial significance to their political development. All were started either by chartered business corporations like the Virginia and Massachusetts Bay companies, by individual proprietors like William Penn, or by parties of migrants from other nearby colonies. The charters and the terms of the proprietary grants gave them wide latitude to regulate their own affairs, as long as they did not establish "laws, statutes, ordinances and directions contrary to the laws of this our realm of England." They were private estates rather than colonies in the usual sense of the term. Of course the King could take control of them and alter their frame of government, with the consent of Parliament. But by the time that happened they had developed traditions of independence that were never extinguished.

Self-government was integral to the English mode of colonization. The question of *who* would exercise the powers of government was less clear. Until 1619, Virginia was ruled autocratically; the governor selected by the directors of the company ruled without consulting the settlers. Many of the proprietors elsewhere also sought to retain as much power as possible in their own hands. William Penn's

TABLE 6-1
Forms of Government in the Thirteen Colonies

Each of the colonies had a governor and a legislature with two houses. The upper house was called the council, the lower the assembly. (Pennsylvania was exceptional with a unicameral legislature.) In royal colonies, the King appointed the governor and his council; assemblymen were chosen by the people. In proprietary colonies, the Crown-appointed proprietor selected the governor and the council, and the assembly was elected by popular vote. In a self-governing colony—early Connecticut and Rhode Island were the only examples of this type—all officials were chosen by the people. In chartered self-governing corporate colonies, directors of the corporation appointed the governor and his council, and freemen elected assemblymen. As can be seen, all the colonies were initially proprietary or self-governing, but most were put under royal rule before the Revolution.

Connecticut	Self-governing 1636–62; self-governing corporate from 1662
Delaware	Dutch and Swedish commercial settlements 1631–64; proprietary 1664–82; part of Pennsylvania 1682–1703; self-governing corporate after 1703
Georgia	Proprietary 1732–54; royal after 1754
Maryland	Proprietary 1632–91; royal 1691–1715; proprietary after 1715
Massachusetts	Self-governing corporate 1629–91; royal after 1691
New Hampshire	Proprietary 1622–41; part of Massachusetts 1641–80; royal after 1680
New Jersey	East and West Jersey proprietary 1664–1702; united and made royal in 1702
New York	Colony of Dutch West India Company 1624–64; proprietary 1664–85; royal after 1685
North Carolina	Part of Carolina proprietary colony 1670–1712; separate proprietary colony 1712–29; royal after 1729
Pennsylvania	Proprietary from 1681
Rhode Island	Self-governing 1636–44; self-governing corporate 1644–63; royal after 1663
South Carolina	Part of Carolina proprietary colony 1670–1712; separate proprietary colony 1712–29; royal after 1729
Virginia	Self-governing corporate 1607–24; royal after 1624

advanced notions about freedom of conscience, for example, contrasted starkly with his ideas about popular government. His first "Frame of Government" provided that the proprietor himself would appoint both the governor and the council and that they would make all the laws. The elected assembly could either approve or reject a law, but it could not amend those proposed or initiate new ones.

The Virginia Company, Penn, and their counterparts in the other colonies, however, were soon compelled to relax their tight grip and allow the settlers a greater voice in government. The Virginia Company felt it necessary to authorize the establishment of a representative assembly to make its precarious colony more attractive to settlers, and the House of Burgesses successfully asserted its rights to legislate when the company collapsed and a royal governor appeared on the scene. The Pennsylvania assembly stridently pressed for greater power, leading Penn to ask in anguish, "cannot more friendly and private course be taken to set matters right in an infant province? For the love of God, me, and the poor country, be not so *governmentish.*" No one listened, and the weary proprietor finally gave in. In 1701 a new "Frame of Government," written jointly by the assembly and council, eliminated the council as well as Penn's right to veto legislation. Throughout the colonies the popularly elected assemblies expanded their powers. They considered themselves local counterparts of the English House of Commons, and claimed privileges that in some cases exceeded those possessed by Parliament at the time—the right to meet without the presence of the chief executive, to elect their own speakers, to set up committees and special commissions to perform functions normally left to the executive, to levy all taxes, and regulate all expenditures of public funds.

The relationship between the new colonial governments and the English governing apparatus was problematical at first, and it was never spelled out in unambiguous terms agreed to on both sides of the ocean. While England was convulsed by the political and religious conflicts that climaxed in civil war and the establishment of a republic under Oliver Cromwell, no one paid much heed to the colonies; they were left free to behave as if they were independent nations. Connecticut and Rhode Island came into being without any formal authorization from English authorities. In 1643 they joined with Massachusetts and Plymouth to form the New England Confederation, again without consulting the authorities at home. The Confederation waged war with the Indians, negotiated with Dutch officials over the boundary between English and Dutch settlements, and even signed a treaty—the 1650 Treaty of Hartford. John Winthrop shrugged off the complaint that the Bay Colony's discrimination against non-Puritans was contrary to English law, saying coolly that "our allegiance binds us not to English law any longer than while we live in England." Virginians in these years engaged in wholesale defiance of earlier royal orders forbidding direct sale of their tobacco to Dutch traders. The House of Burgesses passed an audacious resolution contending that "no law should be established within the kingdom concerning us" without its consent. In 1652 they negotiated a change of government with Cromwell's representatives, a change that gave them extraordinary power until the Restoration. Under the new arrangement, the assembly was empowered to choose both the governor and his council.

Andros and the Dominion of New England

The restoration of the Stuarts to the throne in 1660 brought both a new surge of colonization activity and a move to impose tighter controls over the existing settlements. Primary attention was given to elaborating the mercantilist framework begun with the Navigation Act of 1651. Over the next dozen years the system was expanded and strengthened. The creation of the Lords of Trade in 1675 brought into being a group of career officials, many of military background, who were deeply suspicious of the colonists and disdainful of their talk about their "traditional liberties." After an investigation, they concluded that Massachusetts was the worst offender. In 1680, at their recommendation, the Bay Colony was stripped of New Hampshire, its possession for 40 years. New Hampshire was put under direct royal administration. An even greater blow to Massachusetts fell in 1684, when its cherished charter was annulled.

New arrangements for governing Massachusetts had not yet been worked out when Charles II died the next year and his brother, the Duke of York, ascended the throne as James II. It was not a happy transition for colonists fond of self-government. James was deeply involved in North American affairs as proprietor of New York, and he had resisted the demands of settlers there for an assembly to represent them. Just before his brother's death, he bowed momentarily to popular pressures and agreed to allow a representative body with power over taxes to meet every three years. But after becoming king he vetoed its actions, dissolved it, and gave full legislative power to the Royal Governor and his appointive council.

James then proceeded with a bold plan to merge the New England colonies, New York, New Jersey, and Pennsylvania into a super-colony, a Dominion of New England that would ultimately embrace all the territory from Maine to the northern border of Maryland. (The southern colonies probably would also have been consolidated, had the scheme worked.) He dissolved the assemblies of those colonies and dispatched his close friend Sir Edmund Andros to rule the new Dominion. No new representative institutions would replace the previous ones. Andros and a Crown-appointed council would rule the whole area from their headquarters in Boston, without consulting the settlers. The right of local communities to govern themselves was severely curtailed as well; Andros ordered that only one town meeting a year could be held. He added to his unpopularity by changing Boston's Congregational Old South Meeting House into an Anglican church and by questioning the validity of all land titles within the Dominion.

Had it been fully implemented, it is quite possible that this radical plan would have provoked a full-scale rebellion. Events in England, however, rendered colonial revolt unnecessary. James had ruled at home with the same heavy hand he applied overseas, twisting the law, treating Parliament with disdain, and maneuvering to impose his Catholic beliefs on an overwhelmingly Protestant nation. In November of 1688, parliamentary forces drove the king into exile and replaced him on the throne with William of Orange and his wife Mary. The Glorious Revolution permanently established the principles of parliamentary supremacy and the rule of law. Future monarchs would hold formidable powers for another century, but only within the boundaries defined by the legislature and the courts.

The Power of Royal Governors
in Theory and Practice

The Dominion scheme collapsed with the fall of James, and the assemblies of the various colonies it had embraced quickly reconstituted themselves. Most of the suspended charters were restored by the new English government. New York remained a royal colony, however, and Massachusetts was made into one by the new charter given it in 1691. The trend toward royal rule continued in the eighteenth century. The Crown took over New Jersey in 1702, North and South Carolina in 1729, and Georgia in 1754.

This trend, although significant, did not strengthen the hand of London as much as might be thought. In theory, royal governors had more power than did the executive in England after the Glorious Revolution put an end to Stuart absolutism. They could veto legislation, dissolve assemblies or refuse to convoke them, remove judges, and create new courts without legislative authorization. The King's instructions informed them that colonial assemblies were nothing but "corporations at a distance, invested with an ability to make temporary by-laws for themselves but in no way interfering with the legal prerogative of the Crown, or the true legislative power of the mother state."

In fact, the English government never found the means to bring the assemblies into the strictly subordinate and dependent status assigned to them in imperial theory. One reason was that they were far away, and authorities in London never developed a sufficiently centralized system to keep track of colonial developments and respond forcefully when displeased. The Board of Trade was much weaker than the Spanish Council of the Indies. It was primarily an information gathering body, advisory to the King's council. At first it was empowered to make recommendations on all appointments to the colonial service, but it lost that power in bureaucratic infighting with other branches of the government. The official who actually controlled most of the patronage was a man with broad responsibility for all matters of state in the Western Hemisphere, who had knowledge of the American situation. Other departments—the Army, the Navy, the Treasury, and the courts—also had overlapping claims to jurisdiction over American affairs.

The quality of the men selected to be the King's representatives in the colonies, furthermore, tended to be low. Appointments were made on the basis of birth and connections, not on merit. Governors primarily regarded their posts as sources of personal profit from fees, fines, and land dealings. A not untypical chief executive of New York was an imperious incompetent who owed his position to the fact that his wife was a first cousin of the Duke of Newcastle and the sister of the Earl of Halifax. His reason for taking the job, New Yorkers believed, was "to repair his broken fortune." One of his predecessors, Edward Hyde, Lord Cornbury, was a transvestite who traipsed around the colony in women's clothing "to the universal contempt of the people." Many governors did not even deign to cross the ocean to assume their posts, but remained in England, collecting the rewards of office and paying a pittance to a deputy who did the actual work.

Even governors who were competent and conscientious found their role difficult. Their tenure in office was less dependent on the quality of their performance

THE DIFFICULTY OF GOVERNING MASSACHUSETTS, 1721

Although the government of this province be nominally in the Crown, and the governor appointed by your Majesty, yet the unequal balance of their constitution having lodged too great a power in the assembly, this province is, and is always likely to continue in great disorder. They do not pay a due regard to your Majesty's instructions. They do not make a suitable provision for the maintenance of their governor, and on all occasions they affect too great an independence on their mother kingdom.... An act of assembly...has not a little contributed to the present disorders there, in as much as by the said act it is provided, that no person shall be capable of representing any town or borough where such person is not a freeholder and settled inhabitant; from whence it happens, that the assembly is generally filled with people of small fortunes and mean capacities, who are easily led into any measures that seem to enlarge their liberties and privileges.

—Board of Trade to the King

overseas than on the shifting political winds at home, and turnover was rapid. The average governor served only five years, and good men were often replaced just when they had grasped the intricacies of a colony's political culture. Their capacity to build a supporting political machine through patronage, the glue that held the eighteenth-century English political system together, was substantial at first. But it declined over time, both because ministers of the Crown captured colonial political plums to use for their own purposes and because refractory assemblies refused to make appropriations without attaching strings that gave them a voice in appointments. Although governors urged them to approve long-term appropriations to pay their salaries, assemblies generally resisted making grants of more than one year's duration.

The difficulties governors had in preserving their authority were revealed in their most extreme form in a series of violent political upheavals that occurred in the last quarter of the seventeenth century. Bacon's Rebellion in Virginia in 1676 was a classic example. It began as a dispute between the Crown-appointed Governor, William Berkeley, and Nathaniel Bacon, a prosperous young planter who had arrived from England three years before and been appointed to the governor's council. When Berkeley refused to authorize Bacon to lead a private army of frontiersmen in an attack on the Indians, Bacon took over and forced Berkeley to flee to Maryland. Bacon, however, fell ill and died, and his forces disintegrated before warships arrived from England in response to Berkeley's request for help. Disagreements about how to deal with the Indians in this case precipitated violent combat over a much deeper issue—over the distribution of power and privilege within the colony. Berkeley and his supporters were an entrenched ruling clique who had long expoited their offices for personal gain. Although many of Bacon's troops were small farmers resentful at heavy taxes, his key followers were wealthy planters who were recent arrivals and consequently on the "outs" politically.

The issues that triggered them differed, but essentially similar risings occurred elsewhere in the colonies within the next 15 years—John Culpeper's Rebellion in the Carolinas in 1677, the revolt of the Protestant Association against the ascendancy of the Catholic Calvert proprietary family in Maryland in 1689, a mob revolt against Governor Edmond Andros in Massachusetts the same year, and Jacob Leisler's Rebellion in New York (1689–91). Although the precise causes varied, all represented determined efforts by resentful people who lacked political connections to overthrow establishments that were unresponsive to their wishes.

Violent resistance to the authorities was largely over after the 1690s, but the emergence of an ambitious and adroit native leadership class with a firm hold on the assembly proved a powerful counterforce to the governors' quest for power. In the North, particularly in the Middle Colonies, these elite groups were typically split into competing factions according to economic, ethnic, geographical and family ties. In New York, for example, the Presbyterian Livingston family led a coalition of Hudson River aristocrats, their tenants, and various dissenting religious sects against followers of the De Lanceys—Anglican merchants with a base in New York City and Westchester County. Politically adept governors in colonies with such divided elites were able to maintain some degree of control by siding with one faction or the other. In the southern colonies, their task was more difficult, because the large planters who controlled the assemblies were solidly united on the major issues.

The Zenger Case

The circumstances that led to the famous libel trial of John Peter Zenger in New York in 1735 well illustrate the handicaps governors labored under and indicate the importance of a new political instrument—the popular press. Until then New York had only one newspaper and it was safely in the governor's pocket; its printer was the official printer for the colony and would never criticize the administration for fear of losing that lucrative appointment. William Cosby arrived to assume the governorship in 1731. He was an unusually avaricious man, and proceeded crudely to milk his post for all it was worth. After making an alliance with the dominant De Lancey faction in the assembly, he thought he had the political clout to enrich himself further by suing the former acting governor for half of the salary he had been paid while filling in for Cosby during the preceding year. When Chief Justice Lewis Morris of the New York Supreme Court ruled against him, Cosby suspended him from office and appointed James De Lancey to replace him. Morris was a shrewd and determined political operator who took the issue to the public. He launched a colony-wide petition drive, won the support of the Livingston faction in the assembly, and persuaded a young German immigrant printer, John Peter Zenger, to establish the New York *Weekly Journal* as an opposition organ.

Stung by the *Journal*'s blistering criticisms of his administration, Cosby had Zenger prosecuted for libel in 1735. The prosecution contended that as the King's appointed representative, the governor was "vested with all the prerogatives belonging to the sacred person of his Prince," and had to be protected against character assassination. Morris brought in America's leading trial lawyer, Andrew Hamilton, from Philadelphia for the defense. He argued that the contested passages were true and that truth was a legitimate defense against accusations of libel. Admitting that precedents for his view were absent from English law, he asked "what strange doctrine is it to press every thing for law here which is so in England?" The judge was unimpressed and ruled that the only issue was whether the offending passages had appeared in the *Journal* or not. However, the jury ignored his instructions, and took only a few minutes to find Zenger innocent.

The Zenger case did not, as legend would have it, establish that truth was a defense in libel cases. That did not become accepted American legal doctrine for another half a century. Several newspapers were convicted for "libelous" remarks that were quite true. But the charges were brought by assemblies, not by governors. The real message of the Zenger decision was that unpopular governors could not wrap themselves in the mantle of "the sacred person of his Prince" and persuade American juries to throw their critics in jail. Morris failed in his effort to get London authorities to remove Cosby from office; Cosby died in 1736 in the midst of the struggle. But Morris led the "popular party" to victory in the next elections, and won some major concessions from Cosby's successor—the right of the upper house to meet without the governor in attendance, a guarantee of frequent assembly elections, and an end to revenue grants of more than one year's duration. To make members more responsive to the wishes of their constituents, the assembly began the practice of publishing how each one voted on all assembly divisions. Even

HAMILTON'S ARGUMENT, 1735

I beg leave to insist, that the right of complaining or remonstrating is natural; and the restraint upon this natural right is the law only, and that those restraints can only extend to what is *false*. For as it is truth alone which can excuse or justify any man for complaining of a bad administration, I as frankly agree, that nothing ought to excuse a man who raises a false charge or accusation...against a public magistrate. *Truth* ought to govern the whole affair of libels, and yet the party accused runs risk enough even then; for if he fails in proving every title of what he has written, and to the satisfaction of the court and jury too, he may find to his cost, that when the prosecution is set on foot by men in power, it seldom wants friends to favor it.

—The Zenger Trial Record

more significant than these concrete reforms, perhaps, was the fact that the Morris–Cosby dispute provided the people of New York with experience in mobilizing popular resistance to arbitrary rule. It was not a lesson that would soon be forgotten.

LEADERS AND FOLLOWERS

"The people have got the whole administration in their hands," declared the exasperated governor of South Carolina in 1748, "and the Crown is by various laws despoiled of its principal flowers and brightest jewels." His charge will mislead a modern reader who defines "the people" in terms of contemporary democratic theory. By "the people" the governor meant not the masses of ordinary citizens, but the select and far from representative group of men who controlled the colony's assembly. Neither they nor the people who elected them accepted the egalitarian premises that later Americans would take for granted. Colonial political leadership was exercised by "the better sort," and their lessers expected to defer to them. However, if our point of comparison is not later America but other societies in the same historical era, the colonial political system was strikingly responsive to the popular will.

Neither in South Carolina nor elsewhere in the colonies were *all* the people granted political rights. Slaves, women, and children, it goes without saying, were not allowed to vote or hold office. Nor were indentured servants, free blacks in most colonies, or free white adult males who owned no property. (Early Massachusetts had a religious rather than a property qualification for voting, but shifted to an economic standard by the end of the seventeenth century.) The property requirement, grossly "undemocratic" by later standards, was justfied on two grounds: Only those who had a property "stake in society" were expected to be concerned with the business of government. And they alone had the economic base for making properly independent judgments on public matters. A poor man dependent on his landlord's good favor could be too easily pressured to vote as his superior wished. "Dependence begets subservience and venality, suffocates the germ of virtue, and prepares fit tools for the designs of ambition," said Thomas Jefferson.

Despite this stress on the virtues of independent-mindedness, the social context of colonial politics encouraged voters to follow the lead of wealthy local notables. There was no secret ballot; you had to stand up and be counted on one side or the other. In a classic display of the deferential attitudes that were expected from ordinary voters, a group of "respectable but uninformed inhabitants" of Virginia visited their representative on the eve of his departure for the First Continental Congress in 1774. They said that they understood from him that the British "intended to invade our rights and privileges; we own we do not see this clearly, but since you assure us it is so, we believe it. We are about to take a very dangerous step, but we have confidence in you and will do anything you think proper." That such confidence in traditional leadership was widespread is suggested by the fact that two-thirds of all the men elected to the Virginia assembly between 1680 and 1776 came from one of 23 interrelated planting dynasties.

In the southern colonies, furthermore, the most important officials at the local level were not elected but appointed. The basic institution of local rule was the county court, which had executive and legislative as well as judicial power. It consisted of 8 to 30 judges appointed by the governor. Governors found it politic to choose judges from the local planting oligarchy, and they became a self-perpetuating group. After the late seventeenth-century upheavals in Virginia, North Carolina, and Maryland, political life was tranquil. Smaller farmers deferred to their superiors, and bolstered their egos with the consoling thought that, however poor, they were at least members of the master race.

In New England, so often celebrated as the home of "town meeting democracy," the people elected their local officials as well as representatives to the assembly. The Puritan ideal, however, was a consensual community—one in which everyone thought alike. Strangers who did not conform to local ways were "warned out." Members of prosperous, long-established church families dominated political life. "Go into every village of New England," said John Adams, "and you will find that the office of the justice of the peace and even the place of representative, which has ever depended only on the freest election of the people, have generally descended from generation to generation, in three or four families at most." Seven of the nine new selectmen elected in Northampton, Massachusetts in the 1740s, for example, were the sons of selectmen; their fathers had served an average of more than nine terms apiece. Despite the clear ascendancy of the old families and the ideal of communal harmony, Yankees could be a contentious lot. Many a town meeting sparked bitter quarrels over such issues as where to locate a new road, school, or other public facility or the choice of a minister. Conflict violated Puritan "precepts of peace," however, and community leaders made every effort to smooth it over. Most disputes were resolved by a process of accommodation that ended with unanimous agreement. A study of more than 2,000 meetings in ten eighteenth-century Masachusetts towns reveals that 98 percent of all decisions were taken without recorded opposition. New England communities were certainly democratic in the sense that their governments rested on popular consent. But they were democracies, it has been well said, "devoid of legitimate difference, dissent, and conflict."

In the socially and economically more diverse Middle Colonies, politics was less consensual and less deferential, and competition was more frequent. Elite groups dominated, but they had conflicting views of public policy, and differing constituencies. Conflict was not yet institutionalized in a system of enduring parties with sharply contrasting programs, but there were clear patterns of recurring division in the electorate—between the long-settled coastal areas and the frontier, farmers and merchants, men of English and Scotch–Irish or German stock, Quakers and non-Quakers. The tumultuous and faction-ridden politics of New York and Pennsylvania in particular anticipated the national pattern in the nineteenth century far more than political life in either New England or the South.

American and British Politics Contrasted

These internal differences were significant, but two sharp contrasts may be drawn between colonial politics in general and those in the mother country. First, the right to vote was much more widely available to the citizenry than in England, or indeed anywhere else in the world at the time. It was not because the first settlers intended to design a more democratic and egalitarian policy than the one they had left behind. Most colonies used precisely the same property requirement England had—voters had to possess a 40-shilling freehold (property that could be rented for at least 40 shillings a year). In England, with its masses of tenants and laborers, that standard barred all but a small minority—less than a fifth of the adult males—from exercising any voice in government. In the colonies, with their radically different economic structure, it opened the door to more people than it barred. A majority of the colonial population (about two-thirds when slaves are excluded) had a legal "stake in society." When the actions of external authorities appeared to threaten the independence they cherished, they would not react with passive fatalism.

Both England and America had systems of representative government, but the relationship between the representative and his constitutents that developed in the colonies was also very different from that in the mother country. In the colonies, "direct representation" was the pattern; in England, representation was indirect or "virtual." When it was first created in medieval times, the English House of

Commons was an assembly of delegates who spoke for the interests of the communities they represented (as perceived by the local ruling group). By the time North America was colonized, the ties between Members of Parliament and local communities had become attenuated. English lawmakers were still elected from geographical units—ancient "boroughs" (towns) and "shires" (counties)—but they were not required to come from the districts that elected them. As long as he had the backing of the lord of the manor and influential members of the local gentry, a man from Bristol or Cambridge could win a seat for a district a hundred miles away. Furthermore, Parliament did not redraw the boundaries of electoral districts in accord with population shifts over the centuries. Small towns that had mushroomed into large cities had no seats in the House of Commons, while some that had lost most of their population ("rotten boroughs") still did. In the mid-eighteenth century, 142 boroughs with less than 500 voters each elected more than half of the Members of Parliament.

This was not unfair, according to the prevailing theory of "virtual representation." Members of Parliament, according to this view, did not speak for local interests, and no community, however large, deserved representatives of its own. Each Member of Parliament represented *all* the people of the realm, not just those who cast a ballot for him. Every subject was represented in this virtual sense. Parliament was not "a congress of ambassadors from different and hostile interests, which interests each must maintain as an agent and advocate against other interests and advocates." It was rather "a deliberative assembly of one nation with one interest, that of the whole—where not local prejudices ought to guide but the general good resulting from the general reason of the whole." The colonies, it is important to note, were considered as much a part of the English nation as London or Cambridge. Therefore, Americans were virtually represented in Parliament, although none actually sat in Westminster.

The representative assemblies that developed in each of the North American colonies had a much more parochial and localistic character. Colonists assumed that "local prejudices" should have the right to political expression, and ensured it by requiring representatives to reside in and own property in the communities that elected them. As people poured into underdeveloped western lands, assemblies enlarged their memberships by creating new western seats. These changes were often made slowly and grudgingly, but they were made. The view that farmers on the Massachusetts or Pennsylvania frontier were "virtually" represented by men elected in the East had few supporters. It was taken for granted that any community with a substantial population deserved its own spokesman in the legislature.

Another development that made American representatives far more responsive to the will of the people than their English counterparts occurred late in the colonial period, chiefly in the northern colonies. Until then it was assumed that elected representatives, like Members of Parliament, had the wisdom and judgment to decide what stand to take on issues arising before the assembly. They were superior men capable of discerning "the general good." Around the middle of the eighteenth century that conception came under increasing attack, and towns with strong feelings on particular issues about to come before the legislature began to instruct their representatives how they should vote. Resolutions from local constituencies were not legally binding, but politicians who ignored them were penalized at the polls at the next election.

Conflicting Conceptions of Empire

During the 150 years after the settlement of Jamestown, the political systems of England and her North American colonies increasingly diverged in these fundamental respects. The British government took little notice. With some exceptions—most notably during the brief life of the Dominion of New England—imperial authorities focused their attention on regulation of external trade. They pursued policies of "salutary neglect," leaving colonists free to conduct their own affairs with only the broad constraint that their laws should not be contrary to those of the mother country. That long experience of effective self-determination had unforeseen consequences. Without consciously articulating it, Americans developed a conception of their relationship to central authority that differed radically from the understanding of England's rulers. They came to believe that they were part of an empire made up of self-regulating parts. It had a center, of course, with a King to whom they owed allegiance and a Parliament responsible for making laws to ensure the peace and prosperity of the realm as a whole. But Parliament's power to oversee the entire empire was limited. In the view of Americans, it did not entail the right to intervene in the internal affairs of a colony. There the assemblies, the embodiment of the will of the people, were supreme. Because they saw property as the keystone of their independence, the colonists were particularly adamant in their insistence that no measures affecting property—no form of tax—could be levied without the consent of an assembly representative of the people.

This conception of an empire of self-regulating parts, with a division of power between the central and provincial governments, was a natural outgrowth of the colonists' experience. It bore no resemblance, however, to what British officials *thought* the role of colonies should be. They believed England was the center of a unitary empire that had been established and defended at great cost so as to benefit the mother country. The power of Parliament was not in any way limited, in their view, by competing organs of government in the overseas dependencies. English political and legal theorists were unanimous in their belief that "in sovereignty there are no gradations." Parliament was the supreme authority in every corner of the empire, and every subject was represented in it in the same "virtual" sense as were Englishmen at home. The colonial assemblies were not in any sense miniature Parliaments with sovereignty over their internal affairs; they were mere committees empowered to make "temporary by-laws" pending the arrival of authoritative orders from London.

In short, the "empire of theory" and the "empire of fact" were far removed from each other. After 1763, when the British government began an attempt to exercise its theoretical powers in North America, this difference between theory and fact provoked a conflict that could only be resolved on the battlefield.

SUGGESTED READINGS

The development of the mercantilist system is described in Michael Kammen, *Empire and Interest: The American Colonies and the Politics of Mercantilism* (1970) and Thomas G. Barrow, *Trade and Empire: The British Customs Service in Colonial America* (1967). For a balanced assessment of the economic costs and benefits to the colonists, see Russell Menard and John J. McCusker, *The Development of the Colonial Economy: Needs and Opportunities for Study* (1983). The nature of the British patronage system is analyzed in James A. Henretta, *Salutary Neglect: Colonial Administration Under the Duke of Newcastle* (1972), Alison G. Olson and Richard M. Brown, eds., *Anglo-American Political Relations, 1675–1775* (1970), and Stanley N. Katz, *Newcastle's New York: Anglo-American Politics, 1732–1753* (1968). Stephen S. Webb, *The Governors-General: The English Army and the Definition of the Empire, 1569–1681* (1979) stresses the military considerations governing imperial policy. Bernard Bailyn has written a bold and sweeping overview of *The Origins of American Politics* (1968). David S. Lovejoy, *The Glorious Revolution in America* (1972) is the best analysis of the tensions that erupted over the Dominion experiment.

Jack P. Greene, *The Quest for Power: The Lower Houses of Assembly in the Southern Royal Colonies, 1689–1776* (1963) illuminates the chronic struggles between governors and refractory assemblies. Gary B. Nash, *Quakers and Politics: Pennsylvania 1681–1726* (1968), Patricia Bonomi, *A Factious People: Politics and Society in Colonial New York* (1971), Michael Kammen, *Colonial New York: A History* (1975), Michael Zuckerman, *Peaceable Kingdoms: New England Towns in the Eighteenth Century* (1970), and Robert Zemsky, *Merchants, Farmers, and River Gods: An Essay on Eighteenth-Century American Politics* (1971) are good studies of individual colonies. Edward M. Cook, Jr., *The Face of the Towns: Leadership and Community Structure in Eighteenth-Century New England* (1976) closely examines politics at the local level.

J.R. Pole, *Political Representation in England and America* (1965), and Alison G. Olson, *Anglo-American Politics: The Relationship between Parties in England and Colonial America* (1973) clarify the contrasts between British and American political customs. George Dargo, *Roots of the Republic: A New Perspective on Early American Constitutionalism* (1974) is useful.

Chapter Seven

Resistance and Rebellion

T he 1763 Treaty of Paris brought to a triumphant end England's long war with France, known in Europe as the Seven Years War and in America as the French and Indian wars. To the joyful residents of Britain's North American colonies, England's victory seemed to open a new frontier at a strategic moment. At a time when the supply of unoccupied land within the 13 colonies was nearing exhaustion, France was forced to surrender its enormous American empire. Not only Canada but the entire Ohio and Mississippi valleys—almost two-thirds of eastern North America—was transferred to British rule and would presumably be open to settlement by land-hungry Americans. It was no wonder that delighted colonists danced in the streets in celebration.

Only a few years later, Americans took to the streets again, but this time to express their rage at new policies imposed on them by the British government. After a dozen years of increasingly tumultuous protest activity, a violent climax was reached on April 19, 1775. Bands of minutemen at Lexington and Concord, Massachusetts, refused to give way before regular troops from the strongest army in the world. The "shot heard around the world" that day marked the beginning of a bruising war that dragged on for eight years and ended in full independence for the American colonies.

THE DRIVE FOR IMPERIAL REORGANIZATION, 1763–66

The expulsion of the French from the trans-Appalachian interior seemed a god-send to colonists who clung to the yeomen ideal and dreamed of seeing their children settled on farms of their own. That was becoming an impossible dream

This contemporary drawing of the Boston Tea Party suggests that not all the tea was dumped into the harbor.

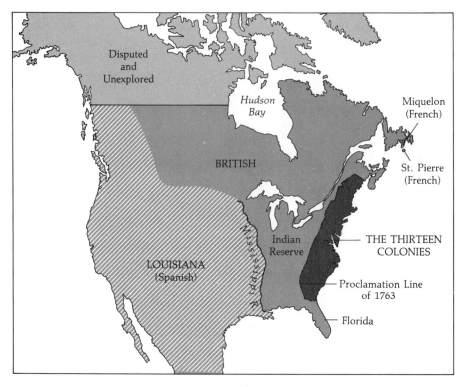

MAP 7-1
North America in 1763

within the existing boundaries of the colonies. The population explosion, resulting from the very high rate of natural increase and a flood of new immigrants, had at last outrun the stock of untilled land. Between 1750 and 1765 the American population increased by as much as it had in the entire preceding half-century. Both individual frontiersmen and large land speculation companies coveted the newly acquired territory.

London officials, however, doubted the wisdom of allowing the colonists to rush into the territories behind the departing French. It wasn't, after all, really a vacuum. Many Indians lived there, both tribes native to the region and others who had moved there under pressure from advancing white settlers. A new surge of settlement could provoke more warfare with the Indians.

That such fears were well grounded was apparent within a few months of the signing of the peace treaty. A major war broke out between British troops and Northwestern tribes that had been allied with France. The Ottawa chief Pontiac, who called for an end to trade with whites and a return to ancient tribal ways, launched a devastating attack to drive all whites out of the Great Lakes and Ohio Valley area. Several British forts were taken and 2,000 whites killed before Pontiac's braves were beaten back at Detroit, Pittsburgh, and Niagara. Pontiac's Rebellion—from the Indian viewpoint, Pontiac's War of National Liberation—was a jarring reminder of the danger of continuing the traditional British policy of allowing individual colonies to handle Indian affairs as they saw fit. "Salutary neglect" in this area could have bloody consequences. Therefore, the British government decided to impose a uniform policy regulating contact between natives and white settlers. King George's Proclamation of 1763 banned white purchases of land west of the Appalachians, ordered the small groups of settlers already there to "forthwith remove themselves," and restricted access to the area to traders licensed by the British government.

The Proclamation was not intended to reserve the entire Midwest to the Indians forever. It was a stalling measure, to provide time to devise an orderly settlement policy that would minimize friction between the races and reduce the danger of another war. In the next few years, the line it drew on the map was moved westward several times to open up portions of Ohio to white farmers from the colonies. But such revisions did not diminish the significance of the policy shift. Power over the pace of westward expansion had always been in the hands of the assemblies. Now such critical decisions would be handed down from on high, by officials beyond the reach of any political influence the colonists might be able to exert.

Even more disturbing than the freeze on settlement was London's decision to enforce it by dispatching a military commander with a standing army of 10,000 troops to the area. Stationing troops in the colonies during peacetime was completely unprecedented. What is more, there were grounds for suspecting that the true purpose of the action was not so much to protect the colonists as to intimidate them. There was some truth in that. The explanations offered by the English government were soothing, but the private correspondence of the key officials involved revealed a quite different motivation. A report to the Board of Trade said that "the keeping of the Indians in subjection and making of roads" were only "pretences," and that the central aim was to "awe the British colonies." Another official remarked with satisfaction that "surrounded by an army, a navy, and hostile tribes of Indians," the Americans would at last have an incentive to give "due obedience to the just and equitable regulations of a British Parliament."

Maintaining a large standing army in North America was not only unprecedented; it was also very expensive. The need for funds to support it, and the English government's determination that the colonists should assume some of the financial burden, was the prime impetus behind the aggressive new imperial policies Britain pursued over the next dozen years. By 1763 British policymakers had come to the conclusion that the Americans' free ride had gone on too long. The war with France had been fought, among other reasons, to defend North American colonies from the French and their Indian allies. Yet colonial governments had made precious little contribution to the cost, aside from raising some militia units. Commanders of British units had frequently ordered assemblies to provide them with supplies, but they rarely got them. Moreover, many American merchants had enriched themselves during the war by trading with the enemy. Britain paid for most of the cost of war by increasing its national debt to a staggering £133 million. The £4.5 million annual interest charges to carry it required heavy taxation. Taxes per head in Britain amounted to 26 shillings per year, as compared with one shilling or less in the colonies. The stiff tax on land hit the large estates of the English landed gentry with special force, and they were the dominant group in Parliament. Having been forced to dig deeply into their pockets to finance an effort that benefited the lightly taxed Americans, they understandably sought ways to force them to pay some of the cost of the North American army.

Tightening the Mercantilist Framework

The most obvious way of raising new revenues from the colonies, and the one most in accord with the traditional imperial relationship, was through regulation of colonial trade. Successive Navigation Acts over more than a century had erected a mercantilist framework; it seemed simple to tighten that framework to Britain's financial advantage. To that end, Parliament passed the American Revenue Act of 1764, commonly known as the Sugar Act. It struck at the lucrative trade between the colonies and the non-English sugar islands of the Caribbean, by imposing steep charges on all foreign wines, coffee, textiles, and indigo imported into the colonies. It lowered, not raised, the prohibitive charges imposed on foreign molasses by the Molasses Act of 1733. The reduction, however, was no boon to the colonists, because for 30 years they had been allowed to smuggle in French molasses without paying any duty at all. A companion measure to the Sugar Act closed the loopholes colonial traders had slipped through in the past. The bill reorganized and greatly enlarged the North American customs service. Every vessel entering or leaving port would henceforth be required to fill out elaborate papers detailing its cargo and destination. The British Navy was ordered to patrol the American coast and search suspect ships. Customs officials were authorized to obtain warrants—"writs of assistance"—to search private property for contraband goods without first showing that they had grounds for suspicion. The customary right of an Englishman to trial by jury was abridged by extending to customs cases the jurisdiction of special vice-admiralty courts with no juries. American merchants feared they would have no defense against being ripped off by greedy "customs racketeers."

Each of these steps had some justification. Britain was hard-pressed for funds, and the disparity between taxation levels at home and in the colonies did seem inequitable. If one granted the English government the right to pass the original Navigation Acts, as colonists had, then surely it had the right to add and enforce new acts. Curtailing an accused smuggler's right to a jury trial was not as indefensible as it might seem; the bitter experience of English offiials had been that trial by jury in a colonial port was "only trying an illicit trader by his fellows, or at least his well-wishers."

From the viewpoint of many colonists, however, this sudden and drastic reshaping of the regulatory system was a menacing challenge to their interests. The Sugar Act threatened serious damage to the vital West Indian Trade, hurting not only the merchants directly involved but the importers of molasses, distillers of rum, and the sailors and shipbuilders who benefited from it. Although they could not deny that Parliament was empowered to regulate trade throughout the British empire, some of them began to argue that the Sugar Act was not truly a "regulation" but a tax. Its explicit purpose, after all, was not to shift the pattern of trade but to raise more money for the British treasury from the existing pattern of trade. The bill's formal title made that intent clear. The Revenue Act was in that sense a tax, a tax levied without the consent of an assembly representative of the people affected by it. A resolution passed by the Boston town meeting in 1764 asked: "If taxes are laid upon us in any shape without ever having a legal representation where they are laid"—without the sanction of the people through their elected representatives— "are we not reduced from the character of free subjects to the miserable state of tributary slaves?" The Massachusetts assembly voted to create a committee on correspondence to sound the call of alarm in the other colonies. Boston's merchants agreed to stop importing British luxury items like gloves, lace, and ruffles, hoping to create economic dislocations in England that would result in agitation for redress of colonial grievances.

Support for the "nonimportation" campaign was limited largely to Boston, however, and the Massachusetts Committee on Correspondence's appeal to the other colonies to complain to London about the Sugar Act did not attract overwhelming support. Five of the thirteen colonies ignored it, and most of the eight that complied did not object on the principled constitutional grounds set forth in the Boston resolution. Instead, they offered pragmatic arguments for easing the regulations—they were bad for American business.

Indeed, 1764 was a bad year for American business, largely because the economy was sliding into a depression following the boom war years. The ending of the stimulating war expenditures was the primary cause, but Americans put the blame on two other sources—the new trade regulations, and the Currency Act of 1764, which banned the issuing of paper money in any of the colonies. Designed to appease the fear of English merchants that colonial paper money would set in motion an inflationary spiral followed by a great crash, the Currency Act put a damper on colonial business transactions by making gold and silver the only legal medium of exchange; these precious metals were always in short supply because of the colonies' chronic trade deficit with the mother country.

The southern colonies had been largely unhurt by the Sugar Act, but the paper money ban struck them with special force, especially Virginia. A number of assemblies made attempts to wriggle around the restrictions, but they failed. The authors of the bill were aware of the many concessions obstinate legislatures had wrung from weary governors in the past, so they included provisions specifying that governors who permitted evasions would be fired, fined the equivalent of $50,000 in today's currency, and made ineligible for any public office in the future. The Currency Act did not provoke immediate large-scale protest like the Sugar Act, but resentment over it smoldered for years after, and it flared it up again and again when Parliament persistently refused pleas for exemption.

The Stamp Act Crisis

From the English viewpoint, the tightening of the mercantilist system worked well, but not well enough to solve the entire financial problem. By 1765 customs duties from America had mounted to £30,000 a year, a fifteenfold increase over the previous level. However, because that was still far below the £300,000 annual cost of the army, something more needed to be done. Parliament therefore passed the Stamp Act which was expected to raise at least another £60,000 annually in the colonies, bringing the colonists' share of the army's upkeep to about a third. The objective seemed modest and reasonable, and the bill sailed through Parliament with hardly a dissenting vote. A similar tax had been in effect in England since 1694, and the rate for the colonies was set lower than the one at home.

It caused an uproar in the colonies. It was the first direct tax Parliament ever levied in America, and a direct repudiation of more than a century's tradition that reserved taxation powers to assemblies elected by the people. And, unlike regulations on foreign trade or currency restrictions, it directly affected the masses of ordinary citizens. All legal documents, newspapers, pamphlets, almanacs, insurance policies, and even playing cards and dice would have to bear stamps sold by imperial authorities. Offenders would be dealt with summarily. Since British officials believed that American juries "in these causes were not to be trusted," suspected violators would be tried in the hated admiralty courts—whose jurisdiction in Britain had always been confined to matters related to navigation. In the eyes of most colonists, the Stamp Act embodied two unconscionable evils—taxation without representation and trials without juries.

Upon hearing the news, the colonists took to the streets. In August of 1765, a Boston crown hanged an effigy of Andrew Oliver, designated to be the stamp distributor for Massachusetts, on the "Liberty Tree," an elm which critics of the British government had chosen to meet under. They destroyed a building that was to become the Stamp Office, attacked Oliver's house, and smashed his furniture. The next day the terrified Oliver renounced his office. The story was featured in the press throughout the colonies, and everywhere the response was the same: People marched with effigies of royal officials, attacked warehouses and homes, and intimidated stamp distributors into resigning. The leadership of local groups calling themselves "Sons of Liberty" consisted of merchants, prosperous artisans, and others from the middle and upper ranks of society, and they sought to keep the protest peaceful and symbolic. The sailors and other workers who tumbled from the taverns to join in frequently got out of hand and burned or looted property. These uprisings paralyzed the royal administration. By November 1, when the law was to take effect, it had been rendered inoperative. North of Georgia, which remained quiescent for special reasons,[1] not a single stamp was ever sold in America. No official dared sell one, and after November 1 the colonists continued to carry on their business as if they had never heard of the Stamp Act.

The Stamp Act provoked not only massive spontaneous civil disobedience but two more measured and deliberate responses as well. It gave new life to the nonimportation campaign that Boston merchants had experimented with in protest against the Sugar Act. Renunciation of British goods spread to other communities and other groups. Artisans spurned English woolens for American leather garments; students swore off English beer and tea; fire companies pledged to eat no more mutton so as to increase the supply of local wool. The boycott quickly began

---

[1]Georgia's proximity to Spanish Florida made its leaders reluctant to challenge British authority throughout the revolutionary crisis.

REACTIONS TO THE STAMP ACT: REASONED PROTEST

We have called this a burthensome tax, because the duties are so numerous and so high, and the embarrassments to business in this infant, sparsely-settled country so great, that it would be totally impossible for the people to subsist under it, if we had no controversy at all about the right and authority of imposing it. We further apprehend this tax to be unconstitutional. We have always understood it to be a grand and fundamental principle of the constitution, that no freeman should be subject to any tax to which he has not given his own consent, in person or by proxy. And the maxims of the law, as we have constantly received them, are to the same effect, that no freeman can be separated from his property but by his own act or fault. We take it clearly, therefore, to be inconsistent with the spirit of the common law, and of the essential fundamental principles of the British constitution, that we should be subject to any tax imposed by the British Parliament; because we are not represented in that assembly in any sense, unless it be by a fiction of law, as insensible in theory as it would be injurious in practice, if such a taxation should be grounded on it.

—Unanimous Resolution of the Town of Braintree, Massachusetts,
September 24, 1765

to bite into Britain's prosperity; exports to America fell 14 percent from 1764 to 1765, and the drop would be even steeper if the figures for the months before and after the Stamp Act were available.

The Stamp Act, furthermore, united representatives of the various colonies in common protest for the first time. Earlier efforts to get the colonies to act in concert had been dismal failures. A conference had been held at Albany, New York in 1754 to consider Benjamin Franklin's proposal for a joint colonial government for purposes of Indian defense and resolution of conflicting claims to western lands. The Franklin plan was endorsed by the delegates, but not a single colonial assembly agreed to it. In 1754 the colonies were but "a rope of sand, loose and disconnected"; they were like "the separate filaments of flax before the thread is formed, without strength." The extent of their separation and insularity is suggested by the fact that when Boston's Sam Adams left for the first Continental Congress in Philadelphia in 1774, he was 51 years old and had never set foot outside Massachusetts! More of the delegates had been to London than to Philadelphia, America's largest city. The shock of the Stamp Act was the first of several that would gradually overcome parochial provincial allegiances and inspire a broader sense of common national identity. The Stamp Act Congress, held in New York, was an important step toward a united America. Nine of the colonies sent delegates, and three of the other four would have but for the interference of their governors. Christopher Gadsden's statement that "there ought to be no New England man, no New Yorker, known on this continent, but all of us Americans," articulated a new national ideal.

The Stamp Act Congress was not a revolutionary assembly. It was attended by moderate men with deep loyalties to the English Constitution, and the protest resolutions it endorsed began with an acknowledgment of "all due subordination to King and Parliament." They went on, however, to assert principles that called into question the meaning of that pledge of "subordination." The Stamp Act was not simply unwise and harmful to business; it violated the "inherent rights and liberties" of Englishmen. It was "inseparably essential to the freedom of a people" that "no taxes should be imposed upon them but with their own consent, given personally or by their representatives." The virtual representation all citizens of the empire supposedly enjoyed was not sufficient; "the people of these colonies are not, and from their local circumstances cannot be, represented in the House of Commons in Great Britain."

REACTIONS TO THE STAMP ACT: THE SONS OF LIBERTY ASSAULT THE STAMP COLLECTORS

After the Effigys were Burnt the Mob Dispers'd and we thought it was all Over. But last Night about Dusk they all Muster'd again, and first they went to Martin Howard's, and Broke Every Window in his house Frames and all, likewise Chairs, Tables, Pictures and every thing they cou'd come across. They also Saw'd down two Trees which Stood before his door and Bro't them and Stuck them up in two Great Guns which have been fix'd at the Bottom of the Parade some Years as Posts. When they found they had Entirely Demolish'd all his Furniture and done what damage they Cou'd, They left his house, and Proceeded to Doctor Moffatts where they Behav'd much in the Same Manner. I Can't say which Came off the Worst, For all the Furniture of Both Houses were Entirely Destroy'd, Petitions of the houses broke down, Fences Level'd with the Ground and all the Liquors which were in Both Houses were Entirely Lost. Dear Doctor this Moment I've Rec'd a Peace of News which Effects me so Much that I Cant write any More, which is the Demolition of your worthy Daddy's house and Furniture etc. But I must Just let you know that the Stamp Master has Resign'd, the Copy of his Resignation and Oath I now Send you. I hope, my Friend You'll Send me the Particulars of your daddy's Misfortune.

—from W. Almy, Newport, Rhode Island,
to Dr. Elisha Story in Boston,
August 29, 1765

The ministers who had drafted the Stamp Act had fallen from the King's favor before the storm broke in America, and their successors drifted for months without a policy. The success of the intimidation campaign of the Sons of Liberty made it clear that enforcement of the act would be extremely difficult. English merchants and manufacturers hurt by the nonimportation campaign urged repeal. Acting as a lobbyist for the colonies, Benjamin Franklin tried to smooth the troubled waters with assurances that colonists did not object to all taxes passed without the consent of an assembly, but only to *internal* taxes imposed by Parliament. Although anyone who took the trouble to sample the barrage of protest literature produced by the colonists in response to the Stamp Act would have seen that Franklin's placating words were simply not true, the Members of Parliament took him at his word—a misconception that would soon lead to further trouble. Eventually the new government backed repeal of the Stamp Act. But it took pains to indicate that the concession was made in deference to English trading interests, not to American hotheads. To puncture American illusions about a division of power between Parliament and colonial assemblies, Parliament unanimously passed an accompanying Declaratory Act asserting that Parliament had the right to make laws to "bind the colonies and the people of America in all cases whatsoever."

The crisis was over, the boycott of British goods was lifted, and the jubilant Sons of Liberty began to disband. Despite the apparent resolution, however, the fissure between the American and British positions had widened substantially. The principles embodied in the resolutions of the Stamp Act Congress had become slogans with deep popular resonance, and Americans had learned that determined extralegal protest activity could force the English government to withdraw an objectionable measure. On the other side of the ocean, anti-American sentiment in Parliament had grown much stronger. The harshly uncompromising and overbearing tone of the Declaratory Act suggested that in the future ministers would have to be careful to avoid giving the impression of being soft on the upstart colonists.

BRITISH AUTHORITY DISINTEGRATES, 1766–76

The calm produced by the repeal of the stamp tax was short-lived. During the turmoil that preceded it, imperial authorities had transferred much of the new North American army from frontier posts to the storm centers of resistance, the major seaports. To support them, Parliament passed the Quartering Act, which ordered colonial assemblies to make appropriations for food and shelter for all troops within their provincial boundaries. A hairsplitting lawyer could argue that these were not actually taxes, but only demands that assemblies agree to tax themselves. But because the legislatures had no right to refuse, and because the size of the necessary appropriation depended on decisions about troop allocations made by the British military commander in North America, it was a distinction without a difference. The heaviest burden fell on New York, where the commander, General Thomas Gage, was headquartered. When the New York assembly defied the quartering order as a form of illegal taxation, the royal governor dissolved the assembly. The physical presence of the troops in New York City also produced tensions; minor violent clashes between "redcoats" and patriots began to erupt in August of 1766.

The Townshend Acts

News of these new acts of American defiance strengthened the elements in the English government who wanted to pursue tougher policies in the colonies. Among them was Chancellor of the Exchequer, Charles Townshend. Townshend was resolved to curry the favor of the English landed gentry by reducing land taxes. To make up the lost revenue, he proposed new charges upon the colonists. In 1767, seizing on Benjamin Franklin's earlier distinction between internal and external taxes, Townshend induced Parliament to pass a bill imposing new tariffs on a number of imports to the colonies—glass, lead, paper, paint, and tea.

As disturbing as the taxes themselves were the uses to which they would be put and the bureaucracy that was to collect them. The Townshend Acts specified that the new revenues could be used to pay the salaries of colonial governors and judges, thereby preventing the assemblies from using their control over the purse strings to keep royal officials in line. Another provision further expanded the customs service and established a new American Board of Customs Commissioners at Boston. Its employees too would be paid out of the duties they exacted from Americans. Since the passage of the Sugar Act, the colonists had seen rapacious customs officers—"customs racketeers"—enrich themselves by accusing merchants of technical violations of that complicated measure. Convicted violators had to forfeit the vessels and cargo, with a third of the value going to the arresting customs officers. The creation of the new American Board of Customs Commissioners promised to enlarge the class of parasites who would prey on colonists in this fashion. Americans could expect that "the least officer employed for the regulation of trade and the collection of revenue will soon be a formidable magistrate, with a stipend of four or five hundred sterling a year." These offices and salaries would increase "as fast as millions of American slaves increase, and can *earn* for them with sweat and hard labor."

The Townshend Acts created another great furor in the colonies. Hardly any colonist accepted Franklin's distinction between internal and external taxes. By 1767 most politically active Americans had arrived at the position set forth in John Dickinson's *Letters from a Farmer in Pennsylvania*: There was no such distinction. Parliament had a right to regulate external trade, and duties imposed for that purpose might raise incidental revenues. But a tax masquerading as a customs duty was still a tax, and was unconstitutional without the consent of colonial assemblies. The Quartering Act, in the view of the colonists, also imposed illegal taxes. Not only economic oppression but political tyranny threatened. The dissolution of the New York assembly, payment of royal officials from customs revenues instead of colonial legislative appropriations, and the bloated customs bureaucracy all seemed part of an unfolding plot to deprive Americans of their liberties.

Townshend's program came under sharp attack from British manufacturing interests as well, who realized that taxing goods they exported to the colonies would reduce sales and encourage colonial production of those items. The colonial reaction was so extreme, though, that Britain felt that it should teach Americans a lesson rather than back down. The government's unbending stance in the face of criticism at home as well as abroad fanned the flames of protest in North America. The nonimportation campaign was revised. Town meetings and assemblies now backed the effort and passed resolutions urging all colonists to follow suit. The names of importers who failed to comply and those who patronized them were published, and the offenders were ostracized. In defiance of the governor's orders, the Massachusetts assembly passed a 1768 circular letter urging other legislatures to join them "in such constitutional measures as are proper" to force repeal. The governor then dissolved the assembly and ruled without it.

Boston crowds harassed and intimidated customs officials. After a ship belonging to resistance leader John Hancock was seized on trumped-up charges in 1768, wild rioting broke out. Four thousand British troops were brought in to restore order. They remained there, a massive and menacing presence in a community of only 15,000 people. Tension between the angry citizens and the soldiers grew until it exploded in the Boston Massacre of March, 1770. When frightened troops were trapped by an advancing crowd, they let loose a volley that killed five Americans. Boston patriots, led by the fiery Samuel Adams, took the massacre as sinister confirmation of the tyrannical aims of the British government, and the colonial press treated it in lurid terms. The news affected English opinion in the opposite way. Parliamentary leaders charged that Boston was in a state of anarchy and said that agitators like Sam Adams should be brought to England, prosecuted for treason, and hanged. The Common Law had long guaranteed Englishmen the right to trial by jury within one's own community, but they defended this astonishing proposal by resurrecting a long-forgotten statute that dated back to the sixteenth century.

Cooler heads prevailed, however. Lord North, Townshend's successor as Chancellor of the Exchequer, had no more respect for the fancied "rights" of the colonists than his predecessors. But he could count. By 1770 it was painfully clear that the Townshend program had failed. Only £21,000 in new duties had been collected, whereas the sale of British goods in America had plunged more than £700,000. Instead of continuing the debacle, and inflaming Americans even more by prosecuting patriot leaders for treason, the North government backed off. It repealed all the Townshend duties but that on tea, retaining it (and the 1764 tax on molasses) as a symbolic reminder that Parliament held fast to its claim to supreme power, including the power to tax. Lord Hillsborough, the Secretary of State for the Colonies, announced that the government had no intention of imposing any new taxes on the colonies. The Massachusetts assembly was permitted to reconvene, and the Quartering Act was ended. British troops in Boston were removed from the city proper and quartered on islands in the harbor, to prevent the recurrence of incidents like the Boston Massacre.

These concessions represented almost a complete reversal of policy in practice, but not an acceptance of the principles patriots had been asserting since the Stamp

Act. At first it seemed that the colonists would keep up their boycott on English imports until the duties on tea and molasses were lifted as well, but the campaign slowly broke down. Imports from Britain soared to £4.1 million in 1771, double the level of any year since 1764. Most Americans had retained a residue of respect and good will toward the mother country, despite the provocations of the past few years. So many of their substantial grievances had been met that ignoring the principle and paying what they regarded as an illegal tax on tea and molasses seemed tolerable.

The Tea and Quebec Acts

Despite such incidents as the Rhode Islanders' burning of the British schooner *Gaspee* when it ran aground while on customs patrol at Narragansett Bay in 1772, and unending quarrels between Massachusetts Governor Thomas Hutchinson and his assembly, the three years following the repeal of the Townshend duties were relatively tranquil. The government refrained from any policy initiatives that raised the great unsettled question of the relative powers of Parliament and the colonial assemblies. But the Tea Act of 1773 suddenly thrust it forward once again.

The English East India Company, a huge quasi-governmental corporation, was tottering on the verge of bankruptcy. Its warehouses were crammed with tea that most Americans refused to buy, drinking cheaper tea smuggled in from Holland instead. The Tea Act authorized agents of the East India Company to bypass American wholesalers and sell the company's tea directly to distributors. Cutting out the wholesaler's profit would make English tea cheaper than the smuggled Dutch variety. In terms of its immediate effect on their pocketbooks, the Tea Act was a boon to Americans; they could keep their teapots filled at a lower price. Only the wholesale merchants would be hurt. The merchants, however, cried "monopoly," and conjured up visions of a great conspiracy to strangle American business. They managed to convince many of their countrymen that granting a tea monopoly to the East India Company was merely the first step in an effort to bring other colonial enterprises under the thumb of the great interests that dominated Parliament. After colonial competitors were driven out of business, they charged, then the English companies would be free to jack up prices as much as they liked. The argument seems farfetched, but tea had became an emotionally charged symbol of compelling power.

When the first English vessels laden with tea pulled into colonial seaports, their captains were met by bands of patriots who advised them to return to England without unloading. In every port but Boston, that strategy worked, making the Tea Act as much a dead letter as the Stamp Act. Boston was different because the imperious Governor Hutchinson was determined to tough it out. He ordered ship captains to remain in port until their cargoes were discharged. On the night of December 16, 1773, under the leadership of Sam Adams—who ironically had been Boston's tax collector earlier in his career—150 patriots dressed as Mohawk Indians obliged the governor by unloading all 90,000 pounds of the tea—right into Boston Harbor.

Many resolute opponents of the Tea Act thought this was going too far. The reservations they felt over their compatriots' unlawful destruction of property, however, were soon overshadowed by their shock at Parliament's bellicose response. The port of Boston was closed to all shipping until compensation was paid not only for the lost tea but for other damages inflicted by earlier mobs. Town meetings were forbidden more than once a year without the consent of the governor, and were to consider only an agenda he approved. The appointment powers of the assembly were curtailed. British officials accused of capital crimes were removed from the jurisdiction of the colonial courts; they would go to England for trial. Unoccupied buildings were made subject to seizure and use for the quartering of troops. The Coercive Acts—in the colonies the "Intolerable Acts"—virtually annulled the charter under which Massachusetts had been governed since 1691. To underscore Britain's determination to rule over the people of Massachusetts as if they were an enemy subdued in war, a replacement for Governor Hutchinson was named—none other than General Gage, Commander of England's North American Army.

These harsh measures were designed to quarantine radical Massachusetts and to stamp out the virus of resistance before the infection spread. It was obvious that Massachusetts alone could not stand up to mighty Britain. The English government failed to understand that the germ had already been spread widely during more than a decade of escalating conflict over imperial power and colonial rights, and that making a lesson out of Massachusetts in this way would only increase American disaffection. By 1774 every colony had organized groups who believed that a threat to one was a threat to all, that after depriving the Bay Colony of its liberties the redcoats would do the same elsewhere.

The colonists' sense of unity was intensified by another major bill passed in the same parliamentary session, a measure just as intolerable as the Intolerable Acts to any colonist who hoped to see American settlement of the trans-Appalachian West. The disturbing Proclamation of 1763 had at least been temporary; the Quebec Act of 1774 seemed to dash those hopes permanently. It enlarged French Quebec to cover the area as far west as the Mississippi and as far south as the Ohio River. The Catholic Church would have privileged status throughout that vast area, and French law would be followed in civil cases. Americans would be free to settle there, but they would not enjoy their accustomed liberties. Their Protestant churches would suffer disabilities. French law meant trials without juries. And there would be no representative assembly to defend the popular interest; Quebec would be governed strictly from the top down by a council appointed by the Crown.

The Crisis of Legitimacy

Although imperial officials strove desperately to keep the lid on, their authority disintegrated rapidly in the summer and fall of 1774. Outrage swept the colonies following the assault on Boston and the handing over of the Midwest to Quebec. New extralegal associations sprang up everywhere, claiming to speak for "the

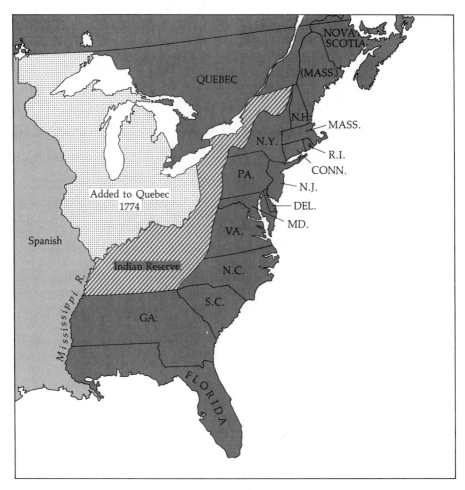

MAP 7-2
Colonial Territorial Claims Denied by the Quebec Act

people." To evade the legal control governors could exercise over their meetings, assemblies transformed themselves into provincial conventions or congresses. After the Governor of Virginia dissolved the House of Burgesses for insubordination in August, 1774, its members proclaimed themselves the Provincial Convention, and pledged a complete ban on trade with Britain. Other colonies followed suit. In Virginia the traditional political elite were solidly in favor of resistance and there was little turnover in leadership. In other colonies members of the conservative establishment who were fearful of antagonizing Britain were shouldered aside by new leaders. Of the 180 people who served on Philadelphia's illicit resistance committees from 1774 to 1776, for example, 90 percent had never held political office before. They were drawn from different social groups than the traditional town leadership; they were middle rather than upper class, and more

A RHODE ISLAND TOWN RALLIES BEHIND BOSTON

We have long felt for the town of Boston; we heartily sympathize with our brethren upon this alarming occasion; we are much pleased with the noble firmness with which this cruel edict is received in Boston. We highly approve the measures taken by the town, and are entirely of opinion that the joint resolution of the Colonies to stop all importations from and exportations to Great Britain and the West Indies, until the Act is repealed, will infallibly produce the desired effect.

This horrid attack upon the town of Boston, we consider not as an attempt upon that town singly, but upon the whole Continent. We are therefore determined to use our whole influence as if the attack had been made on the metropolis of this Colony; and we doubt not but the other Colonies will consider this arbitrary and tyrannical edict in the same light, and heartily unite with friends of liberty in Boston in support of the common cause.

—Committee of Correspondence,
Westerly, Rhode Island
May 19, 1774

representative of the city's ethnic, religious, and occupational mix. The resistance movement thereby acquired a broad popular base.

One unifying theme in the demands that issued from these provincial and local bodies was the need for an intercolonial congress to orchestrate the struggle. The First Continental Congress, which met at Philadelphia in September, 1774, brought together delegates elected by provincial congresses or county conventions. They were united in their distress at recent British policies, but deeply divided about what to do in response. Conservatives, led by Joesph Galloway of Pennsylvania, urged passage of a proposal to negotiate for the creation of an American colonial assembly that would share authority with Parliament; the Galloway Plan failed passage by only one vote. In the end, the Congress endorsed the more militant program set forward in the "Suffolk Resolves," adopted by a convention in Boston after the Congress had started and rushed there on horseback by Paul Revere. Sam Adams and his more cautious cousin, John Adams, joined forces to engineer approval of resolutions that declared that:

1. The Coercive Acts were unconstitutional and should not be obeyed.

2. The people of Massachusetts should form a government to collect taxes and withhold them from royal authorities until the acts were repealed.

3. All trade with Britain should be suspended.

4. Colonists should take up arms and organize militia.

The Congress then issued a sweeping proclamation that no less than *thirteen* Parliamentary acts passed since 1763 were unconstitutional violations of American rights, and would have to be withdrawn before economic sanctions against Britain would be lifted. To enforce the boycott, it created the "Continental Association," which incorporated the extralegal local community organizations that had sprung up spontaneously, and enjoined its members to expose those who continued to trade with Britain as "enemies of American liberty." It was much more widely honored than previous nonimportation agreements; between 1774 and 1775 British exports to North America dived by 90 percent.

After the Congress adjourned, the people of Massachusetts proceeded to do just what the Suffolk Resolves had urged them to do—to form an alternative government. General Gage found that the awesome powers given him by the Coercive Acts had no force beyond Boston, where his troops were garrisoned. The entire countryside was in rebellion. The Massachusetts assembly had reorganized as a provincial congress in defiance of Gage's orders, and was meeting in Concord, 20 miles from Boston. Its agents rather than royal officials were collecting taxes from the towns, and its Committee of Safety was busily storing muskets, powder, and lead. General Gage did not interfere at first, because he wanted to deny the rebels the political advantage of being able to claim that the British had fired the first shot. In early April of 1775, however, he was ordered to strike before the rebels completed their mobilization. Gage accordingly dispatched 700 soldiers to Lexington, to arrest John Hancock and Samuel Adams, and to Concord to destroy the armory. Fighting first broke out at Lexington green, then at the Old North Bridge in Concord, and then all along the route the weary British followed on their way back to Boston. But for the timely arrival of 900 reinforcements when they got back to Lexington, the day would have been an utter disaster for the redcoats. As it was, a third of the original force were killed, wounded, or missing in action, as compared with only 93 of the approximately 4,000 Americans who had taken part in this first battle.

Toward Independence

After the bloodshed at Lexington and Concord, American minutemen surrounded Boston, and administered a punishing defeat to General Gage's forces at the Battle of Bunker Hill in July (see Chapter 8). Both sides, however, made major attempts at conciliation. Lord North offered a plan which pledged Parliament to forbear from levying anything but regulatory taxes on the colonies, so long as their assemblies raised enough revenue for the common defense. The Continental Congress turned it down, but offered the Olive Branch Petition of July, 1775, which pledged loyalty to George III and assured him that "we mean not to dissolve that union which has so long and happily subsisted between us."

Although the delegates to the Second Continental Congress were sincere in their hope that a final break with the mother country could be averted, they were not so imprudent as to count on it. While extending an olive branch with one hand, they reached for the sword with the other. At the same time that it was drafting its humble petition to the King, the Congress also voted to create a Continental Army and named George Washington commander-in-chief. He was a superb choice—dignified, aloof, and utterly unflappable. A great planter with an estate of 15,000 acres and 150 slaves, Washington had distinguished himself in the Virginia House of Burgesses and the Continental Congress. He had acquired considerable military experience as a lieutenant colonel in the French and Indian wars, and was doubly attractive as a southern man. Choosing Washington over the leading Yankee candidate, John Hancock, helped to seal southern support for a movement in which New Englanders had thus far taken the lead.

The colonists were extremely reluctant revolutionaries, however. Not until the summer of 1776, more than a year after Lexington and Concord, did they forswear their allegiance to George III and strike for independence. Major impetus for that decision came from a powerful pamphlet published in January by a recent English immigrant. Thomas Paine's *Common Sense* sold 120,000 copies in three months and was read aloud to untold numbers in taverns and coffeehouses. Paine bluntly denounced George as a "royal brute," and argued that it was absurd for "a continent to be perpetually governed by an island." The only salvation from the tyrannical oppressions of corrupt English aristocrats was American independence and a republican form of government.

The most compelling argument for independence in *Common Sense* was a severely practical one, the force of which became increasingly plain to colonial leaders with each passing day. Other countries, particularly France and Spain, would like to see Britain humbled by the loss of her North American empire. But they would not aid the colonies so long as they were legally part of Britain and lacked standing in international law. The colonies could not conclude treaties of assistance with other powers until they had established themselves as an independent entity capable of making treaties. And military resistance to Britain, it was clear, could not be long sustained without external aid. In June of 1776, Richard Henry Lee introduced in Congress a resolution calling for complete American independence. On July 4, 1776, Thomas Jefferson's declaration was approved without dissent. The colonies, it proclaimed, were now "free and independent states absolved from all allegiance to the British Crown," and "all political connection between them and the state of Great Britain" was "totally dissolved."

UNDERLYING CAUSES OF THE REVOLUTION

Why did this sequence of events culminate in a massive armed struggle for independence that no one had foreseen or desired only a dozen years before? The narrative has a certain logic of its own, a logic of ever firmer response and counterresponse, a logic of escalation common to all revolutionary situations. Men on both sides felt compelled to act as they did to achieve their aims and then, when their actions did not receive the desired response, to take even stronger and riskier action. The great English political philosopher Edmund Burke, a close and sympathetic observer of the colonies as a Member of Parliament, made the point brilliantly in the midst of the unfolding crisis. "The Americans have made a discovery," said Burke in 1769, "or think they have made a discovery, that we mean to oppress them; we have made a discovery, or think we have made a discovery, that they intend to rise up in rebellion against us. We know not how to advance; they know not how to retreat."

That was an astute observation, but we must ask *why* these new conceptions, or misconceptions, of each other's purposes had developed. The notion of "escalation" doesn't really explain anything. Many historical conflicts escalate one, two, or three levels and then subside, as politicians find means of compromising and defusing explosive issues. To understand why efforts at compromise failed in this instance, we must examine some aspects of the imperial relation that are not clear from the foregoing narrative.

British Inflexibility and Insensitivity

After the Peace of Paris, financial imperatives forced Britain to tighten the imperial system. The need was urgent, and the specific acts taken were quite reasonable. The colonists remained in a more enviable situation in many ways than Englishmen at home. The difficulty lay in the high-handed way in which the new measures were adopted—by parliamentary fiat rather than negotiation with the people affected by them. The failure to consult the colonists was no accident. It followed logically from the British conception of the colonies as dependent children who were given generous protection in exchange for unquestioned obedience. If the colonies had been granted some form of representation in Parliament in the early stages of the conflict, a satisfactory compromise might possibly have been reached. But British officials believed that children should have no voice in affairs of state. The colonists, after all, were "virtually" represented in Parliament just as other Englishmen were. To concede that they required direct representation would have been to admit the need for a drastic reform of the entire English electoral system to adjust representation to population, something that would not happen until the Reform Bill of 1832, more than half a century later.

The conception of the colonists as children shaped the British response to their efforts at resistance. They sometimes backed down in the face of protest, as a parent sometimes will to appease a crying child. But the retreat was only strategic, and never led to a serious reconsideration of the essential relationship. Continued resistance therefore provoked sharp anger rather than troubled concern. The colonists, it seemed, were naughty children who needed a spanking to bring them to their senses. "When once these rebels have felt a sharp blow," George III said complacently, "they will submit."

His confidence that only a few sharp blows would result in submission reflected another common misconception in British ruling circles—the belief that the masses of Americans were unswervingly loyal, and that the problem was confined to a few radical hotheads. Even after Lexington and Concord, when virtually all of the adult males in Middlesex county took potshots at the British column from behind stone fences, English authorities minimized the pervasiveness of colonial disaffection. General William Howe, General Gage's successor as commander, assured his superiors that "the insurgents are very few in comparison with the whole of the people." Similarly encouraging and delusory reports continued to flow into London during the years of war that lay ahead. A principal reason for Britain's reluctance to grant American independence for so long was the belief that to do so would be to leave the masses of allegedly loyal colonists in the hands of a fanatic rebel minority.

American National Pride

The colonists had developed a prickly pride that made them resentful of new restraints. Their population had been growing spectacularly and their wealth had been multiplying. It did not take great prophetic powers to see that America was destined to become a power to be reckoned with. In 1751 Benjamin Franklin predicted that within a century "the greatest number of Englishmen" would be "on this side of the water." (The prediction was right on the mark. The 1850 census revealed that the population of the United States exceeded that of Great Britain.) The colonists, said Franklin, were clearly "a rising people." The signs of progress they saw all around them gave them a sense of self-confidence in their ability to manage their own affairs.

They also had a much stronger sense of a common national identity by the 1760s than they had had 50 or a 100 years before. The first settlers had identified first with their own colony, second with the mother country, and hardly at all with the residents of the other colonies. But by the middle of the eighteenth century an incipient American nationalism took shape, a feeling that they were not simply English people living overseas but a new and distinct national group. Newspapers in those years used fewer references of either local identification ("Virginians") or imperial identification ("His Majesty's subjects") than early in the century. Terms of national identification like "Americans" increasingly replaced them.

The growth of American national feeling was revealed in new signs of ambivalence toward the mother country. Admiration for English political institutions and English culture remained enormous, naturally. But some features of British society began to attract unfavorable comment. Colonists who visited England in the seventeenth century and returned to write about it expressed the reverential awe of pilgrims in the Holy Land. Eighteenth-century travelers more frequently emphasized the aristocratic, worldly, decadent features of English life, portraying their own society as pure, simple, and dynamic. Britain was "an old man who has received several strokes of palsy and is tottering upon the brink of the grave," said one smugly, while America was "growing daily towards perfection." Such assertions of moral superiority became increasingly common with the Great Awakening, for every soul the revivalists won for Jesus seemed to make American society seem more pure.

The contrast between American purity and English corruption had especially important implications when applied to the political sphere. Until 1776, Americans believed that the principles of the English constitution were the ultimate in political wisdom, but they were heirs to a tradition of thought that made them suspicious about whether those principles were honored in practice. James II's accession to the throne and the Glorious Revolution it gave rise to spawned an opposition ideology which held that liberty was always endangered by concentrated power. Free institutions were fragile creations, vulnerable to the conspiratorial designs of scheming politicians. This ideology, a minority point of view in Britain, found a much more receptive audience in America. Long before the Revolution it had become a central element of colonial political culture. Again and again the most minor and mundane executive actions were seen as part of a sinister plot to extinguish free institutions. It meshed smoothly with the Puritan belief in the depravity of human nature, and the need for constant vigilance to check man's sinful impulses.

It was this almost paranoid predisposition to see a larger design behind seemingly unconnected events that made Britain's actions in 1763 and after seem so extraordinarily menacing. The professed aims of the government seemed reasonable enough, but what dark purpose was hidden from view? Nothing less than "a deep-laid and desperate plan of imperial despotism for the extinction of all civil liberty," many Americans came to believe. This was absurd, of course. Although historians today still disagree about many aspects of the American Revolution, none believe that British officials were truly plotting to impose despotism upon America. There can be no doubt, however, that American patriots believed that to be the case, and their perception was a crucial part of historical reality. Under the pressure of major shifts of imperial policy, anxious colonists "awakened" to a fresh perception of British purposes with the same fervor with which they greeted the Great Awakening. Thomas Jefferson summed up the emerging revolutionary consensus when he wrote in 1774 that although "a single act of tyranny" might be dismissed as an accident, "a series of oppressions, begun at a distinguished period and pursued unalterably through every change of ministers, too plainly proves a deliberate and systematical plan of reducing us to slavery." This interpretation—or misinterpretation—of British aims was the propelling force that led patriots to risk their lives and fortunes in the struggle for independence.

SUGGESTED READINGS

Edmund S. Morgan, *Birth of the Republic, 1763–1789* (rev. ed., 1977) and James Kirby Martin, *"In the Course of Human Events": An Interpretive Exploration of the American Revolution* (1979) are good, brief overviews. Stephen G. Kurtz and James H. Hutson, eds., *Essays on the American Revolution* (1973) and Alfred Young, ed., *The American Revolution* (1976) include a number of suggestive essays. On the political considerations that underlay changing British imperial policies, see Lewis Namier, *England in the Age of the American Revolution* (1961), George H. Guttridge, *English Whiggism and the American Revolution* (1963), and John Brewer, *Party Ideology and Popular Politics at the Accession of George III* (1976). For an interesting dialogue between a British and an American historian on the causes of the revolution, see Ian R. Christie, *Empire or Independence, 1760–1776* (1976).

Bernard Bailyn offers the fullest treatment of *The Ideological Origins of the American Revolution* (1965). Gary Wills, *Inventing America: Jefferson's Declaration of Independence* (1978) is another stimulating work of intellectual history. Jack M. Sosin, *Revolutionary Frontier, 1763–1783* (1967) examines westward migration and colonial reactions to British restraints on settlement. Edmund S. and Helen M. Morgan, *Stamp Act Crisis: Prologue to Revolution* (1953) is the best account of that major turning point. Pauline Maier, *From Resistance to Revolution: Colonial Radicals and the Development of American Opposition to Britain, 1765–1776* (1972), Dirk Hoerder, *Crown Action in Revolutionary Massachusetts, 1765–1780* (1977), and Philip Reid, *In a Defiant Stance: The Conditions of Law in Massachusetts Bay, the Irish Comparison, and the Coming of the American Revolution* (1977) offer conflicting interpretations of the behavior of revolutionary crowds. Pauline Maier, *The Old Revolutionaries: Political Lives in the Age of Samuel Adams* (1980) traces the evolving views of five leaders of the patriot cause. Jackson Turner Main, *The Upper House in Revolutionary America, 1763–1783* (1967) and James Kirby Martin, *Men in Rebellion: Higher Governmental Leaders and the Coming of the American Revolution* (1973) examine the changing composition of the leadership class. Hilar B. Zobel, *The Boston Massacre* (1970), Richard D. Brown, *Revolutionary Politics in Massachusetts: The Boston Committee of Correspondence and the Towns, 1772–1774* (1970), and Benjamin W. Labaree, *The Boston Tea Party* (1964) reveal the mobilization of the colony that was in the forefront of the rebellion.

The role of economic and social cleavage in generating political discontent is emphasized, perhaps overemphasized, in Edward Countryman, *A People in Revolution: The American Revolution and Political Society in New York, 1760–1790* (1981) and Gary B. Nash, *The Urban Crucible: Social Change, Political Consciousness, and the Origins of the American Revolution* (1979). Richard M. Jellison, *Society, Freedom, and Conscience: The Coming of the Revolution in Virginia, Massachusetts, and New York* (1976) provides fruitful comparisons and contrasts between three colonies. Robert Gross, *The Minutemen and Their World* (1976) views the revolutionary crisis from the vantage point of the common people of Concord, Massachusetts. The anguish suffered by Tories in those years is vividly portrayed in Bernard Bailyn, *The Ordeal of Thomas Hutchinson* (1974). John Shy, *Towards Lexington: The Role of the British Army in the Coming of the American Revolution* (1965) shows how the conduct of British troops helped to precipitate rebellion.

Joseph Keppler's caricature of U.S. Immigration policy, "Welcome to All," first appeared in Puck, *1880.*

Part Two

*From Many Peoples One:
A New Republic*

Chapter Eight

Birth of a Nation

T he Declaration of Independence proclaimed the end of an empire and the birth of a new nation. To attain their freedom from British rule, the people of the 13 rebellious colonies had to win a war against the world's strongest military power. Even after they succeeded, the question of whether they had enough in common to form a viable nation–state remained in doubt for several years. The motto on the seal of the United States, *E Pluribus Unum*, "Out of the many, One," was adopted in 1782. But that was more an aspiration than a description of political reality. If there was an American nation in 1782, it was a nation without a national government except of the most nominal sort. Only after protracted and bitter political struggle did Americans devise a frame of government to make the many in fact one—the federal Constitution that went into operation in 1789.

THE WAR FOR INDEPENDENCE

Taking up arms against mighty Britain was a gamble against long odds. The mother country had a hundred warships for every one in the hands of the rebels, a large and experienced professional army, and abundant funds to hire mercenary soldiers—the usual way eighteenth-century powers expanded their fighting forces. By 1778 almost 50,000 British regulars and over 30,000 German mercenaries were serving in America. George Washington's Continental Army, by contrast, was made up of undisciplined amateurs, who signed up for terms as short as three

George Washington's height is not exaggerated in this 1938 painting, "Inauguration of George Washington at Federal Hall, New York City, 1789" by Keith Shaw Williams. The "father of our country" was six-feet three-inches tall and weighed 220 pounds (at a time when the average height was several inches shorter than it is today).

months and frequently deserted before they were up. The Continental Army could draw from militia units organized by each colony for assistance, but those troops were even less disciplined and more unreliable. Especially frustrating to Washington was their parochial refusal to cross the border into another colony, even when badly needed. Although approximately 400,000 Americans served in the Continental Army or the militia at some stage of the prolonged war, Washington never had more than 20,000 troops under his command at any one time! With only an "untrained rabble" to oppose them, British officers assured their government that they could march from one end of America to the other with only 5,000 men.

The colonists were indeed untrained in the methods of eighteenth century European warfare, but they had other assets the British grossly underestimated. For one thing, they were the best-armed population in the world. Practically every farmhouse had a musket or two hanging on the wall, few of them rusty from disuse. "There is no custom more generally observed among young Virginians," reported a traveler, "than that they all learn to keep and use a gun with a marvellous dexterity as soon as ever they have strength enough to lift it to their heads."

Nor was the colonists' unfamiliarity with the highly formalized rules of traditional European combat the grave disability the British thought it was. To them, a proper battle was a carefully staged confrontation between orderly lines of troops, who moved forward in neat lines at the sound of the bugle, fired a volley, and then closed to grapple with bayonets. In contests fought in this fashion, British professional soldiers with years of experience at close order drill could have easily bested the amateur American troops. But to the frustration of the invading armies, the Americans refused to play by the rules. Instead, they followed the guerrilla tactics they had learned in savage encounters with frontier Indians—to sting quickly and unexpectedly, and then to disappear into what an Englishman sneeringly called "those endless forests which they are too lazy to cut down." The British could not understand how to deal with "an enemy that avoids facing you in the open field." "Never had the British army so ungenerous an opponent," said a stunned officer. "They send their riflemen five or six at a time, who conceal themselves behind trees, etc. until an opportunity presents itself of taking a shot at our advance sentries, which done they immediately retreat. What an unfair method of carrying on a war." Unless a colonist was firing a musket at them, the English couldn't tell whether he was friend or foe, rebel or loyalist. Minutemen wore ordinary clothing.

The hazards of clinging to traditional modes of warfare against an "ungenerous" opponent were revealed most glaringly at the Battle of Bunker Hill—actually fought on adjacent Breed's Hill— in July of 1775, where Britain suffered its heaviest losses of the entire war. Twice redcoats burdened with packs weighing 60 pounds charged up the steep slope in straight lines. The minutemen at the top waited until they could "see the whites of their eyes"—the correct distance for hitting a man with a musket shot—and then mowed them down. A third charge, this time without packs, finally reached the top, but most of the defenders slipped away. It was a British "victory"—they took the position. But more than 1,000 of their soldiers were dead or wounded, a staggering 47 percent of the attacking force—the highest casualty rate in British history.

George Washington's Continental Army was organized along conventional lines and it did not employ the guerrilla tactics of the militia units. His troops wore uniforms, though often ragged ones. But Washington too was careful not to face the British too long in an open field, where their superior forces might be able to deliver a knockout blow. In early 1776 the British abandoned Boston and staged a major invasion of New York, using it as a base from which to drive a wedge through the Middle Colonies and then to mop up resistance in New England and the South. Washington was there to meet them. He was defeated on Long Island, driven off Manhattan, beaten at White Plains, and chased across New Jersey and into Pennsylvania. The Continental Army fought and fell back, fought and fell back again. It was a pattern repeated until the last stages of the war. Washington hardly won a battle, but proved himself a great general by merely keeping his army in existence as a target for the British to pursue across the countryside. One of his chief aides asked him in 1781, "Don't you think we bear beating very well, and that the more we are beaten the better we grow?" Washington well understood that the colonies had no single nerve center, no territory of indispensable strategic significance, that required defense to the last man. For much of the war, the British held every major city south of Boston, but it didn't give them the leverage to end the rebellion. Washington had the entire continent in which to maneuver. He used it to play for time, time to allow the British to succumb to a war-weariness similar to that felt by the United States in the Vietnam War two centuries later.

The British launched a second major offensive in 1777. It resulted in another string of victories, control of real estate that proved meaningless, and one shocking defeat with enormous consequences. The strategy called for General John Burgoyne to lead a major expedition south from Montreal to meet up with General William Howe's forces driving north from New York City, thereby cutting off New England. It was a sound plan, but Howe was less interested in linking up with Burgoyne than he was in capturing Philadelphia. Capturing the capital city, he assumed, would be a mortal blow to the rebel cause, and Washington might be lured into a fatal last ditch stand to prevent it. Howe beat Washington badly in two battles and took the city easily. But the Congress simply moved on, and the Continental Army escaped bruised but far from crushed. By the time Howe acted according to plan and started to move north, it was too late. Burgoyne's southward progress had been slow, in part because the high-living "Gentleman Johnny" insisted on bringing along 30 slow-moving wagons crammed with such "necessary" personal effects as his silver dining service and several cases of champagne. Burgoyne's supply lines to Montreal were stretched so thin that New England militiamen were eventually able to sever them and besiege him at Saratoga, New York. In October he had to surrender his entire army.

The British defeat at Saratoga was the turning point of the war. It not only provided a badly needed boost to American morale; it opened the way to even more badly needed aid from other powers. As soon as independence was proclaimed, France and Spain began secretly to provide the colonists with funds and military supplies, but they avoided large-scale involvement because they doubted that the rebels had a serious chance of winning. The American victory at Saratoga erased those doubts. France immediately extended diplomatic recognition to the United States, and followed with a treaty establishing a Franco-American alliance for mutual defense against Britain. Spain and Holland later entered the fray as well. This broadening of the conflict forced the British to withdraw some troops and ships from the North American theater to protect the West Indies and other vulnerable spots in their far-flung empire.

The French aided the American cause not only by pressuring British outposts elsewhere in the world, but by directly providing troops and ships. The critical nature of their contribution was best illustrated in the climactic battle of Yorktown in October of 1781, the outcome of which at last convinced the British to concede American independence and begin peace negotiations. At Yorktown, Lord Cornwallis' forces were entrapped and overwhelmed by George Washington's advancing army. They could easily have escaped by sea but for the fact that the French Navy had defeated the British fleet and laid down a blockade. Furthermore, from their well-fortified positions, they might well have been able to repel the assault by Washington's only slightly larger 9,000-man American army; but the additional 8,000 French troops under Washington's command gave him the margin of superiority to batter Cornwallis into surrender.

Rebels and Loyalists

The Revolutionary War was fought for independence, for national liberation. It was at the same time a civil war that divided neighbor from neighbor and sometimes even brother from brother and father from son. Benjamin Franklin's son, for example, denounced the rebels and eventually fled to England. The success of the revolution ultimately depended on the ability of its supporters to persuade or intimidate its opponents into changing their minds or at least keeping their reservations to themselves. The political struggle at home was as crucial as the contest on the battlefield.

Although few residents of the colonies (aside from those in imperial service) had defended the British policies that provoked the independence movement, many Americans doubted that the policies were so oppressive as to justify violent rebellion. Just how many is uncertain. A hardcore minimum measure of loyalist support would include the 25,000 colonists who served in the British Army during the war, and the 100,000 who had fled the country by the time independence was won. But clearly the number was much larger. A traditional estimate holds that a third of the population was Tory and another third neutral; a more recent study suggests that 15 to 20 percent were loyalists and that at least half were unaligned and apathetic at the outset of the conflict.

Who were the loyalists? They were strongest in New York and Pennsylvania, and weakest in New England. Not surprisingly, former Crown officials and Anglican clergymen were prominent among them. A comparison of loyalist and rebel leaders in Massachusetts reveals an interesting age difference—American patriots were seven years younger, on the average. Youthful people were more willing than their elders to accept the risks of a future free of the sheltering British presence. In most other respects, however, the two groups were a cross section of society in terms of wealth, occupation, and so on. The painful and dangerous choice of sides was most often determined by older patterns of political cleavage within the colonies. Groups alienated from the previous establishment backed whichever side the established group opposed, on the principle that "the enemy of my enemy is my friend." This attitude helps to explain the Tory leanings of tenant farmers in upstate New York and of the Scotch–Irish and Scotch in the Carolina backcountry.

Committed patriots were clearly a minority of the population at the beginning of the revolutionary war. However, the rebel minority had the energy, political skill, and ruthlessness to win over many of the unaligned and to silence those opposed. In no colony did enough loyalists rally around the Royal Governor to allow him to retain his authority, and in none did they manage to capture the conventions that evolved into the alternative revolutionary governing apparatus. People suspected of disloyalty or even a desire to be neutral were subjected to intense pressure by Committees of Safety. The traditional obligation to serve in the militia was an effective screening device to identify them. For example, 18 men from Framingham, Connecticut were thrown into jail in 1777 for failing to join their militia unit when it opposed a British raid on a neighboring town. To be released they had to swear that they were "now ready and willing to join with their country and do their utmost for its defense," and to be grilled by a committee of the Connecticut legislature until it was satisfied as to their political convictions. In a manner reminiscent of a Puritan laying bare his soul to gain admission to a congregation, they had to declare that they were "penitent of their former conduct" and that their new-found patriotism was truly "a matter of conviction."

Convictions asserted in order to obtain release from jail were not necessarily genuine, obviously. Whenever the British army moved in to take control of an area, hidden loyalists—and many simple opportunists—came out of the woodwork to cheer their arrival, often carrying out harsh reprisals against patriots who had been unable to escape. Most of eastern New York and New Jersey, for example, seemed solidly loyalist after British occupying forces landed in the summer of 1776. The British, however, erred in assuming that such communities would remain pacified after the troops departed. The soldiers had to be withdrawn eventually, of course, because Britain lacked an army large enough to occupy all 13 colonies simultaneously. When they left, the rebels surfaced again and carried out reprisals of their own. In late 1776, for example, British troops were withdrawn from New Jersey. Residents who had publicly declared for the King then had their property seized and "most wantonly destroyed"; "their families were insulted, stripped of their beds, even of their very wearing apparel; they then determined to try the other side." A squad of redcoats could be the finger that stopped up a hole in the dike, but when it had to be removed to plug another hole, the first leaked as badly as before. Well before Britain lost the war on the battlefield, it lost the political war, as opponents of the rebellion concluded that eventually the British would withdraw and the patriots would return and wreak vengeance.

Although the chances of victory in the war for America dimmed after the loss of Saratoga and the consequent entry of France on the rebel side, the British government doggedly kept the fight going for another three years. There were advocates of peace, including the inept Prime Minister Lord North, who argued that the cost of prolonging the war outweighed the benefits that would be gained from a restoration of imperial control. The King and his key advisors held firm, though. To accept American independence, they felt, would be to surrender the masses of presumably loyal Americans to the radical minority of rebels, a cowardly and dishonorable step (see box). They rejected North's "cost–benefit" analysis for a "domino theory." What was at stake was not the mere loss of a few outposts in North America but "the destruction of the Empire." If America was allowed to fall, the dream of national liberation might spread to Britain's other colonial dependencies around the world, and one by one they too might topple. And so the killing continued, until the shocking news of Washington's capture of Cornwallis at Yorktown. "Oh God! It is all over," said Lord North. George III favored further resistance, but disillusionment with the war in Parliament had grown so strong that he was compelled to authorize the opening of peace negotiations.

Britain, France, and Spain were all involved in the diplomatic maneuvering, and it was fortunate for Americans that John Adams, Benjamin Franklin, and John Jay had the skill to play them against each other and obtain highly favorable terms. The January, 1783 Peace of Paris was much more than a British acknowledgment of the independence of the 13 colonies. It undid the Quebec Act, in effect, by extending the new nation's boundaries to the Mississippi River, from the Great Lakes to Florida (returned to Spanish hands by the treaty). The United States in turn recognized British control over a much-shrunken Canada, allowed British navigation rights on the Mississippi, and made a vaguely worded pledge to help

No inclination to get out of the present difficulties which certainly keep my mind very far from a state of ease, can incline me to enter into what I look upon as the destruction of the Empire. I have heard Lord North frequently drop that the advantages to be gained by this contest could never repay the expence. But this is only weighing such events in the scale of a tradesman behind his counter; it is necessary for those in the station it has pleased Divine Providence to place me to weigh whether expences though very great are not some times necessary to prevent what might be more ruinous to a country than the loss of money. Independence is their object. Should America succeed in that, the West Indies must follow them...; Ireland would be reduced to itself, and soon would be a poor island indeed, for reduced in her trade merchants would retire with their wealth to climates more to their advantage; and shoals of manufacturers would leave this country for the New Empire; these self-evident consequences, are not worse than what can arise should the Almighty permit every event to turn out to our disadvantage; consequently this country has but one sensible, one great line to follow, the being ever ready to make peace when to be obtained without submitting to terms that in their consequence must annihilate this Empire and with firmness to make every effort to deserve success.

—George III to Lord North, July, 1779

collect debts owed to British merchants and to encourage the states to compensate loyalists for property losses. Britain's surprising readiness to hand over the trans-Appalachian West did not reflect a generous willingness to let bygones be bygones. It stemmed from fear that a weak America without room to expand might become a pawn for France and Spain, and from confidence that a strong United States would forge binding commercial links to its former mother country.

CONSEQUENCES OF THE REVOLUTION

The American Revolution was not a great social revolution like those that occurred in France in 1789, in Russia in 1917, and in China in 1949. A true social revolution breaks sharply with the past, destroys the institutional foundations of the old order, and transfers power from some social groups to others. It involves a radical, root-and-branch reconstruction of the social order. The American Revolution was

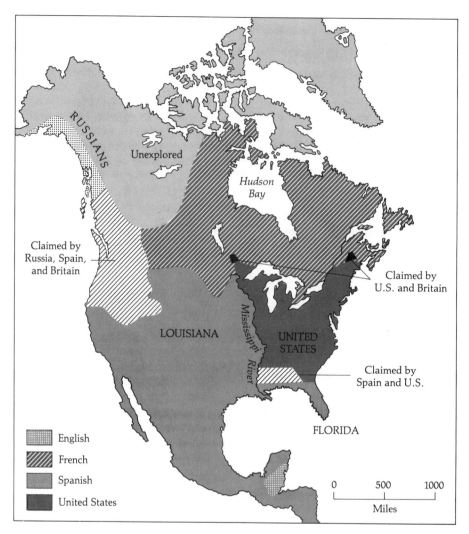

MAP 8-1
North America in 1783

instead a war of national liberation, more a contest over home rule than over who was to rule at home. The freedoms that patriots fought for were traditional freedoms that they believed the King and his ministers were conspiring to take away from them.

The successful War for Independence, however, did set in motion or accelerate some large changes in the life of the nation. The severing of ties with Britain weakened support for traditional English values of hierarchy and deference to authority and stimulated egalitarian and democratic sentiments.

"You and I," John Adams wrote in 1776, "have been sent into life at a time when the greatest lawgivers of antiquity would have wished to live. How few of the human race have enjoyed an opportunity of making an election of government for themselves or their children." Of course in their "election" they could preserve much from their British political heritage, but they were elated at the prospect of purging it of its most evil features—the powerful monarch and the bloated aristocracy that squeezed money from the common people. A simple, frugal, republican government elected by the people, they were sure, would best attain the common good (*res publica* in Latin).

Although there was consensus on the principle of republicanism, Americans differed over how to give it institutional shape. Because the Declaration of Independence voided the old royal charters, the states had to draw up new constitutions to replace them. The conventions that prepared them differed over fundamental issues. Conservatives called for retention of traditional property requirements for voting and a strong executive and upper branch of the legislature to serve as a check against hasty action by the popularly based lower house. Their opponents sought to widen access to the ballot and to limit the power of the executive and the upper house of the legislature, on the grounds that those branches of government were especially susceptible to influence by the rich and wellborn. "The farmers and mechanics constitute 99 out of 100 of the people of America," said a Pennsylvania newspaper. If the new political system was slanted to favor the wealthy, it

TABLE 8-1
Economic Status of Delegates to Prewar and Postwar Assemblies

	North*		South†	
	Prewar	*Postwar*	*Prewar*	*Postwar*
Property holdings				
Over £5,000	36	12	52	28
£2,000–5,000	47	26	36	42
Under £2,000	17	62	12	30
Occupations				
Merchants and lawyers	43	18	23	17
Farmers§	23	55	12	26

*The northern assemblies for which information was available were those of New York, New Jersey, and New Hampshire.

†Maryland, Virginia, and South Carolina

§Slave plantation operators are not classified as farmers here.

asked rhetorically, "would it not be better to acknowledge the jurisdiction of the British Parliament, which is composed entirely of gentlemen?"

The outcome of these political battles varied from state to state. The most democratic of the new constitutions was Pennsylvania's. It eliminated all property requirements for voting, had no governor or upper legislative house, and chose its judges by popular election. At the conservative end of the spectrum was Maryland, which retained a stiff property requirement for voting, an even stiffer one for officeholders, and both a governor and a state senate with considerable powers. Some general trends may be discerned, however. With fresh memories of hated Royal Governors, most states severely circumscribed the powers of the chief executive. And most substantially lowered the property requirement for voting. As more small farmers and artisans flocked to the polls, fewer gentlemen and more common folk were returned to office. The New York assembly, once dominated by Livingstons, Schuylers, and Van Rensselaers, stopped meeting at harvest time; too many of its members were farmers to raise a quorum then. That was typical. The proportion of extremely wealthy men elected to assemblies in the North fell from over a third before the war to only 12 percent after, while the representation of men with small holdings soared from 17 percent to 62 percent. Likewise, merchants and lawyers were much less prominent in the postrevolutionary legislatures, and ordinary farmers far more so. In the South, where elite dominance of colonial politics had been more complete, the change was less dramatic but in the same direction. Small holders increased their share of seats from 12 to 30 percent, while the percentage of extremely wealthy men in the legislatures was cut in half.

Religious Liberty

Well before the Revolution, religious pluralism was a fact of American life. But the traditional European notion that the government should sanction and support a particular church was still in force. Every colony but Pennsylvania and Rhode Island had a legally established church—Congregational in New England and Anglican elsewhere. Dissenters were generally free to hold religious services of the kind they preferred, but some of the taxes they paid went to finance the establishment. When resistance turned into rebellion, patriots were quick to strip the Church of England of its privileged position. A number of the new state constitutions went beyond that simple negative action to assert, as did Virginia's 1776 Bill of Rights, that religion "can be directed only by reason and conviction, not by force or violence, and therefore all men are equally entitled to the free exercise of religion according to the dictates of conscience." The Congregational churches of New England did not have the disability of being associated with George III, but they too had to make important concessions to dissenting groups like the Baptists, allowing individuals to pay their religious taxes to their own churches instead of to central authorities.

There were limits to the growing toleration of diversity. Most state constitutions spoke of the liberties of Christians, and a number imposed disabilities on non-Protestants, such as ineligibility to hold public office. At the end of the revolutionary upheaval the United States had what might be described as a multiple establishment of competing Protestant sects. In revolutionary theory, all men were created equal; in fact, the small numbers of Catholics and Jews in the land were outsiders to a culture whose spiritual cement was Protestant Christianity.

The Denationalization of Slavery

The most glaring and painful anomaly in the land of liberty was that a fifth of its population consisted of enslaved Africans. Or so it would seem to us today. Until the Revolution, however, the striking thing was that very few American whites displayed any awareness of the evils of slavery. A rare exception was the Quaker leader John Woolman (1720-72), who refused to wear cotton or eat sugar because they were the products of slave labor, and traveled widely to urge his fellow Quakers to emancipate their bondsmen. Although 90 percent of the nation's slaves lived in the plantation colonies of the South, slavery was a recognized and generally unquestioned institution in every single colony.

The national consensus on slavery broke down during the revolutionary crisis. The Revolution did not "solve" the problem of slavery, obviously. It created it, by making the existence of slavery problematical for large numbers of Americans for the first time. Some patriots who denounced the alleged British conspiracy to enslave them began to reflect on the plight of their fellow men who were already being literally held in that degrading condition. Thomas Jefferson's Declaration of Independence declared that all men, not all white men, were created equal. The First Continental Congress had urged the member colonies to close the international slave trade, and Connecticut, Delaware, Virginia, Maryland, and North and South Carolina had done so. Although a step far short of abolition of property rights to human beings, it was at least an acknowledgment that continued growth of the slave population was undesirable. Military pressures during the war opened the way to freedom for some bondsmen. The British government shrewdly offered to emancipate the slaves of rebels who ran away and took up arms on the loyalist side, and a number of northern colonies emancipated slaves to reward them for military service. When the conflict was over, the New England and Middle Atlantic states all moved to ban slavery by legislative or judicial action. In the Northwest Ordinance of 1787, Congress ruled that no slaves would be permitted in the trans-Appalachian interior north of the Ohio River. Slavery was transformed from a national to a purely sectional institution.

The antislavery movement, however, made little headway in the South, where nine out of ten American slaves lived. There slaves were the backbone of the labor force, and the source of the fortunes which allowed the planter class to live a life of ease. And the large concentrations of Afro-Americans there posed problems of racial adjustment on a much larger scale than in any northern state. Despite George Washington's urgent pleas that the war would be lost without more troops, planter-dominated southern assemblies refused to offer their slaves the only inducement that might have persuaded them to fight—manumission.

Although slavery in the South survived the revolutionary era unscathed, some whites there expressed significant doubts about the future of the institution. Dur-

MAP 8–2
Conflicting Western Land Claims and Cessions to U.S. Government, 1781

ing the 1780s, 10,000 Virginia bondsmen were set free by their owners. George Washington predicted that slaves would prove to be "a troublesome bit of property," and stipulated in his will that his own were to be freed. Although he saw the evils of slavery more clearly than Washington or any other southern white of his day, Thomas Jefferson believed there was no room for free blacks in American society. Jefferson's *Notes on Virginia* (1785) indicted slavery as "the most unremitting despotism." It undermined "the only firm basis" of liberty, the popular conviction that "liberty is a gift of God." "I tremble for my country," said Jefferson, "When I reflect that God is just" and that "justice cannot sleep forever." On those grounds, he urged that slavery be banned from all the western territory opened up to settlement after the war (see map). But he believed just as firmly that blacks and whites could not live peaceably side by side under freedom; large-scale emancipation would lead to "convulsions" that would result in "the extermination of the one or the other race." Abolition would only be feasible if joined to a scheme to resettle all the freedmen in some other land. Jefferson called for gradual, compensated abolition and colonization like that later favored by the American Colonization Society (founded 1817). He must have realized it was a pipedream before his death four decades later. Although he hated the "unremitting despotism" of slavery, Jefferson was never willing to make the financial sacrifice of freeing his own human property.

The Position of Women

The revolutionary era brought small but significant changes in the position of another dependent element of the population—women. In law and custom, colonial females were subordinate to males—to their fathers until the age of 21, to their husbands once wed. After her marriage, a woman's property became her spouse's. And since the right to vote was confined to property owners, females were excluded from the polls. These basic assumptions remained largely unchallenged during the Revolution; in practice, the Rights of Man meant the rights of men. But many women were forced to take on unaccustomed responsibilities while their husbands and sons were away on military duty, and that experience led some of them to develop a larger sense of their rights within marriage. The richly illuminating correspondence between John Adams and his remarkable wife Abigail reveals her growing pride in her ability as a "farmeress." In her earliest letters to John she referred to the family farm as "yours," in accord with colonial custom; before the war had ended she regularly referred to it as "ours."

It is impossible to say how many anonymous American women likewise began to think of family property as in part their own, or shared the feelings expressed in Abigail's eloquent "remember the ladies" letter (see box). But it is likely that both the libertarian ideology of the Revolution and the experience of coping as "farmeresses" made many question the tradition of feminine subordination. In 1790 a female "Matrimonial Republican" argued that marriage was not "a contract between a superior and an inferior, but a reciprocal union of interest" in which "the obedience between man and wife is, or ought to be, mutual." It would be a long time before women would begin to play an active role in public affairs, but this subtle change in the nature of the marital relationship may have helped prepare the way for the more easily documented advances made by women in later times.

THE AMERICAN CONFEDERATION

The great problem facing patriot leaders in 1776, said John Adams, was to get 13 clocks to strike at once. One way of assuring that coordination would have been to establish a central government with the power to levy taxes, raise an army, and

A DIALOGUE ON THE RIGHTS OF WOMEN
IN THE REVOLUTIONARY ERA

I long to hear that you have declared an independancy—and by the way in the New Code of Laws which I suppose it will be necessary for you to make I desire you would Remember the Ladies, and be more generous and favourable to them than your ancestors. Do not put such unlimited power into the hands of the Husbands. Remember all Men would be tyrants if they could. If perticuliar care and attention is not paid to the Laidies we are determined to foment a Rebelion, and will not hold ourselves bound by any laws in which we have no voice, or Representation.

That your Sex are Naturally Tyrannical is a Truth so thoroughly established as to admit of no dispute, but such of you as wish to be happy willingly give up the harsh title of Master for the more tender and endearing one of Friend. Why, then, not put it out of the power of the vicious and the Lawless to use us with cruelty and indignity with impunity. Men of Sense in all Ages abhor those customs which treat us only as the vassals of your Sex. Regard us then as Beings placed by providence under your protection and in immitation of the Supreme Being make use of that power only for our happiness.

Your ever faithful friend.

—Abigail Adams to John Adams, March 31, 1776

As to your extraordinary Code of Laws, I cannot but laugh. We have been told that our Struggle has loosened the bands of Government every where. That Children and Apprentices were disobedient—that schools and Colledges were grown turbulent—that Indians slighted their Guardians and Negroes grew insolent to their Masters. But your Letter was the first Intimation that another Tribe more numerous and powerfull than all the rest were grown discontented. —This is rather too coarse a Compliment but you are so saucy, I wont blot it out.

Depend upon it, We know better than to repeal our Masculine systems. Altho they are in full Force, you know they are little more than Theory. We dare not exert our Power in its full Latitude. We are obliged to go fair, and softly, and in Practice you know We are the subjects. We have only the Name of Masters, and rather than give up this, which would compleatly subject Us to the Despotism of the Peticoat, I hope General Washington, and all our brave Heroes would fight. I am sure every good Politician would plot, as long as he would against Despotism. Empire, Monarchy, Aristocracy, Oligarchy, or Ochlocracy. —A fine Story indeed. I begin to think the Ministry as deep as they are wicked. After stirring up Tories, Landjobbers, Trimmers, Bigots, Canadians, Indians, Negroes, Hanoverians, Hessians, Russians, Irish Roman Catholicks, Scotch Renegadoes, at last they have stimulated the ladies to demand new Priviledges and threaten to rebell.

—John Adams to Abigail Adams, April 14, 1776

perform the other traditional functions of European states. Some members of Congress favored that, but only a small minority. Most delegates were too fearful of concentrated power and too jealously concerned with protecting the interests of their own states to consider such a drastic step. Although the Declaration of Independence was a proclamation by "representatives of the United States of America" and referred to Americans as "one people," it really created not one new nation but 13. The Continental Congress that issued it was more a debating society than a government in the traditional sense, a forum in which ambassadors from the various states could discuss issues of common concern. Its purpose was to persuade 13 independent sovereign states to cooperate in the national interest; it had no authority to compel any of its members to do anything. The state governments were the source of political authority and the focus of popular loyalty. It did not seem strange to men of the day that Thomas Jefferson, after drafting the Declaration, refused an appointment as American commissioner to France in order to return to his beloved Virginia to help frame its new constitution. "Virginia," he said, "is my country." Such provincial attachments were so strong at the outbreak of the war that the only union that could be arranged was a loose confederation that relied on voluntary compliance by the member states.

While the war was raging, the American confederation worked—well enough, at least, to prevent the British from getting a stranglehold. Although the depth of each state's commitment to the national cause fluctuated with its proximity to invading redcoats, on the whole the states did provide what was necessary. Fear was a potent cement of union. Patriots understood the grim truth of Benjamin Franklin's remark that they had to "hang together or they should surely hang separately." As the British threat receded, the cement began to weaken, to the growing dismay of patriots who had hoped to build a powerful united American nation.

The Articles of Confederation

In 1777 the Continental Congress approved a plan for an enduring American union—the Articles of Confederation. The Articles gave no new powers to the central government, but rather spelled out the basic arrangements already in effect. Congress urged the states to ratify them promptly, to demonstrate national solidarity against the invading foe, but securing unanimous approval for even this shell of a central government was not easy. Several states refused until January, 1779, nine months after the deadline set by Congress, and one—Maryland—held back until early 1781, only a few months before the climactic battle at Yorktown. Instead of impressing the British with American unity, the debate over ratification of the Articles convinced them, as one official put it, that the American people would remain disunited "till the end of time, suspicious and distrustful of each other, divided and subdivided into little commonwealths with no center of union and no common interests."

The most divisive issue delaying agreement of the Articles was whether or not the new central government would be given title to all western lands beyond the frontier. Their issue split the states into two camps with sharply opposed economic interests. Several states, like Maryland and Rhode Island, were "landlocked"; they had fixed western boundaries and no claims to the trans-Appalachian interior. Not surprisingly, they took the high-minded view that all of the West should be part of the national domain. States like Virginia and Massachusetts did have historic claims to borders running all the way to the Mississippi, and were reluctant to surrender them. Further complicating the quarrel were land speculation companies that had purchased large tracts from the Indians before the war. Companies based in landlocked states urged that the land be put in congressional hands to increase the chance that their titles would be recognized; those based in landed states vehemently opposed that proposal.

In the end, it was fear of the enemy that made compromise and final ratification of the Articles possible. In January of 1781, with an invading army approaching her borders, Virginia announced that it would cede its western holdings to the Congress, in hopes that completing the union would contribute to the military effort. Maryland still delayed, because the land speculators who dominated its assembly were furious that Virginia's promise to cede the land was on the condition that all titles based on negotiations with Indians be disallowed. But it then reversed itself and at last approved the Articles, as panic over a projected British invasion spread and Congress promised military aid conditional upon ratification. America's "little commonwealths" were sufficiently "distrustful and suspicious of each other" to take three and a half years to establish a permanent central government with the most minimal powers, despite the menacing presence of a powerful foe. The prospects of their agreeing on much else once that foe was removed seemed slender indeed.

The Articles of Confederation provided the frame of America's national government from 1781 to 1789, which some historians call "the critical period" of American history on the grounds that the survival of the nation was in grave doubt. The Articles were designed to create "a firm league of friendship." How "firm" it would be was doubtful, because they explicitly declared that each member state retained its "sovereignty, freedom, and independence." A Congress that was a carbon copy of the Continental Congress was authorized to make treaties and alliances, declare war, borrow money, and deal with the Indians. The list of powers denied the Congress was longer than the list of those granted it. Congress could not tax the states or the citizens; it could only request that the state legislatures make needed appropriations. Nor was it given the right to raise a national army; it could only specify quotas of men and money to be supplied by the states, and hope that they would be public-spirited enough to comply. The Congress had no power to regulate either foreign or interstate commerce; each state was left free to erect whatever trade barriers would best serve its particular interests. No national judiciary was provided; law enforcement was left in the hands of state courts. To guard against the danger that some future Congress might attempt to step beyond these narrow bounds by amending the Articles, the framers provided that any amendment required the consent of each state.

Out of the conviction that concentration of power in some distant American city was little better than rule from London, the framers of the Articles built in other restraints on the central government. Members of Congress were elected annually, and no representative could serve more than three years out of six, to prevent the emergence of a political elite whose members might place the national interest over the interest of their own states. Delegates were instructed how to vote by their state legislatures, and were subject to recall if they failed to follow orders. No chief executive was provided, only a committee with little power. The most important deterrent to action was that each state was given one vote in Congress, regardless of its size or wealth, and that nine of the thirteen had to approve legislation. Representatives from the five least populous states—Delaware, Georgia, Maine, Rhode Island, and Vermont—could block any measure they disliked, although their constituents comprised only a tenth of the U.S. population. Attendance at congressional sessions was so lax that it was frequently mathematically impossible to secure the consent of nine states to a measure; during one three-month period in 1784, representatives from as many as nine were on hand for only three days!

A trivial but telling indicator of the character of the new government was that Congress was unable to decide on a permanent residence for itself. Until 1783 it sat at Philadelphia, where the Continental Congress had met. Then it had to flee the city ignominiously when confronted by a crowd of angry soldiers demanding their back pay; Pennsylvania state leaders thought so little of the Congress of the United States that they refused to turn out the state militia to assure its safety. Congress subsequently relocated itself in Princeton, Annapolis, Trenton, and New York City. Foreign diplomats with messages for the American government sometimes had to spend weeks discovering where it was to be found.

Westward Expansion and International Rivalries

The most important measures passed by Congress during the Articles period concerned the disposition of the lands in the trans-Appalachian interior. The Land Ordinance of 1784, drafted largely by Thomas Jefferson, guaranteed western settlers self-government on an equal basis and eliminated the possibility that easterners might hold frontiersmen in a permanently dependent colonial status. It divided the West into territories, each to be governed temporarily by its settlers according to the laws of some existing state, and each to be admitted into the union when it had attracted as many residents as the least populous existing state. Jefferson's committee also recommended that slavery be barred from the West after 1800, but Congress defeated the recommendation by a single vote.[1] The Northwest Ordinance of 1787, however, did ban slavery from all territory north of the Ohio River, to make the region more attractive to settlers from northern states in which slavery was coming into disfavor. The agreement to separate the western territory at the Ohio was only a qualified victory for opponents of slavery,

---

[1]Some historians have wishfully speculated that if only the vote had gone the other way and the ban on slavery in the territories had passed, the Civil War might have been avoided. This neglects, among other things, the fact that most territorial land in the Southwest was still formally the possession of slave states. It is impossible to believe that they would have completed deeds ceding the land to the United States without assurances that it would be open to slavery.

however. It implicitly left the Southwest open to settlement by slave-owners and their bondsmen, and laid the basis for sectional tensions that ultimately proved impossible for the American political system to contain.

To legislate for the orderly settlement of the West was one thing; to secure the opportunity to settle in the face of resistance from hostile powers like Britain and Spain was another. The British regarded the American government with undisguised scorn. They refused to appoint an ambassador to the United States, and failed to abide by their treaty promise to abandon their string of military posts from central New York west to the Mississippi. Keeping the forts was a means of ensuring that the flourishing fur trade with local Indian tribes would continue to flow through Canada. It was rationalized by the British on the grounds that the American states had not fulfilled their treaty pledge to repay debts to British creditors and damages for confiscated Tory property.

Lacking the authority to raise an army or to levy taxes, Congress was powerless either to compel the British to evacuate or to buy them off. Although the Proclamation of 1763 and the Quebec Act no longer stood in the way of American settlement, much of the West still remained closed. The last British troops were not removed until 1796, after a diplomatic dispute that almost ended in war (see Chapter 9).

The Spanish in the Southwest were nearly as troublesome as the British in the Northwest. The Mississippi River was the natural route by which western farm products could be shipped to foreign markets, but Spain was afraid that thriving American settlements in the Southwest would menace her trans-Mississippi empire, and consequently closed the Mississippi to American shipping. When this did not deter the frontiersmen pouring into Kentucky and Tennessee, Spanish officials tried to foster secessionist movements, offering access to the Mississippi if settlers would renounce their allegiance to the United States and form satellite states allied with Spain. American fears of involvement with "papists" were too strong for the scheme to work, but Congress had no means of breaking Spain's stranglehold over the crucial interior waterway. Attempts to negotiate a commercial treaty with Spain failed, the Mississippi remained bottled up, and the Southwest continued to seethe with discontent.

Economic Problems

The American economy plunged into a severe depression at the end of the war, and Congress could do nothing to combat it. Britain naturally refused to restore the privileged commercial position of her former colonies after they had won their independence. The British were happy to sell their manufactures in America, but imposed heavy duties on imports from the United States, and barred American meat, fish, and dairy products from the lucrative West Indian market altogether. Without power to regulate foreign commerce, Congress could not use the threat of retaliatory tariffs to force better terms.

American traders, of course, were now free to sell their goods anywhere else in the world. New commercial connections opened up with France, northern Europe, and the Orient in particular, but they were not enough to fill the gap created by the lost British market. Merchants from other lands could count on their governments to follow trade policies that protected their interests; Americans could not. The individual states were not strong enough to bargain with other nations, and the central government was constitutionally barred from regulating trade. In the 1780s the new nation's foreign trade failed to reach the level attained before the war. Because American manufacturing did not increase enough to compensate for the drop, the decline in the foreign trade sector distinctly reduced the standard of living—as much as 20 percent by one recent estimate.

The chaotic state of the nation's finances was another cause of the postwar economic crisis. Because it lacked the power to tax the states or their citizens, the Continental Congress had paid the heavy expenses of the war by the only means available—it issued paper notes that represented promises to pay in the future. By 1780 a total of almost $250 million of these notes were in circulation. At that point, the states picked up a larger share of the burden by providing back pay for their soldiers in the Continental Army. Unable to raise taxes enough to discharge these obligations, they too began issuing paper notes, and ran up a debt almost as large as that of Congress.

With each new issue, the prospect of redemption at face value grew even dimmer, and the value of the paper shrank accordingly. A congressional resolution that anyone refusing to accept its bills in payment should be "published and treated as an enemy in this country" had about as much effect as would an act repealing the law of gravity. By the end of the war it took 150 paper dollars to buy a single dollar in coin. "Not worth a Continental" was a common phrase, and it was said that "a wagonload of money would scarcely purchase a wagonload of goods." The Revolution could not have been fought to a successful conclusion without borrowing through note issue; the states could never have passed the towering taxes needed to pay for it year by year. But the cost was acute financial instability that dampened business activity for years to come.

Class Tensions and Popular Disorder

As the depression became more acute in the mid-1780s, it provoked fierce political conflicts between debtors and creditors, conflicts that convinced some politically active men that a stronger central government was necessary to remedy the evils of "an excess of democracy." Small farmers with shrinking incomes from falling crop prices were threatened with loss of their land for inability to meet their mortgage or tax payments. In states where the political influence of debtors was strong, legislatures granted them relief by issuing paper money for loans to the needy and requiring creditors to accept it at face value. Some assemblies passed "stay" laws as well, preventing creditors from seizing property put up as collateral to secure debts. When paper money was issued with restraints, as in New York and Pennsylvania, it alleviated hardship without depreciating so much as to be cruelly unfair to creditors. When it was not, as in Rhode Island, the results were unfortunate. In "Rogues' Island," as critics called it, merchants were forced to close up shop and hide from people who owed them money to avoid having to accept state paper that was nearly worthless. The Articles government had no power to check legislatures that "soaked the rich" by such methods.

An upheaval in Massachusetts in 1786 was even more disturbing to men of property. The legislature, dominated by commercial interests from the eastern part of the state, had turned a deaf ear on the pleas of western farmers for relief measures, and had instead sharply increased taxes. A band of angry farmers led by a former militia captain, Daniel Shays, then took the law into their own hands. They marched on local courthouses and closed them down to prevent foreclosures and auctions of farms for unpaid taxes. Shays' Rebellion involved very little fighting; when the state militia eventually appeared on the scene the resistance melted away. But for some months the state government in Boston had little more control over the interior areas than General Gage had experienced in 1775. This prolonged resistance to duly constituted authority, in what had been regarded as one of the most conservative states in the union, terrified many people who had previously seen no great need for a stronger central government. "A spirit of licentiousness" had "infected Masachusetts," said one; "anarchy, or rather worse than anarchy, pure democracy" was abroad, and it could spread. "There are combustibles in every state which a spark might set fire to." The response of the Massachusetts legislature was almost equally dismaying to those who feared popular disorder; after peace was restored, it proceeded to extend tax relief. If mob action could make legislators cave in in this way, the "spirit of leveling" could not be held in check.

FORMING A MORE PERFECT UNION

The central government established by the Articles was unable to secure compliance with the treaties negotiated by its representatives, open up the West to free settlement, protect the interests of American traders, create a stable financial structure, or prevent states from pursuing monetary and fiscal policies that benefited the poor at the expense of the wealthy. And the prospect of reform to remedy these flaws was doomed by the requirement that any amendment had to be approved by every single state. By 1782 the leaders of almost every state realized that Congress needed a more reliable source of revenue than handouts from the state governments, and consequently had supported an amendment authorizing a 5 percent duty on imported goods. But almost every state was not enough. Opposition from Rhode Island alone—which had less than two percent of the country's population—was enough to kill the plan. Four years of further haggling produced a revised version acceptable to Rhode Island, but that plan was shot down by New York. The Articles provided a structure of government so rigid, so dependent on unanimous agreement on the part of states with highly divergent interests, that it could not be reformed by legal means. It took skillful extralegal maneuvering on the part of a determined band of nationalist leaders to secure the establishment of a new and radically different national government.

The Convention at Annapolis

The first step in that direction was the Annapolis convention of 1786. It was held as a result of a resolution by the Virginia assembly calling for a convention of the states to consider problems of trade, taxes, and other commercial matters. George Washington, who made no secret of his view that the Confederation was "little more than a shadow without substance," a "rope of sand," a "farce," lent his enormous prestige to the proposal. The driving force behind it, however, was a younger Virginian, James Madison, a lawyer and a three-term veteran of the Continental Congress. Madison was a close student of history and political theory and a master organizer who had thought more fully than anyone about the defects of the Articles and how to remedy them.

The Annapolis meeting was a disappointment. Only five states sent delegates, and none of the New England states were represented. But the fact that such a conclave of state representatives was held at all, when there existed a Congress charged with attending to national problems, was significant. The conclusion reached at Annapolis was that national commercial problems could not be solved without a broader restructuring of the nation's political system. The delegates therefore decided to meet at Philadelphia the next year, to plan a revision of the Articles. After several states approved this recommendation and appointed delegates, Congress endorsed the plan for a convention.

The Convention at Philadelphia

The great majority of the 55 men who attended the Philadelphia Convention were strong nationalists who believed that America needed a much more energetic central government than the Articles had established. They were well-educated, wealthy people with considerable experience at serving their nation; 39 of them had been members of Congress, and 21 had been officers in the Continental Army. It is not surprising that most delegates identified with the nationalist cause; in politics, a wise observer has noted, "those who get appointed to a special committee are likely to be men who supported the movement for its creation." Other politically active Americans were satisfied with the Confederation, but they stayed home, assuming that the Convention would result in nothing more than previous attempts to alter the Articles—a series of amendments that might prove acceptable to most but would in the end be vetoed by at least one.

They were in for a surprise. Madison, Benjamin Franklin, Alexander Hamilton, John Jay, and the others met for four grueling months, with Washington presiding. The convention was held behind closed doors; no public record was made of the proceedings.[2] The outcome of its deliberations, released in September, was breathtaking. Although the resolution of Congress that authorized the convention clearly specified that it was "for the sole and express purpose of revising the

---

[2]Madison fortunately kept a detailed journal, which was made public in 1840, after his death. Most of what we know about the course of debate derives from Madison's account.

Articles of Confederation," the delegates paid no heed to that directive. Instead of revising the Articles, they abandoned them altogether and wrote a new constitution. Furthermore, they declared it would take effect when ratified by popular conventions in *nine* of the thirteen states. Since the Articles of Confederation were still in effect, of course, this ratification procedure was unconstitutional. It placed the power of decision in special conventions rather than in the legislatures, as provided in the Articles, and it replaced the exacting requirement of unanimous approval with one much easier to meet. If members of Congress had chosen to protest the convention's audacious decision to change the rules of the game while it was being played, political chaos might have ensued. But Congress reacted with its customary passivity, accepted the work of the Philadelphia Convention as a *fait accompli*, and submitted it to the states without recommending approval or disapproval. Congress had been so effectively shouldered aside that its members were prepared to allow a majority of the people of nine states to vote it out of existence.

The Federal Constitution

The proposed Constitution provided for a national government clearly separate from and superior to the governments of the individual states. As the product not of the states but of "We the people of the United States," the central government claimed direct authority over every American. As its chief architect, Madison, said, "instead of operating on the states," it operated "without their intervention on the individuals composing them." Its legislature could raise funds through taxes, instead of begging the states for money. It could raise a national army, and call out the state militias as well when it felt necessary. It could regulate commerce, both foreign and domestic, and fix a uniform national currency. In addition to these and other specifically enumerated powers, the Constitution included an "elastic" clause giving Congress the authority to "make all laws necessary and proper for carrying into execution the foregoing powers, and all other powers vested by this Constitution in the government of the United States, or any department or officer thereof."

The states were not abolished, of course, as some of the most ardent nationalists would have preferred. But their power and independence were radically diminished. They were forbidden to conduct negotiations with foreign powers, to print paper money, to pass laws interfering with the obligation of contracts (such as stay laws), or to impede the free flow of goods across state lines through taxes or tariffs. They were required to honor each other's laws and court decisions, to extradite persons accused of crimes in other states, and to grant the citizens of other states "all the privileges and immunities" possessed by their own.

By 1787, memories of the abuses of power by Royal Governors and the Crown had faded, and the framers felt free to provide for a strong, independent chief executive—the President. It was an overstatement to call the Presidency an "elective monarchy," as some did, but it was an office with formidable powers—to execute the laws, veto legislative acts, direct foreign affairs, make judicial and executive appointments, and command the armed services. Debate over the Presidency in

Philadelphia focused less on the breadth of power given it than on the length of the chief executive's term and the mode of his election. Alexander Hamilton, the delegate most sympathetic to monarchical principles, proposed that the President (and senators too) hold office for life, but the majority of framers believed that a four-year term, with no bar to reelection, struck the right balance between executive independence and responsiveness to the popular will. Even that four years was not guaranteed, because incumbents could be removed from office by impeachment for "high crimes and misdemeanors." Fearing that a President elected by direct popular vote would cater too much to mass opinion, the framers resorted to the curious device of the Electoral College. If no candidate received a majority there, the House of Representatives would make the choice from the top five. Since the men at Philadelphia did not anticipate the development of national political parties to limit the number of candidates, they assumed that no one (after George Washington) would be likely to win in the Electoral College, and that the House would normally pick the President.

The lawmaking power of the new government was lodged in the two houses of Congress, the Senate and the House of Representatives. The Senate was like the Congress under the Articles in giving equal representation to each state regardless of size. But senators were given relatively long terms—six years—and could be reelected, so they would be less responsive to parochial interests. It was assumed that men of wealth and status would predominate in the Senate, and that it would be the aristocratic element in the national government. The House of Representatives, as one speaker said at Philadelphia, was to be "the grand depository of the democratic principle of the government." Congressmen would be elected from smaller districts than senators, and would face reelection every two years. They would tend to be less elevated in social rank, would "know and sympathize with every part of the community," and would be more responsive to constituency pressures. It is noteworthy that the Constitution specified that all revenue measures had to originate in the more democratic branch of Congress, and that the House would have usually chosen the President if the Electoral College system had worked as envisaged.

The third independent branch of the federal government provided for in the Constitution was the judiciary. A Supreme Court was to be created, and whatever lower courts Congress deemed necessary. The Constitution was "the supreme law of the land," and the federal judiciary was to enforce it. It was given jurisdiction over all disputes involving the interpretation of the Constitution, laws, and treaties of the United States, and all conflicts between states or the citizens of different states. State judges were made subordinate to its rulings, even if the constitution or laws of their own state conflicted with them.

Although the Constitution designed a central government with vastly enhanced powers, it also limited those powers in significant ways. The most important restraint was the system of "checks and balances" among the three branches of the federal government. Each had its own distinctive function to play, in accord with the principle of "separation of powers." But the separation was incomplete, for each branch wielded some power to check the operations of the others. The President could veto acts of Congress. Congress, in turn, could refuse to appropriate financing for presidential actions it opposed; it could remove a sitting President through impeachment; the Senate could block appointments and treaties proposed by the chief executive. The Supreme Court could declare the actions of either Congress or the President unconstitutional.[3] The Court too was subject to check. Congress could enlarge its membership, allowing the President to make new appointments to alter its political complexion, and judges were susceptible to Congressional impeachment.

The structure of Congress itself was a check against precipitous action. All legislation required the consent of both houses, and agreement was difficult to achieve, because of the differing ways in which membership was apportioned in the two bodies—by state in the Senate, by population in the House. Legislative action required approval both by a majority of the states in the Senate, and by the representatives of a majority of the American people—something quite different—in the House.

Compromises at Philadelphia

That legislative structure was not the product of an abstract commitment of the convention delegates to the principle of checks and balances. It was the result of a practical compromise that bridged a major political division between delegates from the most populous and the least populous states. The former—from Virginia, Pennsylvania, and New York, for example—insisted on making representation proportional to population. Men from places like New Jersey and Delaware demanded instead that each state have an equal number of seats, as in Congress under the Articles. The debate was heated, with representatives of the smaller states threatening to walk out and to "find some foreign ally, of more honor and good faith, who will take them by the hand, and do them justice." Eventually, however, the "Great Compromise" suggested by Franklin was agreed to—a bicameral legislature with one house weighted by population and the other not.

Another major compromise was that between the northern states with few or no slaves and the southern slave states. Southerners argued that the number of seats assigned to a state in the House of Representatives and the number of electoral votes a state could cast in presidential elections should be based on its total population, including all the slaves. Northerners contended that representation should be proportional to the number of free persons only. The solution was the "Three-fifths Compromise," which apportioned both representation and direct federal taxes on the basis of "the whole number of free persons" (including indentured servants) in a state, plus "three-fifths of all other persons"—that is, slaves. A related concession to the South forbade until 1808 federal legislation restricting "the migration or importation of such persons as any of the states now existing shall think proper to admit"—that is, restricting the importation of African slaves. Notice that in forging compromises related to slavery the Founders resorted to evasive euphemisms. The Constitution never once explicitly mentions slaves or

---

[3]This is not explicitly stated in the Constitution. But Chief Justice John Marshall successfully asserted the power in the path-breaking case of *Marbury vs. Madison* in 1803; see page 281.

slavery. The institution, Abraham Lincoln later remarked, was "hid away in the Constitution, just as an afflicted man hides away a cancer which he dares not cut out at once, lest be bleed to death." True, but had they not evaded the slavery issue, the Founders could never have reached agreement to form a stronger union.

As an amalgam of compromises between conflicting interests made by practical men, the Constitution was ambiguous on some points, and open to differing interpretations. Its meaning remained a source of dispute long after, between nationalists and states' rights advocates, between "broad" and "strict" constructionists. But its ambiguity, along with its provision for amendment without enormous difficulty, gave the Constitution a flexibility that allowed it to survive longer than any other written constitution in modern history.

The Struggle Over Ratification

The Philadelphia Convention was packed with delegates predisposed to the nationalist cause; in the end, all but three put their signatures of approval on the Constitution. It soon became clear that selling it to the country would be a good deal more difficult than engineering the agreement at Philadelphia. It took nine months of debate before the necessary nine state conventions ratified the proposal, and even then Virginia and New York—both so large and powerful as to be essential for the plan to work—held back. Supporters of the Constitution did not carry the day in Virginia until late June, 1788, and in New York until July.

In the contest over ratification, the nationalists shrewdly appropriated the label of "Federalist" for themselves, and called their opponents "Antifederalists." The Antifederalists had a better claim to the term "Federalist," since the Articles of Confederation they defended had established a confederation that was "federal" in the usage of the day. The Constitution was less "federal" than the status quo, in that it erected a central government clearly independent of and superior to the states in many spheres. Avoiding a more revealing and politically charged term like "nationalist" was a deft choice that won them votes they otherwise would have lost.

Antifederalists charged that the Constitution was an instrument of tyranny. It would take power from the states and concentrate it in a remote capital. The President would be a monarch in republican clothing. It was obvious that George Washington would be the first chief executive if the Constitution were approved, and Antifederalists asked whether or not George I would be any improvement over George III. The Congress, and especially the Senate, would be far more removed from and unrepresentative of the common people than state legislators. A farmer at the Massachusetts ratifying convention charged that "these lawyers, and men of learning, and moneyed men, that talk so finely, and gloss over matters so smoothly, to make us poor illiterate people swallow down the pill, expect to get into Congress themselves; they expect to be managers of this Constitution and get all the power and all the money into their own hands, and then they will swallow up all us little folks, like the Great Leviathan, just as the whale swallowed up Jonah." Unlike most existing state constitutions, the proposed federal Constitution included no Bill of

Rights to guarantee basic liberties. Having fought against "the iron yoke of British bondage," one Antifederalist said, it would be insane to bend "our necks to as heavy a one of our own make."

In his seminal book, *An Economic Interpretation of the Constitution* (1913), Charles Beard supported the Antifederalist claim that the Constitution was a betrayal of the Revolution, an antidemocratic, counterrevolutionary stroke by rich men primarily concerned with protecting their property from popular assault. Historians have debated the issue ever since, with most recent writers finding the Beardian analysis unpersuasive. The Constitution did not divide the country starkly and simply by class or economic interest. There were well-to-do Antifederalists and poor Federalists, including most commercial farmers and urban artisans, it has recently been shown. However, it does appear that the core of the opposition came from localistic-minded small farmers from subsistence farming areas in the interior. Conversely, the strongest supporters were merchants, professionals, and other city dwellers, who approved the Constitution by margins of four to one or better (see Table 8–2). Wealthy men were likewise more strongly Federalist than those of only moderate means. As a result of their superior status, education, and political experience, the Federalists were much better organized than the opposition. They had greater energy, and fewer scruples about using underhanded tactics to achieve their ends. For example, all but a dozen of the hundred newspapers in the United States were pro-Federalist because well-to-do Federalists bought up the papers and refused to cover opposition arguments.

To note these differences in the social base of the Federalist and Antifederalist movements is not to endorse the claim that the Constitution was a betrayal of the Revolution. Many elements of the population were dissatisfied with the Articles government for many different reasons, and were persuaded that a stronger national government would be beneficial. If fear of an "excess of democracy" in states

TABLE 8-2
Some Indications of Class Differences
Between the Federalists and Antifederalists

Political Alignments of State Senators by Wealth

	Percentage Federalist	Percentage Antifederalist
Wealthy	82	18
Well-to-do	65	35
Moderate means	42	58

Votes of Delegates to Pennsylvania, Connecticut, and New Hampshire Ratifying Conventions, by Occupation

Merchants, Manufacturers, Doctors, Lawyers, Ministers, Large Landholders	84	16
Artisans, Innkeepers, Surveyors, and so on	64	36
Farmers	46	54

like Rhode Island motivated many of the Founders, the Constitution they wrote derived its authority entirely from the popular will. Madison called it "a republican remedy for the diseases most incident to republican government," a means of making democracy safe for the world. In the articles he wrote with Alexander Hamilton and John Jay in defense of the Constitution—the classic *Federalist Papers*—Madison attacked the traditional view that republican government could survive only in small territories like the ancient Greek city-states. Instead, he argued, an "extended republic" like the United States would include such a variety of competing interests as to prevent the formation of a tyrannical majority. That diversity of interests, plus the overlapping powers of the House, the Senate, the Presidency, and the Supreme Court—all selected on different bases—would protect individual liberty and property without abandoning the principle of popular sovereignty.

In the end, the Federalists won. The contest was very close, and the outcome might have been different had not the Federalists wisely agreed to add a Bill of Rights to the Constitution as the first order of business after it had been approved. Their failure to do so at Philadelphia stemmed not from a desire to limit popular liberties but from the framers' assumption that the existing state constitutions already offered sufficient protection. Some delegates feared too that spelling out certain rights of the citizen with precision could be dangerous, in that it might be assumed that the list was exclusive and that citizens had no others. Thomas Jefferson, however, thought otherwise, and campaigned tirelessly for written guarantees of liberty. Jefferson missed the Philadelphia convention and the subsequent ratification debates because he was serving as American Minister to

France, but his letters to Madison and other politically prominent friends persuaded the Federalist leadership to agree to the demand.

Although the Federalists triumphed at every state ratifying convention, they did not win the support of a majority of the American people. Perhaps the most striking thing about the struggle over ratification was the passivity of the general public. Barely a quarter of those eligible to vote for delegates to the state conventions bothered to go to the polls. Most Americans neither desired nor feared a stronger national government; they were simply indifferent, absorbed in personal and local concerns. The Revolution had intruded, often violently, into the lives of millions of ordinary citizens. The issue of whether the Articles of Confederation or the Constitution provided a more adequate frame of government was remote and abstract by comparison. Ratification was a matter of deep interest only to the politically conscious minority.

SUGGESTED READINGS

Many of the titles cited at the end of the preceding chapter are also relevant for these years. Henry S. Commager and R.B. Morris, eds., *The Spirit of '76: The Story of the American Revolution as Told by Participants* (1958) is a collection of primary sources. Howard H. Peckham, *War for Independence: A Military History* (1958) is a brief and lively account of the course of battle. James Kirby Martin and Mark Edward Leander, *A Respectable Army: The Military Origins of the Republic* (1982) discusses the shaping of an American army. Marcus Cunliffe's entertaining *George Washington: Man and Monument* (1958) and James T. Flexner, *Washington: The Indispensable Man* (1974) are useful biographies. John Sky, *A People Numerous and Armed: Reflections on the Military Struggle for American Independence* (1976) and Charles Royster, *A Revolutionary People at War* (1979) examine the social and political dimensions of the armed struggle. On the loyalists, see Mary Beth Norton, *The British-Americans: The Loyalist Exiles in England, 1774–1789* (1972).

The closing chapters of James A. Henretta, *The Evolution of American Society 1700–1815* (1973) summarize the changes wrought by the War and the Revolution. Mary Beth Norton, *Liberty's Daughters: The Revolutionary Experience of American Women, 1750–1800* (1980) is the best treatment of that subject. The experiences of blacks and changing attitudes toward slavery are explored in Donald Robinson, *Slavery in the Structure of American Politics, 1765–1820* (1971), Duncan J. MacLeod, *Slavery, Race, and the American Revolution* (1974), David B. Davis, *The Problem of Slavery in the Age of Revolution, 1770–1823* (1975), Arthur Zilversmit, *The First Emancipation: The Abolition of Slavery in the North* (1967), and Ira Berlin, *Slaves Without Masters: The Free Negro in the Antebellum South* (1981).

Gordon A. Wood, *The Creation of the American Republic, 1776–1787* (1969) is a superb treatment of political and ideological change from the Declaration to the framing of the Constitution. Willi Paul Adams, *The First American Constitution: Republican Ideology and the Making of the State Constitutions in the Revolutionary Era* (1980) examines constitution-making in the states. Merrill Jensen, *The New Nation:*

A History of the United States during the Confederation, 1781–1789 (1948) has a broad sweep, but it minimizes the flaws of the Confederation and exaggerates the antidemocratic inclinations of the supporters of the Constitution. Jack N. Rakove, *The Beginnings of National Politics: An Interpretive History of the Continental Congress* (1979) is more balanced. Charles Beard, *An Economic Interpretation of the Constitution* (1913) took the Framers of the Constitution from the pedestal on which they had long been placed, arguing that they were acting out of class interest and feared democracy. The specifics of Beard's analysis have been demolished by such studies as Robert I. Brown, *Charles Beard and the Constitution* (1956), and Forrest McDonald, *We the People: The Economic Origins of the Constitution* (1958). Some recent investigations, however, find that the debate over the Constitution did split the American people along social lines, pitting "localist" defenders of the Articles against "cosmopolitan" supporters of the Constitution. See Jackson Turner Main, *The Anti-Federalists: Critics of the Constitution* (1961) and *Political Parties before the Constitution* (1974). For the best statement of the view that the Constitution was consistent with the ideals of the Revolution, see Richard Hofstadter, *The Progressive Historians: Turner, Beard and Parrington* (1968), perhaps the best single book to come from the pen of one of the greatest of America's historians. R.R. Palmer, *The Age of the Democratic Revolutions: A Political History of Europe and America, 1760–1800* (2 vols., 1959, 1964) is a comparative study that yields new insights.

Chapter Nine

The Republic In Peril

*I*n January of 1790, after almost a year as President, George Washington remarked that it was "a miracle that there should have been so much unanimity, in points of such importance, among such a number of citizens, so widely scattered and so different in their interests." Considering the fierceness of the battle over ratification of the Constitution, opposition to it had melted away with surprising speed. Only a handful of Antifederalists won election to the first Congress, and Washington was the unanimous choice of the Electoral College. As Woodrow Wilson later observed, it appeared that opponents of ratification had not only been defeated but convinced.

The spirit of union and harmony that prevailed during this honeymoon period did not last long, however. The adoption of the Constitution did not end political argument. Instead, it focused and intensified conflict, and soon polarized the nation far more deeply than the debates over ratification. It was a cruel disappointment to Washington. When he retired to Mt. Vernon at the close of his second term, he lamented the loss of "unanimity" and charged that "the spirit of party" served "always to distract the public councils and enfeeble the public administration." By then, two distinct and sharply opposed political parties were taking shape—Washington's Federalist party and the Republican party organized by Thomas Jefferson and James Madison.[1] In the first quarter of a century under the new

---

[1]Jefferson's Republican party, sometimes also known as the Democratic–Republican party, bears no relationship to the modern Republican party, which was first organized shortly before the Civil War; it was the forerunner of today's Democratic party.

The British fleet bombarded Fort McHenry, Maryland, on September 13, 1814. Francis Scott Key, a witness to the battle, dashed off some verses the following morning under the title "Defense of Fort M'Henry." Within a few days, the lyric was being sung to the tune of an English drinking song, "To Anacreon in Heaven." "The Star-Spangled Banner" did not become the official national anthem until 1931.

Constitution, until the close of the War of 1812 and the collapse of the Federalist party, political clashes were frequently so violent and venomous that the survival of the republic was in doubt. Serious disagreements over domestic policy and even more serious differences over foreign policy brought the nation to the brink of civil war more than once. By 1815, however, America's position in the world had altered fundamentally, and a surge of national feeling had healed the fissures that threatened to break apart the body politic.

THE WASHINGTON ADMINISTRATION

George Washington's first cabinet included two towering figures who were soon to become the focal points of political controversy—his Secretary of the Treasury and close adviser, Alexander Hamilton, and Secretary of State Thomas Jefferson. America's greatest need, in Hamilton's view, was for "energy in government." He had a superabundance of energy himself, a powerful mind, and a clear vision of the nation's future. He thought of himself as the prime minister of the new government, and spoke of "my administration." Hamilton was eager to see the simple, overwhelmingly agrarian America of his day transformed into a rich and powerful industrial nation as rapidly as possible. It mattered little to him whether or not that aspiration was shared by most of his countrymen, for he had nothing but scorn for the common man. On one occasion he confessed that he had "long since learned to hold public opinion of no value." On another he declared that "all communities divide themselves into the few and the many. The first are rich and wellborn, the other the mass of the people. The voice of the people has been said to be the voice of God; it is not true. The people are turbulent and changing; they seldom judge or determine right." Hamilton was determined to reverse the egalitarian and democratic currents that had been set in motion by the Revolution, by creating a powerful consolidated central government securely tied to the "rich and wellborn," making them a "court faction" of sorts. His sweeping economic program, set forth in three brilliant papers in 1790 and 1791, was in large measure successful in establishing that strong central government. But the scheme so offended Jefferson, Madison, and their admirers that it had another unanticipated effect. It provoked widespread opposition, and finally drove Jefferson and Madison to organize an opposition party.

Hamilton's Programs

The first plank of Hamilton's financial program was his plan to establish the national credit securely and to pay off the immense debt left from the Revolution. Congress owed some $12 million to foreign creditors, $27 million to American citizens, and $13 million in accumulated interest; the various state governments owed another $25 million. Hamilton proposed that the federal government assume full responsibility for these obligations, and meet them by issuing new permanent federal notes, bearing interest to be paid through customs duties and taxes. Redeeming those pledges would restore the nation's ability to borrow money abroad, and reassure men of property that the administration respected the sanctity of contracts. Investors holding the new notes would have a powerful stake in the survival of the new government. Because the notes could be bought and sold freely, they would enlarge the money supply and the stock of liquid capital. Assuming the state debts as well as those of Congress would signal the primacy of the central government over the states.

No one in Congress objected to paying off the nation's foreign creditors, but other aspects of the plan were vulnerable to attack. For one thing, few of the unredeemed pledges to pay were by then in the hands of the people to whom they were first issued—for example, the common soldiers who had been given them as pay for military service. So many had been issued that their cash value had plunged to the point at which ordinary people, fearful that they would soon be completely valueless, had unloaded them at a fraction of their face value to speculators who could afford to gamble that they would someday be redeemed. Hamilton's scheme would provide immense profits for these speculators, but do nothing to compensate poorer people for their losses. Madison protested this injustice on the floor of the House, and proposed that speculators be given only what they had actually paid for the notes, with the remainder going to the original holders. Hamilton objected that such discrimination would be too difficult to administer, that quickly establishing a stable national market for the securities was the most urgent necessity, and that the spirit of enterprise shown by risk-taking speculators should be encouraged.

Not only did Hamilton's plan seem to benefit the "wealthy and powerful" and do nothing for "the middling ranks" and "the industrious poor." It also was skewed in favor of one section of the country and against another. Federal assumption of state debts rewarded those states that had been delinquent about paying off the notes they had issued and penalized those that had been more responsible, who would be taxed to finance the scheme. Most of the states that had already discharged the obligations incurred to finance the Revolutionary War were in the South. Moreover, four-fifths of the paper to be redeemed at face value was in the hands of speculators residing in northern states.

Congress eventually passed Hamilton's funding program after some details were altered to favor Virginia and after it was agreed to locate the permanent national capital in the South, along the banks of the Potomac. Jefferson lent it his grudging support. But the prolonged battle began to divide Congress along partisan lines that would soon grow sharper.

The second plank of Hamilton's financial program was his proposal for a huge Bank of the United States, a joint venture between the federal government and private capitalists, clearly modeled on the Bank of England. It would help to support the primitive private banking system and increase the supply of liquid capital available to enterprise. However, it was obviously a carbon copy of an institution that some Americans saw as a pillar of the corrupt and bloated British establishment, an "aristocratic engine." It would concentrate great economic power in the hands of northeastern financial interests and increase their influence over the federal government. And there was a serious question as to its constitutionality. The Constitution does not give Congress any explicit power to create a bank; indeed, a clause authorizing Congress to issue corporate charters had been proposed and defeated at the Philadelphia Convention. Jefferson, Madison, and Attorney General Edmund Randolph all urged Washington to adhere to a "strict" interpretation of the Constitution and to veto the measure. But Hamilton prepared a powerful defense of the "loose constructionist" view, citing some of Madison's *Federalist* writings in support. If the end of a particular measure was legitimate, Congress could constitutionally employ any means to that end that were not specifically barred by the Constitution. Creating a bank was one of the "implied" powers of Congress. Washington was persuaded, and the Bank of the United States became a reality.

Although Hamilton won these two major victories, congressional opposition was too strong for him to secure endorsement of the other crucial element of his economic program—a complex scheme to stimulate American manufacturing by means of high protective tariffs, bounties for domestic enterprises, encouragement of immigration, and federal aid for new roads and other "internal improvements." Although Hamilton's *Report on Manufactures* anticipated most of the policies that later American governments would employ to speed economic development, few congressmen in the 1790s foresaw an industrial future for America. The vast majority of their countrymen were farmers, idealized by Jefferson as "the chosen people of God"; to engineer the growth of cities and factories, with a dependent laboring class, ran counter to the yeoman ideal. Only a low tariff, for purposes of revenue rather than protection, and a 25 percent federal tax on the manufacture of distilled liquor were enacted.

The tax on liquor provoked a popular upheaval that provided Hamilton with an opportunity to test his belief that "government can never be said to be established until some signal display has manifested its power of military coercion." The prime victims of the tax were small farmers in remote backwoods areas, who could only afford to transport their grain to eastern markets by distilling it into much less bulky whiskey. A packhorse could carry 4 bushels of rye grain on its back; it could carry 24 bushels made into whiskey, a liquid much in demand in the hard-drinking young republic. In Pennsylvania and parts of the South, many farmers refused to pay and threatened violence against tax collectors. After Hamilton ordered stricter enforcement, farmers in western Pennsylvania held public meetings in 1794, at which they pledged not to pay and denounced the administration in inflammatory terms. Washington then called out the militia from four states, and 15,000 troops rushed to the scene with Hamilton in the lead. The "Whiskey Rebellion" was anticlimactic, in that the troops met with no resistance at all. It might better be known as the "Rebellion That Never Was". As Jefferson said, "an insurrection was announced and proclaimed and armed against, but could never be found." This attempt to kill a mosquito with an artillery barrage may have "established" the authority of the government more solidly, but it also made the West a prime source of antiadministration votes in future elections.

JEFFERSON vs. HAMILTON ON THE GREATEST MEN IN HISTORY

At a dinner in Jefferson's rooms, Hamilton looked up at the portraits of John Locke, Isaac Newton, and Francis Bacon on the wall and asked his host who they were. Jefferson responded that they were, in his view, "the three greatest men the world has ever produced." Hamilton blinked, shook his head, and declared confidently that "the greatest man that ever lived was Julius Caesar."

An Emerging Republican Opposition

Opposition to Hamilton's plans and distrust of his purposes spread in the closing years of Washington's first term and took an increasingly ideological emphasis. In 1787 Madison had fully agreed with Hamilton on the need for a much stronger central government, and had shared his disappointment at the many compromises that had to be made at Philadelphia to appease defenders of "states' rights." The alternative seemed to him anarchy. After seeing his former close collaborator in action, he lost his enthusiasm for consolidated power and "energy in government," and began to express fears reminiscent of those of the Antifederalists. Jefferson, who had been more dubious about centralization and more concerned about protecting popular liberties all along, reacted the same way. Both suspected that Hamilton and his followers were really monarchists in republican clothing, "aristocrats" and "monocrats" engaged in a plot to reshape American society along English lines. "A sect has shown itself among us," said Jefferson in 1792, "who declare they espoused our Constitution not as a good and sufficient thing in itself, but only as a step towards an English constitution, the thing good and sufficient in itself, in their eye. Too many of our Legislature have become stock-jobbers and King-jobbers. However, the voice of the people is beginning to make itself heard, and will probably cleanse their seats at the ensuing elections."

To see that "the voice of the people" was loud enough to be heard, Jefferson and Madison took the first hesitant steps to build a rival political organization to mobilize the electorate to throw the rascals out. Both shared the common eighteenth-century belief that political parties were evil—a source of discord that would tear apart the body politic, the work of greedy men who fostered dissension for personal advantage. But they felt that the extraordinary menace posed by Hamilton's schemes justified an extraordinary remedy—the building of a temporary popular coalition to end rule by "the monied interest" and the "Anglomen" and restore pure, uncorrupted republicanism. Madison took the lead in orchestrating the formation of a "Republican interest" in Congress. As an administration cabinet member, Jefferson had to be more circumspect, but he was the principal strategist behind the scenes. He quietly subsidized a newspaper highly critical of Hamilton by putting its editor on the State Department payroll, and Madison wrote a series of barbed essays for it.

The Republican opposition was strongest in the South. The dominant planter group and the smaller farmers who deferred to them were repelled by the Hamiltonian vision of a bustling commercial republic. In the North, Republicans tended to be either small farmers from the backwoods or rising men who felt shut out of the establishment. Ethnic and religious affiliations also shaped partisan leanings, with people of non-English immigrant stock and members of dissenting religious groups inclining towards the Republicans, and those of English background and Congregational or Episcopal faith most supportive of the Federalist administration.

The extent of political polarization at the time of the 1792 elections should not be exaggerated. It was still possible for a congressmen to write home, "It is said there are two parties in Congress, but in fact I do not positively know. If there are, I know that I do not belong to either." What were coming to be known as the Republican and Federalist "interests" were hazy in their outlines, and respect for Washington remained a powerful unifying influence. Despite his many clashes with Hamilton, Jefferson still held a key post in the administration and Madison was in close touch with the President. Both urged Washington to run for a second term, hoping that they could dissuade him from backing any more of Hamilton's schemes. Washington was again elected unanimously. Republicans, however, refused to support the administration candidate for Vice-President, John Adams. Their favorite, George Clinton, made a respectable showing, winning two-thirds as many electoral votes as Adams.

"Anglomen" vs. "Gallomen"

During Washington's second term (1793–97), the party divisions that had begun to take shape over the issues posed by Hamilton's economic program sharpened as a result of critical developments in foreign affairs. After war broke out between the new revolutionary republican government of France and Great Britain, Spain, and Holland, Washington proclaimed that the United States would remain neutral, and would insist on its right to trade with any of the belligerent powers. However, a great many Americans cared passionately about the outcome of the struggle. Republicans detested aristocratic Britain and admired egalitarian France. One of their key objections to Hamilton's financial program was that it worked to keep America within England's commercial orbit, and they wished to wrench the national economy out of it. Although they had some qualms about the Reign of Terror then sweeping France, they insisted that the French Revolution embodied the same principles for which their own Revolutionary War had been fought; nothing less than "the liberty of the whole earth" depended on the survival of the revolutionary republican regime. Some recommended military aid to France in accord with the Franco–American alliance of 1778, because "the cause of France is the cause of man, and neutrality is desertion." Jefferson was not ready to go that far, but he did complain that administration policies were not truly neutral and were tilted in favor of Britain. His inability to win over Washington to this view led him to break with the administration finally and resign at the end of 1793.

Federalists tended to be just as ardently pro-British and anti-French. The experience of fighting a long war to win freedom from British rule had not wiped out all the admiration for English culture and institutions that had developed in the colonial years. Economic ties with Britain were much stronger than with France. England was the source of 90 percent of America's imports and the market for three-quarters of her exports, and a good deal of British capital was invested in American public securities. The whole Hamiltonian debt assumption scheme depended on continuing friendly relations with Britain; the bulk of the money that went to pay interest charges on the debt came from tariffs on imports from England, and an Anglo–American war might result in national bankruptcy. Furthermore, many Americans were appalled by the execution of Louis XVI, the murderous excesses of the Reign of Terror, and public attacks on religion by radical advocates of the "religion of humanity." Revolutionary France, said one Federalist, was "an open Hell, still ringing with agonies and blasphemies, still smoking with sufferings and crimes, in which we see perhaps our future state."

Neutrality was easier to proclaim than to maintain, because the contending European powers were not terribly concerned about offending the feelings of a nation with an army of only 3,800 men and a navy with fewer than 1,900. The French made a heavy-handed attempt to compromise American neutrality and manipulate public opinion by sending Citizen Edmond Genet on a diplomatic mission in April, 1793. Genet bungled his mission badly. Encouraged by Jefferson, Genet proceeded to operate as if America were a French satellite to be used as a staging area from which to assault France's enemies. He commissioned privateers to attack British ships, and recruited armies to be used against Spanish posts in Florida and Louisiana. He appointed George Rogers Clark, later to win fame as an explorer, "Commander-in-Chief of the French Revolutionary Legion on the Mississippi River." Genet also helped to organize Republican societies in the United States to serve as pro-French pressure groups. As if this were not enough, in midsummer Genet arrogantly demanded that Washington call Congress into a special session to settle on policies toward France, and declared that if he refused he would appeal to the American people over his head. Washington had Genet expelled after that, but he left behind him a political atmosphere more inflamed than ever before. Republicans denounced their opponents as "British bootlickers," and were called in return "democrats, mobocrats, and all other kinds of rats."

The Genet affair was barely over when a decision of the British government provoked a more serious crisis. American shippers had been conducting a flourishing trade with the French West Indies, but in the fall of 1793 England suddenly tightened its blockade of France by extending it to the Caribbean. Without prior warning or clear justification in international law, the British Navy seized and confiscated 250 American vessels. Britain also asserted its right to stop and search American ships for deserters from the British Navy, and to "impress" suspected deserters back into service. After the British shrugged off the American protest, the only options left open were to take retaliatory action, at the risk of war, or to capitulate. The administration chose capitulation.

John Jay, Chief Justice of the Supreme Court, went to London for several months to arrange terms. (There was so little business for the Supreme Court in these early years that his absence was not missed.) Jay had few bargaining chips, and even fewer in fact than he thought, since Hamilton had secretly informed a British minister that America's threat to join other unaligned nations in a League of Armed Neutrality was just a bluff that could be safely called. The outcome of his mission was Jay's Treaty (November, 1794), an agreement which in effect renounced America's claims to freedom of the seas. It gave Britain virtually as much control over the nation's commerce as it had exercised prior to the Revolution in exchange for very little—British departure from the northwestern forts, limited trading privileges in the British West Indies, and the appointment of commissioners to negotiate some other unresolved issues between the two countries. Although it was a bitter pill to swallow, it accurately reflected the existing balance of power. The state of America's military preparedness was such that when the June, 1796 deadline for British evacuation of the forts came around, the United States didn't have enough troops to garrison them and had to ask the British forces to stay on! Hamilton remarked that "if we can avoid war for ten or twelve years more, we shall have acquired a maturity" that would allow the nation to pursue a bolder foreign policy. In 1794, however, pride was a luxury America could not afford.

After hearing the terms of the treaty, a Federalist congressman predicted quite accurately that "the success of Mr. Jay will secure peace abroad and kindle war at home." Jay's Treaty created a massive public outcry. Jay commented that he could have traveled across the entire country at night by the light of the bonfires lit by crowds that hung his figure in effigy. Hamilton was showered with stones while defending the treaty at a public meeting. "The nation has been secretly divorced from France," declared an opposition paper, "and most clandestinely married to Great Britain. We are taken from the embraces of a loving wife, and find ourselves in the arms of a detestable and abandoned whore, covered with crimes, rottenness, and corruption." Washington put all his prestige on the line to persuade the Senate to approve the treaty. As Jefferson said, it was "the Colossus" of Washington's "merits with the people" that allowed the "Anglomen" to win the day by a narrow margin. Popular discontent with the course of American foreign policy eased shortly after, when Thomas Pinckney concluded a much more favorable treaty with Spain. Spain agreed to open the Mississippi and the port of New Orleans to American shipping and recognized U.S. claims to all territory east of the Mississippi and north of Spanish Florida. Still, the charge that backers of Jay's Treaty were "Samsons in the field" who "had their heads shorn by the harlot England" was a potent Republican argument in the elections of 1796.

FROM ADAMS TO JEFFERSON

By the time of the elections it was very clear that the "unanimity" that George Washington called for in public affairs was irretrievably lost. Even the President, hitherto an almost sacred figure, came under scurrilous partisan attack. Republican papers accused him of "political iniquity" and "legalized corruption," and one even charged that he had been a secret traitor during the revolutionary war, a Benedict Arnold whose crimes had gone undetected! At a meeting in Virginia, Republicans lifted their glasses to toast "a speedy death to General Washington." Washington did his best to tip the election in favor of his chosen successor, John Adams. He delayed his announcement that he would not run for a third term until September, to give the Republicans as little time as possible to drum up support for Jefferson. Even so, Adams edged out Jefferson by only three electoral votes, and Jefferson was elected Vice-President.[2]

Having the leader of the Republican opposition as his Vice-President was a thorn in the side of John Adams. An even sharper thorn, however, pricked him on the other side. There was as yet no tradition of changing the cabinet with the inauguration of a new President, and the men he inherited from the Washington administration were not only mediocre but disloyal to him: Hamilton was not among them, for he had resigned in 1795 to enter law practice. Behind the scenes, though, he played a strong political role as the leader of what became the "High Federalist" wing of the Federalist administration. During the four crisis years of his

---

[2]The Constitution did not provide for a separate vote for Vice-President in the Electoral College; the runner-up for President was made Vice-President. The framers had not worried about the awkwardness of having a President and Vice-President from different parties because they had not anticipated that political parties would develop. This arrangement created even greater difficulties in 1800, as will be seen. After the 1800 elections, an amendment to the Constitution mandated separate ballots for the two offices.

administration, Adams was caught in a withering crossfire between Republicans on his left and High Federalists on his right.

The overshadowing issue that confronted the United States when Adams took office was the rapid deterioration of its relations with France. The French government, flushed by recent military conquests, was in an impatient and aggressive mood. It saw Jay's Treaty as tantamount to an Anglo–American alliance, not altogether without reason, and viewed Adams as pro-British, again not without reason. It rejected the new American minister to France, terminated the 1778 Franco–American treaty, announced that it would hang Americans serving in the British Navy (even if they had been forcibly impressed), and began to seize and confiscate American merchant vessels. When the United States sent a distinguished special commission to France to attempt to resolve the differences, its members were informed that the negotiations could not begin until America paid the French government a huge bribe through anonymous go-betweens known only as X, Y, and Z. Charles Pinckney's response, "No, not a sixpence," would soon be blown up into the legendary and entirely fictitious "Millions for defense, but not one cent for tribute."

Millions were indeed spent for defense, however. News of the XYZ Affair produced war fever in the United States. Adams was not ready to endorse war, but he did support new appropriations to strengthen the armed services. The Navy was enlarged, and Washington was called out of retirement to serve as Commander-in-Chief of an expanded Army. He threatened to resign unless Hamilton was appointed his second-in-command with control over field operations, and Adams reluctantly complied. By the summer of 1798, French warships and hastily equipped American vessels were clashing on the high seas, with 85 French ships taken as prizes of war. The President, however, refused to go further, and kept pressing for a negotiated settlement.

The Alien and Sedition Acts

The wave of anti-French hysteria that swept the country as a result of the XYZ Affair and the commencement of undeclared naval warfare provoked the Federalist administration into striking at its critics, by passing the infamous Alien and Sedition Acts. Because recent immigrants to the United States had shown a tendency to support the Republicans, Congress restricted the access of the foreign-born to the ballot by lengthening the residence period required for citizenship from five to fourteen years. The Alien Act also empowered the President to deport or jail "dangerous" aliens. The Sedition Act made "printing, writing, or speaking in a scandalous or malicious way against the government" a crime punishable by imprisonment and heavy fines. It was written to expire immediately after the next national election.

These repressive measures were patently designed to silence all those who dissented from the Federalist view that "it is patriotism to write in favor of our government" and "sedition to write against it." The editors of several leading

Republican papers were jailed for making critical statements that were far from subversive. One man in New Jersey was arrested after a 16-gun salute to President Adams because he had quipped, "They should have fired through the President's ass." A congressman from Virginia was put behind bars for writing that Adams had an "unbounded thirst for ridiculous pomp, foolish adulation, and selfish avarice."[3]

These were isolated instances, however. The Republican charge that a "Federalist Reign of Terror" was underway was a gross exaggeration. The law was stern, but enforcement was lax. Only 25 people in the entire country were arrested for violations of the Sedition Act, and only 10 of them were actually convicted. The Republican press did not crumble under the assault; the number of opposition papers actually doubled during the three years it was in effect. More energetic enforcement of this repressive legislation was impossible, because the Republicans were not a small minority on the radical fringe. They held almost half of the seats in Congress, and were led by the author of the Declaration of Independence and the principal architect of the Constitution. Imprisoning significant numbers of them for speaking their minds might well have resulted in a civil war. Two state legislatures, those of Virginia and newly admitted Kentucky (1792), voted resolutions denouncing the Sedition Act as unconstitutional, and refused to cooperate with its enforcement. The Kentucky Resolution, drafted by Jefferson, advanced a principle the dangerous implications of which would become clear decades later—that each state was the final judge of the constitutionality of federal actions, and could "nullify" laws it found contrary to the Constitution. No other state responded to Virginia and Kentucky's call for support, but a stronger attempt at enforcement of the Sedition Act would undoubtedly have led some to do so.

In the congressional elections in the fall of 1798, the threat of all-out war with France produced a patriotic atmosphere that gave the Federalists a sweeping victory. But the fruits of victory quickly turned sour, because the quarrel between moderate Adams Federalists and Hamiltonian High Federalists became so venomous. Adams resolutely continued to work for peace with France, and did succeed in negotiating a settlement with Napoleon shortly before the 1800 elections. Hamilton was hell-bent on war with France, and denounced the negotiations as cowardly and treacherous. He saw the French crisis as an opportunity comparable to the Whiskey Rebellion. He wanted a vast enlargement of the army, and clearly hoped that another demonstration of the federal government's "power of military coercion" would intimidate the "Jacobin mobocrats" in the Republican opposition. When Adams refused to go along, Hamilton broke with the administration and worked against Adams' effort to win reelection.

---

[3]Readers may wonder why a law that seems so patent a violation of the First Amendment's guarantee of freedom of speech and the press was not declared unconstitutional by the Supreme Court. Simple politics is part of the answer—the Court was manned by Federalist judges. Beyond that, though, there is evidence that the framers of the First Amendment did not adhere to modern libertarian notions of what these freedoms meant. To them, freedom of the press meant that the government could not exercise *prior* restraint on editors. But they could be punished afterwards for publishing libelous material. The more far-reaching, modern conception of freedom was developed by Republican theorists in response to the Sedition Acts, years after the passage of the First Amendment.

The Election of 1800

Although the split in the Federalist ranks hurt Adams' chances in the 1800 elections, Jefferson's capture of the Presidency and the Republican sweep of Congress reflected deeper forces at work. In the campaign the Republicans proved more skillful at adapting to a changing political universe. Their ideology celebrated the virtue of the common man, and their back-slapping political style appealed to the masses. The Federalist conception of politics was old-fashioned and elitist. They did not "run" for office; they "stood" for office, and trusted that the public would recognize their superior merit. One Federalist candidate went down to defeat after he bluntly told a crowd, "I never will surrender my principles to the opinion of any man, and I wish no one to vote for me who is not willing to leave me free to pursue the good of my country." John Winthrop would have understood perfectly, but the rise of party politics in the 1790s drew to the polls an increasing number of voters who did not. The turnout in typical elections rose from about a quarter to around half of the adult white males over the decade, and many of these newly mobilized voters were repelled by the aloof and austere Federalist brand of deference politics, and attracted by the folksiness of the Republicans. At his inauguration Jefferson made a gesture that nicely symbolized the new political style. He was the first American President to be installed in office without a powdered wig, and he wore pantaloons rather than the traditional buckled knee breeches.

The geography of the voting in 1800 was like that in 1796, in that the Federalists carried New England and the Republicans the southern states. The different outcome was due to the fact that Jefferson won New York and a majority of Pennsylvania's electoral votes as well. In those states the votes of Germans and Scotch-Irish who disliked the English tastes of the Federalists and of frontiersmen who resented the whiskey tax tipped the balance. The swing of the middle states into the Republican camp marked the beginnings of an alliance that was to dominate national politics for much of the first half of the nineteenth century.

The Crisis of Succession

Although it was perfectly clear that Thomas Jefferson was the nation's choice for President, an unfortunate defect in the electoral procedures specified in the Constitution made it uncertain for some months whether he would actually be allowed to take office. The tight party discipline shown by Republicans chosen for the Electoral College led to an unexpected result. Both Jefferson and his Vice-Presidential running mate, Aaron Burr, each received 73 electoral votes, which threw the contest into the House of Representatives.[4] According to the Constitution, the choice of a President in such cases is not made by the newly elected House, which in this case had a strong Republican majority. It is made by the old "lame duck" Congress, which in this case was dominated by Federalists who believed Jefferson to be a fiend in human form (see box, page 194).

---

[4]This can never happen again. The Twelfth Amendment to the Constitution (1804) provides separate votes for President and Vice-President.

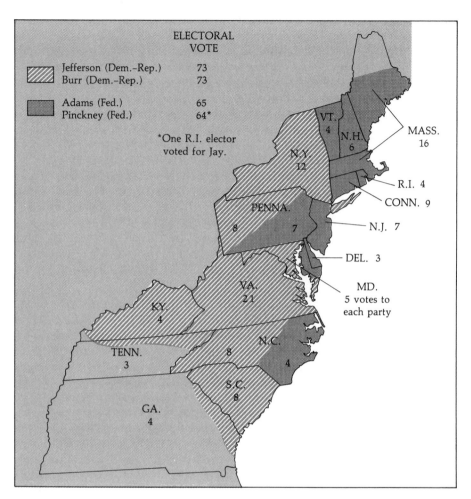

ELECTORAL
VOTE

Jefferson (Dem.–Rep.)	73	
Burr (Dem.–Rep.)	73	
Adams (Fed.)	65	
Pinckney (Fed.)	64*	

*One R.I. elector
voted for Jay.

VT. 4
N.H. 6
MASS. 16
N.Y. 12
R.I. 4
CONN. 9
PENNA. 8 · 7
N.J. 7
DEL. 3
VA. 21
MD. 5 votes to each party
KY. 4
N.C. 8 · 4
TENN. 3
S.C. 8
GA. 4

MAP 9-1
The 1800 Election
The electoral votes of Pennsylvania, Maryland, and North Carolina were split in this election. The tie vote for Jefferson and Burr was resolved in the House of Representatives.

The House divided bitterly and precisely evenly over the choice between Jefferson and Burr. After a week of quarreling, with 35 deadlocked ballots, the national government was paralyzed. A month before the inauguration, it was still unclear who would be President, and there was a real possibility that one side would act unconstitutionally and trigger a civil war. Federalists proposed that the Senate pick a temporary President until a new election could be held. Republicans promised to offer armed resistance if that were attempted, and the Virginia militia made preparations for a march on the capital. At last Hamilton intervened. Although he feared Jefferson, he loathed Burr (and would die at his hand in their famous duel four years later). Hamilton persuaded three Federalist congressmen to abstain from voting for Burr again, and Jefferson was chosen.

A FEDERALIST VIEW OF THE ISSUES IN 1800

Can serious and reflecting men look about them and doubt, that if Jefferson is elected, and the Jacobins get into authority, that those morals which protect our lives from the knife of the assassin—which guard the chastity of our wives and daughters from seduction and violence—defend our property from plunder and devastation, and shield our religion from contempt and profanation, will not be trampled upon and exploded...

In France Danton, Marat, and Robespierre, were flaming patriots—staunch democrats, and great sticklers for the rights of man. Such was the mask they wore, and do you not see that mask, which even French impudence is at present ashamed to wear, now covering the hypocrisy of our pretended republicans? Trace the history of the furious and bloody demagogues of the revolution, and then remark the correspondence with the acts of demagogues at home.... Let these men get into power, put the reins of government into their hands, and what security have you against the occurrence of the scenes which have rendered France a cemetery, and moistened her soil with the tears and blood of her inhabitants?...

—"A Christian Federalist,"
A Short Address to the Voters of Delaware, 1800

The failure of die-hard Federalist attempts to steal the election and frustrate the clear will of a majority of the electorate not only allowed Jefferson to assume the Presidency. The successful and nonviolent transfer of power from one party to another in a period of intense partisan feelings established a vital principle that was new in the history of the world—the principle that organized opposition to governing authorities is legitimate, and that the opposition is entitled to seize the reins of government when its persuasive powers enable it to build a majority constituency. However much the Federalists feared and detested Jefferson, in the end they agreed to play the game by the rules and to defer to the will of the people.

REPUBLICANS IN POWER

Thomas Jefferson liked to refer to "the revolution of 1800." Such terminology may seem surprising, because the policies of his administration certainly did not have the radical and violent character we associate with revolution in the modern world. Jefferson, however, used "revolution" in its eighteenth-century sense, meaning a circling back to an original state of affairs—that is, to the governmental philosophy as it was before the corrupting innovations of Hamilton had been introduced. In that sense, the election of 1800 did lead to revolutionary changes in the role of the federal government.

To Jefferson, that government was best "which governs least." Indeed, the third President believed that the federal government should govern hardly at all. Its functions were to conduct foreign policy and oversee the "mutual relations" of the states. To the states, the units closest to the people, Jefferson preferred to leave "the principal care of our persons, our property, and our reputation." Consequently, he set out to reverse, as much as possible, the Federalist measures enacted over the preceding decade. His energetic and shrewd political leadership of commanding Republican majorities in both houses of Congress allowed him to accomplish much of what he intended.

The grossest Federalist abuse of power had been the Alien and Sedition Acts and the accompanying tightening of immigrant naturalization procedures in 1798. They were one of Jefferson's first targets. The acts were allowed to expire, and Jefferson pressed through Congress a bill that reduced the residence requirement for citizenship from fourteen to only five years. Then he began to whittle down the federal bureaucracy. Although it was tiny in comparison with that of other countries at the time, it was "too complicated" and "too expensive" for Jefferson. He slashed the federal budget by firing tax collectors, simplifying the court system, cutting the armed forces in half, and closing down embassies abroad. Only three diplomatic missions—in Britain, France, and Spain—survived his ax. These economies made it possible for him to eliminate almost all internal taxes collected by the central government, including the hated whiskey tax. Henceforth, the money necessary to run the shrunken federal government would all come from import duties or revenues from land sales.

Of course there were limits to Jefferson's "revolution." Some aspects of the Hamiltonian program were too well entrenched to root out suddenly without causing economic chaos. The Bank of the United States continued to operate, but its influence waned, and congressional Republicans defeated a proposal to renew its charter in 1811. Repayment of the federal debt, which Hamilton saw as a permanent way of ensuring the allegiance of the wealthy classes, was much too large a task to be accomplished overnight. But Jefferson, who viewed an alliance between the wealthy and the central government as a threat to liberty, did his best to whittle down the debt. Federal revenues exceeded expenditures during most of his years in office, and the surplus was used to retire outstanding treasury notes. By the time of his retirement, the debt had been cut almost in half.

The Louisiana Purchase

These were all actions consistent with the principles Jefferson had articulated as leader of the opposition. His most memorable achievement as President, however—the Louisiana Purchase—was not. In 1763, at the close of the French and Indian Wars, France had surrendered the Louisiana Territory to Spain. In 1800 Napoleon demanded it back, and the feeble Spanish government complied. France again was a major power in North America. Extending from the Mississippi to the Rockies, the Louisiana Territory was as large as the entire United States at the time. Many Americans, including Jefferson, had already envisioned that the boundaries

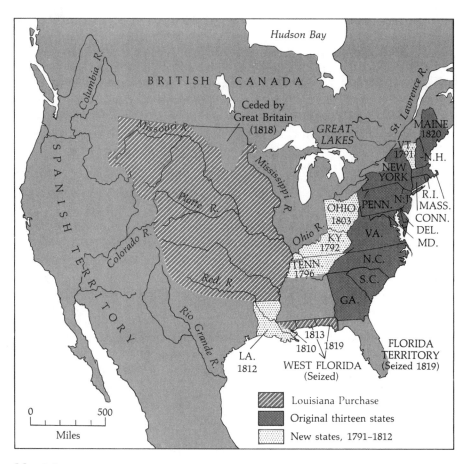

Map 9–2
The Louisiana Purchase and the Formation of New States

of the United States would someday span the continent, an aspiration that could never be achieved if a string of French colonies were planted west of the Mississippi. A more immediate cause for concern was that French possession of New Orleans would give Napoleon a stranglehold on American commerce flowing southward through the Ohio and Mississippi valleys. If France proceeded with its plan to occupy New Orleans, said Jefferson, "We must marry ourselves to the British fleet and nation."

The marriage proved unnecessary. American diplomats dispatched to France to seek assurances that the Mississippi would remain open to American shipping found to their surprise that Napoleon had begun to doubt the wisdom of building a new North American empire. He had become skeptical about holding remote colonial possessions after his best troops had been unable to suppress a slave revolt led by Toussaint L'Ouverture in Santo Domingo, and needed money to resume the war with England. These considerations, plus American threats to support a British attack on New Orleans, resulted in France's surprising 1803 offer to sell the entire Louisiana Territory to the United States for $15 million.

Jefferson was elated at the prospect, but also anguished. In his attacks on the Bank of the United States, the Sedition Acts, and other Federalist legislation, he had always insisted on strict and narrow construction of the Constitution; the powers of the federal government were limited to those explicitly set forth by the framers. And yet the Constitution contained no language authorizing the federal government to acquire territory from another country or to incorporate it into the nation. Jefferson at first sought a way out of this embarrassing difficulty by proposing an amendment to the Constitution authorizing the purchase. He wrote a Senator privately:

> I had rather ask an enlargement of power from the nation, where it is found necessary, than to assume it by a construction which would make our powers boundless. Our peculiar security is in the possession of a written Constitution. Let us not make it a blank paper by construction.

But the amendment procedure is slow, and there was a real danger that the mercurial and devious Napoleon would withdraw his extraordinary offer before it could be completed. Under heavy pressure from his advisers and congressional Republicans, Jefferson swallowed his constitutional scruples and backed the purchase. To secure permanent navigation rights on the Mississippi, a doubling of the national domain, and the withdrawal of a major European imperial power from North America, even the leading exponent of strict construction was willing to risk reducing the Constitution to a "blank paper by construction."

The Failure of "Peaceable Coercion"

Another round in the European war between Britain and France broke out in 1803, posing acute difficulties for Jefferson and finally drawing the country into war in 1812, under his successor, James Madison. Again the United States, the world's largest neutral trader, was caught in the crossfire between great powers fighting a no-holds-barred contest for national survival. Because Napoleon's army was the strongest in Europe, Britain's strategy was to strangle France economically by blockading the Continent. Beginning in 1805 the Royal Navy regularly stopped American ships, searched them, and confiscated those bearing goods to or from Britain's enemies. Napoleon responded with trade restrictions of his own that authorized French confiscation of neutral vessels that had undergone a British search or called at a British port.

Although Britain and France were equally disrespectful of America's neutral rights, Britain came in for more blame. The traditional Republican dislike of aristocratic Britain was as strong as ever, and Britain's naval supremacy made her the greater threat to American shipping. Even more galling, perhaps, was the fact that the British resumed the practice of boarding American vessels and impressing anyone they judged to be British into service in the Royal Navy, whether they held American citizenship or not. British law held that allegiance was "indefeasible" and denied the right of expatriation that was a cornerstone of American law. About 10,000 Americans were spirited away from their ships on these grounds. The British government's determination to strictly enforce its impressment policies was made vividly clear in 1807, when a British man-of-war stopped an American warship, the *Chesapeake*, fired three broadsides that killed or wounded two dozen crew members, and carried away four alleged English deserters.

The news of the firing on the *Chesapeake* inflamed American opinion like nothing since the battle of Lexington. Jefferson, however, resisted the clamor for war, confident that he could protect American rights by means of economic pressure. Again displaying a willingness to interpret the Constitution very broadly when it suited his purpose, he announced a sweeping embargo that made it illegal for American merchant vessels to leave for foreign ports. Through such "peaceable coercion" he believed that Britain and France could be forced to lift their restrictions on American commerce. Jefferson's eagerness to avoid the horrors of war was commendable, but the embargo did not achieve its aim. During the two years it was in effect, the warring superpowers made no meaningful concessions, while American commerce went into a tailspin. The northern ports, especially those in New England, were hit hardest. The sagging popularity of the Federalist Party there was revived by the embargo, and bitter quarrels between "Anglomen" and "Gallomen" resumed again. Federalist leaders were so convinced that Jefferson was a tool of the French that they seriously discussed secession from the Union and carried on secret negotiations with the British Foreign Minister. The Federalist governor of Connecticut took a leaf from the pages of the Virginia and Kentucky Resolutions and asserted his right to prevent federal agents from enforcing the embargo within his state. New England was very close to rebellion by the time the Republicans backed off and relaxed the embargo in March, 1809.

A Republican War

James Madison, who succeeded Jefferson in 1809, continued to believe in "peaceful coercion," but had no more success than his predecessor in making it work. Instead of initiating a complete embargo he attempted first to allow free trade with all nations except Britain and France. Then he authorized trade with the belligerents as well, with the proviso that the United States would bar trade with one of the contending parties if the other lifted its restrictions. Neither policy had the desired effect, and anti-British sentiment grew stronger. The elections of 1810 returned a Congress with a sizable contingent of young expansionist-minded "War Hawks" from frontier states, who argued that war with Britain would provide an opportunity to invade and annex Canada. In June, 1812, an angry and frustrated Madison concluded that to accept continued humiliation on the high seas by the great powers would threaten the ability of the republic to survive in a world of overbearing monarchies. Every Federalist congressman voted against the war declaration, but the large Republican majorities in both houses were sufficient to carry it.

For Americans the war was a sobering experience in many ways. The American militia who invaded Canada in the expectation that they would be welcomed as liberators met with stiff resistance, and were unable to hold an inch of Canadian soil. At sea American gunboats initially won some impressive victories against the Royal Navy, and American privateers captured some 1,300 British merchant ships. Within a year, however, Britain had thrown up a blockade which kept both American warships and trading vessels bottled up in port. The abdication of Napoleon in 1814 freed British troops for the American campaign, and the British began a series of powerful counteroffensives. An assault against ill-defended Washington, D.C. that summer forced Madison and the rest of the government into humiliating flight, and the British set fire to the White House, the Capitol, and much of the rest of the city before moving on. With other powerful British attacks in the planning stage, it began to seem that "the Second War for American Independence" might end in the collapse of the republic—if not the collapse, at least the dismemberment.

New England Federalists were outspoken in their criticism of the war, and refused to provide the militia and war loans for which the administration pleaded. The war revived the secessionist talk first sparked by the embargo, as well as suggestions that the seceded states would make a separate peace with Britain. The climax of the Federalist antiwar drive was a convention that met in Hartford, Connecticut in December of 1814. Although the actual resolutions approved at the meeting were relatively moderate, the Hartford Convention demonstrated the Federalists' unwillingness to rally 'round the flag, even when the nation's capital lay in ashes. Whether that stand would pay political dividends or not would depend upon the outcome of the war.

Fortunately for the Republicans—and the republic—the British chose not to exploit the margin of military superiority they had achieved by the end of 1814. Wearied by two decades of warfare with France and worried about unsettled conditions in Europe, the British government was ready to settle for the antebellum status quo. On Christmas Eve of 1814, American and British representatives concluded a peace treaty at Ghent, Belgium. It left America's boundaries unchanged, but was silent about both impressment and America's rights as a neutral trader. As a Federalist remarked sourly, "We made war, charging the enemy with very gross enormities, and we made peace, saying not one word about them."

The Republicans had nothing to fear from Federalist critics by then, however. The Hartford Convention had given the party a stigma of disloyalty from which it never recovered. If the war really ended in a draw, most Americans were ready to see it as a victory and to credit the Republicans for the accomplishment. The happy news from Ghent coincided with even happier news of a final contest, fought two weeks after the treaty was concluded but before word of it had reached the battlefield. General Andrew Jackson's troops had crushed a British assault on New Orleans, inflicting more than 2,000 casualties on the invaders while suffering only *two dozen* of their own. A tidal wave of patriotic jubilation over the Battle of New Orleans swept the country and obliterated the Federalist party forever.

The War of 1812 was a crucial turning point in American foreign relations. In the first quarter century of the nation's history, European power rivalries forced painful choices that divided the nation into warring camps. In the century between the peace of Ghent and the outbreak of World War I, by contrast, America was left free to concentrate its energies on essentially internal affairs. There were some diplomatic disputes with Britain over the location of the boundary between Canada and the United States, but these were all settled by peaceful negotiation. The vicissitudes of European politics would no longer distract attention from the task of creating what Jefferson called "an empire of liberty" by expanding across the continent.

Tecumseh and the Pan-Indian Movement

The War of 1812 was also a crucial turning point in the history of relations between white Americans and the red men and women who occupied the land that would become the "empire of liberty." Before the war, the Indians of the interior had important external allies to whom they could turn for support against encroaching whites. From their base in Canada, the British had forged alliances with northwestern tribes, believing that a strong Indian buffer state would check temptations Americans might feel to annex Canadian territory. In the Southwest, Spain pursued similar policies to protect their colony in Florida (which included not only present day Florida but portions of Alabama and Mississippi). The Indians had more than allies. They had an extraordinary new leader—the Shawnee brave, Tecumseh—who was beginning to unify them in a campaign to put an end to the further selling of land to whites. The defeat of Tecumseh during the War of 1812 and the abandonment of British and Spanish backing for an Indian buffer state afterwards was a watershed in American history.

The flood of white migration into the trans-Appalachian interior that began after the Revolution provoked conflict with the Indian tribes already residing there. When the Indians resisted the interlopers violently, they were dealt with militarily. After tribes in the Ohio–Indiana area defeated militiamen in several clashes, the U.S. army overcame them at the Battle of Fallen Timbers near Toledo, Ohio, in 1794. Most Indian land, however, was taken with at least a veneer of legality. The dozens of competing tribes were as suspicious of each other as they were of white Americans, and were easily played off against each other. American government officials cajoled, bullied, and bribed petty chiefs into signing over title to lands, often lands to which other tribes had at least as strong a claim. By this means, for example, American settlers obtained title to the entire southeastern quarter of Ohio plus the future sites of Detroit and Chicago for $10,000.

The most farsighted Indian leaders were determined to put an end to the policy of piecemeal cessions. In the Treaty of Greenville after the Battle of Fallen Timbers, the United States pledged that no further land would be purchased from the chiefs of individual tribes; future sales, it agreed, would only be made with the authorization of the whole body of northwestern Indians. In 1804, however, this inconvenient pledge was ignored by William Henry Harrison, the governor of Indiana Territory, who negotiated the transfer of another large chunk of Indian hunting ground to the United States in the customary manner.

This new encroachment was the issue that catapulted into prominence Tecumseh and his brother the Prophet. They preached a revolutionary gospel. Indians should reject all Western cultural influences and return to their ancient ways. They should abstain from firewater, to put an end to the alcoholism that was devastating tribes that had close contact with white traders. And they should insist

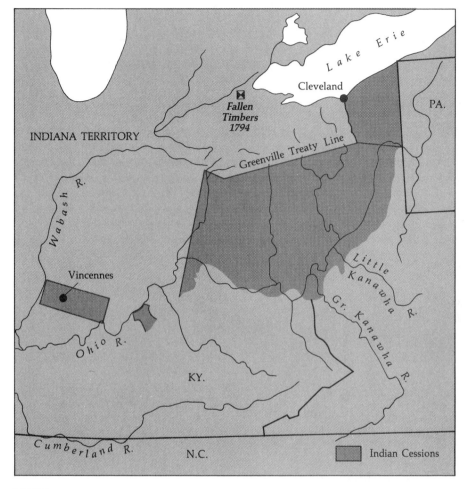

MAP 9-3
Indian Land Cessions in the Treaty of Greenville, 1795

that the United States honor the terms of the Treaty of Greenville. A congress of all the tribes would be created; it would hold all remaining Indian land in common, and no further sales could be made without its approval.

From his base in Indiana, Tecumseh tramped from village to village, from Wisconsin to Florida. He was a magnetic orator who won a startling number of converts. Drunkenness declined; a sense of common purpose that transcended parochial tribal loyalties began to spread. William Henry Harrison warned his superiors in Washington that if Tecumseh could unite the major tribes of the Great Lakes, Ohio Valley, and Gulf Coast behind him, he could build an empire that "would rival in glory Mexico or Peru."

Whether Tecumseh could have completely overcome ancient intertribal rivalries had he been given enough time will never be known. Perhaps not. As it happened, in any event, Harrison forced him into war before he had the oppor-

TECUMSEH'S SPEECH TO GOVERNOR WILLIAM HENRY HARRISON, VINCENNES, INDIANA, 1810

You endeavour to make distinctions [by negotiating with each tribe separately].... You endeavor to prevent the Indians from doing what we, their leaders, wish them to do—unite and consider their land the common property. The way, the only way to stop this evil is for all the red men to unite in claiming a common and equal right in the land, as it was first, and should be now—for it never was divided and belongs to all. No tribe has a right to sell, even to each other, much less to strangers who demand all, and will take no less. Sell a country! Why not sell the air, the clouds and the great sea, as well as the earth? Did not the Great Spirit make them all for the use of his children? How can we have confidence in the white people? When Jesus Christ came upon the earth, you killed Him and nailed Him to a cross. The states have set the example of forming a union among all the fires [states]—why should they censure the Indians for following it?

tunity to cement all the alliances he was trying to build. While Tecumseh was off winning recruits in the South, Harrison took advantage of ambiguous instructions from Washington and marched upon his headquarters along the banks of Tippecanoe Creek. The U.S. Army routed the defenders in the ensuing battle in November, 1811. Although he realized that some tribes were not yet ready to back him, Tecumseh had no alternative but to fight. His army was the closest thing to a united pan-Indian resistance movement in American history, but it was not the solid front he had envisioned. A number of tribes remained loyal to the United States and took up arms against Tecumseh's forces. With the outbreak of the war of 1812, Tecumseh and his men fled to Canada and fought in support of the British. He was killed in battle in 1813.

The death of Tecumseh and many of his warriors was a fatal blow to the pan-Indian cause. No other Indian leader had his breadth of vision and charismatic appeal. Nor would there again be an opportunity for an Indian spokesman to obtain support from other powers hostile to the United States. By the end of the war the British were convinced that Canada was a secure part of their empire, and they abandoned their commitment to the idea of an Indian buffer state. The southern tribes that had looked to Spain for aid were similarly left on their own because of Spain's inability to withstand American pressures on Florida. The United States annexed part of Florida in 1810, another slice during the war, and the remainder after an invasion led by Andrew Jackson in 1818. The withdrawal of the British and Spanish meant that American whites could continue their relentless thrust into the interior without any serious consideration of Indian interests and aspirations.

SUGGESTED READINGS

John C. Miller, *The Federalist Era, 1789–1801* (1960) is a useful overview of political developments in the 1790s. Lawrence S. Kaplan, *Colonies into Nation: American Diplomacy, 1763–1801* (1972) thoughtfully reviews the course of foreign affairs. Richard Hofstadter's *The Idea of a Party System: The Rise of Legitimate Opposition in the United States, 1780–1840* (1969) deftly analyzes shifting political conceptions. Joseph Charles, *The Origins of the American Party System* (1956) and William Nisbet Chambers, *Political Parties in a New Nation: The American Experience, 1776–1809* (1963) reveal more about the concrete issues that divided the two camps. Rudolph M. Bell, *Party and Faction in American Politics: The House of Representatives, 1789–1801* (1974) offers a statistical analysis of party voting patterns in Congress.

For biographies of the two key personalities around whom the conflict focused, see Forrest McDonald, *Alexander Hamilton: A Biography* (1979) and Merrill Jensen, *Thomas Jefferson and the New Nation: A Biography* (1970). The intensity of the ideological battles of the era and the fragility of the Republican experiment are best conveyed in Richard Buel, Jr., *Securing the Revolution: Ideology in American Politics, 1789–1815* (1972), John V. Zvesper, *Political Philosophy and Rhetoric: A Study of the Origins of American Party Politics* (1977), Lance Banning, *The Jeffersonian Persuasion: Evolution of a Party Ideology* (1978), and James M. Banner, *To the Hartford Convention: The Federalists and the Origins of Party Politics in Massachusetts, 1789–1815* (1970). Richard H. Kohn, *Eagle and Sword: The Federalists and the Creation of a Military Establishment in America, 1783–1802* (1975) sheds new light on Federalist aims. On the Federalist attempt to silence the opposition, see James Morton Smith, *Freedom's Fetters: The Alien and Sedition Laws and American Civil Liberties* (1956) and Leonard Levy, *Legacy of Suppression: Freedom of Speech and Press in Early American History* (1960).

Henry Adams, *History of the United States During the Administration of Jefferson and Madison*, 9 vols. (1889–91) is now outmoded on many points, but the author's penetrating insights and brilliant writing make it still worth reading. The first six chapters, published separately as *The United States in 1800* (1955), are splendid reading. Merrill Peterson, *The Jefferson Image in the American Mind* (1960) traces shifting opinion about the third President from his time to the twentieth century. Daniel Sisson, *The American Revolution of 1800* (1974) emphasizes how strongly Jefferson sought to reverse Federalist policies, as does Noble Cunningham, Jr., *The Process of Government under Jefferson* (1978). James S. Young, *The Washington Community, 1800–1828* (1966) is a superb analysis of the weakness of the central government throughout the period. Alexander De Conde, *The Affair of Louisiana* (1976) is a full account of that remarkable bargain. David Hackett Fischer, *The Revolution of American Conservatism: The Federalist Party in the Era of Jeffersonian Democracy* (1965) and Linda K. Kerber, *Federalists in Dissent: Imagery and Ideology in Jeffersonian America* (1970) illuminate the unhappy fate of Jefferson's opposition. On the crisis that led to the second war with Britain, see Bradford Perkins, *Prologue to War: England and the United States, 1805–1812* (1963) and Roger Brown, *The Republic in Peril: 1812* (1964). Clashes with the Indians are treated in Reginald Horsman, *Expansion and American Indian Policy, 1783–1812* (1967).

Chapter Ten

Industrial and Urban Development in the Northeast

*A*t the opening of the nineteenth century, the United States was an economically backward agrarian society. The forces that were transforming Western Europe into an urban, industrial society had barely touched America. There were no giant factories and mills like those of Manchester or Birmingham in the United States. No American city had a population as large as 100,000—the size of Allentown, Pennsylvania and Peoria, Illinois today. Only one American in sixteen lived in a community with as many as 2,500 residents, a third the proportion of city dwellers in France and a fifth that in England. Six out of seven American workers were farmers, as compared with only one Englishman in three; in fact, during the first decade of the new century the fraction of agricultural workers in the labor force actually increased slightly. The farming methods used in Jefferson's republic were nearly as primitive as those employed by the first white settlers two centuries before.

The six decades that followed were an era of extraordinary expansion and transformation. The population grew to a stunning six times its number in 1800. By the time of the Civil War, it had reached 31 million, greater than that of Britain and rapidly approaching that of France. The American people had spilled over the Appalachian barrier and spread across the continent. Less than half a million people lived west of the mountains in 1800; by 1860, more than 15 million people, half of the national total, resided in the West. A new state was added to the Union an average of once every three years in the period, raising the total from 16 to 34.

While millions of Americans were heeding newspaper editor Horace Greeley's advice to "go West, young man, go West," millions of others were leaving the country for the city. The proportion of city dwellers tripled in the most rapid burst

Winslow Homer's 1868 drawing, "Bell-Time," depicts workers—mostly women—leaving the mills at Lawrence, Massachusetts after a 13-hour work day.

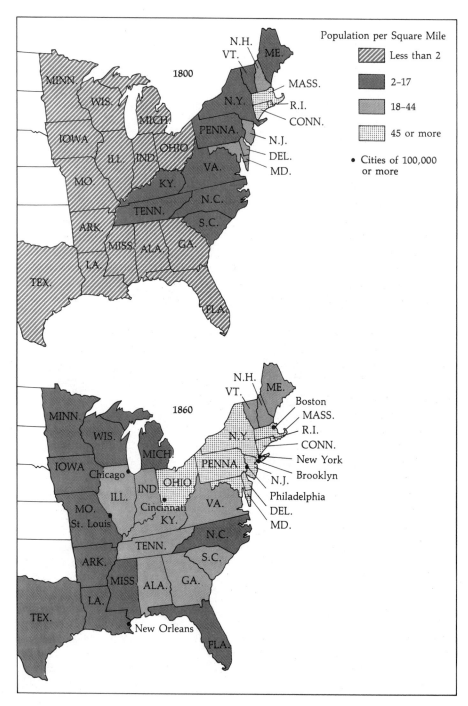

MAP 10-1
Population Density by State, 1800 and 1860

of urban development in American history. By 1860, nine American cities exceeded 100,000 in population, as compared to seven in Britain. Although there was no American London, the sprawling New York–Brooklyn complex had well over a million inhabitants, and Philadelphia over half a million. The simple agrarian republic cherished by Thomas Jefferson had ceased to exist. Indeed, the proportion of Americans who made their living as farmers had dropped from over 80 percent to just over 50 percent, a sharper decline than in any other period of our history. The Industrial Revolution—the most profound change in living and working patterns since man learned to cultivate crops and domesticate animals 10,000 years before—had reached the United States. And the character of American agriculture had changed dramatically as well, from a largely subsistence to a commercial activity. New farming methods and equipment allowed a shrinking proportion of the population to produce enough food to supply the soaring American urban population and a growing export market as well.

Examination of the causes and social consequences of this surge of economic energy must begin with the northeastern section of the United States, which experienced the most sudden and thorough changes in this period. Subsequent chapters on the slave South and the free farming states of the Midwest will portray the very different economic and social structures of those regions and clarify their role in the national economy.

THE INDUSTRIAL REVOLUTION IN AMERICA

In 1851 the eminent Presbyterian minister, Horace Bushnell, visited the small town of Litchfield, Connecticut, near the farm where he had grown up. His address at the town's bicentennial celebration examined the transformation of New England society in the course of his lifetime. He had witnessed, he declared, "a complete revolution in domestic life and social manners." He had been born in what he called "the age of homespun," a time when subsistence agriculture and "domestic manufactures" prevailed in the Northeast. The traditional farmhouse had been "a

TABLE 10–1
Percentage of the American Labor Force
in Agriculture, 1800–60

1800	83%
1810	84
1820	79
1830	71
1840	63
1850	55
1860	53

factory in the field." Its inhabitants spun, wove, cut, and sewed the simple homespun garments worn by ordinary people, and made their own soap and candles, pickles and sausages, furniture, quilts, and coffins. And the farm was "a grower and producer for the house," providing virtually all of the family's food but little in the way of a surplus to be marketed. Money was rarely seen in significant amounts, and there was little need for it except to pay taxes. Work that was beyond the competence of most families and required a specialist—a blacksmith, a shoemaker, or a tanner—was paid for by barter (see box).

Half a century later, when Bushnell spoke, few families of the Northeast grew their own food or wore clothing made from wool grown on their own farms. Large numbers of them had left the farm for the city, and were buying food produced in the West with cash wages they earned in industrial or commercial establishments. The keeper of a diary who noted the clothing worn by women at services in a Northampton, Massachusetts church one day in 1841 saw almost no one in homespun; they were clad in factory-made calicoes, muslins, and silks. An industrial revolution like that which transformed the economy of great Britain at the end of the eighteenth century was well advanced in America by the middle of the nineteenth century.

Technological Innovation

The Industrial Revolution multiplied the productive powers of man many times over because it mechanized production and increased division of labor. Machines driven by water or steam power were substituted for scarce human skills and limited human energies. By 1860 inanimate sources of power were generating five million horsepower of energy in the United States each year—the equivalent of adding 100 million workers to the labor force! The breaking down of work tasks into many discrete jobs, the assignment of each to specialists who did nothing else, and the careful coordination of the work process in factories or large shops also reduced costs and increased output per worker.

America's first technological innovations were borrowed from Britain, the world's first industrial nation. Although British manufacturers and the British government sought to protect their technical secrets in a variety of ways, including a ban on the emigration of skilled mechanics, they were not successful. America's first textile mill was founded by an English immigrant, Samuel Slater, in Pawtucket, Rhode Island in 1790; he built water-powered spinning machinery of a kind familiar to him at home. The large new mill built in Waltham, Massachusetts in 1813 used power looms copied from the latest British models.

The imitative stage soon passed. A group of native American mechanics and engineers emerged to make original contributions to the productive arts. Eli Whitney of Connecticut not only perfected the cotton gin (see Chapter 11). He also developed a revolutionary new method for making muskets with identical interchangeable parts. Until then—even in advanced Great Britain—mass production of complicated items was impossible because each part of the final product was tailor-made and then patiently fitted together by a skilled craftsman. Whitney learned how to make the separate pieces of the musket to such precise tolerances that this slow and costly stage could be skipped. The barrels, stocks, bolts, and triggers that came out of his plant were sufficiently identical to fit together interchangeably. This "American system" of manufacturing was especially well-suited to a country like the United States, which lacked an adequate supply of experienced artisans, and it proved readily adaptable in other industries. It soon was being used to make watches and clocks, sewing machines, farm machinery, and the famed Colt revolver.

There were other important technological breakthroughs as well—Oliver Evans' amazingly modern automated flour mill, Jacob Perkins' nail-making machine, and Charles Goodyear's vulcanization process for toughening rubber, for example. An English visitor at the time of the Civil War marveled:

> We find Americans producing a machine even to peel apples; another to beat eggs; a third to clean knives; a fourth to wring clothes; in fact there is scarcely a purpose to which human hands have been ordinarily employed for which some ingenious attempt is not made to find a substitute in a cheap and efficient labor-saving machine.

A simple statistic indicates that he did not exaggerate. In 1800, only 41 patents were granted to American inventors; in 1860, 4,357, more than a hundred times as many, were issued.

Sources of Industrial Capital

Labor-saving machinery is costly. Five hundred employees of a textile mill equipped with power-driven machinery can produce more cloth per year than five

ELI WHITNEY
(1765–1825)

Eli Whitney was the embodiment of Yankee ingenuity. As a farm boy in Westboro, Massachusetts, Eli was far happier tinkering in his father's workshop than he was at school. He learned to make and repair violins and became skilled at shaping metal into nails, hatpins, and other useful objects. He thought that he needed more formal education, though, and taught school long enough to save the funds to put himself through Yale. After graduating in 1792, he moved to Georgia as an apprentice law student. While living on a plantation owned by the widow of General Nathanael Greene, he spent more time fixing up the place than he did at the law books. Mrs. Greene encouraged him to put his mechanical talents to work at developing a machine to remove the sticky seeds from the short staple cotton plant. In ten days he devised a primitive cotton gin, and by April, 1793 had developed a much-improved model. He obtained a patent on the device, and moved north to New Haven, Connecticut to manufacture it in quantity. The gin was too simple and too easily copied to preserve its inventor's monopoly. Whitney won a series of legal battles against patent infringement, but lost the war. The cotton gin revolutionized the southern economy, but Whitney reaped almost no profits from it.

He did much better financially from his innovations in the production of firearms. In 1798 Whitney was awarded a federal contract to make 10,000 muskets by a radically new method—the manufacture of interchangeable parts. Each copy of a particular part of the gun would be so much like any other that the final product could be assembled speedily and cheaply. It proved exceptionally difficult to build the machine tools required to make the scheme work, and it took him eight rather than two years to fulfill the contract. But he persisted, finally turning out a complex product of high quality without a labor force of skilled gunsmiths. Whitney's "American system" of manufacturing was a godsend in an industrializing country without a class of traditional artisans, and it quickly spread to other industries.

thousand workers turning out homespun with spinning wheels and hand looms. Their superior productivity depends on the expensive machinery they operate, and some individual, group, or institution has to provide the capital to pay for it. Funds to finance industrial development in the Northeast first became available as a result of the economic dislocation caused by Jefferson's trade embargo and the War of 1812. The flow of British textiles into the United States was halted for several years, creating an opportunity for American producers to enter the market sheltered from the competition of well-established English firms. The opportunity seemed especially appealing to Francis Cabot Lowell and a group of other wealthy Boston merchants—"the Boston Associates"—who could no longer carry on their once flourishing foreign trading business because of the conflict. The riches they had reaped from those activities went into the building of the enormous and technologically advanced mill at Waltham in 1813, and later into the creation of the mill towns of Chicopee, Lowell, and Lawrence, Massachusetts.

New institutional sources of industrial capital—banks and insurance companies—became increasingly available at the same time. They encouraged individual saving, and made accumulated funds available to entrepreneurs. In 1800 there were only 28 banks in the entire United States, with a capital stock of $17 million; by 1818 the country had 300 banks, with assets of $160 million; the number exceeded 1,500 by 1860, and their capital stock was over $1 billion. The proliferation of life insurance companies also contributed to the stock of capital available to manufacturers; they sought good long-term investments in order to pay the claims of their customers, and were convinced of America's industrial future.

The Transportation Revolution and the National Market

The greatest single barrier to American economic development at the opening of the nineteenth century was the dismal state of its internal transportation system. No part of Britain is more than 70 miles from the sea, making it relatively easy and inexpensive to transport raw materials to factories and to deliver finished products to consumers. By contrast, a large and growing fraction of the American population lived hundreds of miles from the coast. It cost only $9 to ship a ton of goods across the Atlantic Ocean; it cost that much to send a ton of cargo a mere *30 miles* over the primitive American wagon roads of the day. The country's zooming population meant there was a huge potential market for machine-made items. But without radical transportation improvements, the potential could not be realized.

The first wave of innovation in transportation came early in the new century, with the construction of thousands of "turnpikes" by state governments and private companies that charged a toll for their use. Roads for carriages, stage coaches, and wagons soon connected the coastal cities and extended into the interior. These roads eased interurban communication and trade, and facilitated the westward movement of settlers. But most of these roads were inadequate for shipping heavy commodities economically. One indication of their quality is an Ohio law of 1804, requiring that all stumps *more than a foot high* be removed from

THE STEAMBOAT COMES TO
HANNIBAL, MISSOURI, 1840s

After all these years I can picture that old time to myself now, just as it was then: the white town drowsing in the sunshine of a summer's morning; the streets empty, or pretty nearly so; one or two clerks sitting in front of the Water Street stores, with their splint-bottomed chairs tilted back against the walls, chins on breasts, hats slouched over their faces, asleep—with shingle-shavings enough around to show what broke them down; a sow and a litter of pigs loafing along the sidewalk, doing a good business in watermelon rinds and seeds; two or three lonely little freight piles scattered about the "levee"; a pile of "skids" on the slope of the stone-paved wharf, and the fragrant town drunkard asleep in the shadow of them; two or three wood flats at the head of the wharf, but nobody to listen to the peaceful lapping of the wavelets against them; the great Mississippi, the majestic, the magnificent Mississippi, rolling its mile-wide tide along, shining in the sun; the dense forest away on the other side; the "point" above the town, and the "point" below. Presently a film of dark smoke appears above one of those remote "points"; instantly a negro drayman, famous for his quick eye and prodigious voice, lifts up the cry, "S-t-e-a-m-boat a-comin'!" and the scene changes! The town drunkard stirs, the clerks wake up, a furious clatter of drays follows, every house and store pours out a human contribution, and all in a twinkling the dead town is alive and moving. Drays, carts, men, boys, all go hurrying from many quarters to a common center, the wharf. Assembled there, the people fasten their eyes upon the coming boat as upon a wonder they are seeing for the first time. And the boat is rather a handsome sight, too. She is long and sharp and trim and pretty;

state roads! In a country dependent on such roads, corn and wheat produced in Ohio could not yet be exchanged for textiles and shoes made in Massachusetts.

The steamboat provided a greater spur to long distance trade. Introduced shortly before the War of 1812, steamers soon became the dominant form of transportation on rivers, lakes, and coastal waters. Although it was widely used along the Atlantic and in the Great Lakes, the steamboat had its most dramatic effect in the great valley of the Mississippi, where more than a thousand massive paddle-wheelers were in operation by 1860. To ship 100 pounds upstream from New Orleans to Louisville in a barge pulled by mules cost $5; the steamboat took it for less than 15¢.

Steamboats revolutionized water transportation, but the effect was limited to the supply of waterways. Nature, alas, had not blessed North America with navi-

she had two tall, fancy-topped chimneys, with a gilded device of some kind swung between them; a fanciful pilot-house, all glass and "gingerbread," perched on the top of the "texas" deck behind them; the paddle-boxes are gorgeous with a picture or with gilded rays above the boat's name; the boiler-deck, the hurricane-deck, and the texas deck are fenced and ornamented with clean white railings; there is a flag gallantly flying from the jack-staff; the furnace doors are open and the fires glaring bravely; the upper decks are black with passengers; the captain stands by the big bell, calm, imposing, the envy of all; great volumes of the blackest smoke are rolling and tumbling out of the chimneys—a husbanded grandeur created with a bit of pitchpine just before arriving at a town; the crew are grouped on the forecastle; the broad stage is run far out over the port bow, and an envied deck-hand stands picturesquely on the end of it with a coil of rope in his hand; the pent steam is screaming through the gauge-cocks; the captain lifts his hand, a bell rings, the wheels stop; then they turn back, churning the water to foam, and the steamer is at rest. Then such a scramble as there is to get aboard, and to get ashore, and to take in freight and to discharge freight, all at one and the same time; and such a yelling and cursing as the mates facilitate it all with! Ten minutes later the steamer is under way again, with no flag on the jack-staff and no black smoke issuing from the chimneys. After ten more minutes the town is dead again, and the town drunkard asleep by the skids once more.

—Mark Twain, *Life on the Mississippi*, 1883

gable rivers linking the East and the West; not a single major artery penetrated the Appalachian barrier. But Nature's oversight could be remedied by human action—the construction of canals through which barges, laden with freight, could be cheaply towed. Barely a hundred miles of canals, only three of them more than two miles long, existed in 1817 when the New York state legislature authorized a breathtaking scheme—a 364-mile artificial waterway through the wilderness between Albany and Buffalo, which would connect the Atlantic Ocean with the Great Lakes. A stunning feat of engineering, the Erie Canal was an immediate and spectacular success. After its completion in 1825, freight rates between New York and Buffalo fell by more than 90 percent. A canal building craze swept the nation. Within a year a hundred major canal projects were underway. By 1840 more than 3,300 miles of artificial passages had been created, forging new links between East

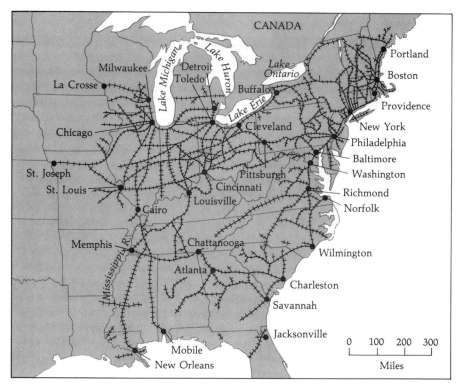

MAP 10-2
The Rail Network in 1860

and West, between the upcountry and the tidewater areas of the eastern states, and between the Ohio–Mississippi River system and the Great Lakes in the agricultural hinterland.

Impressive as they were, these achievements in canal building were soon overshadowed by an almost simultaneous development—the building of a national railroad network. First developed in England in 1825, the railroad proved uniquely well-suited to America, with its vast unsettled plains and its multiplying population. Less than 100 miles of track had been laid by 1830. Only ten years later, the total stood at an amazing 3,328 miles, almost twice the mileage in all of Europe. The rail system was already as extensive as the canal network. Rails could reach points inaccessible by canal, since they were not limited by the location of existing waterways. Unlike the canals, they were not put out of commission by freezing weather. And trains were much faster than boats towed by mules. In 1800 it took four weeks to travel from New York City to Detroit; in 1860 it was an overnight trip. Canal building therefore came to a halt in the 1840s, while the rail network was extended another 5,500 miles. An even more dramatic rail construction boom followed in the next decade, multiplying total track mileage fivefold and making the railroads the nation's first billion-dollar industry by 1860.

The Transportation Revolution made the United States a single, vast market through which goods could flow quickly and cheaply. By the time of the Civil War, approximately ten million people lived in New England and the Middle Atlantic states, the industrial heartland. The industrial transformation of the Northeast could never have proceeded so rapidly had there been only those ten million customers to purchase the textiles, shoes, rifles, clocks, and countless other products of Northeastern factories. But there were more than twenty million people in the West and South who could be reached as well. The larger the potential market, the greater the incentive to produce on a scale large enough to support costly technological innovation. A ten thousand dollar machine that cuts a penny off the cost of manufacturing a carpenter's nail will not pay for itself unless at least one million nails can be sold; if there is a market for several million nails; the machine will yield a handsome profit. The immensity of the national market that opened up to northeastern industry in these years therefore provided a crucial stimulus to development.

The Labor Supply

Some of the workers who toiled in the first American factories were artisans whose special skills became outmoded due to technological advances. Such was the case in the boot and shoe industry in the 1850s, for example, where mechanization and the minute division of tasks into simple operations eliminated the need to hire well-paid workers capable of making a finished shoe by hand. Master craftsmen who refused to accept lower wages and preferred to work in the traditional manner had little bargaining power; employers could replace them with "green hands" who could easily learn how to operate the machines.

The United States, however, did not have a large artisan class. The most important source of labor for the early factories was the countryside. After two centuries of enormously rapid growth, the population of the Northeast had become too dense for the seven children in the average farm family to acquire a farm of their own in the region where they grew up. Furthermore, much of the soil was too poor for farming to be profitable in the face of new competition from western produce flowing in along the Erie and other canals. "There is not a farm in New Hampshire or Massachusetts which I would take as a gift and be obliged to cultivate it," said Senator Isaac Bates in 1844. Some of these surplus young men and women were able to remain in agriculture by moving on to Ohio or Indiana. The open frontier, as the great historian Frederick Jackson Turner later observed, was "a safety valve" preventing economic discontent in the East from building up to dangerous levels. But the valve was too constricted to release all the pressure. Many lacked the financial resources to travel so far and to buy land, seed, livestock, and other essentials. The cotton mills of Lowell and the shoe factories of Lynn, however grim, were more attractive alternatives than living on a farm too small and unproductive to support the younger generation.

Young men who could scrape up enough money to pay the fare West could find work as hired hands, and if they were frugal enough could in time save up enough cash to buy their own farms. Young women could not. That accounts for one of the most striking characteristics of the early factory labor force—it was predominantly made up of young females. By 1832, in firms with 150 or more employees, the majority of workers were women; in the big textile factories, the figure was more than 80 percent. The boarding houses erected by the Boston Associates in Waltham, Lowell, and other mill towns provided a carefully policed environment to appease parental fears that their daughters would be corrupted by an urban environment. Girls who worked in the mills a few years could save a sizable sum, and then frequently boarded a train to rejoin their fiancé in Illinois. Instead of a permanent proletariat, the labor force was made up of a "succession of learners." The boarding house pattern prevailed in northern New England. South of Massachusetts, employers hired workers in family units whenever possible, the larger the family the better (see box). Women and children as young as nine made up the bulk of the factory labor force there, too.

The pool of surplus Yankee women and children began to dry up in the 1830s and 1840s, because the birth rate in the countryside dropped precipitously. The slack was taken up by an influx of European immigrants. Some of the newcomers—Germans and Scandinavians in particular—brought enough funds to travel West and take up farming, or were skilled craftsmen who entered trades that had not yet been mechanized. But most of the Irish fleeing the hideous Potato Famine of the 1840s and a good many of the English, Scottish, and Welsh immigrants in these years arrived with neither capital nor skills. They flocked to the factories, and by the time of the Civil War had largely replaced native women and children.

The character of the labor pool available to American employers shaped the character of industrial development. When England began its industrial takeoff, it had an ample stock of skilled craftsmen, and the technological innovations adopted there tended to be of a kind that took advantage of those skills. Although an English inventor had worked out a plan for manufacturing pulley blocks through the use of interchangeable parts well before Eli Whitney's successful experiment with muskets, the scheme had not caught on in other industries there, because the British had an ample stock of trained artisans which the "American system" rendered superfluous. Consequently, the British economy underwent what economists call "labor-intensive" growth. American industrialization was different, because the available work force was basically unskilled. The scarcity of experienced craftsmen forced American employers to spend large sums on machines that could perform complex tasks when operated by untrained workers. This was a "capital-intensive" pattern of development; technology was substituted for human skills. The level of skill required to work as an operative in the most capital-intensive mechanized industries of the Northeast is suggested by the fact that their workers were referred to simply as "hands."

The Role of Government

It is a common myth that America's extraordinary record of economic growth in the nineteenth century is a tribute to unrestrained, *laissez faire* capitalism, and some argue that the increasing involvement of government in the economy in more recent times is a regrettable departure from earlier traditions. In fact, active government played a vital role in promoting economic development in the antebellum years. Governmental bodies, for one thing, were the key providers of "social overhead capital." Social overhead capital is money that is invested not directly in the production of things, but in improvements without which production and marketing could not take place. Better roads, canals, railroads, docks, and warehouses are examples. Such projects are sometimes undertaken by private firms, but often they entail investments that are so large, so risky, or so remote in their ultimate payoff that they will not be undertaken if left to the private sector.

The Erie Canal, financed and built by the State of New York, is a classic example. Its impact on the entire American economy was enormously stimulating. In the pre-Civil War years state governments supplied about three-quarters of the total funds invested in canals, and roughly half of the capital used to construct the rail network. Local communities and counties were also extremely active in subsidizing transportation improvements. In some cases, like that of the Erie Canal, these developmental efforts were operated as well as financed by governments. It was more common, however, for new ventures to be launched with government funds raised by taxation or the sale of public securities, then placed under private control. Public policy reflected not only widespread confidence in private enterprise, but a determination that it needed spurring to carry out large-scale development projects.

Government actively promoted industrial growth in other ways: erecting tariffs to protect domestic manufacturers from foreign competition; creating new legal arrangements, like the corporation, to stimulate the release of economic energy; and building schools to produce a better educated labor force.

However, government's most important contribution was the development of a vast national market. It was through their government that Americans obtained the territories that enlarged the national domain so dramatically. It was the legal framework provided by the Constitution and enforced by the Supreme Court that prevented individual states from following separate economic policies that might impede the free flow of people, products, and capital throughout the nation. It was government that provided much of the social overhead capital that built the transportation, communication, and trading facilities that made the national market work.

LIVING STANDARDS, STRATIFICATION, AND MOBILITY

The industrial transformation of the Northeast brought dramatic improvements in the standard of living of the average family. The Gross National Product (GNP) per capita more than doubled in the United States between 1800 and 1860. Regrettably, figures broken down by region are not available for the entire period, but at the opening of the century income levels in the Northeast must have been lower than in the South, where agriculture was more commercially developed. By 1840 the industrial surge had lifted income per person in the region 35 percent above the national average and almost double the southern average. Over the next two decades the gap widened a little more. By 1860 earnings of the most industrialized states—Massachusetts and Rhode Island—were two-thirds higher than the average for the United States as a whole.

These gains made life more comfortable and satisfying in many ways. They made possible, for example, a far more varied and healthy diet: less bread and more meat; fruit and vegetables previously available only at harvest time, if at all; more milk for growing children. We naturally assume that farmers in the age of homespun were well-fed, but actually their diet was sharply limited by the nature of the local soil and climate and by the absence of food preservation techniques like canning and refrigeration. It was easier to eat well in Boston in 1850 than on any farm in 1800. There were similar advances in other spheres: larger, warmer, better-lighted homes; machine-made clothing that was both better fitting and easier to launder than homespun garments; a vast increase in the number and

TABLE 10-2
Personal Income per Capita by Region as a
Percentage of the United States Average, 1840–60

	1840	1860
United States	100%	100%
Northeast	135	139
West	68	68
South	76	72

variety of low-cost books, magazines, and newspapers. In his travels through the United States in the 1830s, the perceptive French observer, Michael Chevalier, met an Irish railroad laborer whose job gave him three meals of meat each day plus 75 cents, but whose letters to relatives back in Ireland reported that he had meat three times per *week*. When Chevalier asked why he didn't tell the truth, the laborer answered, "If I told them that, they'd never believe me."

Growing Economic Inequality

Who, though, *was* the average resident of the Northeast—the young woman who toiled 72 hours a week in the cotton mills of Lowell or the Boston merchant who collected fat dividends on his textile stock? The owner of a large tenement in New York or Philadelphia, the man he paid to collect the rent, or the immigrant laborer living in the slum? Averages like "per capita income" or "wealth" figures reveal something, but we must look beyond such generalizations to see whether the "average" experience was, in fact, typical.

The Industrial Revolution divided northeastern society into distinct groups differentiated by economic role, power, and life-style. At the beginning of the century there was relatively little economic differentiation among the people of the northeastern states. True, some farmers had large holdings and some had quite small ones, and a small minority of tenants and farm laborers had no property of their own at all. But the range of wealth among rural residents was quite modest. One common measure of inequality is how much wealth is concentrated in the hands of the richest ten percent of the population—the top decile. In most farming communities, it was only about a third of the total.

There was somewhat greater inequality in the larger towns and cities, with prosperous merchants and professionals at the top of the economic hierarchy and impoverished laborers, servants and sailors at the bottom. But even there, the top decile held no more than half of the wealth, and at most a third of all families were without taxable property at all. The distance between the top and bottom rungs of the wealth ladder was not very great, and most people stood on one of the middle rungs.

In the decades of economic transformation that followed, the picture changed. The population of the Northeast was moving from the country to the city, where inequality had always been greater, and there was a simultaneous increase in the range of the economic inequality *within* the city. By 1860 a substantial majority of the urban population was propertyless. The elite group of manufacturers, merchants, bankers, and others who played a strategic role in the emerging industrial system had succeeded in capturing a generous share of the riches generated by industrialization. The top decile of wealthholders controlled at least 70 to 80 percent of city wealth.

This does not mean, though, that as the rich got richer the poor got poorer. The well-to-do seized a larger share of the pie in 1860 than in 1800, but the pie itself was much larger. The poor were getting richer too, in terms of their purchasing power. Wages rose substantially for most people, even common laborers and domestic servants, and the range of goods and services available to ordinary consumers increased strikingly.

The wealth of the rich, however, was growing faster than that of the poor. The income gap between the classes was widening, and the share of wealth going to those on the low end of the income scale was shrinking. By the end of the age that has often been dubbed "the era of the common man" (because of the intensely democratic flavor of its politics), the extent of economic inequality in the Northeast was as great as in any subsequent period of American history.

Lost Independence

We should resist the temptation to romanticize farm life in "the age of homespun." People worked very hard for precious little material reward. But most of them were economically independent. They owned the land on which they worked, the tools and animals they used at work, and the homes in which they lived. The pace of their labor was dictated by the rhythm of the seasons and their own preferences, and there was some variety in what they did from day to day. In the emerging industrial society of the Northeast, most people worked on property belonging to others—those with capital and entrepreneurial skills—on whom they depended for wages. Their hours of work were fixed by their employers. The peal of a bell or the screech of a siren dictated their arrival and departure from the workplace. Their tasks were set for them by the employer, and departure from the proscribed routine would be severely punished.

The lure of high wages promised a degree of economic security in exchange for acceptance of the regimentation, monotony, and dependence of the factory. The security was all too often illusory, however. Wages were high in good times—well above what could be earned as a hired hand on a farm—but the system of industrial capitalism was highly unstable. Recurrent depressions, the most serious of them in 1819, 1837, and 1857, brought mass unemployment. Philadelphia's cotton mills laid off 90 percent of their workers in the panic of 1819. In New York, the crash of 1837 doubled the number of applicants for charity. The 1857 collapse led to a 68 percent drop in the number of cotton textile jobs in Rhode Island and a 43 percent loss in employment in the iron industry. For many Americans, the danger of being forced to beg for a living as a result of impersonal market forces beyond their control was real and growing.

The Gospel of Mobility

The Industrial Revolution introduced a degree of economic inequality into American life that would have seemed disastrous to an earlier generation. Noah Webster articulated the older ideal well in 1787 when he declared that "a general and tolerably equal distribution of property is the whole basis of national freedom." Judged by that standard, the new order was sadly wanting. A few social critics believed that there was indeed a problem, but these dissenting voices were far outnumbered by those who celebrated economic change and revised their conception of equality. Equality of economic *condition*, they suggested, was an outmoded and impractical ideal. The test of a good society was instead whether or not it offered *equal opportunity to compete*. Enormous disparities in wealth were not unjust if they resulted from free and fair competition. If there were no artificial barriers to social mobility, the most talented would rise to the top and the less worthy would finish in their precise order of merit. If the successful were *self-made*, the unsuccessful likewise had no one to blame but themselves.

The vision of America as a land of opportunity was not a nineteenth-century invention. Expressions of it can be found in the writings of Benjamin Franklin, Hector St. Jean de Crevecoeur, and early Puritan divines like Cotton Mather. But it was propagated with unprecedented intensity at just the point of industrial take-off, in a flood of speeches, sermons, stories, editorials, and tracts celebrating the successful and urging others to emulate their superior industry and frugality. The greatest American philosopher of the era, Ralph Waldo Emerson, summed up the faith:

> Open the doors to talent and virtue and they will do themselves justice, and property will not be in bad hands. In a free and just commonwealth, property rushes from the idle and imbecile to the industrious, brave and persevering.

A country whose citizens had faith in the opportunity ethic could pursue economic growth relentlessly without unleashing class antagonisms over distribution of the fruits. The ideal worker was the textile mill employee from Lawrence, Massachusetts who told a state committee investigating labor conditions: "There is no reason for discontent. Every man in Lawrence is paid exactly what he is worth."

How Much Mobility in Reality?

Did all Americans believe in the gospel of opportunity? We must be skeptical about sweeping claims based on the written records, since they were produced mostly by successful, articulate, middle-class spokesmen with a vested interest in the status quo. Testimony from ordinary working people like the textile worker in Lawrence is rare and of questionable representativeness. It is difficult to believe that all workers were confident that their employers paid them exactly what they were worth. Historians too often generalize about "Americans" on the basis of statements by the select group of people who had access to the press, the pulpit, or the lecture platform. Even so, there are good reasons to believe that the mobility creed did penetrate fairly deeply in the society. Scores of European visitors who differed in their estimates on many other issues agreed that Americans were a driven, striving people, anxious for advancement and optimistic about the future.

We also know from statistical studies of ordinary workers in the nineteenth century that the mobility ideology had a certain plausibility because there was in fact a great deal of movement up and down the social ladder. Cases of movement from rags to riches were rare. The wealthiest and most powerful people, like the "Boston Associates," did not often come from humble homes. But the rise from rags to respectability was exceedingly common. Industrialization did not create the permanently impoverished proletariat that Karl Marx believed was forming in Europe. Instead, the growth and transformation of the U.S. economy opened up a multitude of new jobs on the middle rungs of the class ladder. Unskilled day laborers moved into skilled jobs or opened small businesses like grocery stores and bars. Their children, in turn, had excellent prospects of entering the white-collar world as clerks, salesmen, or supervisors. Although immigrants in general found fewer opportunities than more firmly entrenched Americans, and some immigrant groups—the Irish, for example—were especially slow to rise, these newcomers were not trapped in permanent poverty.

The new order certainly did not offer perfect equality of opportunity. The peak of the social hierarchy was relatively closed to those of lowly origins, and throughout society there were some limits to the range of mobility. It was an advantage to be born into the middle class, a disadvantage to be born into the working class. A laborer's son, for example, was likely to receive less schooling than the son of an attorney, and to find many doors closed to him as a result. But the social system was sufficiently buoyant and fluid to allow most people to improve on their starting positions in life. There was, in short, enough truth in the ideology of mobility to make it plausible, enough opportunity for modest gains to obscure the inequities of the industrial capitalist order.

CITIES AND IMMIGRANTS

In the United States of 1800 there existed fewer than 36 urban communities with as many as 2,500 residents; in 1860 there were 357 of them. The number of city dwellers rose from less than 350,000 to over 6 million. Although some of this urban growth occurred in the South and West, it was heavily concentrated in the Northeast. By 1860 more than one in three northeasterners lived in urban communities, two-and-a-half times as many as in the West and five times as many as in the South. Massachusetts was 60 percent urbanized, Rhode Island 63 percent.

TABLE 10-3
Urban Growth, 1800–60

	Towns of 2,500 to 25,000	Cities of 25,000 to 250,000	Cities of 250,000 or More
Number of places			
1800	30	3	0
1860	357	32	3
Population (in thousands)			
1800	193	129	0
1860	2,455	2,115	1,646
	Northeast	West	South
Population in urban places			
1800	9%	0%	2%
1860	36	14	7

Industrialization stimulated much of this urban growth, as the examples of Lowell and Lawrence suggest. But the connection with urbanization was not as close as might be thought. Most of the nation's early factories were not to be found in New York, Philadelphia, or Boston because these great metropolitan centers were not located along rivers that could be used to turn waterwheels to power machines. The growth of these dominant seaports, and of inland communities like Albany and Pittsburgh, in the antebellum years was based not on manufacturing but on commerce. They were centers for long-distance interregional trade, dispatching southern cotton, western foodstuffs, and northeastern manufactures to their destinations and taking a profit for a wide variety of commercial, banking, insurance, and transportation services. Not until the 1840s and 1850s did improved coal-burning steam engines begin to replace water power in manufacturing, allowing some industries to gravitate into the big cities to take advantage of the cheap immigrant labor force concentrated there.

Urban Disorder

"I look upon the size of certain American cities, and especially on the nature of their population, as a real danger," wrote Alexis de Tocqueville after his travels through the United States in 1831–32. Many Americans shared his apprehensions about the character of life in the mushrooming cities. Bursting at the seams with newcomers, they lacked institutions to impose order on an unruly population or to provide essential services like sanitary water and garbage removal. Professional police forces were nonexistent or in an infant stage; the customary reliance on voluntary watchmen to patrol the streets at night was so inadequate that entire areas of the city like New York's infamous slum, the Five Points, were no safer to walk through at night than is Central Park today. Violent clashes between street gangs and riots were a common occurrence; 200 major riots occurred in New York in the 1834–44 decade alone. Putting out fires was the responsibility of volunteer fire companies, who frequently devoted more effort to fighting a rival company than to fighting the blazes. Neighborhoods deteriorated into slums as landlords converted old mansions and warehouses into tenements into which they crammed as many tenants as possible. Solely interested in milking the building for maximal rental income, slumlords spent nothing on maintenance and let properties deteriorate freely. Expanding pockets of poverty, disease, crime, and vice spread across the city.

These developments seemed all the more unsettling to native city dwellers because of one crucial fact about the slums—they were inhabited chiefly by immigrants from other lands. Fewer than 5,000 immigrants per year entered the United States during the 1820s. In the next decade the figure rose to over 50,000 per year, in the 1840s it was almost 150,000 per year, and in the 1850s over 280,000 per year. Most of these newcomers landed in the major northeastern ports, and a great many of them either remained there or moved on to other smaller cities in the region. In 1860 some 20 percent of the northeastern population was foreign-born, double the average for the nation as a whole. Counting the American-born children of the immigrants—the "second generation"—with their parents, about a third of the people of the Northeast and *more than half* of the residents of its largest cities were alien to traditional Yankee ways. In Boston, New York, Philadelphia, Pittsburgh, Providence, Rochester, Albany, and Buffalo, the immigrant "minorities" were in fact the new majority. Natives of colonial stock were the true minority.

A sudden invasion on this scale was bound to cause tension and conflict in the best of circumstances. In this instance, the shock was compounded by economic and cultural differences between natives and newcomers, and by a selective process that determined which immigrants remained in the Northeast. Those with capital or skills tended to head for the frontier; the poorest and least skilled were more prone to remain where they landed, near their kinfolk, eking out a bare living at menial laboring jobs.

The Irish

The largest single bloc of immigrants to settle in the northeastern cities was the Irish, in flight from a chronically overpopulated and famine-ridden country. They arrived able to speak the language of the land—English had largely replaced the native Irish tongue by then—but were otherwise ill-prepared to meet the challenges of urban life. Largely illiterate peasants, their only attraction in the minds of employers was a strong back. They had to take the lowest paid laboring jobs when they could get work at all. Their minimal incomes forced them to crowd together in dismal cellars and attics; lack of ventilation, clean water, and toilet facilities made the Irish slums breeding grounds of cholera, tuberculosis, and a host of other

killers. By almost any measure of social pathology—the rate of poverty, unemployment, crime, disease, or alcoholism—the Irish stood out.

They stood out in another disturbing way from the Yankee point of view—they
were Roman Catholics. The first half of the nineteenth century witnessed the
intense outburst of evangelical Protestant enthusiasm that came to be known as the
Second Great Awakening. Church membership more than doubled. The United
States became the most religious nation in the world, whether measured by church
attendance, funds donated to religious institutions, or public appeals to religious
values. In the eyes of Protestant evangelicals, Catholicism was not a true religion
but a "promoter of ignorance and low superstition." They also feared it was
innately hostile to republicanism, and that the Irish would vote as instructed by
their priests. Although American Catholicism eventually successfully accommo-
dated itself to republican principles, it was not a wildly implausible fear at the time.
Under Pope Pius IX, the Roman church was a major supporter of reactionary
European monarchs and a staunch foe of republican revolutionaries like the
Hungarian Louis Kossuth, a hero to American democrats but a "red republican" to
church authorities. Nor was it surprising that Yankees believed that Catholics
lacked independent political judgment. They were quick to become naturalized
citizens and to register to vote, and they did indeed vote as a bloc in opposition to
measures favored by Yankee reformers.

One key issue that divided Irish Catholics from Yankee Protestants concerned
alcohol. The temperance movement spread like wildfire from the 1830s onward.
Evangelicals saw the renunciation of strong drink and the taking of the "cold water
pledge" as a crucial sign of personal salvation; employers cheered the movement
on in the hopes of obtaining a more disciplined workforce. As its leaders came to
perceive that converting individuals would not suffice to slay the demon rum, they
turned to coercive means and sought legislation prohibiting the sale of alcoholic
beverages. The use of alcohol, however, was a traditional element of Irish culture,
and the newcomers regarded prohibition as an unwarranted attack on a cherished
custom, an effort to impose alien standards on them. Maine became a "dry" state in

A SECOND DECLARATION OF INDEPENDENCE:
NEW ENGLAND REFORMERS AND THE BATTLE AGAINST LIQUOR

We hold these truths to be self-evident; that all men are created temperate; that they are endowed by their Creator with certain natural and innocent desires; that among these are the appetite for COLD WATER and the pursuit of happiness! that to secure the gratification of these propensities fountains and streams are gushing and meandering from the hills and vales, benignly and abundantly abroad among men, deriving their just powers from their beneficial adaptation to the natures of all the varities of animal organization; that whenever any form of substituted artificial beverage becomes destructive of these natures, it is the right of the recipients to proscribe—to alter, or to abolish it and to return to the use of that crystal element, which alone of all that has come to us from Eden, still retains all its primitive purity and sweetness, demonstrating its benefits on such principles, and testing its powers in such quantities, and under such circumstances, as to them shall seem most likely to effect their safety and happiness.

—Manifesto of the Washington Total Abstinence Societies, 1841

1851, and prohibition became one of the hottest political issues for decades to come. Irish votes were often enough to tip the balance against temperance advocates in these contests.

The issue of public education was also divisive. The Irish arrived in the midst of a great drive to build a compulsory, tax-supported, public school system. Horace Mann, first Secretary of the Massachusetts State Board of Education, and his counterparts in other northern states were convinced that the future of America depended on the education of its children. They worked to develop an elaborate system of schools open to all children, including those whose parents were too poor to pay for their education. Public schools, they argued, would equalize opportunities to get ahead in the world, provide the educated citizenry necessary for democratic government, stimulate economic productivity, and instill needed social discipline.

The reformers got what they wanted, by and large. Thousands of new schools were built with tax dollars; teacher training faculties (state "normal" schools) were created; laws were passed requiring attendance up to a certain minimim age. By 1850 the proportion of youths in school in New England was higher than anywhere else in the world, and the common school movement was spreading rapidly throughout the other northeastern and midwestern states.

The Irish, however, regarded educational reform as anti-Catholic and did their best to block it. Many Irish–American parents lived in such poverty that they needed to put their children to work at an early age to keep the family afloat. They had religious objections as well. The public schools claimed to be nonsectarian, communicating a generalized religious morality on which all Christians could agree. But the Irish feared (with some grounds) that American public schools were thinly disguised Protestant schools that would alienate their children from the true faith. They denied that religion and education could be separated, and insisted on public funding for a system of Catholic-operated schools. Failing in this effort, the Church leadership created independent parochial schools where the children of the faithful would be free from Protestant influence. With their parochial schools and an array of other ethnic institutions like hospitals and orphanages, the Irish created a social world of their own, a tight ethnic enclave separate from the larger society.

For that reason, the violent disturbances that erupted so frequently in the antebellum years very often pitted the Irish against other groups. In 1837 a Yankee mob burned down a Catholic convent in the outskirts of Boston. Street fights between Protestants and Catholics in Philadelphia in 1844 left 13 dead. The bloody climax of decades of urban disorder came in New York City in 1863, when Irish mobs protesting the Civil War draft raged through the streets for several days lynching negroes. Peace was finally established by federal troops, but not before more than 100 lives had been lost.

MEN, WOMEN, AND CHILDREN

In his assessment of the great changes he and his contemporaries had lived through, Horace Bushnell was especially struck with the transformation that had taken place in family life. In the age of homespun, he recalled, farming and domestic manufacturing had been carried on by the family as a unit. There was little specialization of tasks, only a limited division of labor. Jobs requiring considerable physical strength were generally done by the father and elder sons; women and young children prepared food and milked, fed, and cared for domestic animals. Women were legally subordinate, and denied the right to own property, vote, or serve on juries. But the economic roles of the two sexes were not sharply differentiated. The family was a joint productive enterprise.

Industrialization shattered this unity, and altered popular conceptions about sex roles. The shift of production from the household to separate workplaces removed men from the family unit for most of each day; a man's role was that of breadwinner. It took many women and children from low income households out of the home as well, as we have seen. Most manual laborers could not earn enough to support a family without supplementary income from some of their dependents; at the working class level, the family economy remained vital to survival in the new society. But within the expanding middle class, the new ideal was that man was the sole provider; he alone was to venture forth into the impersonal, competitive world to bring home the bacon.

Women were to remain at home, in what Tocqueville called "the quiet circle of domestic employments." According to him, "In no country has such constant care been taken as in America to trace two clearly distinct lines of action for the two sexes." He would not have said so a generation earlier. By the 1830s, particularly among the more prosperous households of the industrializing Northeast, a new sexual differentiation had emerged. In the age of homespun it was assumed, as Bushnell put it, that "women were given by the Almighty not so much to help their husbands *spend* a living as to help them *get* one." In the new society, the saying was reversed; women became specialists in consumption and lost their role in production. Rising incomes and the increasing abundance of goods generated by industrial development provided a new task for the woman: spending her husband's earnings as efficiently and tastefully as possible in order to create an attractive home, a haven to which he could retreat after a long day of bruising encounters with his rivals in the race for success. This explains the great proliferation of new magazines with titles including the words "house" or "home," and of books dealing with household management, etiquette and other such related matters in the province of women in the period.

The other task of women within "the quiet circle of domestic employments" was to raise their children properly. In middle-class homes, the process of child-rearing became both more intensive and more selfconscious. Trusting parental instincts or following traditional customs gave way to a calculated style of socializing the young. There were no counterparts to Doctor Spock's childrearing manual in colonial days, but in the nineteenth century scores of them appeared, ranging from Horace Bushnell's own perceptive and sophisticated *Christian Nurture* to crude tracts revealing how to make children turn out successful. Biographies of popular heroes served this function too. Parson Weems' celebrated *Life of George Washington* attempted to convince children of the virtues of honesty through anecdotes such as the legend of the cherry tree, but it was aimed too at parents who wanted to rear offspring with characters like that of the noble statesman.

The shift in childrearing practices included a heightened emphasis on sexual differentiation, a growing determination to ensure that boys and girls developed along the "two clearly distinct lines" that Tocqueville spoke of. Girls were trained in what historians have called "the cult of true womanhood"; piety, purity, domesticity, and submissiveness were the greatest virtues, and to be independent or assertive was unfeminine. Boys were encouraged to develop the traits to succeed in the marketplace. "The idea instilled into the minds of most boys, from early life," according to an article in *Harper's Magazine* in 1853, was "that of 'getting on.' The parents test themselves by their own success in this respect; and they impart the same notion" to their sons.

Controlling Impulsive Behavior

That anxiety about "getting on" helps to explain two of the most dramatic changes in the private behavior of northeasterners in the antebellum years; they began to drink much less alcohol, and they began to restrict the size of their families. Before

TABLE 10-4
The Shrinking American Family

Average number of children per woman at end of childbearing years:

1800	7.0
1810	6.9
1820	6.7
1830	6.6
1840	6.1
1850	5.4
1860	5.2

Number of children under 5 per 1,000 women 15–50 in selected states:

	1830	*1860*
Heavily Urban		
Massachusetts	502	432
Rhode Island	544	416
Moderately Urban		
New York	700	517
New Jersey	698	556
Frontier		
Indiana	1,112	733
Illinois	1,165	737

the Revolution, Americans were the hardest drinking people in the world. They continued to be in the early nineteenth century, consuming well over a quart of whiskey per week in 1830. Average consumption then suddenly dropped 56 percent over the next decade, and by another 42 percent between 1840 and 1845. The figures are for the nation, not for the Northeast alone, but the Northeast was the stronghold of the temperance movement, and it is reasonable to assume that the decline in drinking was especially great there. Growing numbers of men on the make had learned to deny themselves release through the bottle, and to channel more of their energies into the race for success.

A very similar pattern appears when we examine trends in family size. The number of children born to an average American woman dropped from 7 to 5.2 between 1800 and 1860; most of the change came after 1830, when alcohol consumption also fell abruptly. The figures are not broken down by region, but other evidence makes plain that the trend toward smaller families began first in the Northeast, and particularly in the most urbanized areas of the Northeast. Data on the number of young children per 1,000 women of childbearing age for various states in 1830 and 1860 show that there were fewer births in the most urbanized states and that the number declined over time as urbanization advanced. It is also clear that it was educated, middle-class couples who took the lead in limiting the number of their offspring, and that working class families were slower to adopt the new small family norm.

This new norm, it is important to note, was not the result of a technological advance that made control of fertility a simple matter. Modern contraceptive devices had not yet been developed. Abortion was legal in most states until the Civil War, and one study estimates that as many as a third of all pregnancies to married women were terminated in that way. The major means by which unwanted pregnancies were avoided, however, was by practicing greater sexual restraint—coitus interruptus or outright abstinence. The severe discipline that went into limiting family size in the Victorian age is a clue to the larger meaning of the phenomenon. It suggests a basic value change among the dominant social group, the emergence of a more future-oriented, calculating, rational mentality that was determined to impose tight control over every aspect of life. Parents whose resources were insufficient to educate six or seven children and to launch them in respectable careers or marriages would take the pains necessary to ensure that they had only two or three, and repress the impulses that would lead to more if they gave in to them. That this new pattern emerged during a period of extraordinary economic transformation is not a coincidence. Whether it was the change in values that stimulated economic development or economic development that fostered value change is a chicken-and-egg problem that cannot be resolved here. Perhaps all that can be said is that the two interacted: The rationalization of economic production went hand in hand with what might be called the rationalization of reproduction.

SUGGESTED READINGS

Stuart Bruchey, *Economic Growth of the Modern American Economy* (1975) is a good introduction to economic change in the era. Two recent textbooks by economic historians, Lance Davis, *et al., American Economic Growth: An Economist's History* (1972) and W. Elliot Brownlee, *Dynamics of Ascent: A History of the American Economy* (1979) are valuable. Peter Temin, *Causal Factors in American Economic Growth in the Nineteenth Century* (1975) is brief and lucid. Douglass C. North, *The Economic Growth of the United States, 1790–1860* (1961) is fundamental. Its stress upon regional specialization as the key to economic growth has recently been challenged in Diane Lindstrom, *Economic Development in the Philadelphia Region, 1810–1850* (1978).

George R. Taylor, *The Transportation Revolution, 1815–1860* (1951), Edward C. Kirkland, *Men, Cities and Transportation: A Study in New England History,* 2 vols. (1948), and Albert Fishlow, *American Railroads and the Transformation of the Ante-Bellum Economy* (1965) analyze the emerging national transportation network. On technological innovation, see Constance W. Green, *Eli Whitney and the Birth of American Technology* (1956), Nathan Rosenberg, *Technology and American Economic Growth* (1972), Merritt Roe Smith, *Harpers Ferry Armory and the New Technology* (1977), and David J. Jeremy, *Transatlantic Industrial Revolution: The Diffusion of Textile Technology between Britain and America, 1790–1830* (1981). The crucial role of governmental assistance is shown in Carter Goodrich, *Government Promotion of Canals and Railroads* (1960). Victor S. Clark, *History of Manufactures in the United States, 1607–1860*, 3 vols. (1929) is still the fullest and best account. Caroline F. Ware, *Early New England Cotton Manufacturing* (1931) also remains valuable.

The impact of economic transformation on the lives of ordinary people is described in community studies like Oscar Handlin, *Boston's Immigrants: A Study in Acculturation* (rev. ed., 1959), Stephan Thernstrom: *Poverty and Progress: Social Mobility in a Nineteenth Century City* (1964), Stuart Blumin, *The Urban Threshhold: Growth and Change in a Nineteenth Century American Community* (1975), Alan Dawley, *Class and Community: The Industrial Revolution in Lynn* (1976), Robert Doherty, *Society and Power: Five New England Towns, 1800–1860* (1977), Michael H. Frisch, *Town into City: Springfield, Massachusetts and the Meaning of Community, 1840–1880* (1972), Susan Hirsch, *Roots of the American Working Class: The Industrialization of Crafts in Newark, 1800–1860* (1978), Clyde and Sally Griffin, *Natives and Newcomers: The Ordering of Opportunity in Mid-Nineteenth Century Poughkeepsie* (1978), and Thomas Dublin, *Women at Work: The Transformation of Work and Community in Lowell, Massachusetts, 1826–1860* (1980). Dublin has also edited an interesting volume of documents, *Farm to Factory: Women's Letters, 1830–1860* (1981). John Coolidge, *Mill and Mansion: Architecture and Society in Lowell, Massachusetts, 1820–1860* (1942) is a neglected classic. John F. Kasson, *Civilizing the Machine: Technology and Republican Values in America, 1776–1900* (1977) and Daniel T. Rodgers, *The Work Ethic in Industrial America, 1850–1920* (1978) are extremely stimulating. Edward Pessen, *Riches, Class, and Power before the Civil War* (1973) deals with social stratification. On immigration, see the essays on "American Identity and Americanization," the English, Germans, and Irish in Stephan Thernstrom, ed., *Harvard Encyclopedia of American Ethnic Groups* (1980), and Philip Taylor, *The Distant Magnet: European Immigration to the United States of America* (1971). Changes in family life are analyzed in Robert V. Wells, *Revolutions in Americans' Lives: A Demographic Perspective on the History of Americans, Their Families, and Their Society* (1982), Walter S. Nugent, *Structures of American Social History* (1981), Maris A. Vinovskis, *Fertility in Massachusetts from the Revolution to the Civil War* (1981), Mary P. Ryan, *Cradle of the Middle Class: The Family in Oneida County, New York, 1790–1865* (1981), and several of the essays in Tamara K. Hareven, ed., *Family and Kin in Urban Communities, 1700–1930* (1977).

Chapter Eleven

The Cotton Kingdom

At the opening of the nineteenth century, the South stood proud and strong. Almost half (49 percent) of the American population lived in the southern states, producing more than their share of the country's wealth. Symbolic of its commanding position in the life of the nation was the region's continued domination of the American presidency. A southern slave-owner was President for all but eight of the nation's first forty-eight years. From George Washington through Andrew Jackson, with only the brief exceptions of John Adams (1796–1800) and his son John Quincy Adams (1824–28), the highest office in the land was occupied by men who were products of the distinctive social order of the plantation South.

In the antebellum decades, the plantation order reached its fullest flowering. Like the Northeast, the South grew dramatically in population and material achievements. Like the people of the Northeast, its people were expansive and buoyantly optimistic. But there the similarity ends. The pattern of southern development was anomalous, for the economy of the region and the social structure it spawned rested on the enslavement and systematic exploitation of a large fraction of the population—black Africans and their descendants. The economic interests of the master class, and the racism of much of the nonslaveholding white population together produced a society that was increasingly monolithic, increasingly defensive, and increasingly isolated from the main currents of opinion elsewhere in the United States—indeed, in the world.

By 1820, large versions of Eli Whitney's hand-cranked cotton gin enabled workers to clean 50 times the amount of cotton that could be processed by hand over an equal period.

SLAVES, PROFITS, AND ECONOMIC GROWTH

Textbooks often assert that the southern economy was in deep trouble after the American Revolution because of depressed tobacco prices, and that if Eli Whitney had not invented the cotton gin in 1793 the institution of slavery might well have withered away. These claims are extremely dubious. Tobacco growers were experiencing difficulties, and a few influential planters like George Washington and Thomas Jefferson expressed doubts about the future viability of the slave system. But the vast majority of planters were intensely committed to protecting the investments that had given them abundant profits in the past. No southern state legislature in these years gave a moment's serious consideration to abolition schemes like those then being carried out in the North. The notion that slavery was beginning to fade away is impossible to reconcile with the fact that in the 1780s almost as many bound Africans were imported into the country as in any previous decade of American history. White southerners were resolved to make slavery pay, and were optimistic that it could be done.

The circumstances in which Whitney made his discovery—actually an improvement on someone else's discovery—attest to the optimistic entrepreneurial spirit of the planters and to their responsiveness to changing market incentives. Mechanization of the English textile industry in the late eighteenth century had created a soaring demand for raw cotton, driving up prices precipitously. Most of the cotton produced in the United States then was of the long-staple variety. It was of marvelous quality—$60 shirts are made out of it today—but it required an extremely humid atmosphere like that along the Georgia and South Carolina coast. Attempts to produce it in the interior uplands failed consistently. Another much hardier variety of cotton was known—the short-staple type. It would grow anywhere in the South, but could not be spun and woven into cloth until its sticky seeds were extracted from the fiber, a painfully slow process. Whitney's device broke that bottleneck; one laborer with a gin could clean as much cotton per day as fifty working by hand. If Whitney had never been born, someone else almost certainly would have developed a similar device. Hundreds of mechanics and tinkerers throughout the South were working on the problem. The state of Georgia appointed a special commission to promote such work, and discussions of the subject filled the southern press. A much superior type of gin was invented by a native Georgian only three years later.

The cotton gin and the consequent economic advantage of planting the short-staple variety brought a phenomenal expansion in southern cotton production. From a total of only 3,000 bales in 1790, output zoomed to 178,000 bales in 1810, 732,000 by 1830, and 4.5 million by 1860. The value of the crop increased from $8 million in 1802 to $249 million in 1860. By the 1820s the South was the world's largest supplier of cotton; soon it was producing two-thirds of the total world output.

Cotton was not only the backbone of the southern economy; it was of crucial significance to the national economy as a whole. By the 1830s it accounted for two-thirds of America's exports. Residents of the North and West benefited from the cotton boom in a variety of ways. The textile mills of the North depended on the South for raw material, and the prosperity fueled by cotton made the South a major market for northern manufactures and the western foodstuffs. The merchants of northeastern cities reaped profits for shipping, insuring, and marketing the crop. Senator James Hammond of South Carolina was overconfident when he declared in 1858, "You dare not make war on cotton," because "cotton is king." But he did have substantial grounds for confidence.

Settlement of the Lower South

Much of the land of the coastal tobacco states of the Upper South was depleted from excessive cultivation without proper crop rotation and use of fertilizer. Millions of acres of rich virgin soils superbly suited to cotton cultivation lay westward and southward. The cotton boom resulted in a mass migration into the seven states of the Lower South—South Carolina, Georgia, Florida, Alabama, Mississippi, Louisiana, and Texas. Between 1800 and 1860 the population of the cotton states soared from one-half million to five million.

The spread of cotton production meant the spread of slavery. The number of blacks in the cotton states rose from 200,000 in 1800 to over 2 million in 1860, and all but a tiny minority were slaves. Cotton could, of course, have been cultivated by free laborers on small farms, and to some extent it was. Slaves could have been used for other purposes, and were to some degree—not only as field hands on Carolina rice and Louisiana sugar plantations, but in a variety of skilled occupations as well. But the equation of cotton and slavery is largely correct. The vast majority of southern cotton was produced by slave laborers—93 percent of it in 1850, for example. And the great preponderance of the region's slaves toiled in the cotton fields.

Cotton was well-suited to a slave labor force. As with tobacco, the task of growing, picking, and preparing it for sale could keep "all hands occupied at all times." It was a year-round business: preparation of the ground in the late winter; planting in the spring; thinning and weeding through the summer; picking at the end of the summer; ginning, baling, and carting to market after that. That left only a brief interval in which to cut firewood, repair fences, and the like, before the cycle of cultivation began all over again.

Was Slavery Profitable?

The question may seem silly. Why would the institution have lasted in America for over two centuries if it wasn't? Some historians, however, have asserted that slave labor was innately inefficient, and therefore must have yielded low profits, if any at all. Holding slaves, it has been argued, was a fashionable indulgence, a source of prestige in a social order dominated by aristocrats cut from an almost feudal mold. Others stress that the central function of slavery was to control people thought to be racially inferior and innately dependent. Although many issues concerning the slave society of the antebellum South are still being hotly

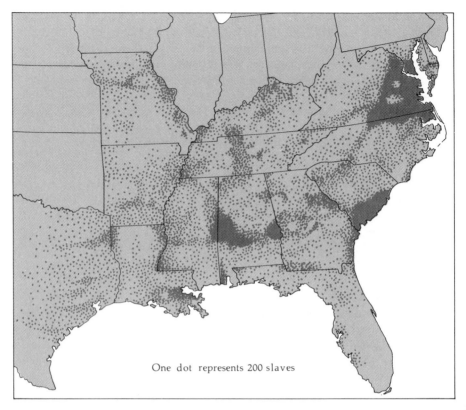

One dot represents 200 slaves

Map 11-1
Concentrations of Slaves, 1860

debated today, the question of profitability is hardly in dispute any more. From the viewpoint of the individual owner, slavery was unquestionably very profitable indeed. Slavery was economically rational for the owner, however repugnant morally. It paid, and paid well, for two reasons: Slaves were a good source of labor, and a good investment.

Contrary to the common belief that unfree labor is innately inefficient, slaves in general performed their tasks quite efficiently. Although some engaged in forms of passive resistance against their masters—dragging their feet, abusing tools and work animals, stealing and the like—it did not happen on a wide enough scale to cut average profits significantly. Some economic historians have even argued recently that the South's slaves were *more* productive than free workers in agriculture, particularly on the larger plantations. This contention has been challenged, and the intricate technical questions at issue in the debate have not yet been resolved.[1] But it is not necessary to believe that slave laborers were actually better workers than their free counterparts to concede that they were induced or compelled to toil with

---

[1]For the contrasting views, see Robert W. Fogel and Stanley Engerman, *Time on the Cross;* Gavin Wright, *The Political Economy of the Cotton South;* and Paul David *et al., Reckoning with Slavery.*

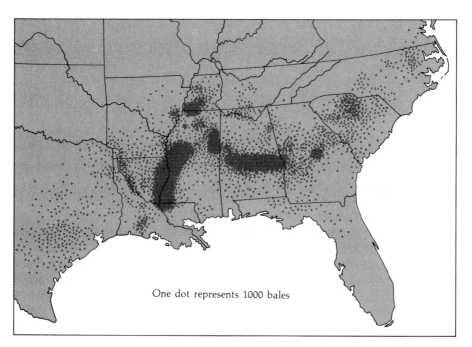

One dot represents 1000 bales

Map 11–2
Southern Cotton Production, 1859

enough efficiency to produce valuable crops in large enough quantities to yield generous profits to the planter.

It was not only the products of slave labor that returned profits. The slaves themselves were capital assets, property that could be sold and that was appreciating in value rapidly through most of the antebellum years. In 1844, for example, a prime Georgia field hand sold for $600. Nine years later, the figure was double that; by 1860 it was up to $1,800. Buying slaves, holding them a few years, and then selling could thus yield spectacular capital gains.

Furthermore, as human beings, slaves were a special kind of capital, because they reproduced at little expense to their owners. Although a typical female slave could not chop as much cane or pick as much cotton as her male counterpart, she could produce offspring—an even more valuable commodity that automatically belonged to the slaveowner and would mature into producers of cotton and perhaps more babies as well. Southern planters bitterly rejected abolitionist charges that they were engaging in systematic slave breeding, but the relative prices of male and female slaves betray the realities of the situation. Because of their lesser strength, female slaves could usually be *rented* from their owners for about half as much as males; the *purchase* price for a female, however, was nearly as high as that for a male (see box, page 238). Whether it was conscious or unconscious, the planters' market behavior showed that they appreciated the value of slaves not only in producing cotton but in reproducing themselves.

PARTIAL INVENTORY OF SLAVES ON A
LOUISIANA SUGAR PLANTATION, 1849

Names	Ages	Value	Remarks
Carter Allen	23	400 00	a Runaway, verry Sloe
Charles Mena	45	500 00	African, verry good
Edmond	40	600 00	A great drunkard
Sam Williams	25	600 00	A good hand
Gallant	45	500 00	rather trifling, but will do
Old Mat M	35	300 00	Sickly consumption
Bill Kenty	45	700 00	good hand
Fleming	45	400 00	a runaway
Simond (Carpenter)	45	800 00	the greatest rascal on plantation
Friday	40	350 00	Sickly Subject to fits
John Davis	45	400 00	Sickly, & a runaway
Letha	20	500 00	good hand
Elmira	25	400 00	sickly
Eliza Ann	18	500 00	good hand
Nanny	16	500 00	good hand
Long Mariah	45	200 00	not much account
Tena	40	400 00	well disposed fair hand
Eliza	20	400 00	fair hand
Amy	35	400 00	fair hand
Jennette	35	400 00	verry good cook
Peggy	30	500 00	good hand
Fanny	18	500 00	good hand
Nancy	16	500 00	good hand
Harriet (Black)	25	500 00	good hand
Olive	20	500 00	good hand

—List and Inventory of the Negroes on the Plantation
of Messrs. Bruce, Seddon, and Wilkings, St. James Parish, La.

Economic Growth

Of course, slavery could have been profitable for the slave-owners without being beneficial to the southern economy. Abolitionist critics of the slave system and many later historians depicted the slave economy as backward and stagnant, providing riches for a few but poverty for the masses. Although per capita income in the South was 20 percent below the national average in 1860, this indicates only that agriculture in general was somewhat less profitable than industry, not that slave-based agriculture was economically inefficient. Personal income in the South in 1860 was 15 percent higher than in the free farming states of the Midwest, which have always been regarded as quite prosperous. In the two decades before the Civil War (the only period for which accurate figures are available), the southern economy was growing at a rate slightly *above* the average for the United States. Had the South been an independent nation in 1860, it would have been the fourth richest country in the world, behind the North but well ahead of such advanced nations as France and Germany!

Impressive though it was, however, the economic growth of the slave South was unique and as important as the devastation of the Civil War in causing the poverty and economic underdevelopment that plagued the region from the end of the war well into the twentieth century. The slave economy was *expanding* rapidly; it was producing rising amounts of a valuable commodity with increasing efficiency. But it was not *growing* in a manner that unleashed economic energies and stimulated innovation across a broad front. In some historical settings, improvements in agriculture trigger the urbanization and industrialization necessary for sustained, long-term economic growth. Not so in the planter-dominated society of the antebellum South; there such qualitative economic advances were conspicuously absent.

It is particularly revealing that the urban revolution which swept over the North between the opening of the century and the Civil War left the South virtually untouched. Cities are historically the sites of innovation and enterprise. By 1860, more than one in three residents of the Northeast lived in a community of 2,500 or more; but only one out of fourteen southerners was a city dweller. On the eve of the Civil War the South remained less urbanized than the Northeast had been at the outset of George Washington's presidency! Perhaps even more striking is the contrast between the South and the Midwest, also a heavily agricultural region. In the first phase of their settlement, the booming free farm states of the West were even less urbanized than the South. As late as 1840, only 4 percent of their residents lived in communities of 2,500 or more, compared with 5 percent in the South. But in the next two decades the number of western city dwellers rose at more than six times the southern rate.

The factory was as alien as the city in the slave South. Although the region contained slightly more than a third of the population of the United States, only 15 percent of the country's industrial establishments were located there in 1860.

TABLE 11-1
Urbanization and Industrialization
in the Slave South, 1860

Southern Share of the Nation's:

Population	35%
Urban population	13
Manufacturing establishments	15
Value of manufactured products	9
Manufacturing labor force	8

Moreover, because southern firms were smaller than their northern counterparts, they employed only 8 percent of the manufacturing work force and turned out only 9 percent of all industrial products.

LIFE IN THE SLAVE QUARTERS

Almost one million Afro-Americans were held in slavery in the South at the opening of the nineteenth century. By 1860 the number had risen to four million. It is difficult to summarize the experience of so many different people, scattered over a vast geographical area, in a few pages. Some worked as field hands or household servants on huge cotton plantations; others toiled on small farms with few or no other slaves as companions. There were slave carpenters and blacksmiths both on the plantations and in the cities and small towns, slave lumbermen, miners, and ironworkers. Adding to the difficulty of generalizing is the fact that the study of American slavery has been one of the most intensely investigated and controversial fields of historical inquiry in recent years, and further important revisions of once accepted views may be expected in the near future. Some basic points, however, stand out clearly.

Subordinate Legal Status

In all of the southern states, slaves were regarded as property, of course, and were completely under the control of their owners. They could not own property themselves, marry freely, make contracts, file legal suits, or testify against their masters in court. They could not travel without a pass, or legally possess whiskey or guns. It was assumed that the intersts of master and slave were identical—that owners would protect their chattels because they were valuable property. The courts sometimes were forced to concede that slaves were property of a unique kind, fellow human beings. "A slave is not in the condition of a horse," said a Tennessee judge in 1846. "He is made after the image of his creator. He has mental capacities, and an immortal principle in his nature." Likewise, a Kentucky court held in 1836 that "although the law of this state considers slaves as property, yet it recognizes their personal existence, and, to a qualified extent, their natural rights." But there was virtually no way for a slave to obtain legal protection for his "natural rights" without the backing of his master. It was against the law, for example, for an owner to murder his slave. But he had very broad powers to "chastise" a "disobe-dient" one. If oversevere "chastisement" resulted in death, conviction was almost impossible because of the inadmissability of slave testimony. The terrible psychological uncertainty created by the vulnerability of slaves to their master's every whim was one of the cruelest features of the peculiar institution.

Longevity and Diet

Fortunately, the interests of master and slave were complementary in some important respects. Southern owners, for one thing, seem to have recognized that it was to their advantage to care for their slaves well enough for them to lead long productive lives. Simon Legree, the brutal overseer in Harriet Beecher Stowe's *Uncle Tom's Cabin*, literally worked his slaves to death. But Legree was a product of Mrs. Stowe's imagination; he had few real life counterparts. In 1850 the life expectancy at birth of a southern slave was 36 years, not far below the 40-year figure for white Americans, and well above life expectancy in crowded urban centers like New York and Boston. (Peasants in nineteenth-century Ireland could expect to live only nineteen years.) The combination of a relatively low death rate and a high fertility rate resulted in a very high rate of natural increase. Between 1808 (when the United States barred new slave imports from abroad) and 1860, the slave population of the South increased three and a half times.

The causes of this striking growth—unique among slave populations in the Americas—are still being debated. Part of the explanation is that tropical diseases—heavy killers farther south—did not flourish in the more temperate climate of the southern United States. But it also reflects differences in the treatment of the enslaved peoples. The planters of the antebellum South understood that working their slaves excessively long hours, underfeeding them, forcing women in the late stages of pregnancy to perform heavy labor, and the like lowered fertility and increased mortality. American slave women reached the age of puberty from one to three years earlier than in any other slave population which has been studied. The onset of puberty is strongly related to nutrition, and the early age in the United States suggests that slaves had a quite nutritious, though terribly monotonous diet. The fact that slaves born in the United States grew to be three inches taller, on the average, than African slaves in Trinidad points in the same direction. Another indication of the concern of planters for the welfare of their chattels is that they avoided using them, whenever possible, for dangerous work. In building or repairing the levees in disease-ridden swamps along the Mississippi, for example, they employed free white laborers, whose illness or death would not threaten a valuable investment.

It is not that southern planters were more benevolent and humane than their Latin American counterparts, less willing to risk the lives of others for profit. It is rather that they did not manifest the same "take-the-money-and-run" mentality, and were more oriented toward reaping profits *in the long run*.

Punishments and Incentives

Slaves seem, on the whole, to have worked hard and well. Why, when the fruits of their labor were expropriated by the owners? Sheer physical compulsion is part of the answer. Slaves toiled in the fields under the vigilant eyes of overseers and drivers who carried whips and did not hesitate to use them. Some masters avoided lashing their charges as much as possible, but the threat of savage physical punishment was essential to plantation discipline.

Masters employed the carrot as well as the stick, however, to induce their bondsmen to work diligently. Although practice varied widely, it is clear that many offered their slaves strong positive incentives to perform their tasks well—released time from work, extra allowances for food or clothing, even cash payments. Another carrot was the opportunity to work at a better job, one that was less

A PLANTER'S INSTRUCTIONS TO HIS OVERSEER
ON THE CASE OF RECENT MOTHERS AND PREGNANT WOMEN

SUCKLERS.—

Sucklers are not required to leave their houses until sun-rise, when they leave their children at the children's house before going to field. The period of suckling is 12 mos. Their work lies always within ½ mile of the quarter. They are required to be cool before commencing to suckle—to wait 15 minutes, at least, in summer, after reaching the children's house before nursing. It is the duty of the nurse to see that none are heated when nursing, as well as of the Overseer & his wife occasionally to do so. They are allowed 45 minutes at each morning to be with their children. They return 3 times a day until their infants are 8 mos. old—in the middle of the forenoon, at noon, & in the middle of the afternoon: til the 12th mo. but twice a day, missing at noon: during the 12th mo. at noon only. On weaning, the child is removed entirely from its Mother for 2 weeks, & placed in charge of some careful woman without a child, during which time the Mother is not to nurse it at all.

REMARKS.—

The amount of work done by a Suckler is about 3/5 of that done by a full-hand, a little increased toward the last.

PREGNANT.—

Pregnant women, at 5 mos. are put in the suckler's gang. No plowing or lifting must be required of them.

Sucklers, old, infirm & pregnant, receive the same allowances as full-work hands.

CONFINEMENT.—

The regular plantation midwife shall attend all women in confinement. Some other woman learning the art is usually with her during delivery. The confined woman lies up one month, & the midwife remains in constant attendance for 7 days. Each woman on confinement has a bundle given to her containing articles of clothing for the infant, pieces of cloth & rag, & some extra nourishment, as sugar, coffee, rice & flour for the Mother.

—"Manual of Rules,"
James Henry Hammond of South Carolina

exhausting or monotonous and more responsible than that of the field hand. Just what proportion of slaves were engaged in managerial, skilled, or domestic tasks is a subject of current debate; estimates range from a high of 26 percent to a low of 11 percent. But even if the lower figure is closest to the truth, it still means that there were tens of thousands of slave carpenters, coopers, blacksmiths, drivers, coachmen, gardeners, stewards, and house servants. The hope of being given one of these privileged positions must have been a significant incentive to a larger number of laborers.

Education

Although there were some chances for ambitious slaves to "get ahead" in these ways, they clearly couldn't rise very far. Among the most important barriers to full development of their talents was that all but a handful were denied the opportunity to learn to read and write. On the eve of the Civil War, all but one or two percent of southern slaves were illiterate, and in plantation areas illiteracy was almost universal. A few slaves taught themselves to read through heroic efforts or were assisted by others, but there was no formal education at all for them. Indeed, in most states, it was illegal to teach a slave to read, since it was feared that literate blacks would be less docile and more rebellious. Even without such laws, few masters would have seen fit to educate slave children when they could put them to work in the field at the age of six. Mass illiteracy was among the most crippling legacies of the slave experience.

Family Life

Slave marriage was not recognized in southern law. But the custom of the plantation encouraged the formation of stable marital unions. Perhaps the most neglected fact about the slave experience in the antebellum South is that slaves had a rich family life of their own.

Slaves normally lived and worked with other slaves. Fewer than 2 percent of slaves were owned by masters who had no other slaves; 95 percent were owned by planters with more than five. Not only did most slaves live in groups with fellow blacks, they typically lived in family units. Slaves were ordinarily housed not in

WHY SLAVES WERE NOT TAUGHT TO READ

If a judgement may be formed from the known conduct of white readers, we may reasonably conclude that the great majority of blacks would prefer other books than the Bible. Is there any great moral reason why we should incur the tremendous risk of having our wives and children slaughtered in consequence of our slaves being taught to read incendiary publications? Religion is as important to the slave as to the master but is the ability to read essential to salvation? Is there no other means of preaching the gospel except by the printed page? Millions of those now in heaven never owned a Bible. To read is a valuable accomplishment, but it does not save the soul. We say it without fear of successful contradiction, that there are more pious persons among the blacks than among any similar class in the world.

—De Bow's Review, 1856

barracks or dormitories, but in cabins, one for each family. Owners who allowed and encouraged such pairing off were usually rewarded with a large number of slave children.

Of course, masters had the unquestioned legal right to break up the slave family at any time, by putting some of its members up for sale. Like Mrs. Stowe's Uncle Tom, all slaves were vulnerable to being sold "down the river," sent off to the booming cotton states of the southwestern frontier. The steady westward spread of the cotton belt required a massive redistribution of the slave labor force. Between 1800 and 1860 approximately one million slaves were forcibly moved from the long-settled coastal states in which they were born to the cotton states of the Lower South. Most, however, traveled with their masters, and consequently remained with their families. Some, though, were sold alone or to separate purchasers, and families were broken up when their members belonged to different masters on adjacent plantations.

Scholars are still debating how common it was for a slave family to be torn apart by the sale of one of its members. Some estimate that the proportion was only 4 percent, but others charge that the true figure is much higher. Two points, however, seem quite clear. One is that even if the true figure was "only" 4 percent, slaves had to live with the gnawing daily fear that it *might* happen to them at any time if their owner suffered economic reverses or if he died and the estate had to split up. The system of slavery denied black people perhaps the most elemental of all human rights—the right to live with one's loved ones. On the other hand, there is strong evidence that a large majority of slaves were in fact able to form stable and enduring unions over many years, despite the ever-present threat of forced disruption. The slave family lacked legal sanction, but for practical reasons it was allowed to be strong.

Rebellion and Flight

In the southern United States as in other slave societies, some slaves found their lot so intolerable that they rose up in rebellion, and many more ran away from their masters in search of freedom. Slave revolts, however, were much rarer in the South than in Latin America. There were serious attempts at insurrection, certainly. In Richmond, Virginia in 1800 a slave named Gabriel planned a violent rebellion. Several hundred of his fellows were apparently ready to fight when the plot was discovered and Gabriel and twenty others were executed. Denmark Vesey, a free black carpenter, organized a revolt in Charleston, South Carolina in 1822, but that effort too was squashed by the authorities. In 1831, a slave preacher, Nat Turner, and dozens of other slaves were able to kill 57 whites in Southampton County, Virginia before the militia overcame them. These and other smaller insurrections give the lie to the slave-owners' claims that blacks were content in bondage. Nonetheless, slave rebellions in the American South were rare and small-scale events by the standards of a country like Brazil.

That fact has led some historians to conclude that American slaves were psychologically crushed by the system, and turned into docile, submissive, dependent creatures, the shuffling "Sambos" of southern stereotypes. The low incidence of slave uprisings, however, can be explained without making such assumptions about the slave personality. Asking why American slaves were not more rebellious is about as sensible as asking why the Estonians don't rebel against the Soviet Union, and the answer is the same: They weren't crazy enough to attempt something so obviously doomed to failure. Many Latin countries had large slave majorities; in the South, whites outnumbered blacks two to one, and the whites had all the guns. Particularly after the Turner uprising, whites had an elaborate system of patrols to monitor any suspicious activity, and to put down any attempted rising. Even if a slave conspiracy had the luck to seize a county or two, planters could count on the state militia and ultimately federal troops if necessary to bail them out. Given the power realities, the relative quiescence of American slaves is hardly an indication that they were truly "Sambos."

Some slaves, of course, resisted oppression in a more individual and less revolutionary fashion—by running away. But the familiar idea that large numbers traveled north via the Underground Railroad, a system to assist fugitives organized by benevolent white abolitionists, is misleading. Most runaways, first of all, seem to have left impulsively for a few days in the woods, with no hopes of permanent escape. Those who were determined to be free fled more often to southern cities than to northern states or to Canada. Despite the myth of the Underground Railroad, there never was a highly organized, elaborately coordinated national network to spirit slaves out of the South. Those fugitives who received aid along the way depended primarily on fellow blacks, slave and free, not on white benefactors. Most important, the number who fled was far smaller than legend would have it.

Although few slaves escaped, it does not follow that most were satisfied with their lot or that they had internalized the values of the system and become childishly dependent on their masters. Flight was exceedingly difficult and dangerous. Blacks could not travel freely in the South without proper papers; even free blacks with proof of their status were harrassed. And at the end of the road for the fortunate few who reached the North was not a Promised Land of freedom and equality, but second-class citizenship amid a generally hostile population. Racism was pervasive in the northern states, which doubtless helps to explain why more than half of the country's free blacks chose to remain in the South despite substantial efforts on the part of southern states to force them out. Family ties were another potent deterrent. To flee alone was difficult enough. To flee with a family was madness. Finally, there were ties beyond the family, attachments and obligations to the broader slave community.

The Slave Community and Culture

We know all too little about slave culture, because a largely illiterate people leave behind few documents for the historian. But scholars have recently discovered in surviving slave songs, folktales, proverbs, aphorisms, and jokes evidence of the richness and complexity of slave culture. The history of slavery is not simply the story of what white masters did to their black victims; it is also the story of how blacks shaped their own lives within the harsh constraints imposed by their powerful oppressors. The great majority of slaves lived in small communities of their fellow bondsmen, and had enough room for maneuver to create quasi-independent cultural institutions that allowed them to interpret their experience in their own ways. Although masters, for example, sought to indoctrinate them in a kind of Christianity that celebrated passive submission, the slaves developed a variant that held out the hope of liberation. The spirituals, work songs, and tales that played such a central role in their culture likewise had subtle subversive meanings that indicated that slaves did not see their oppressed lot as somehow natural and inevitable. Expressions of their alternative world view had to be guarded and subtle, of course, given the crushing force that was directed against the openly rebellious. But slaves did develop a culture that gave them enough sense of pride and group cohesion to survive being treated as less than human without losing a sense of their own humanity. That survival was, as the black novelist Ralph Ellison observes, "one of the great triumphs of the human spirit in modern times."

THE WHITE SOCIAL ORDER

The plantation system and the institution of black slavery on which it rested gave the southern social structure its distinctive shape. It was simpler, more rigid, more starkly hierarchical than society outside the South.

TWO GLIMPSES OF SLAVE RELIGION

You t'inks I'm mistaken, honey! But I know t'ings dat de wite folks wid all dar larnin' nebber fin's out, an' nebber sarches fo' nudder....

No, honey! De good Lawd doan gib eberyt'ing to his wite chilluns. He's gib 'em de wite skin, an' larnin', an' he's made 'em rich an' free. But de brack folks is his chilluns, too, an' he gibs us de brack skin an' no larnin', an' hab make us t' work fo' de wite folks. But de good Lawd gibs us eyes t' see t'ings dey doan see, an' he comes t' me, a poor brack slave woman, an' tells me be patient, 'cause dar's no wite nor brack in hebben. An' de time's comin' when he'll make his brack chilluns free in dis yere worl', an' gib 'em larnin', an' good homes, an' good times. Ah! honey, I knows, I knows.

—Fisk University, *Unwritten History of Slavery*, 1945

F'o de war when we'd have a meetin' at night, wuz mos' always' way in de woods or de bushes some whar so de white folks couldn't hear, an' when dey'd sing a spiritual an' de spirit 'gin to shout some de elders would go 'mongst de folks an' put dey han' over dey mouf an' some times put a clof in dey mouf an' say, "Spirit don talk so loud or de patterol break us up." You know dey had white patterols what went 'round at night to see de niggers didn't cut up no devilment, an' den de meetin' would break up an' some would go to one house an' some er nudder an' dey would groan de w'ile, den go home.

—E.A. McIlhenny, *Befo De War Spirituals*, 1933

The Economic Basis of Planter Domination

At the apex of the southern social structure were the large planters, with their big houses, dozens of slaves, and thousands of acres of prime land. In 1860 some 16,000 families—one percent of the total—had plantations with 40 or more slaves. A third of all slaves were held by this tiny minority, and they were affluent indeed. Although only 22 percent of the American white population lived in the South on the eve of the Civil War, two-thirds of all men with estates valued at $100,000 or more were southerners. Forced labor was the basis of almost every southern fortune.

Another 9 percent of white families had moderately large plantations with from 7 to 39 slaves; they owned just over half of all bondsmen. Five of six slaves (84 percent) therefore belonged to the richest 10 percent of whites; only a small minority lived and worked on farms with few or no other slaves. Land holding was

TABLE 11–2
The Distribution of Slaves in 1860

Number of Slaves Held	Percent of White Families	Percent of Slaves Held
40 or more	1	31
7–39	9	53
1–6	15	16
0	75	0

less concentrated than slaveholding, but distinctly more so than in the free farming states of the Midwest. Three-quarters of white families had no slaves, but the great majority did own their own small farms. The most fertile lands with the best access to transportation, however, were controlled by the planter elite, while slaveless whites scratched out a living on less desirable plots in the backcountry. The richest 10 percent of whites in the Lower South owned almost two-thirds of all farm wealth, far above the 40-percent figure in states like Illinois and Wisconsin. The slave system not only denied equality to blacks; it also promoted greater inequality among the dominant whites than free agriculture. The average slaveholder was five times as wealthy as the average northerner, and more than ten times richer than southern farmers without slaves.

Southern planters liked to think of themselves as "cavaliers," aristocrats who descended from the nobility of seventeenth-century England, heroes out of the pages of their favorite author, the romantic novelist Sir Walter Scott. In fact, on the cotton frontier as elsewhere in the country, blood and breeding counted for less than money. Money and power could be grasped by men of obscure origins, if they had the necessary energy, discipline, and commercial prowess. Descendants of the wealthy planting families of colonial Virginia and South Carolina who inherited capital naturally had an advantage in the competition, but it was not decisive. Some were poor businessmen and lost out, to be replaced by more aggressive and cunning young men on the move and on the make. William Faulkner's 1936 novel, *Absalom, Absalom* is a fictional but true-to-life portrait of one of them.

Social and economic lines in the South were clearly hardening in the antebellum years, and movement into the economic elite from below was becoming rarer. Among the richest 440 planters in South Carolina at mid-century, only one in ten had earned rather than inherited the bulk of his fortune. Opportunities to move up into the ranks of the lesser planters were shrinking as well, because the rising prices of slaves and good land worked to the advantage of those already established. The proportion of white families owning slaves fell from over a third in 1830 to only a quarter in 1860. During the 1850s, all major forms of farm wealth—slaves, land, buildings, and equipment—became concentrated in fewer hands.

TABLE 11-3
Slaveholdings of the Political Elite
of the Lower South, 1860

	Percent Owning Slaves	*Percent with 20 or More Slaves*
White families	38	6
County government officials	53	18
State senators and representatives	68	33
Delegates to secession conventions	83	41

The Political Dominance of the Planters

Although slave-owners were a minority of the southern population, they held more political offices than the slaveless majority; the more important the office, the greater the overrepresentation of the slave interest (see Table 11-3). At a time when the dollar was worth seven or eight times what it is today, the average member of the South Carolina state legislature had a fortune of over $100,000; in Alabama it was $70,000, in Florida $61,000.

These offices were filled by popular election, and it was by no means obvious that the economic interests of the masses of slaveless whites were identical with those of the planters. Nonslaveholders, however, deferred to the residents of the big houses and supported them politically. Challenges to their rule made little headway. In 1857 Hinton Rowan Helper, a farmer from North Carolina, published a powerful assault against slavery, *The Impending Crisis of the South*. Helper's objection to the peculiar institution was not the harm it did to blacks; he was a rabid racist who wanted them all returned to Africa. He argued that slavery debased white labor and prevented economic and social development. Helper's critique did not inspire poor whites to defy their traditional leaders, and he was soon forced to flee to the North. (After Abraham Lincoln became President, he rewarded Helper with an appointment as U.S. consul in Buenos Aires.)

The most important circumstance unifying the white community behind slavery and the leadership of the planter class was racial fear. Slavery was a sure means of keeping blacks in their place. Whites who thought Helper's plan to send the country's four million blacks back to Africa hopelessly impractical—as it surely was—could conceive of only two alternatives. Blacks could be set free to mix with whites—a prospect they found terrifying—or slavery could be preserved. Few hesitated over the choice.

Another factor that fortified the dominant position of the planter class was the undeveloped and undemocratic character of the southern educational system, which perpetuated ignorance and political docility. For the children of the wealthy, education through college was the norm. In 1860 the number of college students

TABLE 11-4
Regional Differences in Education
for Whites Aged 5–19, 1861

	Percent Enrolled in School	Average Percent of Enrolled Attending	Number of Days in School Year	Days of School per Child 5–19 in the Region
Northeast	62	59	150	55
West	76	57	116	50
South	30	45	80	11

per 1,000 whites in the South was three times higher than in the North. But at the primary and secondary levels, the South lagged far behind. The crusade for mass education that swept through the North and West in the antebellum years left the South largely untouched. Half of the white people in South Carolina at mid-century could not read or write. The cause of widespread illiteracy is apparent in Table 11-4. In 1861, only a third of school age whites were enrolled in an educational institution, less than half the proportion in the rest of the country. Those who were enrolled spent much less time there; attendance rates were lower in the South, and the school year was much shorter. Consequently, the average southern white child received only a fifth as much schooling as a child north of the Mason-Dixon Line. When we add the slaves of the region who were given no education at all, except in rare instances, the backwardness of the South stands out even more starkly. The planter elite had a near monopoly on knowledge and the means of communication. This perpetuated planter rule. It also left a legacy of ignorance, a regional scar that would last long into the future.

Ethnic and Religious Homogeneity

The southern social landscape was distinguished also by its lack of ethnic and religious diversity. There were the whites—the dominant group, mostly of Anglo-Saxon background—and there were the blacks. Nineteen out of twenty blacks were enslaved, and those legally "free" were subject to severe discrimination in every sphere of life. Few of the European immigrants who flocked to the New World in the 1830s, '40s and '50s made their way to the South; in 1860 that region contained 35 percent of the country's inhabitants but only 7 percent of its immigrant population. Immigrants were attracted by the job opportunities offered by the burgeoning cities and factories of the industrial North. But even those with the experience and capital necessary for a start in farming preferred Minnesota to Mississippi, probably because they sensed that opportunities for self-advancement were more constricted in a slave society. The complex ethnic mosaic that was taking shape in the Northeast and the Midwest therefore did not develop in the inbred, provincial South.

Southern religious life was also simpler and more homogeneous. The Second Great Awakening there was almost entirely a matter of the growth of the Methodist and Baptist denominations. By mid-century the South was 90 percent Protestant, and 90 percent of the Protestants were Baptists or Methodists. The revivals began with huge camp meetings organized by itinerant ministers. Local churches grew up when enough settlers to support them had arrived. The preachers were not much more educated than their congregations. "We could not," admitted one, "conjugate a verb or parse a sentence and murdered the king's English almost every lick. But there was a Divine unction [that] attended the word preached, and thousands fell under the might[y] power of religion." They preached a simple, fervently emotional creed, with little attention to doctrinal niceties. Whereas many northern evangelists of the day adhered to a kind of "romantic perfectionism" that led them to support social reforms like abolitionism and the common school movement, southern Methodist and Baptist ministers avoided politics and focused all their efforts on individual conversions. Peter Cartwright, one of most famous Methodist circuit riders, was forced to flee the South after he said that slavery was "a domestic, political, and moral evil." When they mentioned slavery at all, southern preachers insisted that it had biblical sanction and was divinely ordained. Instead of challenging the status quo, southern religion celebrated it.

The Violent South

Although generalizations about such large groups as "southern whites" or "Yankees" are always hazardous, there is strong evidence that one distinctive cultural attribute of the whites of the antebellum South was their propensity to resort to violence. The ideal southern gentleman was courtly but hot-tempered, quick to defend his honor with a dueling pistol—and men of every social level displayed what one wise observer described as the "the chip-on-the-shoulder swagger and brag of a boy," an attitude "of which the essence was the boast, voiced or not, that he would knock the hell out of whoever dared cross him." As another commentator put it, "In the South the swagger of the bully was called chivalry, a swiftness to quarrel was regarded as courage. The bludgeon was adopted as a substitute for argument; and assassination was lifted to a fine art." The same tendency was displayed again and again, whether in a duel between gentlemen, in the tavern brawl that ended in a knifing, or in the vigilante mobs taking "justice" in their own hands.

The habit of violence was certainly not confined to the South, of course. But the distinctiveness of the region stands out sharply in the census taker's compilation of the causes of deaths in the year 1860. The homicide rate for the South was triple the rate for the Midwest, and four and a half times as high as in the Northeast! A possible explanation is that in 1860 parts of the South were still not far removed from the frontier stage, and violence is a familiar trait of most frontiers. This doubtless helps to explain why Texas, for example, had a homicide rate 20 times higher than those for the long-settled states of the Northeast. But much of the South was further removed from the frontier than the Midwest. Moreover, if we

TABLE 11-5
Homicide Rates by Region and Selected States, 1860
Homicides per 100,000 Population

Regions

Northeast	1.0
Northwest*	1.4
South	4.5

States Comparably Closer to the Frontier Stage

Massachusetts	1.5	Indiana	1.2	Michigan	1.2
Virginia	2.8	Mississippi	3.4	Arkansas	6.4

*Midwestern farming states, excluding Missouri, Nebraska and Kansas. Missouri was a slave state, and its homicide rate of 4.1 was in the southern range. The even higher rates in Nebraska (6.9) and Kansas (14.9) reflect the violent battle for political dominance that was then being waged by southern and Yankee migrants there.

compare homicide rates for pairs of southern and northern states that were settled at approximately the same time, the South's greater propensity for personal violence stands out dramatically. In 1860 Massachusetts and Virginia both had historical roots reaching back more than three centuries. Homicides were almost twice as frequent in Virginia. Both Indiana and Mississippi gained admission to the Union shortly after the War of 1812. The homicide differential was nearly three to one in favor of the North. And it was wider still—over five to one—between Michigan and Arkansas, which attained statehood in the 1830s.

True, the frontier bred violence. But as the frontier receded, the people of the North shed their cruder, more impulsive characteristics, and developed peaceful means of conflict resolution. In the South, by contrast, the predisposition to violence became a folkway that endured long after the passing of the frontier. It assumed greater significance as the issue of slavery in the republic forced its way ever closer to the center of the political arena. As southerners encountered mounting criticism from outside, they inclined naturally toward a quick and violent solution. By the 1850s, some southerners were beginning to boast that the people of the region had "more aptitude and genius for war" than those of the North. "When the question of honor is raised," said one, the men of the South "rush to the sword, fierce and fearless in a contest. They possess every quality necessary to rule the Northern people." Only a few years later the truth of that bold prophecy would be put to a bloody test.

SUGGESTED READINGS

Willie Lee Rose, *A Documentary History of Slavery in North America* (1976), is excellent. Robert W. Fogel and Stanley Engerman, *Time on the Cross: The Economics of American Negro Slavery* (1974) and Gavin Wright, *The Political Economy of the Cotton*

South (1978) present opposing views of the slave economy. Harold D. Woodman, *Slavery and the Southern Economy* (1966) is a good collection of documents. Robert S. Starobin, *Industrial Slavery in the Old South* (1970) punctures the myth that slave labor was only useful in agriculture. Eugene D. Genovese, *Roll, Jordan, Roll: The World the Slaves Made* (1974), Herbert G. Gutman, *The Black Family in Slavery and Freedom, 1750–1925* (1976), Lawrence Levine, *Black Culture and Black Consciousness: Afro-American Folk Thought from Slavery to Freedom* (1977), and Albert J. Raboteau, *Slave Religion: The "Invisible Institution" in the Antebellum South* (1978) explore slave culture.

For the testimony of former slaves about their experience as bondsmen, gathered by a federal agency in the 1930s, see Benjamin A. Botkin, ed., *Lay My Burden Down: A Folk History of Slavery* (1945), and G.P. Rawick's multi-volume *The American Slave: A Composite Biography* (1972). John W. Blassingame, *The Slave Community* (rev. ed., 1979) draws heavily upon the ex-slave narratives. 2,358 of them are subjected to computerized analysis in Paul D. Escott, *Slavery Remembered: A Record of 20th Century Slave Narratives* (1979). *The Narrative of the Life of Frederick Douglass* (1845) is an absorbing autobiography by an ex-slave. It should be supplemented with Nathan Huggins, *Slave and Citizen: The Life of Frederick Douglass* (1980). Ira Berlin, *Slaves Without Masters: The Free Negro in the Antebellum South* (1974) examines the difficult position of that group.

Ralph A. Wooster, in *The People in Power* (1969) and *Politicians, Planters, and Plain*

Folk: Courthouse and Statehouse in the Upper South, 1850–1860 (1975), analyzes the social characteristics of members of the political elite. Eugene D. Genovese, *The World the Slaveholder Made* (1964) and J. Mills Thornton III, *Politics and Power in a Slave Society* (1978) interpret their thought. Frank L. Owsley, *Plain Folk of the Old South* (1949) examines whites outside the planter group. Other aspects of white society are covered in Carl Degler, *Place Over Time: The Continuity of Southern Distinctiveness* (1977), Donald G. Matthews, *Religion in the Old South* (1977), and Anne Firor Scott, *The Southern Lady* (1970). William R. Taylor, *Cavalier and Yankee: The Old South and American National Character* (1961) treats images of the "Southerner" and the "Yankee" as they emerged in American popular literature.

Chapter Twelve

The New West

*I*f God were suddenly to call the world to judgment," a visitor remarked in 1847, "He would surprise two-thirds of the American population on the road like ants." It was a pardonable exaggeration, for one of the greatest migratory waves in history was then sweeping across the land. "Old America seems to be breaking up and moving westward," an English immigrant en route to Illinois by covered wagon wrote in his journal. "We are seldom out of sight, as we travel on this grand track towards the Ohio, of family groups behind and before us."

At the opening of the nineteenth century, only about 50,000 Americans—less than one percent of the country's population—were to be found in the Northwest Territory beyond the Appalachians. By the time of the Civil War, over 8.5 million Americans—more than a fourth of the population—lived in the nonslave states of the West. In the first 200 years of British settlement in North America, the frontier edged forward at an average rate of less than 2 miles per year; after 1800, it advanced at a rate of 17 miles a year.

DISPOSSESSING THE INDIANS

The "winning of the West" can be viewed as a stirring chapter in the saga of American development. However, it should first be looked at from another vantage point—that of the native peoples who were engulfed and pushed aside by incoming white settlers. The crushing of Tecumseh's pan-Indian movement put an end to the

"The Rocky Mountains," an 1866 print by Currier and Ives, is a romaticized depiction of the difficulties faced by emigrants during the years of westward expansion.

threat of unified Indian resistance to white encroachment. But most of the tens of millions of acres of land between the Appalachians and the Mississippi was still legally held by 125,000 Indians of the area, who were organized into several dozen tribes. Dispossessing the Indians and securing white control of the land therefore had the highest priority for expansionist-minded Americans. The Indians, most thought, were "deficient in intellectual and moral culture," a people who did not "furnish their share of the advancement of society and the prosperity of the world." "There is nothing stationary around us," said the Governor of Michigan. "We are all striving in the career of life to acquire riches, or honor, or power, or some other thing; the aggregate of these efforts constitutes the advance of society." The Indian did not fit in a striving, future-oriented social order:

> *There is little of this in the constitution of our savages. Like the bear, and deer, and buffalo of his own forests, an Indian lives as his father lived, and dies as his father died. He never looks around him, with a spirit of emulation, to compare his situation with that of others, and to resolve on improving it.*

Although virtually all Americans at the time held such ethnocentric beliefs concerning the "backwardness" of Indian society and the superiority of their own civilization, they differed about whether it was possible to reform the Indians and assimilate them to white culture. Thomas Jefferson and other humanitarians insisted that with proper education and guidance Indians could be reshaped in the white Christian mold of settled yeoman farmers. Persuading them to abandon their migrating life of hunting and gathering for settled agriculture would not only bring them the benefits of "higher" civilization, Jefferson said; it would also have the advantage of enabling them "to live on much smaller portions of land. While they are learning to do better on less land, our increasing numbers will be calling for more land, and thus a coincidence of interests will be produced between those who have land to spare and want other necessities, and those who have such necessaries to spare and want lands." As Indians followed white man's ways and acquired property, Jefferson told a tribal delegation, "you will unite yourselves with us, and we shall all be Americans." The red man would disappear in the melting pot.

Inspired by this vision, missionaries and federal agents stepped up their efforts to persuade Indians to cede lands, abandon their customs, and emulate American ways. Their record was spotty. Under pressure the tribes yielded up chunk after chunk of their once vast domains. But few lost their identity and melted away. Those who sought to uplift the Indian underestimated the tenacity and staying power of traditional tribal cultures. People reared to admire the hunter and the warrior and to think of the welfare of the community rather than that of the individual were not easily persuaded that the "spirit of emulation" of a competitive capitalist society was an admirable trait.

Expulsion

Paradoxically, it was the behavior of the minority of tribes who tried hardest to follow Jefferson's advice and emulate white ways that led to the crisis that caused a radical shift in U.S. policy toward the Indians in the 1830s. The Five Civilized

Tribes of the Southwest—the Creeks, Chickasaws, Choctaws, Seminoles, and Cherokees—had long practiced settled agriculture, but in the opening decades of the nineteenth century they began to move even closer to white cultural patterns. The Cherokees became a prosperous society of small farmers growing corn and vegetables. They built schools for their children, developed an alphabet, published a paper in Cherokee and English, and adopted a written constitution modeled on that of the United States. Some even bought slaves, like their southern white neighbors.

Their rapid advance toward civilization American-style, however, did them no good when powerful whites saw an opportunity to profit at their expense. The Cherokees were forced to cede portions of their lands to Georgia farmers and planters moving into their territory on several occasions. When gold was discovered on their remaining land in 1829, they dug in their heels and tried to bar white entry through court action. The Georgia government then declared that the Cherokees had only a "pretended" government and could not keep white prospectors out. Although Georgia's action was a blatant violation of existing treaties between the Cherokees and the United States, the White House was then occupied by Andrew Jackson, who backed Georgia. In his years as a general in the U.S. Army, Jackson had won fame as an Indian fighter. To him they were "wandering savages" who made ridiculous claims to ownership of land "on which they have neither dwelt nor made improvements, merely because they have seen them from the mountain or passed them in the chase." Although this was hardly an accurate description of the settled Cherokees, Jackson had his way. The Cherokees won their suit against Georgia before the Supreme Court, but Jackson simply ignored the ruling and Georgia whites continued to trespass on Cherokee land.

Jackson's refusal to use federal power to protect Indians from state actions that violated treaty rights was a first step toward the radically new federal Indian policy embodied in the Removal Bill of 1830. All tribes east of the Mississippi, whether "civilized" or not, were to be uprooted and relocated in a new Indian territory west of the Mississippi, where they could "pursue happiness in their own way, under their own rude institutions." In theory, the move was to be "voluntary." In exchange for signing a removal treaty, tribes were given title to new land in perpetuity, a year's provisions, and cash. But denial of federal protection from state abuse was clearly coercive. And those who still resisted leaving, as a large faction of Cherokees did, were rounded up by the U.S. Army and forced to walk the "trail of tears" westward.

By 1844, three-quarters of the native peoples of the eastern United States had been removed beyond the Mississippi; most of the remaining 30,000 were in remote spots around Lake Superior, above the line of projected white settlement. The Iroquois Six Nations of New York (the Mohawk, Oneida, Onondaga, Cayuga, Seneca, and Tuscarora) were the only major tribes that escaped the process. The population of the relocated tribes dropped about a third as a result of the hardships of the ill-organized journey and the problems they had adjusting to their new locations. They had to learn how to survive terrains and climates that were often bewilderingly different from anything they had previously known, and to fight off attacks from tribes indigenous to the trans-Mississippi West.

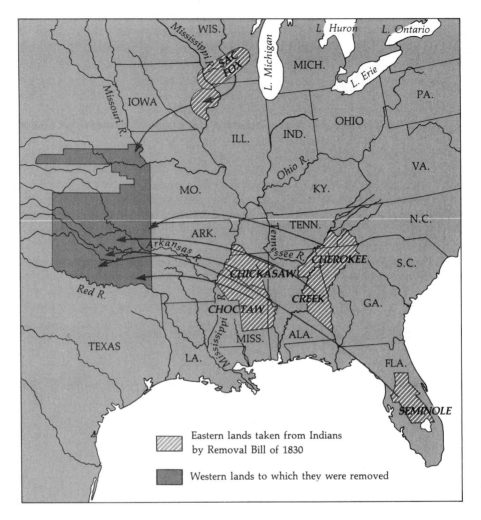

Map 12–1
The Trail of Tears: Indian Removal to the West

Some friends of the Indian denounced the removal policy as a cruel violation of earlier promises. It certainly was, and not the last such violation either (see Chapter 19). Others, however, accepted Jackson's argument that it was necessary to save the tribes from extinction by insulating them from further contact with whites. It would buy time for them, time in which they might "cast off their savage habits and become an interesting, civilized, Christian community." Why such a cultural conversion would be more likely to take place on the plains of Oklahoma than in the forests of Ohio was not made clear. Most ordinary American whites took a simple view of the matter in any event. The new policy removed an awkward obstacle to the expansion of their dynamic, aggressive, materialistic society, at no cost to anyone except the Indians, and they were out of sight and out of mind.

We were at Washington at the time that the measure for chasing the last of several tribes of Indians from their forest homes was canvassed in Congress and finally decided upon by the fiat of the President. If the American character may be judged by their conduct in this matter, they are most lamentably deficient in every feeling of honor and integrity. You will see them one hour lecturing their mob on the indefeasible rights of man, and the next driving from their homes the children of the soil, whom they have bound themselves to protect by the most solemn treaties. The circumstance which renders their expulsion from their own, their native lands, so peculiarly lamentable is that they were yielding rapidly to the force of example; their lives were no longer those of wandering hunters, but they were becoming agriculturists, and the tyrannical arm of brutal power has not now driven them, as formerly, only from their hunting grounds, their favorite springs, and the sacred bones of their fathers, but it has chased them from the dwellings their advancing knowledge had taught them to make comfortable; from the newly-ploughed fields of their pride; and from the crops their sweat had watered.

—Frances Trollope, *Domestic Manners of the Americans*, 1832

THE ECONOMIC DEVELOPMENT OF THE NORTHWEST

Once the Indians had been cleared from the land, American settlers poured in. The advance of the Cotton Kingdom into the Southwest has been discussed in Chapter 11. The remainder of this chapter examines the development of the seven states of the "Old Northwest"—Ohio, Indiana, Illinois, Michigan, Wisconsin, Minnesota, and Iowa. There were, of course, some similarities between the southwestern and northwestern frontiers. But the contrast between the system of family farms operating with free labor and the slave-based plantation economy was of decisive importance in the nation's history.

Acquiring Title to a Farm

Because the federal government had negotiated the transfer of Indian land into white hands, federal policies determined the course of development. One basic decision that left an imprint on the landscape that endures to today was the rectangular land survey provided for in the Land Ordinance of 1785. The West was divided into square townships six miles on each side, and subdivided into 36

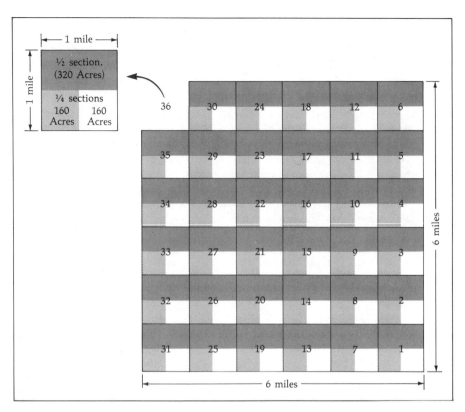

MAP 12–2
The Rectangular Survey System

square sections of 640 acres (one square mile) each. Whatever the contours of the local terrain were, the same monotonous grid was imposed on it, with roads running north, south, east and west. It was a cheap, accurate, and speedy way to divide up the land. Had the cumbersome older system of describing land by metes and bounds been employed instead, it would have produced many odd-shaped parcels and overlapping claims, and the resulting boundary disputes might have discouraged settlement. But the rigid application of the grid made the American West a land of straight lines and produced towns and cities that were stamped out of the same unvarying mold, without the strong center provided by the town green and the meeting house in New England communities.

Federal land disposition policies also exerted a profound influence on the course of western development. Selling federal land on easy terms promoted rapid settlement; selling on restrictive terms inhibited it. In the first years of the young republic, federal land policy was relatively restrictive. In the 1790s the minimum plot offered for sale was a section of 640 acres and the minimum price was $2 per acre. However, 640 acres was too large for a single family to farm, and $1,280 was a sum well beyond the reach of the average American. Most sales were therefore

TABLE 12–1
U.S. Land Distribution Policy

Year	Minimum Auction Price per Acre	Minimum Unit in Acres
1796	$2.00	640
1800	2.00	320
1804	2.00	160
1820	1.25	80
1832	1.25	40

either to well-to-do speculators, who carved up their sections into smaller plots and sold them at a higher price per acre, or to organized groups who pooled their resources and moved west together. A glance at the map of any midwestern state today will reveal how common was group migration from eastern communities, particularly from New England. Ohio, for example, has a Cambridge, a Salem, a Greenwich, a Montpelier, a New Plymouth, and a New Concord.

Public pressure to make available more land to individual settlers with only limited funds was strong, however, and Congress bowed to it by progressively relaxing the terms, lowering both the price per acre and the minimum acreage requirement. By 1820 an aspiring farmer could purchase 80 acres for a mere $100, about what a hired hand could earn, plus his room and board, in a year.

The land was sold at public auctions, and the set price was only a minimum; free bidding could drive the price of desirable plots up considerably more. Since settlement proceeded much more rapidly than the government's land survey, most migrants simply "squatted" on the land when they first arrived and farmed it without any legal claim; two-thirds of the farmers in Illinois in 1828 were squatters. By the time the survey was completed and the auction held, in many cases, the population had become dense enough to drive land values well above the minimum. Consequently, outside speculators often found it advantageous to offer more than $1.25 per acre and snatch away the farms local settlers had worked so hard to develop. To prevent that, spontaneous local associations called claims clubs developed. They exerted social pressure and sometimes violence to keep others from bidding on what they regarded as their property and to ensure that they could secure legal title at the lowest possible price. According to a report from Elkhorn Creek, Wisconsin in 1835, "If a speculator should bid on a settler's farm, he was knocked down and dragged out of the land office, and if the striker was prosecuted and fined, the settlers paid the expense by common consent among themselves." The claims clubs embodied a healthy, egalitarian democratic principle—that the right of common people to a secure living outweighed the right of the wealthy to enlarge their profits. From another perspective, however, the clubs occupy an important place in the American vigilante tradition; such mob action outside established legal procedures has had many uglier expressions since.

The Agricultural Ladder

Even the most militant claims club could do nothing to save the land of a settler who couldn't pay for it once the government put it on the market. Nor was the price of land the only capital needed for a start in farming. A settler had to buy food to last until the first harvest, as well as seed, tools, and farm animals. It is estimated that in 1830, it took about $600 to begin a farm in a well-wooded part of Ohio or Indiana. By the 1850s, settlers on the prairies of Illinois and Iowa needed more like $1,000; in those relatively treeless areas, it took extra money to buy timber for fences and cabins.

Even a penniless newcomer, however, had a good chance of obtaining a farm of his own through hard work and strict economy. Farm labor was in short supply and was relatively well paid. In the 1830s a hired hand could save enough in six months to pay the first year's interest on a $600 loan at 9 percent. Since many farmers bought more land than they could cultivate, in hopes of reaping capital gains in the future, it was also possible to rent a farm for a few seasons and save purchase money that way. We lack adequate studies to know just what fraction of the landless people of the antebellum Midwest actually climbed the rungs of the "agricultural ladder" to full ownership, but it was clearly large. The overwhelming majority of paid farm hands of the West were in their teens or early twenties. As they grew older, they must have either become farm-owners themselves or moved to the city, because there were very few middle-aged farm laborers. That many became independent farmers is suggested by the pattern of age differences in the

---

THE ATTRACTIONS OF FRONTIER ILLINOIS

Come all you good farmers that on your plow depend,
Come listen to a story, come listen to a friend:
Oh, leave your fields of childhood, you enterprising boys:
Come travel west and settle on the plains of Illinois.

Illinois, it is as fine countree as ever has been seen,
If old Adam had traveled over that, perhaps he would say the same,
"All in the garden of Eden, when I was but a boy,
There was nothing I could compare with the plains of Illinois."

Perhaps you have a few acres that near your friends' adjoin,
Your family is growing large, for them you must provide,
Come, leave your fields of childhood, you enterprising boys,
Come travel west and settle on the plains of Illinois.

wealth of Wisconsin farmers on the eve of the Civil War. Well over 40 percent of men under the age of 30 had no property, and fewer than one in seven possessed as much as $1,000 worth. Among farmers in their thirties and forties, however, the proportions were exactly reversed. Only a handful of the older farmers were without property, and a large fraction were quite well-to-do. A simple faith in free competition reigned unchallenged in the new West, and it was based on a dynamic economy that generated ever-increasing wealth for a broad sector of the population.

The Spread of Market Production

Early in the nineteenth century, most of the first settlers of the Midwest had grown up on northeastern subsistence farms in "the age of homespun." They were products of a traditional order in which the best farmer was one "who did everything for himself." The little that he sold in the market was revealingly termed his "surplus"; it was something extra he produced after his real needs—to feed and clothe his family—were met. Farming was much like that in Ohio and Indiana during Jefferson's Presidency. Few residents specialized in the production of a single cash crop and met their other needs through purchase. Those who did not see self-sufficiency as an ideal saw it as a necessity, for they had no means of getting bulky farm products to distant markets at a less than prohibitive cost.

The opening up of new markets—first in the South, then in the Northeast—rapidly reshaped the character of western agriculture soon thereafter. The host of improvements we call the transportation revolution made it possible to sell western farm products outside the region at a profit, and this stimulated farmers to concentrate all their efforts in growing the crop best suited to their area and most in demand. As their incomes rose, they abandoned homespun garments and other products made on the farm for store-bought goods. Their new orientation toward profit made them more jealous with their time and more interested in using it efficiently. A good index of the spread of the market mentality is the growing audience for agricultural journals; the circulation of *American Farmer*, for example, was very small before 1820 but had reached 350,000 by 1860. Through the journals, farmers learned to experiment with improved farm machinery,

TABLE 12-2
**Age Differences in Property Holdings
of Wisconsin Farmers, 1860**

Real Estate Holdings	20–29	30–39	40–49
None	44%	13%	6%
$1,000 or more	15%	39%	39%

At an early period "production for self consumption" was the leading purpose; now no farmer would find it profitable "to do everything within himself." He now sells for money, and it is his interest to buy for money, every article that he cannot produce cheaper than he can buy. He cannot afford to make at home his clothing, the furniture or his farming utensils; he buys many articles for consumption for his table. He produces that which he can raise and sell to the best advantage, and he is in a situation to buy all that he can purchase, cheaper than he can produce. Time and labor have become cash articles, and he neither lends nor barters them. His farm does not merely afford him a subsistence; it produces capital, and therefore demands the expenditure of capital for its improvement.

—New York State Agricultural Society, *Transactions*, 1852

livestock strains, crop varieties, and techniques of cultivation. They read, for example, advertisements for special purpose iron and steel plows, which did a better job for half the effort. It is estimated that those who applied the best methods available in 1850 were able to produce from two to four times as much per year as their predecessors in 1820.

The first external market to open up to midwesterners was in the South. Planters found cotton so profitable that they grew little else, and purchased food from elsewhere. The Mississippi and Ohio rivers and their tributaries together include 50,000 miles of navigable water, flowing generally southward. In the first phase of the transportation revolution, midwesterners laid down a system of roads that enabled them to bring their wagons to a point where crops could be collected by a barge or flatboat. After 1811, when the steamboat appeared in the West, the pace of the West-to-South foodstuffs trade quickened because of rapidly declining freight rates. In the 1820s and 1830s the states of the Lower Midwest—Ohio, Indiana, and southern Illinois—were economically an extension of the Upper South but without slaves. Most farmers grew corn and raised hogs, as they did in Kentucky and Tennessee.

From the 1830s onward, a major reorientation of the western economy took place. New economic links between the West and the Northeast were forged, and the West was wrenched loose from its dependence on the southern trade. Most of the hundreds of artificial waterways that were built after the successful completion of the Erie Canal in 1825, and most of the thousands of miles of rail track constructed in the 1830s, 40s and 50s, were laid along an East–West rather than a North–South axis. They were designed primarily to facilitate the flow of goods between the Northeast and the West rather than between either region and the South. The market for western farm products in the rapidly urbanizing Northeast was growing much more rapidly than the southern market; indeed, southern food needs were increasingly being met by southern producers outside the cotton belt. And the West was conversely a particularly attractive market for northeastern manufactures; the South's population was growing more slowly, and much of it consisted of slaves and whites too poor to purchase factory goods.

The effect of the new canals and railroads on trade flows is clear from figures about the destination of flour and corn exported from the West in the years 1835 and 1853. In 1835, over 67 percent of the flour and 98 percent of the corn went to the South; by 1853, 72 percent of the West's flour and 63 percent of its corn went eastward instead. Another sign of major sectional reorientation is that many midwestern famers in these years abandoned corn and hogs in favor of wheat, cattle, and dairy products, which appealed more to the palates of eastern city dwellers.

Beginnings of Urbanization and Industrialization

In the two decades before the Civil War, urban centers multiplied in the West. The proportion of people living in towns and cities with a population of 2,500 or more almost quadrupled; by 1860, the West was twice as urbanized as the South and about as much so as the Northeast had been in 1830. Cincinnati and St. Louis both had slightly more than 30,000 residents in 1830; by 1860, their populations had grown tenfold. A trading post with a white population of a few dozen in 1830, Chicago could claim over 100,000 inhabitants before the Civil War. Detroit, Milwaukee, and Cleveland grew from nothing or next to nothing to substantial urban centers with close to 50,000 residents each in these same years.

All of these booming cities of the West were located on major waterways, and all established strong rail links to the East as well when the railroad became the dominant form of transportation late in the period. Their primary basis for growth was trade and land speculation. They were the points at which the grain and meat of western farmers was gathered and dispatched to destinations outside the region, and through which manufactures from the East were dispatched to small towns in the countryside. These major centers were at the top of the "urban hierarchy," commanding the trade of the surrounding hinterland linked to them by transportation routes. The merchants of each city fought to extend their hinterlands and siphon away the trade controlled by their rivals.

Hunger for expanding markets and population growth led city promoters to indulge in extravagant "boosterism." A booster of St. Louis declared that his city was "destined in the future to equal London in its population, Athens in its philosophy, art and culture, Rome in its hotels, cathedrals, and grandeur, and to be the central commercial metropolis of a continent." The simple faith that bigger was better was rooted in the elementary fact that population growth brought rising land values and a flourishing real estate market. One choice 80 by 100 foot lot in Chicago sold for $100 in 1832, $3,000 in 1834, and $15,000 a year later.

At the base of the urban hierarchy was a dense network of country towns and villages that functioned as service centers for the farmers of the surrounding area.

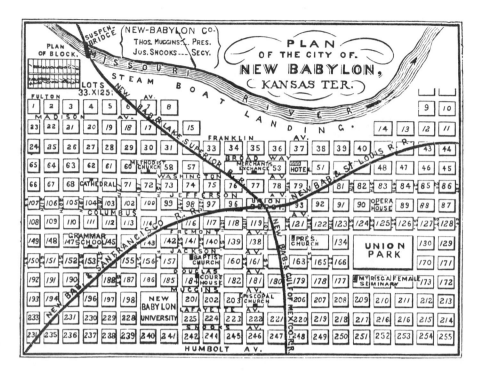

MAP 12-3
Plan of a "Paper Town"

Such places were needed every few miles so that farmers, edging along primitive roads in horse- or oxen-drawn wagons, could get there and back in time to care for their livestock before dark. In the towns farmers could sell their crops and purchase the goods and services they needed. In the boom years of 1835-37, no fewer than 500 new towns were founded in Illinois alone. The competition between them was intense. The most extreme examples of urban boosterism were the hundreds of "paper towns" whose promoters circulated lithographs showing streets crowded with shops and homes, when in fact the lots they were trying to sell were nothing but windswept prairie. The entire town existed only in the mind's eye of the booster.

Although much of the impetus behind urban growth in the antebellum Midwest was commercial, some industrial growth was beginning as well. Most of it involved the processing of raw materials produced in the region—milling grain, brewing beer, tanning leather, and packing meat. The agricultural machinery and implements industry also took firm root in Chicago; in 1860 over $6 million worth of farm machinery, 53 percent of the national total, was produced in the West. That year the West was responsible for almost 20 percent of all American manufactures, substantially less than its share of the nation's population, but double the fraction that could be credited to the South.

Why did the nation's two agrarian regions develop along such different lines in the antebellum decades? The primary reason was the difference in their labor systems. A southern planter who had a good year and wished to invest his profits in hopes of making even more money in the future could easily buy more land and more slaves to work it—hence the emergence of gigantic productive units with hundreds of bondsmen. A midwestern farmer with surplus funds to invest could buy more farmland as easily as in the South, but he faced a severe labor constraint. The supply of hired hands or tenants who could till it for him was very limited, because it was relatively easy for such people to obtain farms of their own. He could hold it vacant in hopes of reaping a speculative gain in the future, but that was by no means a sure thing. Consequently, prospering farmers in states without slaves were much more alert to alternative investment opportunities than their counterparts in the South. Their surplus capital therefore flowed into canal and rail construction projects and into urban commercial and industrial enterprises, stimulating an economic transformation that the South, with all its wealth, failed to experience.

SOCIAL STRUCTURE

"A pleasing feature of western life," boasted one settler in 1850, "is the perfect social equality." A dour visitor from New England remarked with less enthusiasm that in the Indiana backwoods the people were divided into two classes—"the superior and the inferior; the former shaved once a week, the latter once in two weeks." Later historians have been somewhat more cautious in their generalizations, but most accounts have stressed the basic unity and homogeneity of western communities in the antebellum years, and the democratic character of the region's economic, social, and political arrangements. This picture is oversimplified.

It is true that a substantial majority of western residents owned and operated their own family farms. Even after the impressive urban and industrial development of the 1840s and 1850s, farm operators remained the dominant element in the

TABLE 12–3
The Growth of Western Cities, 1830–60
(Population in Thousands)

	1830	1840	1850	1860
Cincinnati	25	46	115	161
St. Louis	6	14	78	161
Chicago	—	5	30	109
Detroit	2	9	21	46
Milwaukee	—	2	20	45
Cleveland	1	6	17	43

TABLE 12–4
The Concentration of Wealth in Three Farming Areas, 1860

	Percent of Farm Property Held by the Richest 10 Percent of Owners
Southern black belt counties	64
Trempealeau County, Wisconsin	39
11 Vermont counties	38

population. In addition to these independent yeomen, between 20 and 30 percent of the farm population were tenant farmers or paid farm hands, who had good prospects of obtaining farms of their own as they grew older. On the other hand, sharp differences in wealth holding had already begun to appear in the farm-owning group. The richest 10 percent of the farmers in a Wisconsin frontier county in 1860 controlled 40 percent of all the property there, precisely the same proportion as in eleven Vermont counties at the same time. That was a much less unequal distribution than in southern plantation areas, where the figure averaged above 60 percent. But it does indicate that the degree of "economic democracy" fostered by the frontier has often been exaggerated. The price of farmland was lower in the West, and it was clearly easier than in the East to work one's way up from hired hand to farm operator. But among those who did own land, the gap between the richest and poorest farmer, surprisingly, was no less in the West than in the East.

Nor were the rapidly growing western cities and towns notably more egalitar-

TABLE 12–5
Poverty and Wealth in a
Northeastern and a Western Town, 1860*

	Jacksonville, Illinois	*Northampton, Massachusetts*
Percent of adult males with no real estate	69	68
Percent of real property held by richest 10 percent	80	72

*The student who compares this table with the preceding data on the concentration of wealth in farming areas might be surprised to discover that the holdings of the top 10 percent of city dwellers seem to have been substantially larger than those of rich southern planters. This is misleading, however, in that the figures are not comparable. The urban figures given here apply to all adult males in the two communities. The data on farming areas, by contrast, apply only to *farm-owners* and leave out those without property. The difference is particularly important for the South, because so many of the people of the black belt were slaves, who of course had no wealth. If better figures, including slaves and landless whites, were available for the South, the concentration of wealth there would doubtless be even more unequal than in northern cities.

ian in an economic sense than eastern cities. These booster towns with grandiose expectations of future greatness, it has been argued, were knit closely together by their citizens' common interest in further population growth, which would drive up land values and produce speculative profits. In the communities that flourished—thousands vanished from the map within a few short years—such profits did indeed materialize. But the gains did not go to the majority of the population. Like eastern cities in these years, the typical midwestern community contained large masses of people with no property beyond their clothing and other personal possessions, and small clusters of extremely wealthy individuals. In Jacksonville, Illinois, a frontier boom town with about 5,000 inhabitants in 1860, over two-thirds of the people owned no real estate. There were almost precisely as many poor people in Jacksonville as in Northampton, Massachusetts, a community of about the same size in the supposedly more stratified Northeast. Furthermore, the wealthy of this Illinois frontier community actually had a somewhat larger share of the town's riches than the wealthy in Northampton.

In both the farming and the urban sectors of western society there was a good deal less than "perfect social equality," and social divisions were based on more than how often a man shaved.

Woman's Lot

Needless to say, western women had no more political and legal rights than their sisters in the East. Their economic role, however, was not the new one of middle-class urban women—that of the specialist in consumption and childrearing. There was too much backbreaking farm work to be done, especially in the pioneering stage of farm building. Aside from helping out in the field when necessary, women (and children when they were old enough) had full responsibility for doing all the cooking, making and repairing clothing, and laundering. They tended the garden and the chickens, cut firewood, carried water, and made cheese, butter, soap, and candles. And of course they bore and looked after the children. The round of toil was unending. An 1862 report by the U.S. Commissioner of Agriculture declared that "a farmer's wife, as a general rule, is a laboring drudge. On

TABLE 12-6
Limiting Family Size in the Old Northwest
(Number of children under 5 per 1,000 women aged 15-50)

	1830	1860
Ohio	933	644
Indiana	1,112	733
Illinois	1,165	737
Michigan	945	627

three farms out of four, it is safe to say, the wife works harder, endures more, than any other on the place; more than the husband, more than the farm hand, more than the hired help of the kitchen." An apt frontier aphorism of the time was: "This country is all right for men and dogs, but it's hell on women and horses."

Some of the burden was lifted from their shoulders after the pioneering phase was over, when rising incomes from increased market production allowed farm families to substitute store-bought goods for domestic manufactures, but it was still heavy. Gradually, however, the women of the West were able to escape from the punishing round of regular pregnancies and huge broods of children. Between 1830 and 1860, the size of the average family in the Old Northwest dropped by a third. When a state filled up to the point at which it became problematic to settle grown children on their own farms, farm families deliberately restricted the number of their offspring. As was the case with the earlier trend in the Northeast, parents developed a more rational, calculating attitude toward giving birth to more children than they could properly launch on a career. Consequently, fewer farm women died in childbirth or reached menopause in broken health.

The Daniel Boone Syndrome

The American frontiersman of legend was a rugged individualist, fleeing civilization and venturing alone into the unknown wilderness. His incessant mobility preserved his freedom and independence. A perfect example was Natty Bumpo, the hero of James Fenimore Cooper's immensely popular Leatherstocking novels (1823–41). His historical counterpart was Daniel Boone, whose wanderings inspired many tales. According to one, he pulled up stakes and moved on whenever he could spy the smoke from a neighbor's chimney. Another has it that Boone once said that he was compelled to travel on because "a damned Yankee came and settled within a hundred miles of me."

The extraordinary transiency of its population was indeed one of the most important characteristics of western society. Restless movement from place to place was common throughout nineteenth-century America; it was much more common in the West, however. Approximately half of the residents of eastern communities were not to be found in the same city on two successive censuses ten years apart; in the Midwest, three out of four people moved away over the course of a decade. According to these statistics, Daniel Boone was a representative figure.

It was not primarily, however, a desire for solitude and personal independence that kept so many westerners on the move. Some transiency was the result of ignorance of proper farming methods, particularly crop rotation and the use of fertilizer. Although such knowlege was spreading among the class of farmers who read the agricultural press, many continued in the old way, mining the land rather than cultivating it wisely. As one scholar describes it, "When the surface treasures had been skimmed, the process was repeated in another place where Nature's bounty was as yet untouched." There may have been truth as well as humor in the boast of an oldtimer to a younger man: "Why, son, by the time I was your age I had wore out three farms."

THE FOOTLOOSE FARMERS OF THE WEST, 1836

I have spoken of the moveable part of the community, and unfortunately for the western country, it constitutes too great a proportion of the whole community. Next to hunting, Indian wars, and the wonderful exuberance of Kentucky, the favourite topic is new countries. They talk of them. They are attached to the associations connected with such conversations. They have a fatal effect upon their exertions. They have not motive, in consonance with these feelings, to build "for posterity and the immortal gods." They only make such improvements as they can leave without reluctance and without loss. I have every where noted the operation of this impediment in the way of those permanent and noble improvements which grow out of a love for that appropriated spot where we were born, and where we expect to die. Scarcely has a family fixed itself, and enclosed a plantation with the universal fence,—split rails— reared a suitable number of log buildings, in short, achieved the first rough improvements, that appertain to the most absolute necessity than the assembled family about the winter fire begin to talk about the prevailing them,—some country that has become the rage, as a point of immigration. They offer their farm for sale, and move away.

Another incentive to move was a desire to reap profits from rising land values, coupled with a faith that there were greener pastures farther west. Many prospective settlers, European immigrants to a strange land in particular, were reluctant to move all the way to the edge of the frontier, even though land was cheapest there. To avoid all the difficulty involved in starting a farm in the wilderness—clearing the land of trees in wooded areas, breaking the tough prairie sod for the first time, building a cabin and shelter for work animals, erecting fences—they would pay a

ILLINOIS FOLK WISDOM

I will tell you a good sign to plant corn. You go home, take down your pants, sit you down on the ground for five minutes, then get up, and if you don't take cold the next day it is time to plant your corn.
—Henry Hyatt, *Folk-Lore from Adams County, Illinois,* 1965

premium to buy a going operation. The more restless first settlers sold out to them and hit the road again.

The transiency of the population critically affected the character of community life. "Everything shifts under your eye," wrote one pioneer. "The present occupants sell, pack up, depart. Strangers replace them. Before they have gained the confidence of their neighbors, they hear of a better place, pack up, and follow their predecessors." Transients, he said, found it difficult to gain "the confidence of their neighbors" and remained outsiders socially. From the earliest years of western settlement, newcomers set about building institutions like those they had known in the East. When 23-year-old Abraham Lincoln first arrived in New Salem, Illinois in 1831, the town had fewer than 150 inhabitants but already boasted a school, a Sunday school, and even a debating society. The associational life of such communities, however, was dominated by the settled, propertied minority. The visible community—the people who were later to be celebrated in the town histories—was substantially smaller and socially quite different from "the community" defined as all persons located by the census-taker.

Entrepreneurial Politics

The prosperous settled class dominated politics. The average member of the Wisconsin State Senate in 1860 held property worth $6,500, at a time when the average adult male in the state owned only $425. The same was true of politics at the local level. Only 8 percent of the men in Jacksonville, Illinois had property worth $1,000 or more, but between 1833 and the Civil War that tiny group occupied more than half of all town offices. The two-thirds of local residents who were propertyless, by contrast, were virtually unrepresented in town government.

The role of wealth in politics, however, was far less commanding than in the antebellum South, where the average South Carolina state senator was worth more than $100,000. Politics was the province of a broad class of hustling entrepreneurs, who battled and maneuvered to advance the interest of their communities and themselves. That was because government decisions and policies crucially affected the course of economic development, and were of major concern to anyone eager to see his community grow. The "county seat" wars that raged in every midwestern state, for example, were struggles between local communities who pressured the legislature to locate or relocate the county seat, improving the business prospects of the victorious contender and putting its rivals at a disadvantage. The route followed by a new road, canal, or railroad critically affected which towns would grow and which would stagnate or decline. The massive "internal improvement" programs untaken by the states from the 1830s onward poured public funds into transportation projects. They were the result of intense local pressures for developmental aid, and the precise shape they took was determined by an enormous amount of wheeling and dealing and logrolling. The political system was broadly based, competitive, and highly responsive to local entrepreneurial interests. Transients who lacked an abiding interest in the future of the communities they were passing through remained largely outside it.

Dreams of growing prosperity and personal advancement—and the "spirit of emulation" which the Governor of Michigan had found so lacking in the Indians—united the residents of the Old Northwest. Even so, they differed in other important ways because they came from areas with differing cultural traditions. Although the massive "Yankee Exodus" from the Northeast is most familiar, newcomers from both the southern United States and from Europe also flocked to the West in large numbers. In 1850, migrants from the Northeast were slightly outnumbered by non-Yankees. Some 47 percent of the 2 million migrants living in the West had been born in the Northeast, 25 percent in the South, and 28 percent in Europe. Indiana had twice as many southerners as Yankees. In Illinois the three groups were in almost perfect balance—37 percent northeasterners, 34 percent southerners, and 29 percent Europeans. These ethnic differences were a source of recurrent conflict.

Transplanted Yankees were eager to recreate institutions to promote an orderly and "virtuous" community life. They were respectful of law, and inclined to use it to effect social betterment—to force children to attend the public schools, to ban the sale of alcohol, or to prevent shopkeepers from doing business on Sundays. In religion they sought to preserve the New England tradition of an educated ministry that would help to "dispel ignorance, check vice, and create a pure public opinion favorable to sound morals and true religion." Politically they leaned toward the party of order, the Whig party and its successor, the Republican party.

Southern migrants tended to settle in the southernmost portions of the states in the Lower Midwest, but they also entered communities with Yankee residents. Yankees found southerners more individualistic and more impulsive, distrustful of institutions and impatient with authority. Compulsory school attendance laws, for example, were viewed by southerners as improper meddling in a sphere best governed by the individual parent. The school, declared a newspaper from a southern Illinois county, was "a petty monarchy which would even seek to enter into the secrets of the family and sway its controlling sceptre there." Their stance toward the uplifting efforts of their Yankee neighbors was well summed up by the observer who complained that "matters have come to such a pass that a peaceable man can hardly venture to eat or drink, to go to bed or get up, to correct his children or to kiss his wife" without the benevolent guidance of some reform organization. The churches that appealed to southerners most—the Baptists and the Methodists—lacked an educated ministry or strong central organization, and preached a highly individualistic doctrine of sin and salvation, virtually devoid of any broader social ethic. Politically they found the radical individualism espoused by the Democrats most congenial. Although many had no liking for slavery, and had indeed moved to free states to escape it, they had no fondness either for black people or for those who urged governmental interference with the rights of individual slaveholders.

It is harder to generalize about the European immigrants who poured into the West in such large numbers, because they came from several different national cultures—English, Irish, German, Swedish, Dutch, and so forth. In some respects, they adapted quickly and smoothly to American ways. For example, they did not carry over European farming techniques. They chose to grow the same crops as their American neighbors with the same methods, and had the same rational acquisitive attitudes towards the land. There were other points of difference, however.

One was religion. Almost all of the Irish and about a third of the German newcomers were Roman Catholics. Yankee Protestants in the West were as anti-Catholic as their brethren in the East. Indeed, the fear of a Catholic plot to subvert republican institutions was even stronger in the West, because its society was still in the process of formation. "The great battle in the West," thundered the leading Yankee missionary journal in 1839, was between "truth and error, between law and anarchy, between Christianity with her Sabbaths, her ministry, and her schools, on the one hand, and the combined forces of Infidelity and Popery on the other." Associating such attacks with the Whig–Republican reform tradition, Catholics aligned themselves with the Democratic party, the party of individualism and personal freedom.

Many non-Catholic immigrants found themselves at odds with Yankees over cultural issues as well. German and Swedish Lutherans and members of the Dutch Reformed church were suspicious of public schools, and sought public funds for their own parochial institutions. Many groups attempted to pass along a knowledge of their native tongue to their children, a practice deplored by Yankees whose ideal was a homogenous English-speaking community. The Yankee crusade against alcohol and their efforts to enact Sunday "blue laws" repelled immigrants from cultures in which drink was accepted and where "continental Sundays" were celebrations. They too tended to favor the Democrats.

There were, of course, many exceptions to these broad generalizations about group attitudes and values. Although Abraham Lincoln was born in the South to southern-born parents, he was a quintessential "Yankee" as the term has been used here. Conversely, although Stephen Douglas, Lincoln's greatest political rival, was born in Vermont and educated in New York, he was a "southerner" in this sense. Nevertheless, cultural predispositions brought into the West by migrants from different regions and countries were the major source of social and political division.

Not only was the West divided politically; it was divided very evenly. The southerners and the immigrants, who together made up slightly more than half of the population, leaned strongly to the Democratic party, whereas Yankees leaned strongly in the opposite direction. The defection of even a relatively small fraction of voters from the pattern common to their group would be enough to tilt the balance decisively in one direction. That is why the political struggle to win the West was so intense and so critical in the turbulent decade preceding the Civil War. It was no accident that the West was the spawning ground of the new political party that arose then from the ruins of the Whig party, and no accident that both of the leading contenders for the Presidency of the United States in 1860 were from the state of Illinois.

SUGGESTED READINGS

Richard A. Bartlett, *The New Country: A Social History of the American Frontier. 1796–1890* (1974) and Malcolm J. Rohrbough, *The Trans-Appalachian Frontier* (1979) are good syntheses. The classic interpretation of the significance of the frontier in shaping the character of American life is Frederick Jackson Turner, *The Frontier in American History* (1920); Turner believed the frontier was a "great leveler" and the source of the American democratic spirit. Ray Alan Billington's *America's Frontier Heritage* (1966) and *Westward Expansion* (1974) are written within a Turnerian framework. For alternative views, see Richard Hofstadter and Seymour Martin Lipset, eds., *Turner and the Sociology of the Frontier* (1967) and Margaret Walsh, *The American Frontier Revisited* (1978). On Indian removal, see Bernard Sheehan, *Seeds of Extinction: Jeffersonian Philanthropy and the American Indian* (1973), Wilcomb E. Washburn, *The Indian in America* (1975), and Charles Hudson, *The Removal of the Southeastern Indians* (1978).

Paul W. Gates, *The Farmer's Age: Agriculture, 1815–1860* (1960) and Clarence Danhof, *Change in Agriculture: The Northern United States, 1820–1870* (1969) describe the evolution of the agricultural economy. Richard Wade, *The Urban Frontier: The Rise of the Western Cities, 1780–1830* (1959) clarifies the role of urban centers in the development of the West. Allan G. Bogue, *From Prairie to Corn Belt: Farming on the Illinois and Iowa Prairies in the Nineteenth Century* (1963), Paul W. Gates, *The Illinois Central Railroad and its Colonization Work* (1934), and Robert P. Swierenga, *Pioneers and Profits: Land Speculation on the Iowa Frontier* (1968) are excellent monographs. Merle Curti, *The Making of an American Community: Democracy in a Frontier County* (1959) is a pioneering quantitative analysis, limited by the author's preoccupation with the Turner theory. Don H. Doyle, *The Social Order of a Frontier Community: Jacksonville, Illinois, 1825–1870* (1978) is a much livelier and more satisfying statistical community study. The Doyle book and Richard L. Power, *Planting Corn Belt Culture: The Impress of the Upland South and the Yankee in the Old Northwest* (1953) suggest patterns of cultural conflict.

Chapter Thirteen

Politics and Reform, 1815–45

I n the aftermath of the War of 1812, the Federalist party collapsed, bringing to an end the "first party system." The stigma of having opposed the war and having flirted with secession at the Hartford Convention was Federalism's death sentence. The Federalist candidate in the 1816 presidential election received only 34 electoral votes, as opposed to 183 for the victor, James Monroe; in 1820, the Federalists got only one, and the party gave up the ghost. During the so-called "Era of Good Feelings" (1817–25) almost every signficant public figure identified with the Jeffersonian Republican tradition. A second party system, however, emerged during the Age of Jackson. Although Jacksonian Democrats and their opponents, the Whigs, quarreled rancorously, the development of two great parties with national constituencies allowed the political system to compromise or sidestep issues that could polarize the nation into antagonistic sections and threaten the Union. Radical reformers who called for drastic changes in American social arrangements were frustrated at the way party politicians evaded and muffled questions that were of burning moral importance to them, but until the mid-1840s the reformers were voices in the wilderness.

POLITICS WITHOUT PARTIES

The experience of waging a war on American soil led many Republicans to abandon temporarily their Jeffersonian attachment to minimal central government, and to support policies that could be considered "Hamiltonian." For example,

Robert Cruickeshank's lithograph, "All Creation Going to the White House," humorously depicts the festivities surrounding Andrew Jackson's inauguration as President in 1829.

Republicans in Congress had cheered when the charter of the Bank of the United States expired in 1811, believing as they did that America needed no corrupting, "aristocratic" counterpart to the Bank of England. They soon learned how difficult it was to run the national government without an institution that could store its revenue, transfer funds from place to place, issue paper money, and regulate the activities of banks chartered by the states. Accordingly, in 1816, a second Bank of the United States was authorized by Congress and approved by James Madison, despite his doubts that it was constitutional by the "strict construction" standard he favored.

A second expression of the new economic nationalism was the passage of a 25 percent protective tariff the same year. American industry had been greatly stimulated by the shelter from foreign competition provided by the embargo and the war. With the coming of the peace, many of these infant industries found themselves unable to deliver their goods as cheaply as well-established British firms. The moderate subsidy provided by the 25 percent tax on imports gave them the needed margin for survival and encouraged further industrial development. Representatives from every part of the country, including the agrarian South and West, areas that later came to view tariffs as harmful to agriculture and beneficial to industry, supported the tariff. John C. Calhoun of South Carolina argued for it vigorously, thinking it would boost manufacturing in the South.

A third proposed new departure was federal aid for internal improvements. Wartime difficulties in moving troops through the interior exposed the pitiful state of the nation's transportation system, and created a clamor for a system of national roads. When Congress responded with a major appropriation for federal road building, Madison vetoed it on constitutional grounds. However, he called for a constitutional amendment authorizing such aid in the future.

For a time, then, many Republicans were prepared to endorse the three principles that were at the heart of what Speaker of the House Henry Clay later called "the American System": 1) a centralized national banking system, 2) a high protective tariff, and 3) federal aid to internal improvements. This surge of economic nationalism proved short-lived, however. As the unifying memory of the struggle against the British faded, congressional enthusiasm for energetic government waned and Jeffersonian localism reasserted itself. When a two-party system re-emerged in the 1830s, the party that claimed the mantle of Jefferson—the Democrats—would oppose all these measures, while Henry Clay's Whigs would favor them.

The label "Era of Good Feeling" commonly applied to the period of James Monroe's Presidency (1817–25) is apropos only insofar as it suggests an absence of organized *partisan* political conflict. In other ways, feelings in Washington were anything but good. When the need for Republican solidarity against the Federalist enemy disappeared, vicious personal, factional, and sectional squabbles erupted. By 1824 the political scene was so disorganized that the Electoral College divided between four candidates, with none close to having a majority; the winner (John Quincy Adams) had to be chosen by the House of Representatives after months of wrangling and horse-trading. Neither Monroe nor Adams was able to impose any order on a chaotically fragmented Congress, and neither achieved anything significant in domestic affairs.

John Marshall and the Supreme Court

One of the few strong forces for national unity in this period of political stalemate was the Supreme Court under Chief Justice John Marshall, who presided over it from 1801 until his death in 1835. When Marshall, a Federalist Congressman from Virginia, was appointed by John Adams, the Court was a feeble institution with limited and uncertain authority. The Constitution lodges "the judicial power of the United States" in the Supreme Court, but does not spell out what the "judicial power" is. In the first dozen years of the Court's existence, its members showed little interest in defining and extending their authority. They took few cases—none at all in the first three years—and disposed of them on the narrowest legal grounds. One justice found the job so unchallenging that he resigned to take up a position on the South Carolina Supreme Court; Chief Justice John Jay spent almost a year in England negotiating a treaty without worrying that he might be needed on urgent court business at home. But Marshall's brilliant and aggressive leadership over the first third of the nineteenth century transformed an almost moribund body into a vital national institution with sweeping powers.

Marshall took his first decisive step toward this end in his opinion in *Marbury vs. Madison* (1803), which asserted for the first time the Supreme Court's power to overrule an act of Congress it deemed a violation of the Constitution. Marshall shrewdly decided the immediate issue at stake—whether or not the Federalist William Marbury was entitled to a federal judgeship—in the way the Jefferson administration wanted, thereby protecting himself from the charge that he had been swayed by his Federalist biases. But he did so by a cleverly circuitous route, declaring that Marbury deserved his office but that the Court lacked the authority to order the President to give it to him. The Judiciary Act of 1789, which clearly authorized the Court to do that, was unconstitutional. By giving in to the Republicans on the concrete question and by surrendering a minor power granted to the Court by Congress, Marshall seized a much larger power that is not explicitly contained in the Constitution—the power to decide the constitutionality of the actions of the other two branches of the federal government.

Although *Marbury vs. Madison* was of great historic significance, it was the only time the Marshall Court overturned an act of Congress, Marshall was less interested in testing the power of the Court against other branches of the federal government than he was in curbing the actions of state legislatures and state courts, to establish the supremacy of the national government and eliminate state barriers that impeded entrepreneurial freedom. *Flectcher vs. Peck* (1810) struck down Georgia laws that impaired the freedom of contract guaranteed in the federal Constitution and implicitly held the states responsible for due process in their internal affairs. *Martin vs. Hunter's Lessee* (1816) and *Cohens vs. Virginia* (1821) made state court decisions susceptible to review by the Supreme Court. *Gibbons vs. Ogden* (1824) denied the state of New York the right to grant a steamboat monopoly on its waters on the grounds that the Hudson River was an artery of interstate commerce, and that only the federal government was constitutionally empowered to regulate interstate commerce. *Dartmouth College vs. Woodward* (1819) prevented the state of New Hampshire from imposing new controls over the college, because its initial royal charter was a contract whose sanctity was guaranteed by the Constitution.

The effect of all these decisions was to circumscribe the ability of state governments to regulate the economic activity of individuals and corporations, and to create a uniform, predictable environment in which enterprise could flourish.

A final landmark decision by John Marshall decisively repudiated the Jeffersonian states' rights, strict constitutionalist position. *McCulloch vs. Maryland* (1819) reviewed Maryland's decision to impose a heavy tax on the Baltimore branch of the Second Bank of the United States. It hinged on two key questions. Did Congress have the power to charter a national bank in the absence of explicit authorizing language in the Constitution? Can a state tax federal property? Speaking for a unanimous Court, Marshall endorsed a Hamiltonian "loose constructionist" reading of the Constitution. The power was there, not explicitly, but *implied*. Congress was authorized to "make all laws necessary and proper" for executing its responsibilities, and the bank was an appropriate means towards a legitimate end. A state could not tax federal property because "the power to tax involves the power to destroy." If states could exact revenues from federal agencies operating within their boundaries, they could tax them out of business and make the Constitution's statement that it was "the supreme law of the land" into "an empty and unmeaning declamation." Although the Federalist party had vanished from the scene, Hamiltonian nationalism had a powerful defender in the highest court of the land.

Storm Over Missouri

One of the functions of the two-party system that developed in the 1790s was to check the tendency for political sentiments to follow strictly sectional lines, lest they reach the danger point at which a section whose representatives were consistently on the losing end in policy disputes might decide to pull out of the Union. Federalists from Massachusetts could identify with Federalists from South Carolina and appreciate their interests and concerns; both New Yorkers and Virginians could agree on a satisfactory Republican program. When the Federalist party lost its base outside New England during the Jefferson and Madison administrations, it lost its ability to perform that unifying function, and New England went to the brink of secession during the War of 1812. The single-party politics of the postwar years was highly vulnerable to disruptive sectional conflict, as the crisis that led up to the Missouri Compromise of 1820–21 made clear.

In the 1780s, when the Mississippi River was the country's western border, the Confederation Congress had settled the question of slavery in the West by allowing it south of the Ohio River and banning it to the north, in effect making the Ohio an extension of the Mason–Dixon line. Slavery, they sensed, was an issue that could split the Union into warring sections; the Ohio River compromise was a way of cooling it. Having barred slavery from their own states, northerners assumed that it was a strictly southern problem and hoped that it would eventually fade away. The addition of the immense Louisiana Territory, stretching almost to the Rockies, did not disturb this understanding, and the admission of Louisiana to the union as a slave state in 1812 provoked little controversy.

Over the next few years, however, migration patterns to the West failed to conform to the simple line drawn in the post-Revolutionary settlement. Although it lay north of the Ohio, Missouri had proven itself attractive to large numbers of newcomers from the South, who brought 10,000 slaves with them. When Missouri applied for statehood with a constitution that sanctioned slavery, a New York Congressman, James Tallmadge, Jr., threw a bombshell that began a fierce sectional debate that paralyzed Congress for more than a year. Tallmadge's amendment to the statehood measure sought to freeze slavery in Missouri and gradually phase it out. It barred further importation of bondsmen into the state, and set free all children born into slavery there at the age of 25.

The Tallmadge bill passed the House, where the North's population edge gave it a majority of seats. But it stalled in the Senate, where the South had a slight advantage. The stalemate lasted for the rest of the congressional session and part of the next, while the contestants exchanged furious charges and countercharges. With a confidence fueled by their rapidly multiplying cotton fortunes, southerners claimed that Congress had no power to deny Missourians the right to hold slaves. Slavery, they insisted, was not an evil, as some in an earlier generation had conceded; it was a positive good, the only suitable status for an inferior race incapable of governing itself (see box). The plantation was a school to instruct blacks in the only tasks for which they were suited. Slaves were happy to be "moulded to their master's will"; when he returned from a trip he saw only "glad faces and a hearty shaking of hands." "Christ himself gave a sanction to slavery. He admonished them to be obedient to their masters." If meddling northerners tried to interfere with any aspect of their splendid system, speaker after speaker threatened, the slave states would secede. "Like a fire bell in the night," wrote an aging Jefferson in the midst of the crisis, "the momentous question fills me with alarm." It was, he feared, "the knell of the Union."

The votes on the Tallmadge bill followed sectional lines almost perfectly. No Senator from the South, and only 2 of the 66 Representatives from slave states (both of them northern-born), supported it. The North was almost as strongly in its favor. Although some northerners denounced slavery as a violation of the Declaration of Independence, concern over the sufferings of enslaved blacks was not the primary force at work. Although every northern state had eliminated slavery, none had gone very far toward ensuring racial equality. Free negroes were second-class citizens throughout the Northeast, and third-class citizens in most of the Old Northwest. Illinois, for example, barred the immigration of blacks and regulated the lives of those already there with a harsh Black Code. Freezing and phasing out slavery in Missouri, in any event, would not do anything to check the rapid spread of slavery in all the land south of the Ohio.

The dynamic behind the restrictionist impulse was not so much egalitarian resentment at racial oppression as a new northern sectional consciousness, a feeling that slavery was economically harmful and that the influence of slaveholders in the nation was increasing. The South, many argued, was more powerful in national politics than it should be because the "three-fifths" clause of the Constitution counted five slaves as the equivalent of three free men in apportioning congressional representatives and electoral votes. Jefferson, it was argued, would have lost to John Adams in 1800 without this unfair advantage. Admitting Missouri as a slave state would unbalance the sectional seesaw, making twelve slave and only eleven free states. To allow slaves into Missouri, in the same latitude as Illinois and Iowa, would be a step toward opening up the entire West to a black invasion. It should be preserved as "white men's country."

In the end, the artful wheeling and dealing of Henry Clay made possible the passage of a two-part compromise measure. Missouri was allowed entry into the union as a slave state, balanced by the admission of Maine as a free state. Second, it was provided that no further intrusions of slavery would be permitted in states as far north as Missouri. A line drawn through the southern border of Missouri, at $36°30'$, would be the boundary between slavery and freedom. The potentially most divisive question before the American people would be safely removed from the political arena. The "compromise" was really a victory for the South, and it taught them a dangerous lesson. If they dug in their heels and screamed secession loudly enough, they concluded, their northern opponents would be intimidated and back down.

The young republic was growing as fabulously as Paul Bunyan or some other hero from the popular tall tales of the day. Its population was swelling, its economy was surging, and it was beginning to develop muscle that could intimidate other

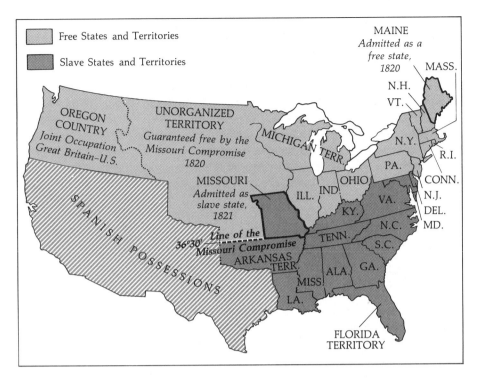

MAP 13–1
Results of the Missouri Compromise, 1820–21

powers. In 1819, after Andrew Jackson led the U.S. Army into Spanish Florida on the pretext of retaliating for raids into American territory by Seminole Indians, the Secretary of State, John Quincy Adams, negotiated the remarkable Transcontinental Treaty, in which Spain ceded not only Florida but its claims to the Pacific Northwest to the United States. Four years later, President Monroe announced his famous doctrine: The United States would henceforth be the guarantor of the independence of the Latin American countries that had recently won their freedom from Spain, and no further colonization in the Western Hemisphere by European nations would be permitted. The crisis over Missouri, however, had revealed a massive fault line beneath the surface of a confident, expansionist society. The first tremors of a mighty earthquake to come had been felt.

JACKSONIAN DEMOCRACY AND THE EMERGENCE OF THE SECOND PARTY SYSTEM

The election of Andrew Jackson to the Presidency in 1828 opened a new era in American politics. "Old Hickory" was a poor boy who had made good. The first American President born west of the Appalachians, he grew up on a small farm in

North Carolina and fought the British in the Revolution as a boy of 13. Although he had little schooling, he amassed a tidy fortune through law practice and land speculation in Tennessee, and lived in the finest mansion in the state (the Hermitage), prospering from the labor of more than 100 slaves. The Battle of New Orleans made him a national hero. Despite his wealth, he claimed to be a man of the people, a symbol of the vigor and determination of the rough-hewn frontiersman. He had more presence, more charisma, than any President since George Washington, and he inspired fanatic devotion in his supporters.

He also inspired bitter hatred. Jackson was overbearing, hot-tempered, and pugnacious. He once killed a man over a racetrack quarrel, and fought several other duels. As a friend remarked, he was "apt to regard the terms 'opponent' and 'enemy' as synonymous." John Quincy Adams said, with pardonable exaggeration, that Jackson was "a barbarian who could not write a sentence of grammar and hardly spell his own name." The opposition called him "King Andrew." His stormy eight years in office polarized American politics, bringing into being a second party system that lasted until the eve of the Civil War.

Jackson was one of four candidates for the Presidency in 1824. Although he won a plurality of the votes in the Electoral College, John Quincy Adams won the contest in the House with Henry Clay's support. Convinced that he had been cheated of office by a "corrupt bargain," Jackson set out to build a national network of support, "a Jackson party." In 1828 he easily defeated Adams, whose supporters called themselves "National Republicans."

The two organizations that had taken shape by 1828 were not yet fully developed political parties, with names, slogans, and platforms to distinguish them. The only issue on which Jackson took a stand was the alleged "aristocratic" and "monarchist" tastes of his opponent, and his supporters in the various states attributed to him whatever views they thought would win the most votes. The main lines of division in the electorate were regional. Jackson got 56 percent of the national vote, but carried most southern and western states by two to one or more; Adams won equally lopsided victories in the Northeast. In the average state, the difference between the winner and the loser was a huge 36 percent; the victor drew 68 percent of the vote, his opponent only 32 percent. Jackson had no need to be attentive to the concerns of northeastern voters, since his cause there was hopeless; the same was true for Adams with respect to southern and western voters.

By the time Jackson retired to the Hermitage in 1837, two modern political parties had developed, each with a genuine national base. Jackson was the head of the Democratic party, and picked his successor, Martin Van Buren. The "National Republican" organization had become the Whig Party, led by Henry Clay, Daniel Webster, and Adams. The two parties were quite evenly balanced, and neither was mainly sectional in its appeal. In the average state in 1836 the winning margin was 56 to 44; a shift of a shade more than 6 percent of the electorate would have tipped the balance the other way. Both parties therefore had a strong incentive to appeal to as many interest groups as possible, and not to write off any particular bloc of states as hopeless. As long as that remained the case, the fratricidal sectional divisions that loomed up during the Missouri crisis would be held in check.

TABLE 13-1
Presidential Voting, 1824–44

	Total Voters	Percentage of Eligible Voters Who Cast Ballots	Democratic	Whig
1824	356,038	27	NA	NA
1828	1,155,350	58	56.0	44.0*
1832	1,250,799	55	56.9	43.5
1836	1,505,278	58	50.9	49.1
1840	2,402,405	80	46.9	53.1
1844	2,700,861	79·	50.7	49.3

*National Republican

The Growth of Mass Politics

"Jacksonian Democracy" is familiar shorthand for the growth of mass democratic politics in the first half of the nineteenth century. But it would be a mistake to believe that much of the credit should go to Andrew Jackson himself. The trend was underway before Jackson entered national politics and continued after his retirement. Jackson benefited from it; he did not cause it. One reason that the electorate was expanding was the disappearance of traditional property require-ments that barred poor people without a "stake in society" from the polls. Between 1810 and 1821, six western states with only minimal or no property qualifications entered the union, and four older states approved new constitutions that provided for nearly universal white male suffrage.

As significant as the lowering of legal barriers to political participation was the abrupt jump in the proportion of those legally qualified who actually exercised the right to vote. Barely a quarter of the eligible voters turned out in the elections of 1824; it was up to 58 percent in 1828, and a striking 80 percent by 1840, nearly as high as in any election in all of American history. The effect of these two changes—the growth in the pool of eligible voters and the increasing participation rate of those eligible—was dramatic. Only 356,038 people cast a ballot for one of the four candidates for President in 1824; in 1840, the figure was 2.4 million. Although the population grew only 57 percent during those years, the number of voters increased by 700 percent.

To a considerable extent, the increase was due to the innovative efforts of party workers to mobilize the electorate. Party workers eager to elect their candidates and gain their shares of the "spoils" of office labored tirelessly to convince voters that it would be calamitous if the opposition won. Jackson supporters were the first to learn the game of mass politics. They backslapped their way through boisterous picnics and rallies, denouncing the Whigs as aristocrats who had only contempt for the common man. The Whigs quickly learned to emulate their opposition. In the 1840 elections, they waged an intense campaign with party songs, slogans, badges, parades, and mass rallies. Obscuring the wealthy origins of their candidate, William Henry Harrison, with pictures of the log cabin in which he had allegedly been born, and trumpeting his successes as an Indian fighter—"Tippecanoe and Tyler too"—they swept to victory.

The broader inclusion of the masses into politics had its limitations, of course. Women were excluded. Indians were excluded. And in this period the position of free blacks in the North deteriorated. In states where they had the right to vote if they met the property requirement, when the requirement was eliminated for whites it was either retained for blacks or they were barred from voting altogether. In 1840 only 7 percent of northern blacks were allowed to vote on an equal basis with whites. The term "Jacksonian democracy" would have seemed bitterly ironic to blacks, because the Democratic party took the lead in pressing for these regressive measures.

Nor did increasingly broad popular participation in politics mean that the influence of the wellborn or well-to-do elite diminished. Andrew Jackson was fond of claiming "the road to office" should be "accessible alike to the rich and the poor," but his appointment record indicated that this was mere rhetoric. Jackson discharged hundreds of federal officeholders who remained on from the Adams administration and replaced them with loyal Democrats. But none of the newcomers were poor men. In wealth, occupational rank, and education they closely resembled the members of earlier administrations back to the days of George Washington.

Indians, Internal Improvements, and the Bank War

Jackson was an exceptionally forceful and active President. There can be debate about the wisdom of his policies, but no dispute about the fact that he enlarged the powers of the Presidency. His predecessors, for example, exercised the veto power only when they believed a congressional act was unconstitutional. Jackson exerted it against any measure he disapproved of, forcing Congress to look over its shoulder at the White House when it considered any bill. Jackson was the first chief executive to claim that the President alone spoke for all the people. His ties to the electorate were closer than those of any previous President, and his influence over the other branches of government was greater.

Upon his retirement, Jackson said that one issue had been "the most arduous part of my duty, and I watched over it with great vigor." It was not one of the familiar questions stressed in most textbooks; it was his ruthless and successful campaign to drive the Indians beyond the Mississippi, described in the previous chapter. Although downplayed or not mentioned at all by sympathetic historians, the Indian removal bill was, as an Alabama Congressman remarked, "the leading measure" of the Jackson administration.[1] It was a one-sided contest. The Indians had no political power, and their appeals to the conscience of the nation were heard by few. The Whig opposition in Congress sniped at particular provisions of the various removal treaties, but were afraid—correctly, no doubt—that principled objection would cost them too many votes in the South and West. When they came to power after the election of 1840, the Whigs completed the last remaining removals in the same fashion as their Democratic predecessors. Jacksonian Democracy was built on Indian graves.

Ready though he was to use federal power against the Indians, Jackson had a Jeffersonian fear of strong central government in other realms. In particular, he was hostile to the Whig program of federal aid for internal improvements to foster economic development. When Congress agreed to subsidize a turnpike from Maysville, Kentucky to Louisville in 1830, Jackson vetoed the plan. Such aid, he claimed, was beyond the power of the federal government by a strict interpretation of the Constitution. The taxes needed to pay for it would bear "severely upon the laboring and less prosperous classes of the community." "Retrenchment" and "economy" in Washington were necessary to preserve "state's rights." The Maysville Road veto came at a crucial time, on the eve of the great canal and railroad building era. It meant that Jackson and the party he led would act in accord with their belief that "the best government is that which governs least," and would do all they could to prevent the federal government from guiding and promoting the development of the nation's transportation system.

Jackson also gave a resounding "No" to the Second Bank of the United States. He was a firm hard money man. He had a primitive fear of banks in general, believing that the issuance of paper money was responsible for speculative booms and financial panics. But the Bank of the United States was particularly wicked, in his mind. With $35 million in capital, headquarters in Philadelphia, and branch offices across the land, it was by far the largest corporation in the United States. It held federal funds and could exert considerable power over the hundreds of smaller banks chartered by the states, and yet only a fifth of its directors were federally appointed; the four-fifths who set policy were wealthy private parties who received dividends out of the bank's profits. The president of the Bank was Nicholas Biddle, a Philadelphia gentleman with aristocratic tastes and a great many Whig friends in Congress. Jackson called it "the Monster" and set out to "kill" it by vetoing Congress' attempt to recharter it in 1832.

The veto message was a savage attack on "the rich and powerful," who "too often bend the acts of government to their selfish purposes." The Bank was a "monopoly," whose "exclusive privileges" served to make "the rich richer and the potent more powerful." The existence of such a center of power was an invasion "of the rights and powers of the several States," who should be left "as much as possible to themselves." Despite John Marshall's ruling in *McCulloch vs. Maryland* that the Second Bank was constitutional, Jackson insisted that it was not. "Each

---

[1]Although Arthur Schlesinger, Jr.'s admiring *The Age of Jackson* is over 500 pages long, it doesn't even mention Indian removal.

public officer who takes an oath to support the Constitution," he asserted, "swears that he will support it as he understands it, and not as it is understood by others."

Jackson was wildly misguided in claiming that the Second Bank of the United States benefited the rich at the expense of the poor and was the major source of the speculative fever that periodically gripped Americans. If anything, the Bank's efforts to see that the paper notes issued by state banks were backed by an adequate amount of gold or silver seriously dampened speculation. On the other hand, recent studies of the exceptionally complex banking question by economic historians make it appear that the Bank of the United States was neither as wisely run nor as essential for a sound national financial system as its defenders—and many later historians—have maintained. The traditional account held that Jackson's 1833 decision to transfer all federal funds from the Bank to Democratic state banks—"pet banks"—led to the tremendous speculative boom of 1834–36 and the depression of 1837. Other causes too complex to relate here, having to do with trade with Britain and China, actually seem to have been responsible for the surge and the collapse.

Whatever the merits of the economic arguments of the contestants in the Bank War, Jackson reaped political capital from it. His veto of the recharter bill was the central issue of the 1832 campaign, waged against Henry Clay. Clay defended the bank as a central component of "the American system," denounced Jackson for refusing to defer to the Supreme Court's judgment as to its constitutionality, and attacked the veto of a measure strongly backed by Congress as an abuse of executive power. How much the results were due to the continuing charisma of "Old Hickory" and how much to public acceptance of his arguments is uncertain, but he won by a comfortable 57:43 margin.

The Nullification Crisis

For all of his attachment to "states' rights," Andrew Jackson was an ardent patriot. When the two causes came into conflict, as they did in a crisis that erupted in South Carolina in 1832, his commitment to the Union proved stronger. The planters of South Carolina had been in an uproar ever since the passage of a high tariff bill—the "Tariff of Abominations"—in 1828, which they claimed would further depress their already sluggish economy. Jackson refused to commit himself to a major scaling down of the rate, and a new bill passed in 1832 offered only slight relief. By this time, many leading South Carolinians had convinced themselves of the truth of a "compact" theory of the Constitution. Building on premises asserted by Jefferson and Madison in the Virginia and Kentucky Resolutions of 1798, they argued that the Union was only a compact between sovereign states, who surrendered certain powers to the central government for their convenience. Since the states had created the central government, it was up to them to decide when it had overstepped its authority and infringed on their freedoms. A tariff for purposes other than revenue was unconstitutional, they asserted, and South Carolina therefore had the right to nullify it and to forbid federal agents in the state to collect the duties. Urged on by Vice President John C. Calhoun, the South Carolina legislature passed an Ordinance of Nullification in November of 1832, and swore to secede from the Union if the federal government used force against it.

It might seen an extreme action to take in response to an issue of dollars and cents; the planters of the state were not exactly languishing in dire poverty. But the tariff was a symbol of a series of other broader developments that had profoundly unsettled them. Calhoun abandoned his earlier economic nationalism to take up the extreme states' rights position because he concluded that manufacturing would not develop in the South, and that anything that would contribute to more rapid economic and demographic growth in the North was a threat to the southern way of life. Once the North became clearly predominant in the national government, sentimental northern "innovators" and "enthusiasts" would be tempted to tamper with "the institutions of our forefathers," reducing the people of South Carolina to the condition of "the unfortunate colonists of the West Indies" (whose slaves were being freed by the edict of the British government). People who battled to keep slaves out of Missouri would someday concern themselves with the lot of those in South Carolina, once they had the power.

Even before they had the power they could do grave damage, because the mere discussion of the issue could dangerously affect the slaves. Denmark Vesey, a free black caught and executed for organizing a slave revolt in Charleston in 1822, claimed to have been inspired by antislavery speakers during the Missouri debate. Vesey's plot was at least foiled. At the very time that the nullification drive was gathering steam, the largest slave revolt in American history broke out in the Virginia tidewater. In the summer of 1831, Nat Turner and his followers managed to slaughter 57 white men, women, and children before he was captured. It was the frenzy of fear over the future of their society that led South Carolinians to make the absurd claim that it was possible to have one government for the Union and yet leave its powers susceptible to 24 interpretations.

Jackson would have none of it. He instructed South Carolina Congressmen leaving Washington for home in the summer of 1832, "Tell them from me that they can talk and write resolutions and print threats to their heart's content. But if one drop of blood be shed there in defiance of the laws of the United States, I will hang the first man of them I can get my hands on to the first tree I can find." He dispatched fresh troops to federal forts in South Carolina, and naval vessels to patrol the coast. When the Nullification Ordinance was passed anyway, he issued a blistering proclamation that the power of nullification was "incompatible with the existence of the Union, contradicted expressly by the letter of the Constitution, unauthorized by its spirit, inconsistent with every principle on which it was founded, and destructive of the great object for which it was formed." Attempts to dissolve the Union by force were treason, he warned, and would be treated as such. He asked Congress to authorize him to use force to collect the customs if necessary, but declared that if refused he would act anyway on the basis of his obligation to carry out the laws of the land.

There was no doubting Jackson's absolute determination, and the nullifiers had to back down. No other southern state was willing to support them, once Jackson made his position plain; Jacksonian Democrats were prepared to follow their President. South Carolina was hardly likely to win a war against the other 23 states.

A compromise tariff bill that lowered the tariff substantially but gradually, over a ten-year period, allowed the state to save face while it rescinded the Nullification Ordinance. With a last defiant gesture, though, it at the same time nullified the Force Bill Congress had passed at Jackson's request. That act of nullification had no more legal force than the earlier one, of course. The Force Bill was still on the books when Abraham Lincoln entered the White House 29 years later, to confront a similar but much graver crisis that had also begun in South Carolina.

THE AGE OF UPLIFT

"What a fertility of projects for the salvation of the world," exclaimed Ralph Waldo Emerson in 1844. He spoke in the midst of a period that witnessed an extraordinary proliferation of social movements aimed at human betterment. The buoyant optimism and extravagant hopes of the day were nicely summed up in H.C. Wright's call for a "World Convention for the Discussion of All Wrong," to be held in Boston "where great historical movements naturally commence." These efforts at uplift were so varied and wide-ranging—from abolitionism to vegetarianism—that no attempt to catalogue them can be provided here. One historian, Alice Felt Tyler, has devoted a 600 page book to that task. Only a few generalizations about some of the major antebellum reform efforts can be offered.

The reform impulse was closely connected with the rapid growth of evangelical Protestantism. During the Second Great Awakening, bands of revivalist ministers traveled the land gathering in souls for Christ. The only existing statistical measure of their success is crude but nonetheless revealing: Between 1800 and the Civil War the number of churches in America grew twice as rapidly as the total population. The evangelists abandoned fatalistic Calvinism, with its emphasis on predestination and the impotence of human will, and preached a far more hopeful and energizing message. All men and women had an equal opportunity for salvation; it was a matter of free will. Charles Grandison Finney, one of the most eloquent and popular of them, insisted that "sinners ought to be made to feel that they have something to do, and that is to repent; that it is something which no other being can do for them, neither God or man, and something which they can do and do now. Religion is something to do, not something to wait for."

If, as revivalists preached, God had "made man a moral free agent," it followed that sin was a voluntary, avoidable act. Christians freed of the burden of original sin exchanged it for the quite different and perhaps equally heavy burden of constantly displaying the pure state of their souls through moral action. Under this injunction, evangelicals created the dense and far-flung network of voluntary associations known as "the benevolent empire." It included the American Bible Society (founded in 1816), which aimed to put the scriptures into every home in the nation, the American Sunday School Union (1824), and the American Tract Society (1825). The latter circulated millions of religious tracts throughout the country, and by 1837 claimed no less than 3,000 affiliated local organizations. The

SONG FOR A YOUTH TEMPERANCE GROUP

This youthful band
Do with our hand
The pledge now sign—
To drink no wine,

Nor brandy red
To turn the head,
Nor whiskey hot,
That makes the sot,

Nor fiery rum
To turn our home
Into a hell
Where none can dwell
Whence peace would fly

Where hope would die
And love expire
'Mid such a fire:—
So here we pledge perpetual hate
To all that can intoxicate.

"benevolent empire" carried on crusades against any form of behavior it considered sinful, and it had a quite expansive conception of sin. Organizations like the Connecticut Society for the Reformation of Morals sought to "discountenance immorality, particularly Sabbath-breaking, intemperance, and profanity; and to promote industry, order, piety, and good morals." The misnamed drive for "temperance" was the worldly cause dearest to the evangelical heart. It began as a true effort at temperance—using alcohol only temperately—but evolved into a crusade for total abstinence, and then into a campaign to force abstinence on everyone by prohibiting the sale of alcohol. Evangelical demands for stricter observance of the Sabbath, including a ban on the movement of the U.S. mails, revealed the same eagerness to impose a uniform moral code on an increasingly diverse society.

Other attempts at uplift focused on people on the fringes of society. Until the 1820s and 1830s it was customary to imprison defaulting debtors, making it impossible for them to earn funds to secure their release; most states ended this barbaric practice after it was attacked by reformers. The deaf and blind benefited from new institutions to educate and care for them. The lot of the insane improved after a pioneering investigation by Dorothea Dix in 1841–43 revealed that mentally ill people in Massachusetts were being kept in "cages, closets, cellars, stalls, pens. Chained, naked, beaten with rods and lashed into obedience." The state appropriated funds to develop a much improved system of asylums, and others soon followed suit. Prison reformers likewise successfully called for new penal institutions in which first offenders were separated from hardened criminals, and for detention schools for juvenile delinquents. If they were moved by a fear of social disorder, as some historians have recently emphasized, they were also highly optimistic in their faith that exposure to the right kind of environment could effect rehabilitation. With their stress on solitary confinement and martial discipline, the new prisons were in many ways harsher than what they replaced, and it is doubtful that they achieved more in the way of rehabilitation. But they were viewed as models both in America and elsewhere; Alexis de Tocqueville, for example, came to the United States in 1831 to examine the country's penal institutions for the French Minister of Justice.

The most important new institution of social betterment, in terms of the number of people it affected and the length of their exposure to it, was the public school. The drive to develop a system of universal, compulsory, tax-supported education won support from many quarters for a variety of reasons. Education could be seen as an instrument of liberation for the children of the poor, rescuing them from a legacy of crippling ignorance and giving them a more equal chance to compete against children whose parents could afford to educate them privately. Employers thought a more educated work force would be more productive, and favored educational reform on those grounds. From another perspective, schools could be seen as a necessary source of authority in a society that was changing with bewildering speed. "Without intelligence in the people," said Horace Mann, "a republican form of government must be on a mass scale what a mad-house without a superintendent or keepers would be on a small one—universal anarchy." Schools would be the antidote to anarchy. They would cultivate "intelligence"—not so much mere book learning as character traits like honesty, obedience, punctuality, and discipline. As the 1844 report of the school committee of a Massachusetts mill town put it, schools were "moral and intellectual machines which spin and weave the very warp and woof of a well-regulated and order-loving community."

As might be expected from what has been said earlier about the different world views of Jacksonian Democrats and their Whig opponents, Jacksonians were generally hostile to these reform efforts and Whigs usually supportive. Jacksonians tended to be pessimistic about mankind's capacity to attain perfection, and distrustful of powerful institutions. They were more tolerant of cultural styles that deviated from that of middle class evangelicals, and less eager to secure a morally homogeneous America. Andrew Jackson and his followers had nothing but contempt for the evangelical Anti-Dueling Society (1809), nor did many of them take the "cold water pledge." In considerable measure, Jacksonian Democracy can be seen as a backlash against the reform impulses radiating from "the benevolent empire."

The Women's Movement

One of the most important effects of the Second Great Awakening was that it drew women into public activities more fully than ever before. At the same time that the developing "cult of true womanhood" was enjoining women that their proper place was in the home, they were finding new opportunities for action in the world through missionary societies, temperance groups, and a host of other activities organized under the aegis of "the benevolent empire." Many women joined the abolitionist movement (discussed later in this chapter) and some, like Angelina and Sarah Grimke, broke the customary taboo against females speaking before mixed audiences. "The investigation of the rights of the slaves," said Angelina Grimke, "has led me to a better understanding of my own." Her *Letters on the Condition of Women and the Equality of the Sexes* (1838) are a classic feminist attack on "subordination to man," an assertion that both sexes had the "same rights" and the "same duties." The mill girls of Lowell and other New England towns who waged strikes in the 1830s and 1840s and established the short-lived Female Moral Reform Association also challenged male authority.

The climax of these tendencies was the first national meeting to discuss "the social, civil, and religious rights of women," held at Seneca Falls, New York, in 1848. It was attended by 250 women, led by Elizabeth Cady Stanton and Lucretia Mott, and 40 men. The Seneca Falls Declaration was a ringing manifesto modeled on the Declaration of Independence. "We hold these truths to be self-evident: that all men and women are created equal." It further asserted that the history of mankind was "a history of repeated injuries and usurpations on the part of man toward woman, having in direct object the establishment of absolute tyranny over her." It was time for the American woman to break out of "the circumscribed limits which corrupt customs and perverted application of the Scriptures" had marked out for her, and to enter an "enlarged sphere" as man's equal in every respect.

The immediate effects of the Seneca Falls meeting were minimal. Its demands for equal educational opportunities, an end to laws that made married women mere appendages of their husbands, "equal participation in the various trades, professions, and commerce," and the right to vote were utterly visionary by the standards of the time. Although one can say that the "women's movement" began in antebellum America, it is doubtful that as much as one percent of the female population supported its aims, doubtful indeed that that many had even heard of it. Seneca Falls sowed seeds that would bear significant fruit much later, but the nutrients they needed to grow would not become available for decades.

The Unpopular Cause of Abolitionism

If the extent of its popular following and its ability to secure the adoption of its program are the test of a social movement's success, the crusade to rid antebellum America of slavery was a dismal failure. However, if the test is the extent to which it raises moral issues to public consciousness and stirs up passions, abolitionism achieved its ends. Even on the eve of the Civil War, only a small fraction of the people of the North were outright abolitionists; most were only "free soilers" who wanted slavery kept out of the western territories. But without the abolitionist movement, it is difficult to believe that many millions of Americans would have come to believe that "free soil" was the most important issue facing the nation.

The first national antislavery organization in the United States was respectable and innocuous. The American Convention for Promoting the Abolition of Slavery was founded in the 1790s. Based largely in the South, it sought to persuade slaveholders to phase out the system of bondage gradually. As was clear from its only major project, the American Colonization Society, it was as much antiblack as it was antislavery. Contending that Negroes could never live on an equal plane with whites, the society proposed to ship them all back to Africa. The scheme had the endorsement of figures like Henry Clay and President Monroe and got some federal funding to create the new African Republic of Liberia. Most of the 234,000 free blacks in the country had no interest in returning to their roots, however, and denounced the colonization plan. And very few slaveholders proved willing to release their property for the purpose. In ten years of effort, the society managed to transport only 2,228 blacks to Liberia. Since that was fewer people than were born into slavery in the South in a typical *month*, it is obvious that the colonizers had not found the long-term solution to the problem of slavery in a free society.

A genuine national antislavery movement was born in the 1830s. Much of the inspiration for it came from developments across the Atlantic. After winning Parliamentary approval for a ban on importation of new slaves into the West Indies in 1807, a year before the United States abandoned the international slave trade, British evangelicals launched a drive for "immediate emancipation" of enslaved blacks in the Caribbean. Even before their final victory in 1833, their campaign convinced a growing number of Americans that slavery was a barbaric relic that had no place in an enlightened and progressive society.

The most famous of them was William Lloyd Garrison. Garrison began his career as the editor of a weekly newspaper, which failed. He then tried his hand at running a temperance paper. In 1831, at the age of 26, he launched an antislavery organ, *The Liberator*. Garrison was absolutely certain that "God and His truth, and the rights of man, and the promises of the Holy Scriptures" demanded the immediate and complete destruction of the slave system, with no compensation to the owners. In response to the criticism that his furious assaults on slavery were immoderate, he replied:

> No! No! Tell a man whose house is on fire to give a moderate alarm; tell him to moderately rescue his wife from the hands of her ravisher; tell the mother to moderately extricate her babe from the fire into which it has fallen—but urge me not to use moderation in a cause like the present.

Garrison took the lead in the formation of the New England Anti-Slavery Society in 1832, and participated in the formation of the American Anti-Slavery Society in 1833, but his influence as an organizer has often been exaggerated. The most important recruiters to the abolitionist cause were young evangelical minis-

> ## INSTRUCTIONS FROM THE EXECUTIVE COMMITTEE OF THE AMERICAN ANTI-SLAVERY SOCIETY TO A NEWLY APPOINTED AGENT, 1833
>
> Our object is the overthrow of American slavery, the most atrocious and oppressive system of bondage that has ever existed in any country. We expect to accomplish this mainly by showing to the public its true character and legitimate fruits, its contrariety to the first principles of religion, morals, and humanity, and its special inconsistency with our pretentions as a free, humane, and enlightened people. In this way, by the force of truth, we expect to correct common errors that prevail respecting slavery, and to produce a just public sentiment, which appeals both to the conscience and love of character of our slave-holding fellow citizens, and convince them that both their duty and their welfare require the immediate abolition of slavery.
>
> You will inculcate everywhere the great fundamental principle of IMMEDIATE ABOLITION as the duty of all masters, on the ground that slavery is both unjust and unprofitable. Insist principally on the SIN OF SLAVERY, because our main hope is in the consciences of men, and it requires very little logic to prove that it is always safe to do right. To question this is to impeach the superintending Providence of God.
>
> Do not allow yourself to be drawn away from the main object to exhibit a detailed PLAN of abolition; for men's consciences will be greatly relieved from the feeling of present duty by any objections or difficulties which they can find or fancy in your plan. Let the *principle* be decided on, of immediate abolition, and the plans will easily present themselves. What ought to be done can be done.

ters like Theodore Dwight Weld, followers of Charles Grandison Finney for whom the gospel of Christ and the gospel of abolition were one. They were "immediatists" too. According to them, slavery was a monstrous sin, and the wicked men who profited from it should renounce it, just as drinkers should renounce the Demon Rum. By 1838, the American Anti-Slavery Society had approximately a quarter of a million members in 1,300 locals, and had been able to gather over 400,000 signatures on antislavery petitions to Congress. It included many blacks, among them escaped slaves like Frederick Douglass, Sojourner Truth, and Harriet Tubman. White women like the Grimke sisters were prominent in the movement, too. Many white male abolitionists, however, did not share Garrison's beliefs in either women's rights or full equality for blacks. They wanted an end to slavery, but continued sexual and racial subordination.

Although the antislavery campaign had become highly visible by the late 1830s, it attracted much more hostility than support. Not surprisingly, abolitionist speakers could find no audience in the South, where the slave-owners they were trying to convert lived. They couldn't even deliver their messages by pamphlet after 1835, when a Charleston mob broke into the post office and destroyed antislavery literature. Although three years before he had forcefully asserted the federal government's authority to collect customs, Jackson thought that abolitionists had no right to disseminate their unpopular message through the U.S. mails, and he gave local postmasters the right to ban their publications.

Abolitionists were also widely regarded as crazy and dangerous fanatics throughout most of the North, an important fact that southerners failed to understand. Garrison was dragged through the streets of Boston with a rope around his neck in 1835 and narrowly escaped with his life. In 1837, another abolitionist editor, Elijah P. Lovejoy of Alton, Illinois, was killed by a crowd set on destroying his printing press. Movement leaders proclaimed him "the first martyr to American liberty," but a more typical reaction was that of the Attorney General of Massachusetts who told a large audience in Boston that the killing of Lovejoy was a valiant act for a just cause, in the tradition of direct popular action started by Samuel Adams and other patriots. The strength of the consensus that abolitionists were lunatics was reflected in the fact that Congress refused even to discuss the antislavery petitions that flooded in; in 1836, with bipartisan support, it adopted a "gag rule" that prevented any consideration of them. Each year John Quincy Adams, who returned to the House of Representatives after retiring from the Presidency, carried on a strenuous campaign to lift the gag rule, but he was unsuccessful until 1844.

In 1840 the American Anti-Slavery Society split, partly because of personal animosities created by Garrison's confidence that he and he alone knew God's plan, partly over his insistence that women's rights and pacifism were an integral part of the cause, and partly over the issue of political involvement. Garrison would have nothing to do with politics; he was a Christian anarchist who denounced the Constitution as a "covenant with death and an agreement with Hell." According to him, mankind would attain perfection when all institutions had been eliminated, and that could only be accomplished by "moral suasion."

Other, more pragmatic, figures within the abolitionist camp were unwilling to wait for the coming of the millennium, and they decided to put the issue of slavery before the electorate. Working within one of the two major parties—which had cooperated on the gag rule to keep the question silenced—seemed hopeless, so they formed a new third party. James G. Birney, the Liberty Party's candidate for the Presidency in 1840, drew only a pathetic 7,053 votes, .3 percent of the total. In 1844 the Liberty Party called for other reforms in addition to abolition, and Birney ran rather better, drawing 62,300 ballots. Still that was but 2.3 percent of the total. The prospect of putting a militant abolitionist in the White House in the foreseeable future was obviously a very dim one.

In 1844 the vast majority of Americans still regarded slavery as a nonissue. In that sense, the abolitionists had failed. Slavery was dead in the northern states, very much alive in the South, and present or absent in the territories depending on whether or not they lay north or south of the 36°30′ line. On the other hand, abolitionist agitators had been successful in stirring up sectional feelings. South-

FREDERICK DOUGLASS
(1817–1895)

I n the eyes of the law, slaves had no family name and no one bothered to register their births. About all that can be said about the early
history of the man who became known as Frederick Douglass is that he
was born into slavery on the Eastern Shore of Maryland around 1817, the
son of a slave woman and an unknown white man. As a youth he was
fortunate enough to be hired out as a house servant to a Baltimore
woman who taught him to read and write in violation of the state's slave
code. When he was sent back to work as a field hand, he persistently
rebelled against the drivers' attempts to "break him." Eventually his
master allowed him to return to Baltimore and hire himself out as an
apprentice ship caulker. At the age of nineteen, he borrowed the papers
of a free black sailor and fled to the North, where he took the name of
Frederick Douglass.

He was living in New Bedford, Massachusetts in 1841 when he
attended a meeting of the Massachusetts Anti-Slavery Society and overwhelmed the audience with his eloquence. A denunciation of slavery by someone who had felt the lashes of the slavedriver's whip had far
greater power than the fulminations of a Garrison or a Weld. Douglass
spoke tirelessly for the anti-slavery cause across the country and in
Britain, edited the leading black newspaper of the period, *The North Star*
(later called *Frederick Douglass's Newspaper*), and wrote a powerful autobiography, *The Narrative of the Life of Frederick Douglass, an American Slave,
Written by Himself* (1845). During the Civil War, Douglass recruited black
troops for the Union Army and urged Lincoln along the path that led to
the Emancipation Proclamation. After the war, Douglass held a number
of federal appointments while he struggled to advance the cause of his
people. By the time of his death in 1895, however, most of the fruits of
Emancipation and Reconstruction had turned sour.

erners not only seized on Garrison's most extreme statements and assumed that all antislavery activists were sheer anarchists; they began to think that he was a typical moralistic Yankee fanatic who enjoyed far greater support than he did. Northerners, who were not terribly concerned about the lot of slaves in Alabama, in turn, were repelled by mail censorship, the gag rule, and the ever more strident southern defenses of slavery as a positive good that poured forth in response to abolitionist attacks. In this sense, as one historian puts it, the unbending "immediatist" stance of the abolitionist "helped to set off the emotional chain reaction that led to the Civil War and the destruction of slavery."

SUGGESTED READINGS

George Dangerfield, *The Era of Good Feelings* (1952) and *The Awakening of American Nationalism, 1815–1828* (1965) are brilliant and highly readable. On the growing authority of the Supreme Court, see Francis N. Stites, *John Marshall: Defender of the Constitution* (1981). James S. Young, *The Washington Community, 1800–1828* (1966) offers penetrating insights into the politics of the period. Arthur M. Schlesinger, Jr., *The Age of Jackson* (1945) celebrates Jackson and his supporters in sparkling prose. Its basic assumptions about the character of Jacksonianism are undermined by the quantitative studies of Lee Benson, *The Concept of Jacksonian Democracy: New York as a Test Case* (1964), and Ronald P. Formisano, *The Birth of Mass Political Parties: Michigan, 1827–1861* (1971). Marvin Myers, *The Jacksonian Persuasion: Politics and Beliefs* (1957) and John William Ward, *Andrew Jackson: Symbol for an Age* (1955) are imaginative and incisive studies of the thought of the period. Edward Pessen, *Jacksonian America: Society, Personality, and Politics* (rev. ed., 1978) is a broad-ranging survey. Richard P. McCormick, *The Second American Party System: Party Formation in the Jacksonian Era* (1966), William C. Shade, *Banks or No Banks: The Money Question in the Western States, 1832–1865* (1973), Robert V. Remini, *Andrew Jackson and the Bank War* (1967), and Daniel Walker Howe, *The Political Culture of American Whigs* (1980) examine key political issues. Robert Kelley, *The Cultural Pattern in American Politics: The First Century* (1979) is a useful synthesis. On the issue of slavery and nullification, see Donald L. Robinson, *Slavery in the Structure of American Politics, 1765–1820* (1971), William Freehling, *Prelude to Civil War: The Nullification Controversy in South Carolina, 1816–1836* (1966), and William J. Cooper, *The South and the Politics of Slavery* (1978).

Ronald G. Walters, *American Reformers, 1815–1860* (1978) is the best introduction to reform in the era. Clifford S. Griffin, *Their Brothers' Keepers: Moral Stewardship in the United States, 1800–1860* (1960) is a fuller general account. David Brion Davis, ed., *Antebellum American Culture: An Interpretive Anthology* (1979) is a fine collection of pertinent documents. Perry Miller, *The Life of the Mind in America: From the Revolution to the Civil War* (1966) offers many insights into the changing intellectual and cultural climate. Paul Johnson, *A Shopkeeper's Millennium: Society and Revivals in Rochester, New York, 1815–1837* (1979) sheds light on the social sources of the Second Great Awakening. On temperance, see W.J. Rorabaugh, *The Alcoholic*

Republic: An American Tradition (1979) and Ian R. Tyrell, *Sobering Up: From Temperance to Prohibition in Antebellum America* (1979). Educational reform is analyzed in Michael B. Katz, *The Irony of Early School Reform* (1968), Lawrence A. Cremin, *American Education: The National Experience* (1980), Carl F. Kaestle, *The Evolution of an Urban School System: New York City, 1750–1850* (1973), and Carl F. Kaestle and Maris A. Vinovskis, *Education and Social Change in Nineteenth-Century Massachusetts* (1980). For the women's rights movement, see Carl Degler, *At Odds: Women and the Family from the Revolution to the Present* (1980). Ronald G. Walter, *The Antislavery Appeal: American Abolitionism after 1830* (1976), William H. Pease and Jane H. Pease, *They Would Be Free: Blacks' Search for Freedom 1830–1861* (1974), and Lewis Parry and Michael Fellman, *Antislavery Reconsidered: New Perspectives on the Abolitionists* (1979) treat abolitionism.

Chapter Fourteen

The Road to Disunion

In 1846 the United States attacked a weak neighbor, Mexico, won an easy military victory, and stripped her of her northern provinces. Fifteen years later, largely as a result of political conflicts stirred up by those acquisitions, the nation went to war again. Only this time it was American against American, Confederate against Unionist, Rebel against Yankee. The American people have the oldest written Constitution in the world, and have again and again displayed a gift for papering over major disagreements and making deals that no one really likes but all can live with. A pragmatic, "let's split the difference," "you scratch my back and I'll scratch yours" mentality made the original charter of union at Philadelphia possible, and allowed Americans to peacefully resolve many highly contentious issues on later occasions. The only issue that proved too much for the politicians to dispose of in the customary compromising fashion was slavery. The passions it stirred shattered the second party system, inflamed sectional fears and hates, and led finally to a war that destroyed slavery and killed 600,000 men. The chain of political events that culminated in that unprecedented crisis is therefore of compelling interest.

THE FRUITS OF MANIFEST DESTINY

In the early 1840s the United States experienced the surge of expansionist energy known as "Manifest Destiny." The western third of what is now the United States was in the hands of other powers—Britain laid claim to the Pacific Northwest, and

Bloodhounds pursue Eliza Harris across the icy Ohio River in this poster advertising a melodrama based on Harriet Beecher Stowe's 1852 novel, Uncle Tom's Cabin.

Mexico to the Southwest from Texas to California. Much of the best land within America's borders had come under the plow, and the population was growing at the same dizzying speed as before. The new rail network had already penetrated the Appalachian barrier and was advancing along the prairie, and the idea that iron rails might span the continent from the Atlantic someday soon was no longer a fanciful vision. And who could be sure that other remarkable transportation innovations would not follow? In 1846 one company advertised that it was about to produce a "windwagon" with mast and sail to carry settlers to Oregon at 15 miles per hour; in 1849 an "Air Line to California" was announced, promising a three-day journey from the East Coast to San Francisco in a hot-air balloon for $50 "with wines included." In this heady atmosphere, the editor of the *Democratic Review* declared that the drive to the Pacific was "the inevitable fulfillment of the general law which is rolling our population westward." It was our "manifest destiny to overspread the continent allotted by Providence for the free development of our yearly multiplying millions."

The Pacific Northwest was acquired peacefully. The Oregon Territory, comprising present-day Oregon, Washington, Idaho, and parts of Montana, Wyoming, and British Columbia, had long been open to settlement. Both Britain and the United States claimed sovereignty over it, and citizens of both countries had the right to settle there. Efforts to delineate a boundary between the United States and Canada were unsuccessful, so the two parties agreed to postpone the question. For many years the boundary was a moot issue, because only a few hardy American fur traders and some missionaries to the Indians were willing to risk the perils of the Oregon Trail, which wound through 2,000 miles of wilderness from Independence, Missouri to the Pacific. In the late 1830s, however, news filtered back that the missionaries had found rich soils and a temperate climate, and "Oregon fever" broke out in the Midwest. Thousands of farmers loaded their possessions on covered wagons and made their way across the barren plains and over the mountains. The trail was soon lined with the carcasses of horses and oxen, abandoned goods, and more than a few graves. As the number of Americans in Oregon grew, so did the clamor to have the whole Northwest up to the Alaskan border—the 54°40' line—annexed to the United States. The Democratic party backed this claim, and used "Fifty-four Forty or Fight" as a slogan in the 1844 campaign. After threatening to abide by his party's platform and go to war, the victorious Democratic candidate, James K. Polk, accepted a compromise that divided the area at the 49th parallel, the present boundary between the state of Washington and British Columbia.

The Mexican War

Polk showed no such compromising spirit in his dealings with Mexico. Mexico had won its independence from Spain in 1821, but it was an economically and socially underdeveloped country with a population less than half that of the United States and a tradition of unstable government. Its northern provinces—Texas, New Mexico, and California—contained more than half a million square miles of land, but only one percent of the Mexican population. And few in that one percent had much loyalty to Mexico. Communications between Mexico City and the provinces were terrible, and inhabitants of colonial Spanish origins resisted efforts to link them more closely with Mexico. Native "Californios," for example, attempted no less than ten revolts against Mexican governors between 1828 and 1843, and by the time Polk took office had won a de facto but unacknowledged independence.

Texas had been even more restive under Mexican rule because so many of its settlers were Americans. In the 1820s, Mexican authorities offered generous land grants to Americans who agreed to settle in the almost empty province and develop it. The evident restlessness of these settlers and offers from the U.S. government to buy Texas led the Mexican government to reverse the policy in the early 1830s, but by then it was too late. When General Santa Anna proclaimed himself dictator in 1834 and sought to impose tighter controls over the provinces, including a ban on slavery, the Texans rose up in arms. Although they suffered a crushing defeat at the Alamo at San Antonio in 1836, losing every man, they prevailed on the battlefield after that and won their independence. At gunpoint, Santa Anna concluded a peace treaty that set the Texas border at the Rio Grande, 150 miles south of the traditional boundary of the province, the Nueces River. That added millions of new acres to Texas, and the Mexican Congress naturally refused to endorse the treaty.

The Americans who won independence for Texas did so with the expectation that they would soon be admitted to the United States. That did not happen until 1845. Since Mexico insisted that Texas was a rebellious province, not an independent nation, and objected especially vehemently to its claims to the Rio Grande boundary, successive administrations hesitated to take an action that might provoke war. Another reason for caution was that Texas was so huge in territory that it could easily be carved into three or four new slave states. Southerners looked forward to that, northerners feared it, and neither side pressed the issue. For nine years the Republic of Texas remained an independent nation.

In the 1844 campaign, finally, the Democratic party called for the annexation of Texas as well as all of Oregon to the Alaskan border, and a bill authorizing it scraped through Congress on a straight party vote in early 1845. Congress ducked the thorny question of the status of all the land between the Nueces and the Rio Grande. It was left to the incoming President, Polk, to decide whether to back the Texans' claim to an area more than twice the size of the Mexican province of Texas, a claim plainly contradicted by American and European maps of the day. Although he knew that no Mexican government could survive the humiliation of surrendering the entire disputed area, Polk believed that might makes right and ordered the U.S. Army to march to the Rio Grande. When he heard of a minor skirmish between Mexican and U.S. forces, he asked Congress for a declaration of war, on the grounds that "Mexico has passed the boundary of the United States and shed American blood on American soil." Although this specious assertion was later challenged by Whigs and some Democrats in Congress (see box), the war resolution was approved with only a few dissenting votes.

Polk wanted not only an enlarged Texas for the United States. He wanted the entire Southwest, including New Mexico and California. He dispatched the army to drive the ill-prepared Mexican defenders from the whole area, which they

WHIGS QUESTION POLK'S RATIONALE FOR THE MEXICAN WAR, 1847

Whereas this House desires to obtain a full knowledge of all the facts which go to establish whether the particular spot of soil on which the blood of our citizens was shed was, or was not, our own soil at that time; therefore

Resolved by the House of Representatives, that the President of the United States be respectfully requested to inform this house—

Whether the spot of soil on which the blood of our citizens was shed, as in his messages declared, was or was not within the territories of Spain until the Mexican revolution.

Whether that spot is, or is not, within the territory which was wrested from Spain by the Mexican revolution.

Whether that spot is, or is not, within a settlement of people, which settlement had existed ever since long before the Texas revolution.

Whether the People of that settlement, or a majority of them, or any of them, had ever, previous to the bloodshed mentioned in his messages, submitted themselves to the government or laws of Texas, or of the United States, by consent.

Whether our citizens whose blood was shed, as in his messages declared, were, or were not, at that time armed officers and soldiers sent into that settlement by the military order of the President.

---

accomplished easily in a few months. When Mexico refused to accept the legitimacy of the conquest, Polk had General Winfield Scott lead an invasion of central Mexico and capture Mexico City. Mexico had to sue for peace and "sell" the Southwest to the United States for $15 million. The 1848 Treaty of Guadalupe Hidalgo transferred the northern half of Mexico to the United States and filled in her present continental borders, except for a portion of southern Arizona and New Mexico purchased from Mexico in 1853 (the Gasden Purchase).

It can be argued that this outcome, or something much like it, was inevitable. Mexico's hold over its northern provinces was exceedingly weak and America's expansive energies were great. American occupying forces met with little resistance from local residents; most thought that becoming part of the great democracy to the north would be advantageous to them. Throughout history strong powers have ignored the rights of their weaker neighbors when it suited them, and it is perhaps unrealistic to expect anything different from nineteenth-century America. Nevertheless, it was a morally dubious war, and Polk shamelessly misrepresented the facts of the situation to win congressional approval for it.

The seizure of the Southwest, an area larger than the entire United States before the Louisiana Purchase, seemed a spectacular achievement. It seemed even more

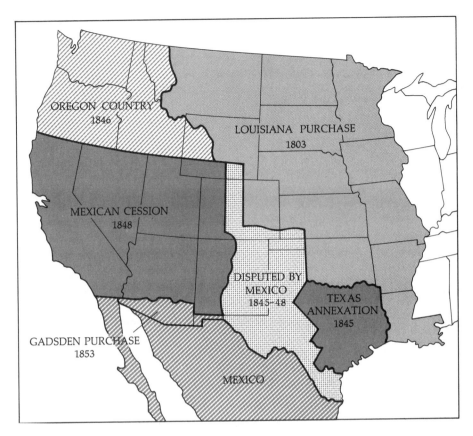

MAP 14-1
Manifest Destiny

spectacular when prospectors struck immense gold deposits in California and the furious westward rush of the "forty-niners" began. Ironically, however, this national triumph was a Pandora's Box—from it issued the problem that tore the nation apart—the issue of slavery.

The Wilmot Proviso

Most of the territory added to the United States as a result of the Mexican war was south of the 36°30′ line, and would be open to slavery if the line drawn by the Missouri Compromise were extended all the way to the Pacific. The prospect of several new slave states in the Union was disquieting to northerners who were becoming convinced that the South already had too strong a voice in the national government. Another consideration was that Mexico had outlawed slavery in the area (although it hadn't been able to enforce the ban). If a country as backward as Mexico in American eyes was advanced enough to recognize the superiority of free labor, many reasoned, it would be criminal for the world's greatest democracy to permit the regressive peculiar institution to be introduced. To prevent it, in the summer of 1846, a Congressman from Pennsylvania, David Wilmot, introduced a bill excluding slavery from any lands taken from Mexico. The Wilmot Proviso passed the House, dominated by representatives from the populous North and West, but was beaten in the Senate. It was reintroduced several more times over the next four years, with the same stalemated result.

Although it was never enacted, the Wilmot Proviso had enormous consequences, because it began to undermine the firm partisan allegiances that made the second party system work. Before the Mexican war, Congressmen had generally voted with their party, even on issues that had sectional implications. A good many southern Whigs, for example, followed the party line to vote down a Democratic proposal to admit Texas into the union as a slave state in 1844, even though southern public opinion ran in favor of it. On the repeated votes on the Wilmot bill, however, party discipline broke down and sectional loyalties asserted themselves. Wilmot himself was a Democrat, and his antislavery measure won the support of more than half of the northern Democrats in Congress. Likewise, most southern Whigs rejected the Whig party line and voted in the negative like southern Democrats.

The problem of what to do with the lands ceded by Mexico dominated the 1848 elections. The Democratic candidate, Governor Lewis Cass of Michigan, rejected the Wilmot Proviso, and proposed instead that the slavery question be resolved by popular or "squatter" sovereignty. The Whigs had great difficulties in settling on a candidate. Southern Whigs and northern "Cotton" Whigs—so called because many were cotton manufacturers dependent on raw materials from the South— were reluctant to antagonize the slave interest. Northern "Conscience" Whigs were firmly against the extension of slavery in the Mexican cession. When General Zachary Taylor, a southern slave-owner and a hero of the Mexican war, won the nomination, many Conscience Whigs defected to a new antislavery third party, the Free Soil party. Although many of the abolitionists who had founded the Liberty party backed it, it did not call for immediate abolition. It stood for "free soil, free labor, and free men"—a ban on the expansion of slavery into new territories. Confining the slave system within its present limits, Free Soilers thought, would force gradual abolition in the future when southern soil became too depleted for plantation agriculture. The Free Soil candidate, ex-President Martin Van Buren, drew almost 300,000 votes, 10 percent of the total and enough to throw the election to General Taylor. Antislavery sentiment was becoming a potent force in northern politics.

The Compromise—or Armistice—of 1850

The future of Mexican lands was at last settled in 1850, with the famous compromise. It cheered Free Soilers by abolishing the slave trade in the District of Columbia, and admitting California to the Union as a free state, despite the fact that its lower half was below 36°30'. The most important concession to the South

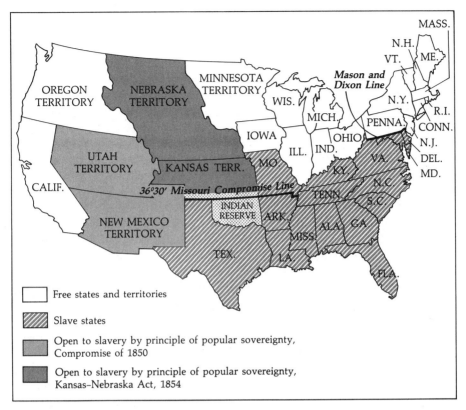

MAP 14–2
The Compromise of 1850 and the Kansas-Nebraska Act of 1854

was a strict federal law to facilitate the capture and return of runaway slaves, one that placed the burden of proof on accused black fugitives rather than the whites who claimed them. The status of slavery in the remainder of the Southwest—the territories of Utah and New Mexico—was left to be determined by squatter sovereignty.

The congressional debates over the Compromise of 1850 are legendary. They were dominated by three figures whose political careers began in the early years of the republic—the great triumvirate of Daniel Webster, Henry Clay, and John C. Calhoun. Webster and Clay spoke with florid eloquence of the need to bury sectional issues that threatened the survival of the Union. Their efforts were successful, in the short run—the compromise measures carried.

Calhoun was more pessimistic and, as it turned out, more prescient. He bitterly warned that the sectional divisions that had been opened up by "agitation of the slavery question" had already snapped some of the most important bonds uniting the states under one government. Palliatives like the measures offered by the compromisers were not solutions but evasions. The root problem was that political equilibrium had been destroyed because population growth was greater in the northern states and because the northern majority was determined to impose its will on the mortally threatened southern minority. Nothing less than a guarantee that southerners had equal rights in the Union—which meant the right to bring slaves into *all* the territories—would suffice to protect them from the assaults of abolitionist fanatics.

Calhoun and his supporters therefore agreed with their greatest enemies—supporters of the Wilmot Proviso and the Free Soil principle—on one crucial thing. It was necessary to have a uniform national policy toward slavery in the territories. Because neither of these militant "all or nothing at all" groupings dominated Congress in 1850, the great compromise was passed. But it was not a true compromise, if by that we mean that the contending forces agree upon a package that gives something to each side, and accept the bargain as basically satisfactory. It might better have been called the armistice of 1850. Most southern Congressmen voted against those elements of the "compromise" sought by the North; likewise, most northern congressmen voted against the provisions the South demanded. Only one of the six bills that made up the package was approved by *both* a northern and a southern majority, and that in only one house of Congress and by the slenderest of margins. (This was the admission of New Mexico under the popular sovereignty formula, in which 11 of the 21 northern senators joined the 16 southern senators who approved it unanimously.) The swing vote of a small group of moderates tipped the balance in every other vote.

Senator Thomas Hart Benton of Missouri summed up the situation in a vivid metaphor. The Wilmot Proviso ban on the extension of slavery and Calhoun's demand for its unrestricted expansion were like the two blades of a pair of scissors, Benton said. Neither one alone could cut; together they could sever the bonds of the Union. The measures concocted by desperate Congressmen in 1850 temporarily slowed the closing of the scissors, but nothing more.

PARTY DISINTEGRATION AND REALIGNMENT, 1850–56

In the 1840s, the Whig and Democratic parties both had solid roots in all sections of the country, and the balance between them was exceedingly close. The Whigs won the Presidency in 1840 and 1848, and lost by a hair's breadth in 1844. The margin of victory in the three contests averaged a mere 4.1 percent of the popular vote. The Democrats had a slight edge in Congress, controlling the Senate in four out of five congressional sessions and the House in three out of five, but there too the contests were close. In the fall of 1848, for instance, 112 Democrats, 109 Whigs, and 9 Free Soilers were elected to the House.

Within a few years, however, that balance was destroyed, and the shape of the American political universe was transformed. By the mid-1850s the Whig party was defunct. The Democratic Party was in mortal danger too, not of disappearing but of splintering into northern and southern wings. And two brand new political organizations had been formed, one-issue parties unaccustomed to the give and take of traditional politics.

JOHN C. CALHOUN
(1782–1850)

John Caldwell Calhoun was perhaps the most brilliant and certainly the most unbending and obstinate American statesman of the nineteenth century. When he was born in South Carolina in 1782, the states had just surrendered their conflicting claims to western lands and had begun to forge a closer union. Calhoun's early career as a Congressman, beginning in 1810, reflected the strength of these nationalizing impulses. He was a militant "War Hawk" before the War of 1812, and at its end favored an energetic central government, supporting national aid for internal improvements, a national bank, an expanded military force, and protective tariffs. Under John Quincy Adams, a strong nationalist, he served as Vice-President without evident discomfort from 1825 to 1829.

Re-elected to serve a second term as Vice-President in 1828, Calhoun made an about-face and supported the objection of many Southerners to the "Tariff of Abominations." He secretly drafted the "South Carolina Exposition" that held that states were empowered to "nullify" legislation they regarded as unconstitutional, and in 1832 went public with his opposition to the Jackson administration and resigned his Vice-Presidency. Although the effect of the tariff on the South was the ostensible reason for the outcry, the deeper fear that impelled Calhoun and his supporters to resistance was that a strong central government might someday interfere with slavery. The rise of abolitionist and Free Soil sentiment in the 1830s and 1840s made Calhoun insist ever more shrilly that slavery was not an evil but a positive good and that "Southern Rights" were imperilled by the more rapid economic and demographic growth of the North. In his treatises, *Discourse on Government* and *Discourse on the Constitution and Government of the United States,* Calhoun used his formidable powers of argumentation to defend the rights of a minority against a majority, but he assumed that a large minority of the people of the South—its four million slaves—had no rights at all. In the furious Congressional battle over the disposition of the land acquired as a result of the Mexican War, the aging and sickly Calhoun summoned up his last energies to plead that all territory be left open to slavery and to urge that the South secede rather than settle for anything less. He was disappointed when the Compromise of 1850 temporarily laid the issue to rest. However, the intransigence he embodied prevailed in Southern ruling circles after Abraham Lincoln's election to the Presidency in 1860.

Decline of the Whigs

The deaths of both Henry Clay and Daniel Webster in 1852 were an omen of the imminent demise of the Whig Party they had created. Although the Whigs had been the principal architects of the Compromise of 1850, the party derived no political advantage from it. To the contrary, that fall they lost almost a fifth of their seats in the House of Representatives, and in 1852 they suffered further disaster. The Whig presidential candidate managed to carry only four states and, in the newly elected House, Democrats outnumbered Whigs by a crushing seven-to-three margin.

At first Whig losses were concentrated in the South. In 1852 the Whig share of the presidential vote fell in every slave state. The party lost three southern states it had carried in every election since Andrew Jackson's retirement in 1836—North Carolina, Maryland, and Delaware—and two others it had lost but once in those years. The Whigs were not truly committed to the protection of slavery, southerners were coming to fear. Militants who opposed the Compromise of 1850 resented the Whig role in engineering it. More moderate southerners who grudgingly accepted it were dismayed that so many northern Whigs denounced it for giving away too much to the South. Furthermore, President Zachary Taylor had not been as solicitous of southern interests as they had expected.

Soon, however, northern Whig voters began to turn away from the party for just the opposite reason. Masses of northerners who had never seen an abolitionist tract began to think about slavery in a new way as a result of reading Harriet Beecher Stowe's remarkable novel *Uncle Tom's Cabin*, serialized in 1851 and published as a book in 1852. It was an astonishing success. By 1861 the American sales had exceeded a million copies, one for each five families in the entire country. For those who missed reading the book, several dramatizations toured the North after 1852, some of them altering the fact that Simon Legree, the villian of the piece, was a northerner from Vermont, not a southerner. Readers today may find *Uncle Tom's Cabin* lurid and sentimental, and be offended by the racial stereotypes it contains. But it is a work of remarkable power. The first American novel to focus on black people, it convincingly portrayed the humanity of the slave and the inhumanity of the condition in which he was held.

Mrs. Stowe was moved to write her book out of outrage at the passage of the new national fugitive slave law in 1850. As federal authorities began to enforce the measure and ship hundreds of blacks back to the South without a trial, many other northerners came to feel the same way. Federal troops had to be brought in to keep mobs in Boston, Chicago, Detroit, and other cities from rescuing accused fugitives who had been arrested by "man-stealers." Several northern states impeded enforcement of the federal law by enacting personal liberty laws guaranteeing alleged runaways the right to counsel and a jury trial. The government of Wisconsin went so far as to refuse to permit the return of fugitives after the U.S. Supreme Court ordered it to do so. Militant opponents of slavery began to sound like John C. Calhoun, arguing that the ultimate source of political authority rested with the individual states rather than the federal government. Two could play at the game of nullification.

Nativism and the "Know Nothings"

Already weakened by intramural warfare between its "Conscience" and "Cotton" factions, the Whigs suffered a final fatal blow when they misjudged the depth of nativist anti-immigrant resentment in the 1850s. An unprecendented three million newcomers arrived in the years 1846–54. They were free to vote after meeting the five-year residency requirement, and increasing numbers of them were exercising the privilege. Most were Irish or German and favored the Democrats, perceiving the Whigs as nativist and anti-Catholic. In 1852, just the time that hostility to the newcomers was surging, the Whigs cast aside their traditional nativist themes and made a bid to win the immigrant vote. They not only failed; they drove many of their supporters into a new party.

The American Party, a secret patriotic society formed in New York in 1849, became a major political force almost overnight. By 1854 it controlled most New England states and was strong in New York, Pennsylvania, and the South as well. Members were called "Know Nothings" because they were pledged to say that they knew nothing when asked about secret party rituals. Playing on popular fears of immigrants and Catholics, the Know Nothings insisted that "Americans must rule America." They proposed that the naturalization requirement be extended to 21 years, and that Catholics be barred from holding political office.

The remarkable, if short-lived, spread of Know Nothing sentiment revealed the profound anxiety that the immigrant flood had unleashed in many parts of the country, even in places like the South that had attracted very few newcomers. For many, the foreigner had become the symbol of every ill besetting American society. It also revealed that a great many Americans had come to believe that the old parties had become corrupt and unresponsive to mass sentiment, and that a new and radically different political organization was needed. The star of the American Party, however, faded as quickly as it rose. Its leaders were inexperienced and inept. The principle of secrecy limited its appeal by giving the movement a conspiratorial image. It took no position on slavery, hoping to transcend sectional divisions by convincing the electorate that it was the Pope and not the Slave Power that truly threatened the Republic. In 1854, at the height of its influence, a major bill passed by Congress thrust slavery back to center stage and provided the impetus for the creation of another new party, one that would soon absorb the Know Nothings and many disaffected northern Democrats as well.

The Kansas–Nebraska Act

The Kansas–Nebraska Act provided a framework for the settlement of the entire Great Plains region from the western borders of Minnesota, Iowa, and Missouri, not just those portions of it now occupied by Kansas and Nebraska. The land had been reserved as Indian territory and barred to white settlers, so the bill authorized federal agents to once again pressure the tribes to yield up their lands and move on. Although all of it lay north of the 36°30′ line specified in the Missouri Compromise, the Kansas–Nebraska Act did not close the territory to slavery. It explicitly repealed the Missouri Compromise, and left the question of slavery to be determined by popular sovereignty.

The architect of the bill was Senator Stephen Douglas of Illinois. An ardent expansionist, he had long been frustrated by the unwillingness of southern Congressmen to allow the organization of territories in the region because they were earmarked to become free states. He was equally ardent in his hopes to see a transcontinental railroad line built along a route that would connect with Chicago and stimulate its development, and was worried that proponents of an alternative southern route from Memphis through Texas and New Mexico might have their plans approved instead. He was morally indifferent to slavery, and was convinced in any event that the climate and soil of the Great Plains were utterly unsuited to slave-based plantation agriculture. Consequently, it seemed to him a master stroke to win southern acceptance of the opening up of the Kansas–Nebraska territory by repealing the historic ban on slavery there. It was a symbolic gesture that would win needed southern votes without disturbing anyone but the most fanatic Free Soilers, he thought. It seemed perfectly evident to Douglas that the great majority of pioneers who would flock into the area would be from free farm states and would vote slavery out at the earliest opportunity.

Douglas knew how to count votes, and the bill went through. But he greatly underestimated the effect it would have on public opinion. It created a political firestorm in the North. "We went to bed one night old-fashioned, conservative, compromise, Union Whigs," wrote one Massachusetts mill-owner, "and waked up stark mad Abolitionists." The pattern of congressional voting followed sectional more than party lines. Although it was a Democratic measure, southern Whigs supported it almost to a man. Northern Whigs who voted against it were joined by about half of the northern Democrats.

Douglas may have misjudged northern reaction to a measure that could spread slavery across the Great Plains because he reasoned that there was a precedent for the squatter sovereignty principle in the Compromise of 1850. The situations, however, differed in three key respects. The 1850 arrangement made important concessions to Free Soil sentiment, making California free despite the fact that much of it was below the 36°30′ line, and abolishing the slave trade in the nation's capital. Furthermore, the territory at issue in 1850 had just been added to the national domain, and there had been no prior agreement among Americans as to its status vis-à-vis slavery. But all of the area now in question lay within the Louisiana Purchase north of 36°30′, and had been explicitly guaranteed free forever by the terms of the Missouri Compromise. Finally, Utah and New Mexico did not border on thickly settled states. They were far beyond the existing line of settlement, and their populations would remain relatively small for a long time to come. (In 1890 the population of the area covered by the Kansas–Nebraska Act was more than ten times larger than that of Utah and New Mexico.) The possibility of the new territories becoming slave states was remote and abstract; the future of Kansas was immediate and concrete.

The prospect that the Kansas–Nebraska Act would permit slavery to sink roots in a vast area long regarded as permanently closed to it was appalling to people of conscience who opposed slavery on moral and humanitarian grounds. It was appalling, too, to a larger group who opposed slavery out of a mixture of racism and self-interest. Their main objection to the expansion of slavery was that it would bring large numbers of blacks into areas that should be reserved for the homes of free white Americans. The introduction of slavery there would not only force whites into contact with a race they regarded as inferior. The next step, the logical outcome of the philosophy of the master class, might well be enslavement of the white worker, as southern social theorists like George Fitzhugh had actually proposed. A popular poet of the day summed up the fear:

> Wy, it's jest as clear ez figgers,
> Clear as one an' one make two,
>
> Chaps that make black slaves o' niggers
> Want to make white slaves o' you.

The Kansas–Nebraska Act started a political revolution in the North. Spontaneous "anti-Nebraska" mass meetings were held everywhere, meetings at which former Whigs, Know Nothings, and Democrats discovered a common interest more compelling than their many differences—an interest, as they perceived it, in preserving free society against a "Slave Power" conspiracy that was striving to extend its tentacles over the entire West. Within six weeks of the bill's passage, a new anti-Nebraska organization called the Republican Party was formed.

The fall elections of 1854 registered an extraordinary political upheaval. The Democrats suffered a smashing defeat and lost almost half their seats in Congress. Because those losses were all in the North, the balance of power within the Democratic congressional delegation tilted decisively toward the South. In the previous Congress, northern Democrats outnumbered southern Democrats; after 1854 they were a distinct minority until the Civil War. The Congress that met in 1856, for example, had 63 southern and only 25 northern Democrats. The capacity of the Democratic party to speak on behalf of the national interest transcending sectional differences was drastically diminished as a result.

Although the Democrats had lost, it was not so clear who had *won*. The infant Republican party carried Wisconsin and Michigan, but in most states the successful candidates ran on "fusion" tickets, negotiated between Whigs, Know Nothings, Free Soilers, anti-Nebraska Democrats, and Republicans. Whether these fragile coalitions could be built into enduring alliances, and if so which party could successfully incorporate them, was yet to be seen.

Polarization Continues

In the next two years the passions stirred by the Kansas–Nebraska Act rose even higher, as the country witnessed squatter sovereignty in operation in Kansas. The slaveholders of Missouri were understandably eager to see Kansas, directly to their West, develop along southern lines. A Senator from Missouri told a meeting bluntly: "You know how to protect your own interests; your rifles will free you from free soilers. You will go there, if necessary, with the bayonet and with blood."

Northern antislavery forces were just as determined to see the territory won for free labor, and formed a New England Emigrant Aid Company to stimulate migration of right-minded settlers. They were prepared for violence as well. One said, "When I deal with men made in God's image, I will never shoot them; but these proslavery Missourians are demons from the bottomless pit, drunken orangutangs who may be shot with impunity."

It soon became apparent that more Yankees than southerners found Kansas attractive. When it did, slave-owners showed they were more attached to slavery than they were to democratic principles. They won an election for the first territorial legislature in 1855 by stuffing the ballot box; although a census counted only 2,900 eligible voters, more than 6,000 ballots were cast, most of them by Missouri men who had only come over for the day. The fraudulently elected legislature then proceeded to expel the few antislavery men who had won seats, and made it a felony to argue the Free Soil cause publicly, and a capital crime to assist a fugitive slave. The Pierce administration, strongly pro-South in its sympathies, endorsed the provisional government. Free Soilers denied its authority and organized their own rival regime with headquarters at Topeka. Their new constitution, revealingly, banned both slavery *and* the entry of free black migrants into Kansas.

Kansans were armed to the teeth, and in early 1856 a small-scale civil war broke out. A mob of southern men burned the Free Soil town of Lawrence. Although no one was killed at Lawrence, the news enraged John Brown, a 56 year-old fanatic abolitionist of questionable sanity, who believed that "without the shedding of blood there is no remission of sins." Convinced that he was God's avenging angel, Brown and his sons took five unarmed southern men—none of them slave-owners—captive at Pottawatomie Creek, chopped off their hands, and then stabbed and bludgeoned them to death. In the guerrilla war that followed, marauding bands burned farm buildings and crops, stole livestock, and tarred and feathered, tortured and murdered their enemies. When strangers met each other in Kansas, a traveler reported, they approached with pistols in hand, and asked in salutation, "Free state or proslave?" The answer was sometimes followed by a gunshot. The awful climax of this vicious struggle came during the Civil War when a Kansas settler led a band of Confederate troops into Lawrence, burned it to the ground, and systematically murdered 183 unarmed male civilians, many of them mere boys.

The killing in Kansas was featured in superheated and slanted accounts in the northern and southern press. It was a clash of good and evil, and which side was which depended only on where the paper was printed. The same held true for the reporting of an ugly incident in the halls of Congress in May, 1856. Massachusetts Senator Charles Sumner gave a blistering two-day speech on the evils of southern society, and denounced Senator Andrew Butler of South Carolina for his devotion to "the harlot, slavery." When it was over Butler's nephew, Representative Preston Brooks, beat Sumner on the head with a heavy cane, doing enough damage to leave him an invalid for the next three and a half years. Northern papers described the incident with horror. The southern press, by contrast, said that the "elegant and effectual caning" was justified by Sumner's "cowardly vituperation," and suggested that it was Sumner who should be ashamed for having fallen to the floor "an inanimate lump of incarnate cowardice."

The elections of the fall of 1856 revealed the same intense sectional polarization exhibited in these divergent reactions to the attack upon Sumner. The Democrats retained the Presidency with another "Doughface" candidate, a northern man of proslavery principles. James Buchanan of Pennsylvania managed his victory by sweeping the South and carrying only five of the sixteen free states. In the Northeast and the West, the Whig party had disappeared and the Know Nothings, who had fallen under proslavery control, were collapsing as well. The contest there was between Buchanan and the Republican choice, the explorer John C. Frémont. Frémont ran astonishingly well, carrying eleven states—but not one of them was southern. His name did not even appear on the ballot in eleven of the fifteen slave states, and in the four in which it did he polled a grand total of 1,251 votes. Despite the fact that Republicans were utter anathema in one entire region of the country, they could have won the contest with a switch of less than 100,000 votes in Pennsylvania and Illinois or Indiana. The dizzying rate of population increase north of the Mason–Dixon line would clearly soon deprive the South of the dominant role it had played in presidential politics since the birth of the nation.

Buchanan's victory made irrelevant the preelection threats of southern leaders—that if a purely sectional party won, "the Union cannot and ought not to be preserved." But it was evident that the test would come again four years later, unless the Democrats could agree on an attractive candidate who could hold the South without alienating the masses of northern voters.

FROM DRED SCOTT TO JOHN BROWN, 1857–59

Neither the executive nor the legislative branch of the federal government had been able to defuse the explosive issue of slavery in the territories. In March 1857, the Supreme Court tried to do so in its ruling on the Dred Scott Case. Scott, a Missouri slave who had lived with his master for several years in Illinois and in the Wisconsin Territory, sued for his freedom on the grounds that slavery was illegal in both places. The justices could have resolved the immediate questions raised by Scott's appeal on narrow grounds, but instead they rashly seized the opportunity to address the larger issue, naively confident that an authoritative judicial pronouncement would remove this divisive matter from politics once and for all. Scott, declared the majority of six (five of them slave-owners or former slave-owners themselves), could not claim that his constitutional rights had been violated because he was not a citizen. Blacks, whether slave or free, were a "subordinated and inferior class of beings . . . who had no rights or privileges but such as those who held the power and the government might choose to grant them." Furthermore, slaves were not persons but property, whose security was guaranteed by the Fifth Amendment to the Constitution. Congress therefore had no right to bar this species of property from any territory. In specifying that lands north of the 36°30′ line were to remain free, the Missouri Compromise had been unconstitutional.

The Court's overruling of the Missouri Compromise was irrelevant, in a way, because the Kansas–Nebraska Act had already accomplished that three years before. But the decision had other possible implications that were profoundly disturbing to Free Soilers. Although the justices did not say so explicitly, their opinions left open the possibility that the popular sovereignty formula employed in the Compromise of 1850 and the Kansas–Nebraska Act was likewise unconstitutional, for territorial legislatures were creations of the Congress of the United States and as such were bound by the same Constitution. One possible reading of the confused and ambiguous majority opinion was that the people flocking into the Kansas and Nebraska territories could not legitimately ban slavery, even if 99 percent of them wanted to. The Court's logic might even lead to a still more extraordinary conclusion. "Does the Constitution make slaves property?" asked an outraged Republican. "If so, slavery exists in Ohio today, for the Constitution extends over Ohio, doesn't it?"

The Dred Scott Decision naturally delighted most southerners. The highest judicial body of the land had endorsed a principal demand of the most militant proslavery spokesmen. In effect, it had also declared that the main objective for which a new party that had narrowly missed winning the Presidency had been formed was unconstitutional. The judges sorely miscalculated the impact of their action on northern opinion. The Supreme Court can indeed use its prestige and moral authority to shape opinion. When the Court dramatically intervenes in matters that are regarded as political rather than judicial, however, the results can be counterproductive. The masses of committed northern Republicans, and a good many undecided moderates as well, took the decision as proof that the "slave power" had a stranglehold on the national government. A conspiracy to "renationalize" slavery was unfolding.

The Lecompton Constitution

Further evidence seemed to point in the same direction. In the summer of 1857, the proslavery regime, by then centered in Lecompton, Kansas, held an election to choose delegates to a state constitutional convention, so that Kansas could be admitted to the Union. The election was boycotted by the antislavery forces loyal to the rival Topeka government. Since defenders of slavery were by then heavily outnumbered, the framers of the Lecompton Constitution refused to submit it to a popular referendum. Instead, they cunningly requested admission after a popular vote with only two narrow options. The only choice offered concerned the importation of more slaves in the future. The voters could elect to prevent that, but would have to tolerate the continued enslavement of blacks who had already been brought into the territory. Such a procedure was unprecedented. But President Buchanan succumbed to heavy southern pressure, his desire to end the prolonged wrangling over Kansas, and his feeling that antislavery men had brought the Lecompton Constitution on themselves by boycotting the election, and pressed vigorously for its acceptance in Congress.

The Dred Scott Decision and the Lecompton Constitution posed the most awkward of political difficulties for Stephen Douglas and the moderate northern wing of the Democratic party. To endorse them might alienate northern voters and drive them into the Republican ranks. To oppose them, however, might bring equally damaging defections in the South. The middle ground on which Douglas Democrats stood was shrinking rapidly.

Although Douglas' central political objective was to prevent the national Democratic party from splintering—and to win the Presidency as its nominee in 1860—the first hurdle to be cleared was in his own state of Illinois. There he had to defeat a Republican challenger and win reelection to the U.S. Senate in 1858. Identification with the "Doughface" President and extremist southern supporters of the Lecompton Constitution would have been a serious, perhaps fatal, handicap in that contest. Douglas was forced to break with the Buchanan administration and to join hands with Republican congressional opponents of the Kansas measure.

This maneuver outraged southern Democrats, but it served Douglas' immediate needs very well. Leading spokesmen of the national Republican party, like Horace Greeley, editor of the *New York Tribune*, took his anti-Lecompton stance as a hopeful sign and urged Republican support for Douglas and other anti-Lecompton Democrats.

Lincoln Challenges Douglas

The hope that Douglas could be won over to the Free Soil cause was folly. The difference between a Douglas Democrat and a true Republican became clear to the nation during a series of seven great debates in different Illinois cities and towns in the fall of 1858, the Lincoln–Douglas debates.

Abraham Lincoln was an attorney who loved politics, and had been involved in it since he was first elected to the Illinois state legislature in 1834 at the age of 26. He had served there eight years, and had one inconspicuous term as a Whig Congressman from 1847 to 1849. During the 1850s he suffered several political reverses without losing his ambition for further office. When the Republican party sprang up in the wake of the Kansas–Nebraska Act, Lincoln kept his distance from it until he was sure that the Whigs would not be able to rebound, but by 1856 he declared himself a Republican and in 1858 was recognized as the party's leading spokesman in the state of Illinois. In his famous speech accepting the senatorial nomination that year, Lincoln argued eloquently that "a house divided against itself cannot stand," that "this government cannot endure permanently half slave and half free." Why not, when it had already done so for well over half a century? Because, in Lincoln's view, a conspiracy to renationalize the slave system was well underway, and further compromise with the "slavocracy" would only embolden the conspirators. Unless slavery was set on "the course of ultimate extinction," its advocates would push it forward, till it shall "become lawful in all the states, old as well as new—North as well as South." If in hindsight this seems an unlikely possibility, it was no more farfetched than the similar perception of the patriots of the revolutionary generation that the new British trade regulations represented a "conspiracy against liberty." Taken together, the Kansas–Nebraska Act, the Dred

Scott Decision, and the Lecompton Constitution suggested that an aggressive "slave power" was having everything its way. It was that perception on the part of Lincoln and the swelling ranks of the Republican party that made the seemingly limited issue of slavery in the territories assume such immense significance.

Lincoln did not call for immediate abolition of slavery throughout the nation. Far from it. It would have been political suicide to do so; moreover, he genuinely opposed such action. Lincoln believed in gradual abolition with compensation to owners, a process that would take decades in his estimate. He was deeply pessimistic about whether or not free blacks would ever become fully integrated into American society, and considered colonization a possible long-term solution. When pressed on the issue of social and political equality for blacks before audiences in southern Illinois, Lincoln denied that he favored it and declared himself "in favor of having the superior position assigned to the white race." Nevertheless, the cornerstone of Lincoln's thought and the central premise of Republican ideology was the radical insistance that all people, black and white, were created equal, and that no man had the moral right to enslave another. If he was cautious and conservative compared to a radical egalitarian like William Lloyd Garrison, Lincoln's insistence on this fundamental moral principle struck at the very foundations of the southern social order.

Throughout the debates Lincoln insistently challenged Douglas to say whether he favored the further spread of slavery—and if not, how he proposed to check it, given the Dred Scott Decision. Douglas displayed no concern for the morality of slavery—to him it was simply a business proposition, and would and should exist wherever it was profitable—but he realized that many voters favored its containment, some on moral grounds and some from racist motivations. Unable to echo the Republican condemnation of the Dred Scott Decision, which he had firmly endorsed when it was first announced, Douglas attempted to squirm out of the difficulty in the debate at Freeport by arguing that the Court had only forbidden *legislation* against slavery. Popular sovereignty could still operate to prevent its introduction into areas in which a majority of settlers were hostile to it. Slavery could not actually exist, he asserted, "unless sustained and enforced by appropriate police regulations and local legislation prescribing adequate remedies for its violation." Although the Supreme Court had denied both Congress and the people of a territory the right to say *no* to slavery, he argued, it did not require them to say *yes*, and without positive legal protection the institution would inevitably collapse.

Douglas' ingenious "Freeport doctrine" was a successful ploy in the short run, for he did stave off Lincoln's challenge and was returned to the Senate. It was hardly an impressive victory for Douglas, however. The Republicans gained ground not only in Illinois but in virtually every northern state, and had captured 22 more seats than the Democrats in the new House of Representatives. Lincoln would have won but for the fact that the Illinois state legislature, which made the choice, was apportioned in a way that gave more weight to Democratic than Republican votes. The campaign catapulted Lincoln, hardly known outside his own state before then, into national prominence. The duel with Douglas made him a serious contender for the Republican presidential nomination in 1860. And it greatly improved the prospects of the new party in the next presidential contest.

I do not believe that a negro is a citizen or ought to be a citizen. I believe this government of ours was founded and wisely founded, upon the white basis. It was made by white men for the benefit of white men and their posterity. I freely concede that humanity requires us to extend all the protection, all the privileges, all the immunities, to the Indian and the negro which they are capable of enjoying consistent with the safety of society. You may then ask me what are those rights. My answer is that this is a question for each state and each territory to decide for itself.

—Douglas

These arguments that are made, that the inferior race are to be treated with as much allowance as their condition will allow, that as much is to be done for them as their condition will allow. What are these arguments? They are the arguments that kings have made for enslaving the people in all ages of the world. They always bestrode the necks of the people, not that they wanted to do it, but because the people were better off for being ridden. Whether it come from the mouth of a king, an excuse for enslaving the people of his country, or from the mouth of men of one race as reason for enslaving the men of another race, it is all the same old serpent. Let us discard all this quibbling about this race and that race and the other race being inferior, and therefore they must be placed in an inferior position. Let us discard all these things, and unite as one people throughout this land, until we shall once more stand up declaring that all men are created equal.

—Lincoln

Douglas' "Freeport heresy"—his insistence that slavery could in fact be blocked from areas in which it was unpopular despite the constitutional protection afforded it by the Dred Scott holding—was as offensive to southern and Buchanan Democrats as his anti-Lecompton stance. Douglas supporters would probably control the 1860 Democratic convention, but the odds were good that the anti-Douglas minority would bolt the party and divide the opposition.

John Brown's Raid

Southern slave-owners viewed the rising strength of the Republicans with apprehension not only because the new antislavery party might capture the national government before long. A more immediate and terrifying danger, in their minds, was that relentless northern attacks on slavery might inspire blacks to stage a violent rebellion. Such fears were brought to a new pitch of intensity in October, 1859, when John Brown and 19 of his followers seized the federal arsenal at Harpers Ferry, Virginia. By capturing the weapons there, Brown thought he could trigger a great slave revolt. The revolt did not materialize. Within three days, federal troops under the command of Colonel Robert E. Lee easily recaptured the arsenal, and Brown and the other five surviving members of his party were promptly hanged for treason.

It was a mad scheme, executed with a breathtaking disregard for the realities. Lincoln accurately said that John Brown's raid was "not a slave insurrection. It was an attempt by white men to get up a revolt among slaves, in which the slaves refused to participate. In fact, it was so absurd that the slaves, with all their ignorance, saw plainly enough it could not succeed."

John Brown's attempt to engineer a slave revolt failed, and he lost his life for it. However, the raid was a success in a larger sense. It sent a wave of terror and rage through the South that strengthened the position of secessionist hot-heads and brought closer a civil war that would result in the death of slavery. Southern whites surrounded by large numbers of black slaves were not reassured by those who dismissed John Brown as insane. Other "insane" abolitionists might succeed where he failed. It was quickly apparent that Brown's scheme had been backed by a number of key abolitionist leaders—though exactly what they knew about his plan was unclear. Some prominent northern intellectuals saluted Brown as a martyr to the cause of liberty. Ralph Waldo Emerson called him "an idealist" who "believed in his ideas" to the extent that he "put them all into action." Henry David Thoreau compared him to Jesus Christ, who had nobly given his life that others might live. Boston minister Theodore Parker spoke of "the fire of vengeance" that would soon run "from man to man, from town to town" throughout the South. "What will put it out?" he asked. "The white man's blood." The song "John Brown's Body"—set to the same old folk tune used for "The Battle Hymn of the Republic"—would become one of the most famous Civil War songs of the Union army.

Such views were those of but a small northern minority. Anti-Brown meetings and demonstrations in the North attracted much larger audiences than organized efforts in support of him. Southerners were too traumatized to see that. Many moderates who had been committed to the Union as well as to the southern way of life concluded that the two objectives were incompatible. They became convinced that there was indeed a conspiracy afoot—not a "slave power" conspiracy to renationalize slavery but a "Black Republican" conspiracy to enslave the South and take away their slaves. Although Lincoln forcefully condemned the Harpers Ferry raid, they were sure that he would work for the same unthinkable end if he won the Presidency in 1860.

The congressional session that opened a few days after Brown's execution was the most rancorous in history. For three months the House was so paralyzed by sectional discord that it was unable even to elect a new Speaker. The debate was bitterly abusive, and many Congressmen came to the sessions armed. It was said that the only members who didn't attend with a revolver and a knife were those who carried two revolvers.

THE FINAL CRISIS, 1860-61

The same atmosphere prevailed at the Democratic party convention that met in Charleston, South Carolina in April, 1860. The conflict between southern extremists and Douglas Democrats proved irreconcilable. Douglas was finally nominated by the northern wing, but southern militants spurned him, walked out, and selected a rival Democratic candidate of their own—John C. Breckinridge of Kentucky. The single most important remaining institution for accommodating and adjusting regional differences between Americans, the Democratic party, broke in two.

Lincoln's Election

The nomination of Lincoln by the Republicans, and the formation of a mainly southern fourth party—the Constitutional Unionists—made the election of 1860 a four-cornered contest. But it is a myth that it was only the splintering of the Democratic party and the split in the opposition vote that allowed Lincoln to triumph in November. The continued existence of a unified Democratic party might possibly have altered the course of events that followed Lincoln's election. It would not, however, have altered the outcome of the election itself. Although Lincoln received much less than a majority of the popular vote—slightly under 40 percent, as opposed to just under 30 percent for Douglas and a bit over 30 percent for the two southern candidates together—his strength was concentrated in the heavily populated states that counted in the Electoral College, and he therefore won a solid 60 percent of the electoral vote. Had the entire anti-Lincoln vote gone to Douglas or to any of his other rivals, it would have subtracted a mere eleven electoral votes from Lincoln's total and left him a decisive victor still.

For the first time in American history, the highest office in the land had been won by a man who lacked any voter support whatever in an entire region of the country. A more purely sectional candidate than Lincoln, who carried only two of the 1,109 southern counties, is hard to imagine. The Republican party was not even on the ballot in ten of the southern states. There could be no greater blow to southern pride. The South, which had contributed so notable a share of the nation's political leadership in the early days of the Republic, seemed to have become a permanent powerless minority. And it was faced with living under a chief executive whose central conviction was that the institution upon which the southern way of life rested must be set on a course toward "ultimate extinction." Lincoln was moderate, cautious, and flexible in his views of *how* the elimination of slavery might be achieved. He had no power to directly interfere with it in the states. The Republicans had not captured Congress. No Republicans sat on the Supreme Court, which could prevent unconstitutional attacks on slavery. But slave-owners nevertheless did have something direct and immediate to fear from living under a Lincoln administration—a decline in the value of their enormous capital investment in slaves, stemming from fears that abolition was on the way (see

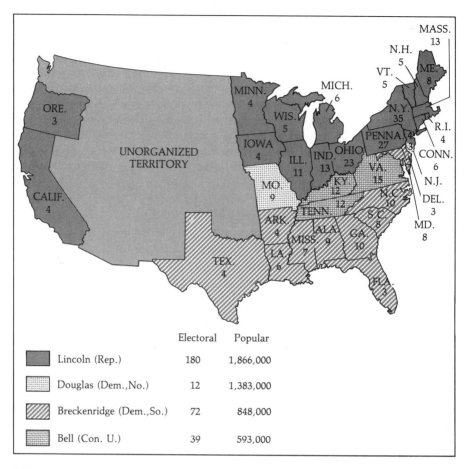

MAP 14-3
The 1860 Election

	Electoral	Popular
Lincoln (Rep.)	180	1,866,000
Douglas (Dem.,No.)	12	1,383,000
Breckenridge (Dem.,So.)	72	848,000
Bell (Con. U.)	39	593,000

box). Even if Lincoln *did* nothing unfavorable to slavery, anxieties that he *might* would send slave prices tumbling.

Secession

In the 1860 campaign many southern orators had warned that they would rather sever their ties with the Union than tolerate Abraham Lincoln as President. Threats to secede, however, were nothing new, and most northerners were complacent about the future. With the election over and the Cotton Kingdom's bluff called, they felt confident that the slave states would bluster and then back down. "As to disunion," said one in late November, "nobody but silly people expect it will happen." But happen it did, of course. On December 20, a South Carolina convention repealed the state's ratification of the Constitution of the United States and voted to withdraw from the Union. By February 1861, a month before Lincoln's inauguration, six other states of the Lower South had followed suit, and had joined together to create a rival nation—the Confederate States of America.

That was but seven of the fifteen states in which slavery was legal in 1861, all of them located in the Lower South. Four more—Virginia, North Carolina, Arkansas and Tennessee—joined the Confederacy only after the Lincoln administration began to attempt to subdue it by force. The other four—Delaware, Maryland, Missouri, and Kentucky—remained within the Union. (So did the western part of Virginia, which refused to join the Confederacy and became the new state of West Virginia.) What explains those differences between early seceders, late seceders, and nonseceders? The chief determinant of their behavior seems to have been the extent of their economic dependence on slavery (see Table 14–1). Those states that gave up on the Union before Lincoln even took office had the heaviest concentration of slaves and largest proportion of white families whose fortunes depended on slavery. The states that joined the Confederacy later were significantly less dependent on slavery, but notably more so than those remaining loyal. Commitment to the Union varied inversely with commitment to slavery.

Slave-owners, however, did not form a majority of the white population anywhere, even in South Carolina or Mississippi. Although planters led the secessionist movement everywhere, they needed some support—or at least passive acquiescence—from the non-slaveholding majority. They encountered significant internal resistance in some places. Class divisions within southern white society, obscured in the past by the unifying ideology of white supremacy, appeared in the pattern of voting in the secession conventions. Not only did the states most heavily committed to slavery show the greatest readiness to leave the Union. Within the states, plantation areas were most militantly secessionist, whereas representatives from the hill country—where farms were small and there were few or no

TABLE 14–1
Slaveholding and Political Behavior, 1861

	Percentage of Slaves in Population	Percentage of White Families Owning Slaves
Early Seceders		
South Carolina	57	47
Georgia	48	38
Florida	44	35
Alabama	45	35
Mississippi	55	49
Louisiana	47	31
Texas	30	29
Late Seceders		
Virginia	31	27
North Carolina	33	29
Tennessee	25	25
Arkansas	28	2
Loyalist		
Delaware	2	4
Maryland	13	15
Kentucky	20	24
Missouri	10	13

slaves—were lukewarm or opposed. But the differences were not very sharp, and large numbers of the slaveless followed the lead of their "betters." Traditions of deference to the planter class and fears of what freedom for blacks would mean remained strong.

The secessionist thrust might have met greater resistance within the South but for a common misconception of what the northern reaction would be. Just as northerners entertained illusions that secession could never happen, many southerners were naively optimistic that they would be allowed to go their separate way peacefully. One South Carolina firebrand declared that if secession led to a war, he would "eat the bodies of all those slain in the struggle." The Union depended upon the freely given consent of all parties. The southern states had the same right to independence that Americans had exercised when they renounced their allegiance to Crown and Parliament less than a century earlier. If a house divided could not stand, why not recognize the division and build a permanent partition to prevent further conflict?

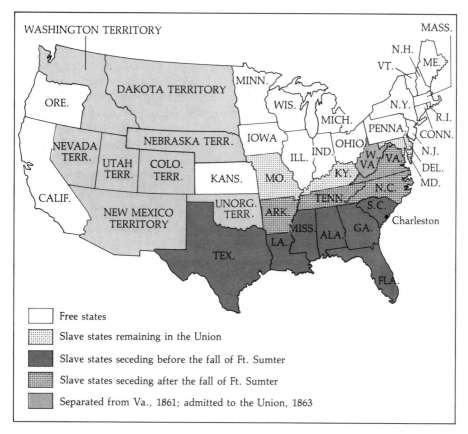

MAP 14-4
Choosing Sides in 1861

Coming of the War

Few northerners saw it that way, least of all the man on whom the burden of the momentous decision rested. Lincoln was as iron-willed as Andrew Jackson had been when he faced down the South Carolina nullifiers a generation earlier. To allow the South to leave the Union would shatter the national market that had allowed growing national prosperity. The trade of the Ohio and Mississippi Valley system would be hostage to a hostile power controlling New Orleans. An independent Confederacy could inflate the price of southern cotton needed for northern mills through export duties, and keep northern goods from southern markets with tariff barriers. Without natural geographic barriers separating the two countries, endless border conflicts and recurrent warfare would be likely.

Beyond these compelling practical considerations were deeper moral and philosophical ones. Few Americans could have articulated them as Lincoln did, but many shared his faith in "government of the people, by the people, and for the people" and his conviction that to accept the dissolution of the Union was to confess that the republican experiment launched at Philadelphia was a failure, as European reactionaries had often charged. To "prove that popular government was not an absurdity," Lincoln said, it was necessary to establish that the power to govern lost by ballots in a free election could not be won back by bullets. "The central idea of secession" was "the essence of anarchy. If a minority will secede rather than acquiesce, they make a precedent which in turn will divide and ruin them; for a minority of their own will secede from them whenever a majority refuses to be controlled by such minority." A year and a half before his election, speaking of the execution of John Brown, Lincoln made his position crystal clear. "We cannot object," he said, "even though he agreed with us in thinking slavery wrong. That cannot excuse violence, bloodshed, and treason. If constitutionally we elect a President, and therefore you undertake to destroy the Union, it will be our duty to deal with you as old John Brown has been dealt with."

Lincoln was absolutely firm on that point, but cautious and conciliatory on everything else. His great First Inaugural, delivered on March 4, 1861, promised that he would strictly abide by the Constitution in every respect, and would consider accepting amendments that would explicitly forbid the federal government from interfering with "the domestic institutions of the states, including that of persons held to service." It closed with the stirring plea:

> We are not enemies but friends. We must not be enemies. Though passion may have strained, it must not break our bonds of affection. The mystic chords of memory, stretching from every battlefield, and patriot grave, to every living heart and hearthstone all over this great land, will yet swell the chorus of the Union, when again touched, as surely they will be, by the better angels of our nature.

But war was only five weeks distant. Lincoln was careful not to fire the first shot and make the Union appear the aggressor. When he heard that Fort Sumter, a federal outpost in Charleston Harbor, was about to run out of supplies, he dispatched naval vessels there, and advised the governor of South Carolina that the ships contained "provisions only," not reinforcements or arms and ammunition. That threw the ball in the court of the Confederacy, giving it the choice of either striking the first blow or accepting the humiliation of an indefinite federal military presence commanding the traffic of one of its great harbors. On April 12, Confederate guns opened fire on Sumter. The fort fell in a day and a half, without a single casualty. It was a curiously pacific beginning for a convulsive struggle that would grind on for four years and shed rivers of blood.

SUGGESTED READINGS

David Potter's masterful *The Impending Crisis, 1845–1861* is a detailed political history rich in insights. A fuller account with a somewhat broader focus is Allen Nevins, *The Ordeal of the Union* (2 vols., 1947) and *The Emergence of Lincoln* (2 vols., 1950). Michael F. Holt, *The Political Crisis of the 1850's* (1978) is a fine synthesis of the recent literature stressing the ethnic and religious roots of political conflict in the past. Robert Swierenga, ed., *Beyond the Civil War Synthesis* (1975) and Eric Foner, *Politics and Ideology in the Age of the Civil War* (1980) are stimulating collections of essays.

Frederick L. Merk, *Manifest Destiny and Mission in American History* (1963) is an excellent overview of the expansionist thrust of the 1840s. Merk's *The Monroe Doctrine and American Expansionism, 1843–1849* (1966) is a detailed account. Gene M. Brack, *Mexico Views the Mexican War* (1976) makes it possible to view the story from the Mexican perspective. See also David M. Pletcher, *The Diplomacy of Annexation: Texas, Oregon, and the Mexican War* (1973).

The strain of the war and the Wilmot Proviso on party loyalties is clear in patterns of congressional voting, analyzed in Joel Silbey, *Shrine of Party: Congressional Voting Behavior, 1841–1852* (1967), and Thomas J. Alexander, *Sectional Stress and Party Strength* (1967). Ronald P. Formisano, *The Birth of Mass Political Parties: Michigan, 1827–1861* (1971); Paul Kleppner, *The Cross of Culture: A Social Analysis of Midwestern Politics, 1850–1900* (1976); and Michael F. Holt, *Forging a Majority: The Formation of the Republican Party in Pittsburgh, 1848–1860* (1969) examine popular voting at the state and local levels.

Robert W. Johannsen's massive biography of the framer of the Kansas–Nebraska Act and Lincoln's chief rival for the presidency, *Stephen A. Douglas* (1973), sheds new light on many key issues of the period. The racist basis of the Free Soil and Republican movements is overstressed in Eugene Berwanger, *The Frontier against Slavery: Western Anti-Negro Prejudice and the Slavery Extension Controversy* (1967). Eric Foner, *Free Soil, Free Labor, and Free Men: The Ideology of the Republican Party before the Civil War* (1970) and Richard H. Sewell, *Ballots for Freedom: Antislavery Politics in the United States, 1837–1865* (1976) are more balanced, sympathetic, and penetrating. Harriet Beecher Stowe, *Uncle Tom's Cabin* (1852), should not be missed.

The Lincoln–Douglas debates, available in various editions, are another key document of the era that can be read with great profit and enjoyment, enjoyment mixed with dismay about the level of political discourse in our own time. For a brief and well-written biography of Lincoln, see Oscar and Lillian Handlin, *Abraham Lincoln and the Union* (1980). Donald E. Fehrenbacher's *Prelude to Greatness: Lincoln in the 1850's* (1962) is concise and penetrating. Fehrenbacher has also written the definitive study of *The Dred Scott Case: Its Significance in American Law and Politics* (1979), abridged as *Slavery, Law and Politics: The Dred Scott Case in Historical Perspective* (1981). Stephen B. Oates' sympathetic biography of John Brown, *To Purge This Land of Blood* (1970) may be compared with David Potter's treatment in *The Impending Crisis* and C. Vann Woodward's essay in *The Burden of Southern History* (1960). Roy F. Nichols, *The Disruption of American Democracy* (1948) is a superior study of the crises during the Buchanan administration.

Southern reactions to the election of Lincoln are analyzed in Ralph Wooster, *The Secession Conventions of the South* (1962); Steven Channing, *Crisis of Fear: Secession in South Carolina* (1970); and William L. Barney, *The Road to Secession* (1972) and *The Secessionist Impulse: Alabama and Mississippi* (1962). On the northern side, David Potter, *Lincoln and His Party in the Secession Crisis* (1942) and Kenneth M. Stampp, *And the War Came* (1950) are classics.

Chapter Fifteen

The Union Shattered

T he American Civil War was a prolonged and extremely bloody struggle. In casualties it ranked as the worst war in the world in the century that elapsed between the close of the Napoleonic wars in 1815 and the outbreak of World War I in 1914. At its outset, however, both sides were confident of quick victory.

THE BALANCE OF FORCES

Given the ultimate outcome, it is easiest to understand the grounds for northern confidence. When Robert E. Lee finally surrendered his battered army at Appomattox in April 1865, he sorrowfully acknowledged that he was "compelled to yield to overwhelming numbers and resources." Indeed, the Union forces had enjoyed a formidable advantage in both. The population of the eleven Confederate states totaled less than 9 million, compared to more than 22 million in the rest of the country. And more than a third of the men in the South were slaves; they could hardly be expected to risk their lives to keep themselves in bondage. In January of 1862, the Union army was two and a half times larger than that of the Confederacy; by 1865 the North held a four-to-one edge in troop strength.

In its capacity to produce modern war material, the North had an even more lopsided advantage. In 1860, 470 railroad locomotives were built in the United States, only 17 of them in the South; just 3 percent of U.S. firearms were produced

Civil War deaths exceeded 600,000—more than the combined U.S. casualties of the First and Second World Wars.

TABLE 15-1
Troops "Present-for-Duty," January 1

	Union	Confederate
1862	527,204	209,852
1863	698,808	253,208
1864	611,250	233,586
1865	620,924	154,910

in the South. Pennsylvania and New York *each* turned out manufactured goods more than double the entire output of the Confederate states. Even much smaller Massachusetts outpaced the South in manufacturing. A May, 1861 survey of the contents of all southern arsenals found only 160,000 small arms of any kind; at the same time, the U.S. government had enough weapons to equip half a million men.

In numbers and industrial capacity the North was clearly superior; no wonder the northern armies were eventually victorious, we might conclude. But that is hindsight. In reality, those assets were not decisive. Southerners, after all, could read the census returns, too, yet they failed to draw the "obvious" conclusion. In fact, most knowledgeable observers abroad expected a Confederate victory. There were good reasons.

First, the Confederacy faced a far easier military task than the Union. To achieve their objective—independence from the United States—the men in grey did not need to conquer one inch of northern territory. All they had to do was discourage the invading forces. The North, by contrast, had to attack and subdue the people of an area almost as large as Western Europe. Three-quarters of a century earlier, Britain's superior numbers and resources had not sufficed to put down the resistance of an American people determined to be free. Many Confederate orators boasted, reasonably, that the southern war for independence would inevitably end the same way.

Furthermore, at the outset of the war, the Union was not a military giant comparable to Britain in the revolutionary years. The U.S. Army numbered only 16,000 men, their fighting experience largely confined to conflicts with small Indian war parties. Only two of its officers had ever commanded substantial numbers of troops in battle, and one of them was 77, the other 75. Many of its most promising younger leaders—Robert E. Lee, Joseph E. Johnston, and P.T. Beauregard—were southerners who sided with the rebels. In plantation society, with its code of chivalry, military careers had a status they lacked in the business-minded North. Almost all the West Pointers who were destined to play key roles in the Union military effort were pursuing civilian business careers at the outset of the war. Ulysses S. Grant was tending a store in Galena, Illinois; George B. McClellan was a railroad executive; William T. Sherman, having failed in banking in San Francisco and in law practice in Kansas, was running a small military academy in Louisiana. The peacetime army had few attractions for an ambitious northerner. To mobilize

MAP 15–1
Political Regions in the Civil War Era

the people of the North into disciplined, well-equipped, and well-led fighting units would be an immensely difficult task.

In 1861, the possibility of such a transformation was far from clear. It would take rare organizational skill and careful planning. Revolutionary advances in transportation and communication had created a national market, but otherwise American society was hardly centralized. For example, no one in Washington even knew how many draftable males lived in the loyal states. The population recorded in the 1860 census was divided into broad categories: 15–19, 20–24, and so forth. There was no way of telling how many of those in the 15–19 group were under 18 and too young for the army. The U.S. Department of War had no detailed maps of the landscape of the Confederate states it was supposed to invade. In addition, there was no standard time and no standard time zones. Each American community set its own time by the sun, and railroads had their own separate time systems. In a city served by two railroads, there could be three different "correct" times, varying by as much as an hour. Imagine trying to coordinate troop movements over long distances without knowing exactly what time it was *anywhere*. It would take an organizational revolution to build and supply a fighting machine that could crush the militant South.

Some southerners were sure that their opponents lacked the necessary courage and determination to win. "Just throw three or four shells among those blue-bellied Yankees and they'll scatter like sheep," assured one. Johnson's *Elementary Arithmetic* posed its young Rebel readers problems like this: "If one Confederate soldier can whip seven Yankees, how many soldiers can whip 49 Yanks?" Others, more thoughtful and less arrogant, simply believed that war-weariness would eventually divide the North and lead to a successful peace movement there, as would happen a century later during America's involvement in the Vietnam War.

Confederate leaders were also mindful that all of the cotton used in northern textile mills and four-fifths of that used in Europe came from the South. Much as OPEC ministers today talk about employing the "oil weapon," they thought the "cotton weapon" would be decisive. Withholding their crops from market, they calculated, would devastate northern industry, and create such economic hardship abroad that European powers would be compelled to recognize the independence of the Confederacy and supply it with the manufactures it needed to fight the Union. If the North imposed a naval blockade on the seceded states, Britain and France needed cotton so badly that they would break it, and might even join the war as fellow belligerents. "The Confederacy has its hands on the mane of the British lion," the Richmond *Whig* said cockily, "and that beast, so formidable to all the rest of the world, must crouch at her bidding."

The southern cause did not seem hopeless from the beginning, but in the end the South was ground into submission. Atlanta lay in ashes. The Georgia and Carolina countrysides were littered with dead livestock and the shards of a demolished society. Richmond was scarred from nine months of seige and starvation. The loyal Union states had successfully mobilized their assets against the Confederacy. But that end was not achieved—could not have been achieved—without sweeping changes in the organization of American life.

The Death Toll

The Civil War stands out as by far the bloodiest military conflict in American history. Barely 4,000 Americans died in service during the entire Revolutionary War, but in the Battle of Gettysburg alone more than 7,000 men were killed, 33,000 were wounded, and another 10,800 were listed as missing in action. In all, more than 600,000 died in the struggle, more than the combined U.S. casualties of the First and Second World Wars. The chances of death for the average soldier were three times greater than in World War I, nine times greater than in World War II, thirteen times greater than in the Vietnam War. One out of every four young men who wore a uniform failed to return home.

The conflict was uniquely murderous partly because of outdated military strategy. Generals often tend to fight the last war, misapplying old lessons to new

TABLE 15–2
The Terrible Costs of the War

	Union	Confederacy
Total forces	1,556,678	1,082,119
Died from wounds	110,070	94,000*
Died from disease	249,458	164,000
Death rate	23%	24%
Wounded	275,175	100,000

*Confederate statistics on casualties are less accurate than those for the Union, but are definitely not overestimates.

circumstances. But this was particularly true in the Civil War. The crucial new reality was a revolutionized weaponry. When Lee and Grant were comrades-in-arms in the Mexican War, their soldiers had used the traditional smooth-bore musket. It was slow to reload, and accurate only at short ranges. "At a distance of a few hundred yards, a man could fire at you all day without your finding out," said Grant. Civil War troops were issued new and far deadlier rifles. The Springfield .58 and the Enfield .577 had grooved barrels that gave a bullet a spin and kept it on a dead straight course for half a mile or more. The new artillery was more lethal too. Sending a massive frontal assault against such firepower was inviting a slaughter, but military doctrine was slow to grasp this. Massed attacks had succeeded against the Mexican Army; therefore, massed attacks remained the key strategy. Thanks to a highly developed and efficient rail and steamboat system, more troops than ever before could be transported to a battle site. The result was carnage of monstrous proportions.

The Civil War was as much a public health as a military calamity. The germ theory of disease and modern antiseptic techniques had not yet been discovered, so infection and death frequently followed the most minor wounds. Over-crowded camps that lacked a supply of pure water and proper sanitary facilities spawned microbes as deadly as bullets. The average regiment lost almost half of its fighting strength through disease the first year; without fresh recruits it vanished altogether within three years. The 800 men of the 4th Ohio Regiment landed in Virginia in July of 1862; by November, it had only 120 men fit for duty, even though it had suffered only 11 combat casualties. For every soldier who lost his life as a result of a wound in battle, two succumbed to an infectious disease of some kind. One soldier wrote truly, "Big Battles is not as bad as the Fever."

THE WAR FOR THE UNION, 1861–62

From the beginning, the Civil War was *about* slavery. It was provoked by the conviction of a majority of northerners that slavery must not spread further into new territories. The war did not begin as a war to *abolish* slavery throughout the land, however. Lincoln had said repeatedly that he had "no purpose, directly or indirectly, to interfere with the institution of slavery in the States where it exists." At his inauguration a month before the first shot was fired on Fort Sumter, he repeated that pledge. The war, Lincoln declared, had to be brought to a quick end before it degenerated into a "violent and remorselessly revolutionary struggle." It should be a limited war for limited objectives, and "the utmost care" was to be taken "to avoid any devastation, and destruction of, or interference with, property." It was clear that property, in this context, included slaves. "The Battle Hymn of the Republic," with its extraordinarily self-righteous injunction, "as He died to make men holy, let us die to make men free," was written by Julia Ward Howe in 1861. But freedom for all people, white and black, was not yet the question.

Abolitionists, of course, besieged Lincoln with complaints that merely restoring the Union, with continued slavery, was intolerable. But they had little influence on national politics. In July of the first war year, Congress passed almost unanimously (117 to 2 in the House and 30 to 5 in the Senate) the conservative Crittenden Resolution, which declared, "This war is not waged...for the purpose of over-throwing or interfering with the established institutions of those States, but to maintain the States unimpaired; and that as soon as these objects are accomplished, the war should cease."

Keeping the Border States in the Union

Lincoln's caution stemmed from genuine conviction. He believed that a gradual emancipation program, with compensation to slave-owners, could bring slavery to "ultimate extinction" without chaos and bloodshed. But he also had a compelling practical motive for taking this stance at the outset of the war. To abolish slavery, it was necessary to defeat the Confederacy. And that task, Lincoln felt, would be well-nigh impossible if the critical border areas, initially uncommitted to either side, were alienated. In a belt from roughly 36°30′ to 41° lived almost five million people, a group almost as large as the white population of the states already in the Confederacy. Kentucky, Delaware, Maryland, and Missouri were slave states. If they joined the Confederacy, the strategic balance would tilt sharply. Washington, D.C. would have to be abandoned as the national capital, and Confederate troops could take up strong defensive positions along the southern banks of the Ohio River, instead of much more vulnerable posts farther South. It was critical for the Union not to antagonize those states to the point of defecting. Lincoln's supposed remark that while he *hoped* to have God on his side he *had* to have Kentucky is apocryphal. But he did indeed say: "I think to lose Kentucky is nearly the same as to lose the whole game."

In addition to this military consideration, a broader political concern suggested the need to confine the definition of war aims. Abolitionism was anathema not only in the four nonaligned slave states, but in southern Ohio, Indiana, Illinois, and Iowa as well. Many of the people there had migrated from the South and had southern racial attitudes. They might support a war to restore the Union, but not a military crusade to root out slavery. A radical definition of Union war aims would drive such people into the antiwar "Peace Democrat" or "Copperhead" camp. Lincoln's political instincts were acute, and for him winning the war was at least as much a political as a military problem.

The Union did not lose Kentucky, nor any of the other border states. It might have done so had John C. Frémont, the 1856 Republican presidential candidate, had his way. Frémont was placed in command of the Union army on the Western front, and rashly proclaimed in August 1861 that the property of disloyal citizens in Missouri was to be confiscated and their slaves set free. Lincoln immediately countermanded the order, thereby infuriating radical antislavery men. Powerful Congressman Ben Wade remarked bitterly that Lincoln might next recommend rewarding all rebels with 160 acres of free land! But if Lincoln was right about the strategic and political necessity of keeping the good will of the border areas, at least until the North could establish military superiority over the Confederacy, he was right to insist that the issue be defined as the preservation of the Union rather than the destruction of slavery.

Men and Supplies: The North

At first, optimistic northerners thought that 75,000 men from the state militias, committed to a mere three months' service, could put down the rebellion. The first major battle, at Bull Run in northern Virginia in July of 1861, punctured that illusion. Raw Union troops panicked under Confederate fire and fled back to Washington, limping back bleeding, covered with mud, without their packs and guns. This disaster shocked Lincoln into calling for a citizen army of half a million men serving for three years.

The needed men flocked to the call, for war fever at first ran high. But equipping and maintaining them was a gigantic task. It was estimated, for instance, that the average soldier wore out a pair of shoes in two months and a uniform in four, which meant that 3 million pairs of shoes and 1.5 million uniforms were required each year. The troops would need weapons and ammunition, ships with armor and guns, blankets, tents, compasses, and countless other things in numbers vastly in excess of the normal output.

Thanks to the earlier transformation of its economy, the North was well able to meet the needs of war. Now the famous Yankee energy and inventiveness put on an awesome display of productive power. Ready-to-wear clothing was just becoming available as a result of the newly invented sewing machine, and the sudden demand for uniforms was a tremendous stimulus to that industry. There was a similar revolution in the boot and shoe industry—a dramatic increase in firm size, division of labor, degree of mechanization, and productivity per worker. Advances like these were not so colorful as the progress of Union troops marching on Confederate positions, but they made the eventual successes possible.

Men and Supplies: The South

Mobilization was a great challenge for the Confederacy, too. Responsibility for it lay with the Confederate Congress and President Jefferson Davis, in the capital at Richmond, Virginia. The Constitution of the Confederate States of America repeated most of the language of the United States Constitution. Its framers claimed to be the true heirs of Washington and Jefferson, protecting traditional American liberties against an oppressor as dangerous as George III had been. It differed in two respects from the Philadelphia Constitution, however. First, the Founders had been too embarrassed by slavery to mention it, while the Confederates made support of slavery an explicit aim of government (see box). Second, the Confederate Constitution was more deferential to states' rights than the federal Constitution. It circumscribed the powers of both the Congress and the chief executive more narrowly—limiting the President, for example, to a single six-year term. The weakness of central government was to hamper the Confederate war effort throughout the conflict. Of the men Jefferson Davis chose for his first cabinet, only one actually took the post. Davis' own Vice President, Alexander Stephens of Georgia, was the leader of a faction that considered the "tyranny" of Richmond as dangerous as the Union army, and did much to paralyze the administration.

Raising the troops to carry out armed resistance was the first task of the new government. The South did not need as many fighting men as the North, of course, because its armies could achieve their fundamental objective by simply repelling the invader. In most Civil War battles, the attackers needed to outnumber the defenders by at least 50 percent to have much chance of success. But the South's manpower pool, of course, was much smaller. During the first year of war there were plenty of volunteers, but as their first twelve-month enlistment term drew to a close, enthusiasm waned dangerously. Ironically, the Confederacy—whose central political principle was the supremacy of states' rights—found itself compelled to act in violation of its own Constitution: In April of 1862, it passed a conscription act to force white males between 18 and 35 into the army.

Conscription did bring in enough men to avert the immediate crisis, but the act had many loopholes. A wide range of occupations, thought important to the war effort, were exempted. A later amendment, to the anger of many, exempted planters holding 20 or more slaves. More important than the loopholes in the law were the problems of enforcement. Reaching potential soldiers in local communities depended on the cooperation of state governors. Many gave it grudgingly at best, partly because Davis was a prickly character who was incapable of wheedling and cajoling state politicians, but largely because of southern fears of central authority. Given these obstacles, it was remarkable that the South did not suffer from graver shortages of troops until the latter part of the war.

Much of the same could be said about other aspects of Confederate mobilization—securing weapons, equipment, transportation, and food for the army, and financing the whole effort. The political machinery was inadequate to deal with these complex problems in a systematic way, and widespread suspicion of centralized decision making made for further chaos. Nevertheless, the absolute necessities were indeed acquired. Although southern manufacturing was much too underdeveloped to meet the needs of a massive war machine, an ample supply of

CONSTITUTION OF THE UNITED STATES OF AMERICA

We the People of the United States, in order to form a more perfect Union, establish Justice, insure domestic Tranquillity, provide for the common defence, promote the general Welfare, and secure the Blessings of Liberty to ourselves and our Posterity, do ordain and establish this CONSTITUTION for the United States of America.

Article I.

Section 2.... Representatives and direct Taxes shall be apportioned among the several States which may be included within this Union, according to their respective Numbers which shall be determined by adding to the whole Number of free Persons, including those bound to Service for a Term of Years, and excluding Indians not taxed, three-fifths of all other Persons...

... No Bill of Attainder or ex post facto Law shall be passed....

Article IV.

Section 2. The Citizens of each State shall be entitled to all Privileges and Immunities of Citizens in the several States....

CONSTITUTION OF THE CONFEDERATE STATES OF AMERICA

We, the People of the Confederate States, each State acting in its sovereign and independent character, in order to form a permanent Federal Government, establish justice, insure domestic tranquillity, and secure the blessings of liberty to ourselves and our posterity—invoking the favor and guidance of Almighty God—do ordain and establish this Constitution for the Confederate States of America.

Article I.

Section 2.... Representatives and direct taxes shall be apportioned among the several States, which may be included within this Confederacy, according to their respective numbers, which shall be determined by adding to the whole number of free persons, including those bound to service for a term of years, and excluding Indians not taxed, three-fifths of all slaves....

....No bill of attainder, ex post facto law, or law denying or impairing the right of property in negro slaves shall be passed....

Article IV.

Section 2. The citizens of each State shall be entitled to all the privileges and immunities of citizens in the several States, and shall have the right of transit and sojourn in any State of this Confederacy, with their slaves and other property; and the right of property in said slaves shall not be thereby impaired....

war materials was obtained from abroad during the early years of the conflict. The Confederacy had 2,500 miles of coastline, far too great an area for the tiny Union navy to police. Although Lincoln ordered a blockade to seal off the flow of supplies to the South, an estimated 90 percent of the ships that attempted to run it got through in 1861, and over 85 percent in 1862.

Military Stalemate

In 1861 and 1862 the Union and Confederate armies clashed repeatedly, with inconclusive results. The theater of war that attracted the most attention was the East, where the Army of the Potomac confronted Robert E. Lee's Army of Northern Virginia. There the course of battle was profoundly discouraging to Union supporters. Richmond was only 100 miles from Washington, D.C., but a series of campaigns to march on Richmond and seize the Confederate capitol ended in disaster.

After a humiliating trouncing at Bull Rull in the first summer, the Army of the Potomac was placed under a new commander. General George B. McClellan was young and dynamic, a superb organizer and administrator, and a master at shaping raw recruits into an efficient fighting force. He proved to have very little aptitude, however, for actually leading them into battle. A perfectionist, he was unwilling to leave anything to chance, and habitually exaggerated the strength of the enemy by a factor of two or three. He was no match for the brilliant and daring Robert E. Lee and Thomas "Stonewall" Jackson. Perhaps he himself knew it, for he procrastinated for almost a year before marching toward Richmond. A frustrated Lincoln complained that McClellan had "the slows," and quipped that if McClellan was not going to use his army he would like to borrow it for a while.

When McClellan finally did go on the offensive, under heavy pressure from the White House, he failed to sustain it. In the Battle of the Seven Days (June 25–July 1, 1862) not far from Richmond, his troops inflicted substantially more casualties on the enemy than they received, but afterwards McClellan's excessive caution led him to retreat to Washington instead of pressing on to Richmond against the outnumbered foe. He showed the same indecisiveness at the helm ten weeks later at the Battle of Antietam. Lee had gone on the offensive by marching boldly into western Maryland. McClellan cornered him with a force almost 50 percent larger, and some of the bloodiest fighting of the entire war ensued. There were more than 21,000 casualties. Fields of slain soldiers lay in rows just as they had stood firing in ranks moments before. Had the contest continued, there was a real possibility that Lee's Army of Northern Virginia would have been destroyed. But McClellan had no instinct to go for the jugular, and he let the enemy slip away without further bloodshed. He congratulated himself on having repelled Lee's invasion of the North—not much of an accomplishment in a war to conquer the South.

McClellan obviously had to go. His successor, General Ambrose Burnside, soon demonstrated that rashness could be as ruinous as timidity. In mounting a new drive on Richmond two weeks before Christmas, Burnside chose to cross the Rappahannock River at the splendidly fortified town of Fredericksburg, where he sent wave after wave of troops into a sea of blood before impregnable positions.

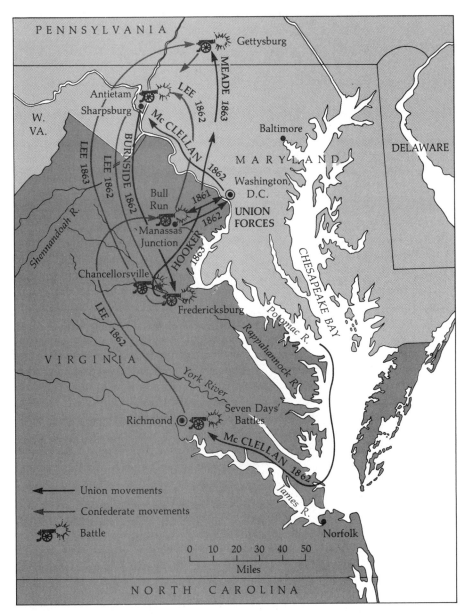

MAP 15-2
The War in the East, 1861–63

Union casualties exceeded Confederate losses by more than three to one, and no ground was gained. A corporal from New York who survived that hideous day wrote home: "Alas, my poor country. It has strong limbs to march and meet the foe, strong arms to strike heavy blows, brave hearts to dare. But the brains, the brains—have we no brains to use arms and limbs and eager hearts with cunning?"

THE SCENE AFTER THE BATTLE OF ANTIETAM

On coming near the brow of the hill, we met a party carrying picks and spades. "How many?" "Only one." The dead were nearly all buried, then, in this region of the field of strife. We stopped the wagon, and, getting out, began to look around us. Hard by was a large pile of muskets, scores, if not hundreds, which had been picked up, and were guarded for the Government. A long ridge of fresh gravel rose before us. A board stuck up in front of it bore this inscription, the first part of which was, I believe, not correct: "The Rebel General Anderson and 80 Rebels are burried in this hole."

Other smaller ridges were marked with the number of dead lying under them. The whole ground was strewn with fragments of clothing, haversacks, canteens, cap boxes, bullets, cartridges, scraps of paper, portions of bread and meat. I saw two soldiers' caps that looked as though their owners had been shot through the head. In several places I noticed dark red patches where a pool of blood had curdled and caked, as some poor fellow poured his life out on the sod.

—Oliver Wendell Holmes, *Pages from an Old Volume of Life*, 1904

West of the Appalachians, the war went better from the Union point of view, but the advances made there were far from decisive. The Union army succeeded in holding Missouri against determined efforts by Confederate sympathizers and invading forces from the South. In early 1862, they drove into Kentucky and Tennessee. In February General Ulysses S. Grant, still a relatively obscure figure in the war, forced them out by capturing Fort Henry and Fort Donelson along the Tennessee–Kentucky border. Grant pushed on so rapidly toward Mississippi that he fell into an almost fatal trap at Shiloh two months later. A surprise attack by a larger Confederate army pinned his troops against the Tennessee River and nearly wiped them out before reinforcements arrived and the Confederates had to fall back.

Washington received encouraging news in April, when Flag Officer (later Admiral) David Farragut's fleet smashed the feeble defense of New Orleans, capturing the Confederacy's largest city and closing the Mississippi River to southern trade for the rest of the war. This opened the way to Union capture of the entire Mississippi Valley, splitting the Confederacy in two by cutting off communications between Arkansas, Louisiana and Texas and the eight rebel states east of the river.

During the rest of the year, no significant progress was made. Although Grant was the most intelligent and aggressive fighting general yet to appear on the Union side, he was kept on a short leash by his superior, General Henry Halleck. Overall commander for the western theater, Halleck assumed direct command of Grant's army and other Union forces in the West after Shiloh. He was traumatized by that near calamity, and began to act as if he too had "the slows." He took an entire month to move the 20 miles between Shiloh and Corinth, Mississippi, and then indecisively dispersed his forces instead of making the concentrated thrust down the Mississippi that Grant pleaded for. The 1862 campaigns in the West forced the South to surrender significant amounts of territory, but did very little to undermine its determination and capacity to resist.

THE WAR FOR FREEDOM

As the fighting dragged on and the casualty lists grew, the political character of the war changed. The basic objective of the Confederates remained the same: southern independence and the preservation of the slave system. In the North, however, the long war radicalized public opinion. What began as a war against a society of slaveholders was transformed into a war against slavery as well. The war for union became a war for freedom.

The transformation was gradual, but it became irreversible in September of 1862 when President Lincoln announced that the Emancipation Proclamation would take effect on January 1, 1863. It declared the nation's slaves "forever free." It did not actually eliminate the institution of slavery throughout the entire United States. Both the border slave states and those areas of the Confederacy already under Union control—Tennessee, southern Louisiana, and western Virginia—were specifically exempted from its provisions. To some people, the proclamation seemed like a hollow gesture, because it freed slaves who were living behind Confederate lines and left in chains those who actually within the jurisdiction of the federal government. The principle, commented an English journal disgustedly, "is not that a human being cannot justly own another, but that he cannot unless he is loyal to the United States."

Although for the moment it did not affect loyal slaveholders, or even those slave-owners in conquered parts of the Confederacy, the Emancipation Proclamation entailed a crucial change in northern war aims. It was obvious that slavery could not survive long in Missouri and Maryland once it had been rooted out of Mississippi and the rest of the Lower South. Lincoln had not given Unionist planters a lifetime guarantee of their property; he had offered them a last chance to push their states toward a program of compensated emancipation. Congress had passed such a plan for the District of Columbia in 1862. One way or the other, a Union victory would certainly mean abolition throughout the land.

The grant of freedom to slaves in rebel territory was not really meaningless. Now every advance of the Union army would free the slaves of another area. Daring slaves now had a stronger reason to aid the Union by passing on information about the routes and locations of Confederate forces. This kind of help proved important to Grant in his successful Vicksburg campaign a few months later. More important, the promise of freedom stimulated slaves to escape and run for Union lines. There are no accurate records, but an estimated half-million slaves fled, draining away sorely needed southern manpower.

Pressures for Emancipation

What influenced Lincoln to take this bold step? One crucial consideration was the international scene. The South had found that "the cotton weapon" did not have the overwhelming power they thought it would have. Although Britain and France were hurt economically by the loss of most of their southern supplies of raw material, they hesitated to recognize the Confederacy out of a fear that it might embroil them in war with the United States. But the possibility that they might do so, break the blockade, and provide the South with unlimited military supplies was still there. Because no European nation condoned slavery, redefining the war as a contest between freedom and slavery made it less likely that southern diplomats would be able to win the recognition they sought.

The sheer fact that the war was dragging on so inconclusively was another reason for Lincoln's escalation of its aims. Many thousands of lives had been lost and many millions of dollars spent, without a single clear Union victory on the eastern front. Political discontent over what was coming to seem an unwinnable war was growing. A desperate Lincoln concluded, "We had about played our last card, and must change our tactics or lose the game." Attacking slavery, and transforming the war into the "violent and remorseless revolutionary struggle" he had warned of in his First Inaugural, was his last card.

Abolitionists had been urging such a course of action since the war began, but Lincoln came to the conclusion that it was necessary only gradually. As late as August, 1862 he still professed publicly that the object of the war was to save the Union and not to destroy slavery. "If I could save the Union without freeing *any* slave I would do it," he declared, "and if I could save it by freeing *all* the slaves I would do it; and if I could save it by freeing some and leaving others alone I would also do that. What I do about slavery, and the colored race, I do because I believe it helps to save the Union; and what I forbear, I forbear because I do *not* believe it would help to save the Union." But Lincoln was a complex and subtle man, and this statement, like many others he made, cannot be taken quite at face value. He had already written a draft of the Emancipation Proclamation when he said this, in fact, and only a month later he issued it. He was providing in advance a highly conservative rationale for an extremely radical action: that whatever he did would be out of sheer necessity to keep the nation intact. The action he planned to take was certain to win praise from radicals; Lincoln was developing a justification that would be acceptable also to moderates and conservatives. This also explains why he justified emancipation on military rather than moral grounds (see box).

Blacks in Blue

Transforming the war into an attack against slavery would weaken the Confederate war machine. Might liberated slaves not also be used to strengthen the Union forces? Racist sentiments in the North were strong, and at first even free blacks

WHY LINCOLN JUSTIFIED EMANCIPATION ON MILITARY GROUNDS

It seems to me very important that the ground of "military necessity" should be squarely taken. Many of our strongest Republicans, some even of our Lincoln electors, have constitutional scruples in regard to emancipation upon any other ground, and with them must be joined a large class of Democrats, and self-styled "Conservatives," whose support is highly desirable, and ought to be secured where it can be done without any sacrifice of principle.

I know that you and many others would like to have it done upon higher ground, but the main thing is to have it done strongly, and to have it so backed up by public opinion that it will strike the telling blow, at the rebellion and at slavery together, which we so much need.

I buy and eat my bread made from the flour raised by the hard-working farmer; it is certainly satisfactory that in so doing I am helping the farmer clothe his children, but my motive is self-preservation, not philanthropy or justice. Let the President free the slaves upon the same principle, and so state it that the masses of our people can easily understand it.

He will thus remove constitutional scruples from some, and will draw to himself the support of a very large class who do not want to expend their brothers and sons and money for the benefit of the negro, but who will be very glad to see Northern life and treasure saved by any practical measure, even if it does incidentally an act of justice and benevolence.

Now I would not by any means disclaim the higher motives, but where so much prejudice exists, I would eat my bread to sustain my life; I would take the one short, sure method of preserving the national life,—and say little about any other motive.

—John Murray Forbes to Charles Sumner, December, 1862

were considered unfit for service. The Union army, like the Confederate army, was initially for whites only.

Early in the war, the North could easily afford to indulge its prejudice, because its black population was small—fewer than 50,000 black males of military age in the entire region. The massive slave population behind Confederate lines was out of the picture. When these areas began to fall into Union hands, there was no coherent policy on how slaves were to be treated. Their legal status was unclear, and Washington showed every desire to duck this explosive issue as long as possible. Some commanders declared slaves "contraband of war" and put them to work building fortifications and performing other jobs under military supervision. One general actually armed the slaves, but was denied authority to muster them into official service.

Toward the end of 1862, however, the Union was growing hungrier for manpower. The target of half a million volunteers had been reached. But the three-year terms of the 1861 enlistees would be expiring in 1864, and a sober awareness had sunk in that the war could easily grind on longer. Congress therefore passed a general conscription law in March, 1863, a year after the Confederacy had been forced to do so. Necessity also dictated the opening up of the Union army to blacks. In July of 1862, Congress invited the President to enlist black troops, and the Emancipation Proclamation announced that black recruits would be welcomed into the armed services.

Black volunteers answered the call with enthusiasm. By the end of the war almost 180,000 had served in the Union army, a tenth of total enlistments. Most were former slaves who had escaped or been liberated as the Union army advanced. They were treated as second-class citizens, were segregated into black units led by white officers, and—until the final months of the war—were paid a third less than their white comrades. Some commanders flatly refused to use black troops at all; others assigned them noncombat tasks like cooking and loading wagons. When given the chance to fight, however, black recruits proved as brave as anyone.

It took particular courage for black soldiers to take the field because of the barbaric treatment they could expect in case of defeat. The Confederates refused to exchange black prisoners of war, on the grounds that they were not persons but property. Some did forced labor and others were not even taken captive but slaughtered on the spot. After the rebels stormed Fort Pillow, Tennessee, in April of 1864, 60 percent of the defending white troops but only 20 percent of the black soldiers were marched away as prisoners. A Confederate sergeant who was there wrote home that surrendering blacks would "run up to our men and fall upon their knees and with uplifted arms scream for mercy, but were ordered to their feet and then shot down."

The North reacted with outrage to such inhumanity. Lincoln ordered that for every Union soldier executed a rebel prisoner would meet the same fate, and for every captured Unionist put to work at hard labor a Confederate would be so treated. The rebels remained adamant in their refusal to exchange black prisoners; however; as a result, exchanges stopped altogether during the last two years of the war.

Total War

A dramatic shift in military policy reflected the total war attitude of the Emancipation Proclamation. In the early stages of the conflict, traditional distinctions had been observed between soldier and civilian, between combatants and noncombatants. Union commanders respected the property rights of the population in occupied territory, or at least were expected to do so. In April of 1863, a new general order announced that military necessity "allows of all destruction of property . . . and of all withholding of sustenance of means of life from the country," and the "appropriation of whatever an enemy's country affords necessary for the subsis-

Dec. 10th.... You can form no idea of the amount of property destroyed by us on this raid. All the Roads in the state are torn up and the whole tract or country over which we passed is little better than a wilderness. I can't for the life of me think what the people that are left there are to live on. We have all their Cattle, Horses, Mules, Sheep, Hogs, Sweet Potatoes and Molasses and nearly everything else. We burnt all the Cotton we met which was millions of pounds. Our teams with all their hard driving are better today by about 200 percent than they were when we started because we have more than ⅔ new mules, besides all the old ones we could bring with us. Those that couldn't travel we killed and the road is lined with those that died. A tornado 60 miles in width from Chattanooga to this place 290 miles could not have done half the damage we did.

—W. F. Saylor to his father

tence and safety of the Army." Now it was legitimate not only to forage for supplies and live off the land, but to destroy anything that might be of use to the rebels.

The most famous demonstration of what this meant (though by no means the only example) was General William Tecumseh Sherman's march through Georgia in late 1864. His army cut a swath of destruction 60 miles wide and 300 miles long, from Atlanta to the coast, doing more damage than a plague of locusts. One of Sherman's objectives was traditional strategy—to cut the supply lines between the lower South and Lee's army in Virginia. The other goals were special to modern total war—to shatter the enemy's economic system and weaken civilian morale. In Sherman's own words, to bring "the sad realities of war home to those who have been directly or indirectly instrumental in involving us in its attendant calamities." Sherman's famous remark that "war is hell" obscures the fact that some ways of waging war are more hellish than others. The doctrine of total war he and other Union commanders formulated, with its slippery notion of "indirect" civilian responsibility, is one of the most important and morally ambiguous legacies of the Civil War.

The Military Balance Shifts

1863 was the decisive year in the military history of the war. It opened wretchedly, from the Union viewpoint. In May, Lee outmaneuvered the Army of the Potomac at Chancellorsville, Virginia. Although outnumbered two-to-one, his forces ad-

WALT WHITMAN ON THE CARNAGE AT CHANCELLORSVILLE, MAY 1863

The night was very pleasant, at times the moon shining out full and clear, all Nature so calm in itself, the early summer grass so rich, and the foliage of the trees—yet there the battle raging, and many good fellows lying helpless, and every minute amid the rattle of muskets and cannon the red life-blood oozing out from heads or trunks or limbs upon that green and dew-cool grass. Patches of the woods take fire, and several of the wounded, unable to move, are consumed—quite large spaces are swept over, burning the dead also. Then the camps of the wounded. There they lie, from 200 to 300 poor fellows—the groans and screams, the odor of blood, mixed with the fresh scent of the night, the grass, the trees—that slaughter-house! One man is shot by a shell, both in the arm and leg—both are amputated—there lie the rejected members. Some have their legs blown off—some bullets through the breast—some indescribably horrid wounds in the face or head, all mutilated, sickening, torn, gouged out—some mere boys.

ministered a punishing defeat. Lee then launched his most daring offensive. He marched into Pennsylvania in hopes of either winning a great battle on northern soil and discouraging the Yankees, or at least triggering the long-awaited intervention of Britain and France. He found his great battle, but not his great victory, at Gettysburg on the first three days of July. At the climax, 15,000 rebels made a suicidal advance now known as Pickett's Charge. They marched across an open field almost a mile wide, into the teeth of massive Union troop and artillery concentrations along Cemetery Ridge. The few who survived the hail of lead thrown at them could only surrender or retreat. The next day a Union officer reported, "I tried to ride over the field but could not, for dead and wounded lay too thick to guide a horse through them." The inept Union commander, General George Gordon Meade, bungled in the end by letting the remnants of Lee's forces retreat unpursued. But total Confederate losses were nearly 25,000 in killed, wounded, or missing, and the South had not the men to replace them. Lee would never again command so large a force. He would never again mount a major offensive.

In the West, on July 4, Grant won a victory as important to the Union cause as Gettysburg. Vicksburg, Mississippi fell after a brilliant and brutal seven-month campaign. Confederate territory west of the Mississippi was now split away from the heartland of rebellion, and helplessly isolated for the remainder of the conflict. Another vital triumph came in November, when Grant's forces repelled a rebel attack upon Chattanooga, Tennessee. A thrust from Tennessee through Georgia to the sea would split the Confederacy further; Sherman achieved that the next year.

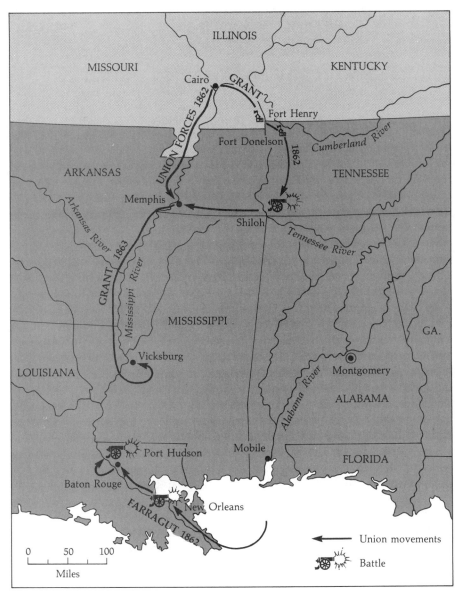

MAP 15-3
The War in the West, 1861–63

The military initiative had passed over to the North. At last Lincoln had commanders who would exercise it boldly. Early in March, 1864 he called Grant in from the West and named him General-in-Chief in charge of all Union forces. Like the President himself, Grant struck polished easterners as lacking in social graces. He had "no gait, no station, no manner," complained one. He originally left the army in 1854 to avoid a court-martial for his heavy drinking, and was still fond of

Consecrate to the holy cause not only the incidentals of life but life itself. Father, husband, child—I do not say give them up to toil, exposure, suffering, death, without a murmur—that implies reluctance. I rather say, urge them to the offering; fill them with sacred fury. Be large and lofty. Count it all joy that you are reckoned worthy to suffer in a grand and glorious cause.

—*Atlantic*, March, 1863

the bottle. When Lincoln was asked why he chose him, he responded simply: "He fights." When someone criticized Grant's drinking habits, Lincoln said if he knew the general's brand he would send every other commander in the Union army a barrel of the whiskey. Grant had a singleness of purpose, a will to victory, that none of his predecessors displayed. When a worried subordinate warned him that Lee might take advantage of an apparent weak spot in his invasion plan, he said, "I am heartily tired of hearing what Lee is going to do. Some of you always seem to think he is going to turn a double somersault, and land in our rear and on both flanks at the same time. Go back to your command and try to think what we are going to do ourselves, instead of what Lee is going to do." When he began his campaign against Lee's forces, it was clear that he meant it when he said that he would "fight it out along this line if it takes all summer."

Grant had the insight to see that by the time he took command the South had lost the ability to make good its losses in manpower and materials, and could be hammered into submission by a focused and sustained attack on her two main armies—Joseph E. Johnston's Army of the Tennessee, and Lee's Army of Northern Virginia. He personally took charge of the campaign against Lee and sent Sherman to deal with Johnston. Although Lee's forces were somewhat depleted, they had the advantage of being on the defensive in the rough Virginia countryside they knew so well. Grant threw all his forces into the assault and paid no attention to the body count. In May of 1864—"bloody May," it soon came to be called—the two armies fought a series of bitter engagements. Grant's Army of the Potomac suffered 55,000 casualties, and inflicted only half as many on the rebels. The Union had replacements for the fallen men, however, and the South did not. The Confederates fell back steadily, and by mid-June Grant was in the outskirts of Petersburg, where he began a siege designed to destroy Lee's supply and communications line.

It was a sound plan, and eventually a successful one. The drawback was that it took time—nine months—and Grant's time seemed to be running out. Lincoln's reelection was in serious jeopardy because of popular discontent over the course of the war. How much more bloodshed would they tolerate to restore the Union?

Viewing one battle site during "bloody May," a northern senator confessed, "If that scene could have been presented to me before the war, anxious as I was for the preservation of the Union, I should have said: 'The cost is too great; erring sisters, go in peace.'"

Political Choices

That sense of war weariness was the principal asset of the Democratic opposition as the 1864 campaign began. In many societies, politics as usual would be suspended during a major civil war. The holding of free elections would be regarded as a dangerous luxury; those who disagreed with the administration would be forcibly silenced. The Lincoln government did at times feel compelled to take actions that infringed on civil liberties. During the war some 1,300 persons suspected of collaborating with the enemy were imprisoned (in most cases briefly) in violation of their constitutional right of habeas corpus. Martial law was in force for a short time in some areas, and there were instances of press censorship. On the whole, however, basic political freedoms were unhampered to a surprising degree. Scheduled elections almost always took place, and the most extreme antiwar faction of the Democratic party was allowed to submit its case to the voters.

For much of 1864, it seemed a strong possibility that a war being won on the battlefield would be lost at the polls. The Democratic party platform denounced the war as "four years of failure," and called for an immediate truce, to be followed by a national convention that would somehow restore the Union peaceably. In effect, this plan would have amounted to recognition of southern independence, because the military effort to subdue the South would have been halted and the Confederate states would have been under no requirement actually to attend the convention. The Democratic presidential nominee, General George McClellan, was unwilling to endorse this portion of the platform. He adopted a basically compromising stance toward the rebels, however, making it plain that he was willing to see any state returned to the Union "with a full guarantee of all its constitutional rights"—including the right of its citizens to hold slaves.

Lincoln also faced serious political opposition from the opposite quarter—from radicals who fervently supported the war but insisted that the southern social order be reconstructed along northern lines. He had recently sponsored the creation of what he considered acceptable loyal governments in three captured Confederate states—Tennessee, Louisiana, and Arkansas. He had, moreover, requested that their elected representatives be seated in Congress. As Commander-in-Chief, he argued, he had primary responsibility for restoring legitimate government in regained territories. The terms Lincoln offered the subdued states were mild. Once 10 percent of their voters (with the temporary exclusion of high civil and military officials from the former regime) had pledged their future loyalty to the Union, elections could be held. The loyalty oath entailed acceptance of recent presidential and congressional actions concerning slavery. To take it would be to affirm that slavery was defunct, but would not in itself amount to formal abolition. That the states could accomplish subsequently.

Lincoln considered his plan appropriately flexible and conciliatory; growing numbers of Congressmen saw it as a sellout. They insisted that Congress, not the President, should regulate the reinstatement of rebel states, and the requirements should be far stiffer. The loyalty oath should affirm past as well as future allegiance to the United States, so that no one who had voluntarily taken up arms in the Confederate cause would be eligible to vote or hold office. Half, rather than a mere 10 percent, of the electorate should take it. And the states should write new constitutions abolishing slavery and permanently disenfranchising former Confederate leaders. Congress refused to recognize the three states that had qualified under Lincoln's "10 percent plan," and passed a measure mandating its strict terms, the Wade–Davis Bill. Lincoln vetoed it, leaving the whole issue of reconstruction policy at a stalemate.

In the summer of 1864, there was such strong anti-Lincoln feeling among the radicals that even Lincoln's own party's nomination was uncertain. He was nominated as a candidate of the National Union party—a temporary label adopted by the Republicans to gain broader support from former Democrats—with a loyalist southern Democrat, Governor Andrew Johnson of Tennessee, as his running mate. There was some backstage maneuvering to induce Lincoln to resign in favor of a more radical candidate, and a movement was organized to run John C. Frémont on a third party "Radical Democracy" ticket. The Democrats' extreme antiwar platform, however, and their choice of the hated McClellan as a candidate, moved the Republicans to close ranks behind Lincoln.

The Democratic threat soon diminished as well, as new military breakthroughs discredited the "four years of failure" slogan. In late August, Farragut captured Mobile, the Confederacy's largest remaining Gulf port, and in early September, Atlanta fell to Sherman's army. The taste of victory heartened war–weary northerners, and Lincoln won in November by a solid 55 to 45 margin.

TRIUMPH FOR THE UNION

Lincoln's annual message to Congress in December of 1864 called attention to an extraordinary fact: "The steady expansion of population, and governmental institutions over the new and unoccupied portion of our country have scarcely been checked, much less impeded or destroyed by our great civil war, which at first glance would seem to have absorbed almost the entire energies of the nation." Sales of public lands in the West had continued strong, there had been new discoveries of precious minerals, and construction had begun on that crucial link to the far west, the transcontinental railroad. "We have *more* men *now* than we had when the war *began;* we are not exhausted, nor in process of exhaustion; we are *gaining* strength, and may, if need be, maintain the contest indefinitely. This as to men. Material resources are now more complete and abundant than ever before."

Recent statistical studies suggest that on the whole the war actually retarded economic growth somewhat. The Civil War decade appears the poorest of the nineteenth century by a number of different indexes. But the high output levels of those years were a tremendous productive achievement, with so many men with-drawn from the labor force and so many resources destroyed by pillaging armies.

Under the stimulus of the war, the federal government moved to foster development more vigorously than ever before. The House and Senate passed a number of key measures previously defeated by southern votes. Tariffs to protect American industry from foreign competition were raised sharply; by 1864 they were two and a half times the 1860 level. A new national banking system was established, both to finance the war and to achieve the long-term objective of a uniform national currency. Railroad promoters succeeded in winning lavish federal land grants to finance new construction. The government gave away more federal land to subsidize internal improvements in 1865 alone than in the entire previous history of the United States. Congress also consigned large parcels of land to state governments as sites for land grant colleges to offer training in agriculture, engineering, and military science. Perhaps the most dramatic land grant measure was the 1862 Homestead Act, which assigned parcels of 160 acres of land to prospective settlers. Any citizen, or any alien intending to become a citizen, could receive title to the land free of charge after farming it for five years. The public policy legacy of the Civil War was federal activism to benefit industry and agriculture. It created lines of cleavage between the Republican and Democratic parties that would remain visible for more than a generation.

The Confederacy Collapses

By 1864, no responsible southern spokesman could have uttered anything approaching Lincoln's boast, "We are *gaining* strength." The shortage of fighting men was desperate. Although both sides had to resort to conscription, the South drafted boys as young as 17 and men as old as 50; the Union, by contrast, took only married men from 20 to 35 and single men from 20 to 45. So great was the South's need for men that in the closing months of the war it was forced to contemplate the unthinkable—using slave troops. In March of 1865, the Confederate Congress actually authorized this, although it could not bring itself to promise the slaves their freedom to motivate them to fight. Even going as far as they did testified to the acuteness of the manpower shortage. Drafting slaves into the Confederate army was a step that one representative called "revolting to Southern sentiment, Southern pride, and Southern honor."

Even when men were found to put on the grey, it was difficult to supply them. Despite great efforts to foster manufacturing at home, the Confederacy remained basically dependent on its vessels' success in running the Union blockade. A crash program to expand the Union navy made that far more difficult to do. By 1864, it is estimated that at least a third of the Confederate ships running the blockade were seized and confiscated; the next year, it was fully half of them. The uniforms of a typical brigade told the story. "In this army," reported a Texan in June of 1864, "one hold in the seat of the breeches indicates a captain, two holes a lieutenant, and the seat of the pants all out indicates that the individual is a private." Perhaps worst of all was the increasingly grave shortage of food. Army rations, never generous,

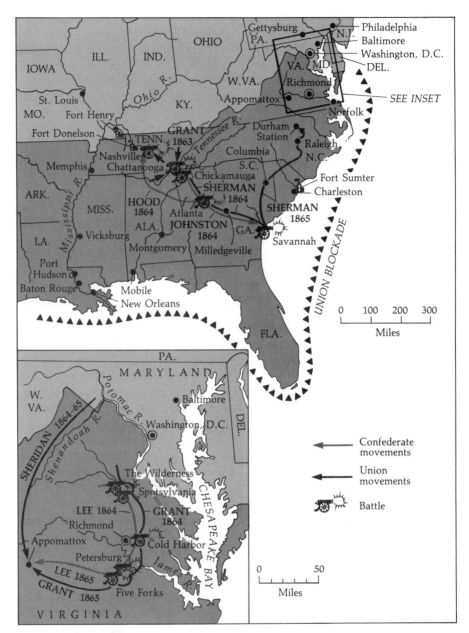

MAP 15–4
The War, 1863–65

had to be cut. "There is more to fear from a dearth of food than from all the Federal armies in existence," declared a Mississippi newspaper. "Who can fight starvation with hope of success?"

The economic strangulation of the Confederacy affected civilians too, and their suffering sapped troop morale. The latter days of the war saw a high rate of desertion. One Alabama soldier wrote to his wife that he was requesting a furlough, but if refused was "coming home enny how, for I can't stand to hear that you and the children are sufren for Bread."

These wounds weakened the Confederacy until further resistance was impossible. There was no grand climactic battle. The Confederacy simply collapsed. In April of 1865, Lee's army, shrunk now to a mere 25,000 men, was forced to evacuate Petersburg and Richmond, and its escape route was cut off. On Sunday, April 9, Lee surrendered his sword to Grant at Appomattox.

One more gun was still to be fired—not by a soldier but by a demented young actor from Virginia. On the evening of April 14, Lincoln attended a play at Ford's Theater in Washington. There John Wilkes Booth crept up in the darkness and shot the President in the head. The war was won, the indivisibility of the American nation was established. It was left for the living, as Lincoln had said in his Gettysburg address, to take up the "unfinished work" and give the country "a new birth of Freedom." The war's outcome opened the way to revolutionary changes in the American pattern of race relations. Whether those changes would actually take place depended on the interplay of forces and personalities in the years of reconstruction that followed.

SUGGESTED READINGS

Many of the titles cited at the end of the previous chapter are also pertinent here. Peter J. Parish, *The American Civil War* (1975) is the best one-volume introduction, and includes an extensive bibliographical essay. Allen Nevins' four volumes, *War For the Union* (1959–1971) are masterful, but neglect the Confederate side of the story, for which see Emory M. Thomas, *The Confederate Nation* (1979) and Paul D. Escott, *After Secession: Jefferson Davis and the Failure of Confederate Nationalism* (1978).

David Donald, ed., *Why the North Won the Civil War* (1960) offers stimulating answers to that perennial question by leading authorities. On the actual fighting, Bruce Catton, *Mr. Lincoln's Army* (1951), *Glory Road* (1952), and *A Stillness at Appomattox* (1953) are lively accounts written from a Unionist viewpoint. Shelby Foote's three-volume *The Civil War* (1958–74) is more sympathetic to the Confederates. More scholarly and analytical articles on military aspects of the conflict are to be found in John T. Hubbell, ed., *Battles Lost and Won* (1975). For the experience of the ordinary soldier, see Bell Wiley's *The Life of Johnny Reb* (1943) and *The Life of Billy Yank* (1952), and Henry S. Commager, ed., *The Blue and the Grey: The Story of the Civil War as Told by Participants*, 2 vols. (1950).

A good starting point for wartime politics may be gained from David Donald, *Lincoln Reconsidered* (1956) and Richard Current, *The Lincoln Nobody Knows* (1958), both rich in ideas and broader than their titles suggest. More recent collections of articles are Robert Swierenga, ed., *Beyond the Civil War Synthesis* (1975), and George M. Fredrickson, *A Nation Divided: Problems and Issues of the Civil War and Reconstruction* (1975). Eric McKitrick's essay on the Union and Confederate Governments in William N. Chambers and Walter D. Burnham, eds., *The American Party System* (1975) offers highly suggestive comparisons and contrasts. James L. Sundquist, *Dynamics of the Party System* (1973) is illuminating on party alignments. James A. Rawley, *The Politics of Union: Northern Politics During the Civil War* (1974) is a brief overview. Herman Belz, *Reconstructing the Union* (1969) and the opening chapters of Michael Les Benedict, *A Compromise of Principle: Congressional Republicans and Reconstruction, 1863–1869* (1974) trace the issues of the Reconstruction era back into the war years. Harold Hyman, *A More Perfect Union* (1973) is a magisterial study of the constitutional and legal questions raised by the war.

Basic works on blacks and their role include John Hope Franklin, *The Emancipation Proclamation* (1963); James McPherson, *The Struggle for Equality: Abolitionists and the Negro in the Civil War and Reconstruction* (1964); Dudley Cornish, *The Sable Arm: Negro Troops in the Union Army* (1956); Eugene Genovese, *Roll, Jordan, Roll* (1974); Herbert Gutman, *The Black Family in Slavery and Freedom* (1975); and Lawrence Levine, *Black Culture and Black Consciousness: Afro-American Folk Thought from Slavery to Freedom* (1977). McPherson's *The Negro's Civil War* (1965) is a fine collection of primary sources that reveal black reactions. V. Jacques Voegeli, *Free But Not Equal: The Midwest and the Negro During the Civil War* (1967); George M. Fredrickson, *The Black Image in the White Mind* (1971); and essays in C. Vann Woodward, *American Counterpoint: Slavery and Racism in the North–South Dialogue* (1971) stress the pervasiveness of white racism.

On literary and intellectual aspects of the war and its aftermath, see Edmund Wilson's fascinating *Patriotic Gore: Studies in the Literature of the American Civil War* (1962); Daniel Aaron, *The Unwritten War* (1973); and George Fredrickson, *The Inner Civil War: Northern Intellectuals and the Crisis of the Union* (1965). The best novel written about the war from first-hand experience is John W. DeForest's *Miss Ravenel's Conversion* (1867), a coolly realistic account still worth reading today.

Chapter Sixteen

Reunion and Reconstruction

T he Civil War was a revolution that destroyed the Old South and struck the chains from four million black people. Once the military struggle was over, however, the victors treated the vanquished with a mildness rare in the history of revolutions. Mass executions for political crimes and confiscation of vast lands and other wealth accompanied great social revolutions in France, Russia, and China. The dozen years of "reconstruction" following the American Civil War, by contrast, saw remarkably little vengeance. Although Union troops had marched into battle singing, "We'll hang Jeff Davis on a sour apple tree," the chief political leader of the rebellion merely went to prison for two years. Robert E. Lee was never even arrested. Of the hundreds of thousands of rebels who took up arms against the federal government, none was forced into exile. Only one was tried and executed, and that not for treason but for war crimes—his administration of the ghastly prison at Andersonville, Georgia, where thousands of Union captives died. The only significant bloodshed after Appomattox was caused not by the winners but by the losers—southern whites who banded together in the Ku Klux Klan and similar organizations to topple the recently established Republican regimes through systematic terrorist raids.

The planters, it is true, lost $2.5 billion worth of human property. But they generally managed to hang onto their land, and a new system of sharecropping allowed them to continue to exploit black labor. New modes of political and social control were devised to put the freedmen back "in their place."

The impressive resilience of the southern social order was testimony not only to the fierceness of the resistance displayed by its defenders but to the weakness of

"The First Vote" of freed Negroes is depicted in this drawing by A.R. Waud for an 1870 issue of Harper's Weekly.

the radical impulse in the triumphant North. There were moments when truly fundamental changes seemed possible, changes that would radically and permanently alter not only southern society but the place of black people in American life. But beneath the turbulent surface was a bedrock consensus that was missing in convulsive social upheavals in other countries. Some visionaries, like Senator Charles Sumner of Massachusetts and Representative Thaddeus Stevens of Pennsylvania, challenged it, but in the end white Americans agreed on the sanctity of private property, the limited right of the central government to intervene in state affairs, and the inferiority of the black race. A dozen years after Appomattox, the reconstruction effort had faltered, and proponents of white supremacy were back in power in all the ex-Confederate states. The Union was restored, but the South was not drastically reconstructed.

PRESIDENT JOHNSON'S RECONSTRUCTION PROGRAM

Three major questions faced the nation in 1865. On what terms would the defeated rebel states be brought back into the Union as normally functioning states? Could the ruling Republican party retain its national ascendancy once that happened? What would be the place of the millions of "freedmen" in southern society? These contentious and intricately interwoven issues provoked a prolonged political struggle that almost resulted in the removal of a President from office for "high crimes and misdemeanours."

Slavery was, of course, dead. The Emancipation Proclamation had not done the job completely, because it only applied to areas not under Union control in January of 1863. Congress had completed the task by approving the Thirteenth Amendment. It was ratified by the necessary three-fourths of the states and became the law of the land in 1865. Once blacks were no longer slaves, however, what were they? Were freedmen full citizens with all the rights enjoyed by white Americans? Could they vote, hold political office, serve on juries, testify in court, own property, move freely from place to place, attend school, enter any occupation? In 1865 southern whites obviously were not prepared to grant their former servants equality in all these spheres. What is less obvious, and crucial to an understanding of the period, is that many northern whites were not either. Only 7 percent of northern blacks lived in states that allowed them to vote. Most states forbade blacks to join the militia, to serve on juries, and to testify against whites in court. Housing was segregated. So were public transportation, hotels, restaurants, theaters, schools, hospitals, prisons, and cemeteries. Only a year before the Emancipation Proclamation, Lincoln's own state of Illinois approved a referendum forbidding blacks from entering the state by a two-to-one margin.

Such racist policies did not go unchallenged in the Reconstruction years. Radical Republicans committed to egalitarian ideals led courageous campaigns to extend the franchise to blacks and to protect them from discriminatory treatment throughout the North. But a lot of courage was required, for the issue was politically dangerous. Between 1865 and 1869, Republicans sponsored eleven referenda on black voting rights in northern states; nine were defeated.

Democratic politicians found white supremacy their best issue, practically their only issue. In the 1867 Democratic campaign in Ohio, a parade of young girls, in white dresses, carried banners reading, "Fathers, Save Us from Negro Equality." The Democrats roundly defeated the Republican equal suffrage proposal that year and captured both houses of the Ohio legislature as well. In 1868, the Democratic literature for the presidential contest included a pamphlet called "White Men Must Rule America." A Democratic victory, it pledged, would "maintain the supremacy of the white race at all hazards, and restore negroes to that condition where they can exist in accordance with the laws of their being and where they will become in the future as they were in the past, the happiest and most valuable race of subordinates on earth." The widespread racial prejudice to which the Democrats appealed was felt by a good many Republicans as well. It was a powerful constraint on the policies that Republicans could devise for the South. The 1868 Republican platform avoided entirely the issue of black suffrage in northern states.

The Freedmen's Bureau

After passing the Thirteenth Amendment in early 1865, Congress took another significant action. Most of its members regarded the centralization of power in Washington that had taken place during the war years as a temporary aberration, the product of an emergency that was now over. The Constitution delegated only certain powers to the central government and left such matters as education, control of crime, and preservation of law and order to states and local communities. The enormous disruptions caused by the war and the freeing of the slaves, however, seemed beyond the capacity of the individual states to manage. Consequently, Congress reluctantly created a temporary agency to provide assistance to the war-torn South, and to ease the transition of black Americans from slavery to freedom—the Freedmen's Bureau. The Bureau was to administer relief for the needy, and in its five years of existence it supplied more than 20 million free meals, a quarter of them to impoverished southern whites. It established schools and hospitals for freedmen.

The central aim of the Freedmen's Bureau was to assist blacks to find employment. General O.O. Howard, its head, told a group of former slaves that he would "promise them nothing but freedom, and freedom means work." Bureau officials wanted freedmen to have the same rights as northern workingmen—to bargain for wages and freely choose their employers. However, the major source of work was obviously in the cotton fields, and planters pleaded that they lacked the capital to pay regular cash wages. As a transitional measure, the Bureau printed contracts committing plantation owners to provide food and shelter to ex-slaves in exchange for labor from all able-bodied members of the family, who were put to work in gangs as they had as slaves. Blacks were pressured to sign these agreements by the threat that no more rations would be forthcoming from the Bureau. There were provisions for what the contracts referred to as "wages," but they were not truly wages, a fixed sum for a given unit of time. Freedmen would receive income only if the plantation returned a profit at the end of the season, which was of course quite beyond their control.

The legislation authorizing the Freedmen's Bureau also pointed to another more promising solution to the problem of black employment. The bill empowered the Bureau to "set apart for the freedmen" abandoned lands in plots of 40 acres at nominal rents, with the option to purchase later. Two similar efforts to create a class of independent black yeoman farmers had already begun under military auspices during the war. After the fall of Vicksburg, General Grant had resettled some 2,000 blacks on former plantation land at Davis Bend, Mississippi, and allowed them to farm the land cooperatively. Likewise, General Sherman had set aside a portion of the South Carolina and Georgia coasts for 40,000 ex-slaves, and had given them temporary titles to farms. When a Carolina planter returned to claim his estate, his former slaves greeted him with "overflowing affection," but told him, "We own this land now. Put it out of your head that it will ever be yours again." Congress now seemed prepared to move further in this direction. Although the Freedmen's Bureau had only enough abandoned plantation land for 20,000 out of almost one million families, the principle was vitally important; the federal government was beginning to assume responsibility for satisfying the freedmen's ardent desire for "forty acres and a mule."

Johnson Takes Command

Congress adjourned in March of 1865, not to reconvene until the end of the year. When southern military resistance collapsed in April, the task of reconstructing the governments of the rebel states fell to the President, who would have a free hand for eight months. Andrew Johnson, a life-long Democrat from Tennessee, had been made Vice President in 1864 in a gesture of wartime bipartisanship. That responsibility fell to him, thanks to Lincoln's assassination. The situation was doubly ironic. The victorious North now had a southern chief executive, and a former slaveholder at that. The Republican Party which had directed the war effort had to contend with a Democratic President. Although Johnson claimed that his reconstruction policies would adhere strictly to the guidelines established earlier by Lincoln, he had none of Lincoln's flexibility and gift for compromise. He was the most rigid and obstinate man ever to occupy the White House. Congress had already made plain its determination to play a powerful role in the formation of Reconstruction policy. Johnson rashly ignored this. He assumed that if he could establish new regimes in the rebel states before Congress returned in December, the legislators would have to accept them as a *fait accompli*.

Before the year was out, governments acceptable to Johnson had been created in all but one of the former Confederate states. But the character of these new governments shocked and infuriated many northerners. They were led, almost without exception, by the same planters who had steered the South down the road to secession. The men southern voters elected to the new Congress included four Confederate generals, five colonels, six Confederate cabinet officers, fifty-eight

A BLACK CODE

All freedmen, free Negroes and mulattoes in this State, over the age of eighteen years, found on the second Monday in January, 1866, or thereafter, with no lawful employment or business, or found unlawfully assembling themselves together, either in the day or night time, and all white persons so assembling with freedmen, free Negroes or mulattoes, on terms of equality, or living in adultery or fornication with a freedwoman, free Negro, or mulatto, shall be deemed vagrants, and on conviction thereof shall be fined in the sum of not exceeding, in the case of a freedman, free Negro or mulatto, fifty dollars, and a white man two hundred dollars, and imprisoned at the discretion of the court, the free Negro not exceeding ten days, and the white man not exceeding six months. . . .

And in case any freedman, free Negro or mulatto shall fail for five days after the imposition of any fine or forfeiture upon him or her for violation of any of the provisions of this act to pay the same, that it shall be . . . the duty of the sheriff of the proper county to hire out said freedman, free Negro or mulatto, to any person who will, for the shortest period of service, pay said fine and forfeiture and all costs. . . .

—Laws of Mississippi, 1865

Confederate Congressmen, and the Vice President of the Confederate States of America! Almost all were Democrats, with predictably negative stances on the tariff, federal aid for railroads, river and harbor improvements, and other developmental expenditures. Some of the conventions at which these new regimes were formed were so unrepentant that they refused to fly the Stars and Stripes. Republicans who hoped that the South could generate a more moderate, loyal, progressive leadership group were appalled at the return of the old guard.

The actions the Johnson-sponsored governments were taking toward the freedmen were equally troubling. Although the President had made ratification of the Thirteenth Amendment a condition for readmission to the Union, some states did so with great reluctance and much defiant rhetoric. And if they grudgingly conceded the end of slavery, they seemed determined to recreate it in everything but name by passing restrictive Black Codes. It was not terribly disturbing to most northern Republicans in 1865 that every one of the secessionist states denied blacks the right to vote. The average Republican favored, at best, only a qualified suffrage for a black minority—those who were literate, owned property, or had served in the Union Army.

The Black Codes, however, denied far more than black suffrage. They were often lifted from the old slave codes, with the word "negro" for "slave." In

Mississippi, Negroes were denied the right to purchase or even rent land. In South Carolina, they needed a special license to hold any job except that of field hand. Almost all the state codes contained restrictions protecting white labor from black competition. Most denied blacks the right to purchase or carry firearms, and even the right to assemble after sunset. Most brutal were the typical vagrancy provisions. Any black discovered by the authorities "wandering or strolling about in idleness" could be arrested and put to work on a state chain gang, or auctioned off to a planter and forced to work without pay for as long as a year. Freedmen were therefore forced to remain with their employers, normally their former masters, because they could not travel in search of better opportunities.

The Black Codes, a Louisiana newspaper explained, created "a new labor system prescribed and enforced by the state." General Howard had advised freedmen to "begin at the bottom of the ladder and climb up," but powerful whites were determined to keep them on a quite separate ladder with only one rung. They believed, as one said candidly, "The general interest both of the white man and the negro requires that he be kept as near to the condition of slavery as possible, and as far from the condition of the white man as is practicable." As a northern traveler said, the codes were "a striking embodiment of the idea that although the former owner has lost his individual right of property in the former slave, the blacks at large belong to the whites at large." President Johnson, nonetheless, defended them as measures "to confer upon freedmen the privileges which are essential to their comfort, protection, and security."

Congressional Reactions

When Congress convened in December of 1865, Johnson declared that the task of reconstruction had been completed, and requested that the duly elected representatives of the ex-Confederate states be allowed to take their seats. Not surprisingly, outraged Republicans refused. Instead, they created a special joint Senate and House Committee, the Committee of Fifteen, to develop an alternative program. After hearing testimony on what was happening in the South, they proposed two measures. One bill enlarged the power and extended the life of the Freedmen's Bureau. Another, the Civil Rights Act of 1866, was the Republican answer to the Dred Scott Decision and the Black Codes. It extended citizenship to blacks and guaranteed them equal protection of the laws.

The angry President vetoed both measures and denounced the Congress in intemperate terms. They were unconstitutional federal intrusions into matters best left to the states, he said, the work of fanatics who aimed to "destroy our institutions and change the character of our Government." Although he was undoubtedly sincere in his constitutional scruples, he was also influenced by the fear that the bills threatened white supremacy. In his view, blacks had "shown less capacity for self-government than any other people. Whenever they have been left to their own devices they have shown an instant tendency to lapse into barbarism." After a meeting with Frederick Douglass and other black leaders, he told his private secretary: "I know that damned Douglass; he's just like any nigger, and he would sooner cut a white man's throat than not."

Because representatives from the former Confederate states had been denied their places, the Republicans had the votes to override the vetoes by the required two-thirds majority. But the measures were threatened from a different quarter as well—the Supreme Court had the power to strike them down as unconstitutional. To guard against that, Congress sought to write the necessary safeguards for equal rights into the Constitution itself via the Fourteenth Amendment. Republicans pushed it through Congress, and required that rebel states ratify it *before* they were readmitted to the Union. The Fourteenth Amendment extended citizenship to blacks, and forbade any state to "abridge the privileges and immunities" of citizens, to deprive citizens of "life, liberty, or property, without due process of law," or to "deny any person within its jurisdiction the equal protection of the laws." This seemed to rule out the most obnoxious features of the Black Codes, although the Supreme Court was later to ignore the clear meaning of this language, and also to find in it other quite unanticipated meanings.

Another important provision of the Fourteenth Amendment barred from federal or state office anyone who had taken a federal oath of office and then participated in the rebellion. This was a blow at the South's traditional leadership, of course. It specified, however, that such persons might be pardoned by a two-thirds vote of Congress.

The Fourteenth Amendment also protected the black man's right to vote, albeit in a rather sneaky way. Some Republican radicals had argued for equal political rights for the freedmen all along. By the summer of 1866, when the amendment was framed by Congress, others had come to favor it out of fear for the future of their party. The Democrats were experiencing a resurgence in the North. They would obviously grow even stronger when the South reentered the Union, if only whites were allowed to vote. The South had been solidly Democratic since the 1850s. The Republicans had long complained of the disproportionate political clout the three-fifths clause of the Constitution gave the South. The end of slavery, ironically, only increased it more. Because the entire black population—not just three-fifths—would count in apportioning seats in Congress and the Electoral College, the South would gain 24 additional Representatives and electoral votes. The only hope of making the Republican party a contender for those seats would be to open the polls to the freedmen, who would surely favor the party that gave them their freedom. It was an issue, said a Republican official, in "which the highest requirements of abstract justice coincide with the lowest requirements of political prudence."

Given the racist climate in the North, the "lowest requirements of political prudence" ruled out a straightforward provision barring racially discriminatory voting laws anywhere in the land. Idealistic proposals to do that were rejected in Congress, as were the pleas of Susan B. Anthony to delete the word "male" from the voting provision. A devious compromise measure was adopted instead. The states would control the franchise, as was traditional, excluding blacks from the polls if they wished. However, they would lose congressional seats in proportion to the number of persons so excluded. With its large black population, the South could expect its congressional delegation to shrink by at least a third, whereas no northern states had enough black residents to lose any seats at all as a result of racially restrictive policies. Northern Republicans could thereby weaken southern Democrats without incurring the wrath of their constituents who shuddered at the thought of blacks voting in Philadelphia or Chicago. Either the rebel states would be forced to extend the vote to blacks, who would probably vote overwhelmingly Republican, or there would be a good many fewer southern Congressmen in Washington.

The Failure of Compromise

The congressional Reconstruction program of 1866 was less generous with the South than President Johnson would have wished, but its terms—readmission to the Union in exchange for acceptance of the Fourteenth Amendment—were far from harsh. Most members of the pre-Civil War southern political elite—perhaps 25,000 people—were barred from political office. These people could still vote, however, and were eligible for future pardon. (All but 500 were pardoned by 1872.) The elementary human rights denied former slaves by the Black Codes would have to be granted, but the vote could be withheld, although at the cost of losing congressional representation.

Most reassuring of all to southern leaders, there would be no serious attempt to redistribute rebel property to the freedmen. This was partly because the President had quickly crippled the experiments of Grant, Sherman, and the Freedmen's Bureau in settling ex-slaves on the plantations. Within a few months of the war's end, Johnson offered amnesty to the owners of most of these estates and allowed them to reclaim their property. Officials of the Bureau were forced to evict the unbelieving freedmen from the land.

It was Johnson who ordered the Freedman's Bureau to put an end to the land redistribution effort. But the President, of course, had no monopoly of political power. Congress found much of his Reconstruction program wanting when it came back into session. It could have passed legislation mandating a continuation, or even a drastic expansion, of the land distribution experiments, and it did not. The betrayed freedmen petitioned Congress in protest, but only a few isolated legislators on the radical fringe supported them. Thaddeus Stevens, the most dedicated egalitarian in the House, argued the case at every opportunity. Although he favored the granting of full political rights to blacks as well, he had no doubt about what the priorities should be. "In my judgment we shall not approach a measure of justice until we have given every adult freedman a homestead on the land where he was born and toiled and suffered. Forty acres of land and a hut would be more valuable to him than the immediate right to vote." To obtain the necessary land, Stevens proposed to confiscate 400 million acres of land belonging to 70,000 Confederate planters with estates of more than 200 acres. This program would have brought a true social revolution to the South, but such an assault on private property was unthinkable to most Americans of the day.

The Reconstruction effort would probably have ended with the Fourteenth Amendment had the new Johnson-sponsored state governments been wise enough to bend with the wind and accept the bargain as the best they could expect. Encouraged by President Johnson, however, all but Tennessee rejected the amendment. Northern opinion was further outraged by a mounting wave of southern violence against blacks and white sympathizers. In April of 1866, a white mob in Memphis attacked black neighborhoods, killing 47 men, women, and children and burning down four churches and twelve schools. In July, white New Orleans police fired on a convention of black suffrage advocates, killing 48 and wounding 200. Convinced that the organizers of the meeting were part of a radical Republican conspiracy to stir up the "passions and prejudices of the colored population" and stage a *coup d'etat*, Johnson refused to condemn the perpetrators of the New Orleans massacre. The "cause and origin of the blood that was shed," he said, was the actions of "the radical Congress."

CONGRESSIONAL RECONSTRUCTION

The campaign preceding the congressional elections in the fall of 1866 was as vicious as any in American history. Johnson went on an extended speaking tour, denouncing his opponents as "a common gang of cormorants and blood-suckers," and comparing himself to a persecuted Christ. Thaddeus Stevens responded with a quite different biblical metaphor, saying:

> You all remember that in Egypt He sent frogs, locusts, lice, and finally demanded the first-born of every one of the oppressors. Almost all of these have been taken from us. We have been oppressed with taxes and debts, and He has sent us worse than lice, and has afflicted us with an Andrew Johnson.

The election was a referendum on the conflicting reconstruction policies of the President and congressional Republicans, and the verdict was clear cut. A Republican landslide gave them 42 of 53 Senate seats, and a House of Representatives with 143 Republicans to 49 Democrats. With margins of command like that, the President's veto power was an empty threat and the Republicans were free to do what they wished with the South.

That smashing victory marked the beginning of what is usually termed Radical Reconstruction. Radical it was in certain ways—in its assertion of congressional supremacy over the executive, in its determination to transform the political complexion of the rebel states, in its assumption of the superiority of Yankee ways. The "spirit of the North," declared the most influential religious journal of the day, must become "the spirit of the whole country." A popular poem summed it up:

> Make 'em Amerikan, and they'll begin
> To love their country as they loved their sin;
> Let 'em stay Southun, an' you've kep' a sore
> Ready to fester ez it done afore.

But Radical Reconstruction was not very radical in the dictionary sense of the term—"going to the roots or origins"—if one accepts Thaddeus Stevens' view that the root problem was the continued economic dependence of the freedmen on the master class that held the land. The abolition of serfdom by the Russian Czar in 1861 did not give the freed serfs political rights, but it did provide them with some of the land they had worked. The reverse was true in America. At the height of "radical" Reconstruction, equal political rights were granted and enforced by Union soldiers. But after Johnson torpedoed the first land redistribution experiments, nothing further was done to assure the preservation of those political rights once the troops were withdrawn. The dominant view was that all men would be rewarded fairly in the marketplace, and that interference on behalf of particular disadvantaged elements of the population was unnecessary. One of the most powerful Senate Republicans declared that giving land to freedmen was "more than we do for white men," and was unmoved by Charles Sumner's response, "white men have never been in slavery." Once they were granted equal political rights, declared the leading liberal journal, *The Nation*, blacks were "on the dusty and rugged highway of competition," and henceforth "the removal of white prejudice against the Negro would depend almost entirely upon the Negro himself." Any "attempt to justify the confiscation of southern land under the pretence of doing justice to the freedmen," said the *New York Times*, "strikes at the root of all property rights in both sections. It concerns Massachusetts quite as much as Mississippi."

Congress had been able to block Johnson's plan for restoring the Union on easy terms, by failing to seat the representatives the old guard regimes had sent to Washington. But those white supremacist governments were still operating as the supreme authority in their respective states. Had they read the 1866 election returns correctly and promptly ratified the Fourteenth Amendment, they might well have won readmission to the Union without further conditions. But only Tennessee did so. The intransigence of the other ten forced sterner measures— Military Reconstruction. In February of 1867, *The Nation* summarized the political dynamics that caused it:

> Six years ago, the North would have rejoiced to accept any mild restrictions upon the spread of slavery as a final settlement. Four years ago, it would have accepted peace upon the basis of gradual emancipation. Two years ago, it would have been content with emancipation and equal civil rights for the colored people without the extension of suffrage. One year ago, a slight extension of the suffrage would have satisfied it.

The Reconstruction Act of 1867 declared that "no legal State governments or adequate protection for life or property now exists in the rebel States." It divided the South into five military districts, and empowered Union Army officers to supervise the actions of state and local governments, conduct military trials, and remove officeholders for misconduct. Military Reconstruction was not as draconian as is sometimes alleged. There were less than 20,000 federal troops available to supervise a population of more than ten million, and no one proposed expanding the army. But to the intransigent southern whites it was an astonishing and appalling extension of federal power.

The act provided that military rule would end after the states held conventions to prepare new constitutions. Delegates were to be elected by universal suffrage, without racial bars. Former rebels denied political office by the terms of the Fourteenth Amendment could not serve in them, although the amendment itself had not yet been ratified by enough states to make it part of the Constitution. The conventions were to be followed by elections for new state governments. Once their legislatures had approved the Fourteenth Amendment, their representatives would be accepted in Congress.

Johnson raged at Military Reconstruction. It was "an act of military despotism," a "tyranny as this continent has never witnessed." Equal suffrage would give power to a race of men "corrupt in principle and enemies of free institutions." "Of all the dangers which the nation" had yet encountered, "none are equal to those which must result from the success of the effort now making to Africanize the half of our country." Because the military commanders responsible for enforcement were subject to his authority as Commander-in-Chief, he did his best to obstruct the implementation, removing the four of the five he found too vigorous in defending the rights of the freedmen. He could not, however, prevent the holding of conventions and the creation of new governments chosen by universal suffrage, and that soon happened throughout the South.

Impeachment

Johnson's resolute efforts to frustrate congressional Reconstruction made his supporters a dwindling minority on Capitol Hill, and brought him within a hairsbreadth of losing his office through impeachment. The storm that almost drove him from the White House began with his February, 1868 decision to fire Secretary of War Edwin Stanton, the last surviving member of Lincoln's cabinet and a favorite with congressional radicals. This was arguably a violation of the Tenure of Office Act passed by Congress the year before to prevent Johnson from purging the government of Republican civil servants. The act was loosely worded and of questionable constitutionality, and it was unclear that it even applied to Stanton, who had not been appointed by Johnson. But Republican rage at the President had reached such a peak that they were ready to use the pretext that he had violated the law to throw him out. In three days, the House approved an impeachment resolution by a vote of almost three to one.

Johnson's six-week trial before the Senate focused on the issue that resurfaced again more than a century later in the Watergate era—whether the "high crimes and misdemeanours" that the Constitution refers to were to be defined in narrow legal or broad political terms. Can a President be unseated only for a serious criminal offense, or is it sufficient to establish that his actions had been "subversive of some fundamental or essential principle of government or highly prejudicial to the public interest?"

The result of the trial was seemingly a victory for Johnson and the office of the Presidency. In May of 1868, he was acquitted, although the prosecution failed to obtain the two-thirds majority needed for conviction by only one vote. The claim that that single vote "marks the narrow margin by which the Presidential element in our system escaped destruction" seems exaggerated, but a conviction of Johnson would doubtless have diminished the independence of subsequent chief executives.

In an important sense, however, congressional Republicans achieved much of what they had sought. If in the end they had to live with Johnson for the remaining months of his term, they had tamed him. The President had persuaded a group of conservative Republican senators to vote for acquittal by promising that he would refrain from further interference with congressional Reconstruction and would enforce the Reconstruction Acts properly, and he lived up to that promise. Many Americans would later take the decision as a precedent that no President could be impeached unless caught holding "a smoking gun," but the immediate political lesson suggested otherwise. A chief executive who failed to faithfully execute laws approved by a strong majority in both houses of Congress could suffer a punishing political defeat. Johnson hoped to win a second term in the 1868 elections, and angled for the Democratic nomination, but he won only a handful of southern votes at the convention and had to return reluctantly to Tennessee.

The Fifteenth Amendment

In the November, 1868 elections the Republicans retained their lopsided majorities in both houses of Congress, and elected their presidential candidate, General Ulysses S. Grant. With that hurdle cleared, Congress proceeded to pass the last major constitutional change of the period—the Fifteenth Amendment, which provided that the right to vote could not be denied any citizen "on account of race, color, or previous condition of servitude."

This amendment fell considerably short of what the most devoted egalitarians wanted. It did not forbid racial barriers to the holding of political office, only to voting. It did not provide national control of the suffrage and federal protection of voting rights, but only specified something states could not do. Most important, it did not bar a variety of techniques that could be employed to restrict the access of black people to the polls—property requirements, poll taxes, literacy tests and a host of others that were in fact soon to be used successfully for that purpose. Despite these limitations, however, the Fifteenth Amendment was a great step forward: it struck a blow for equality in the North as well as in the South. At the time it was passed, all but seven northern states denied blacks the franchise, and it was courageous of the Republicans to make it a matter of national policy. After strenuous organizational efforts by Republican state machines, the necessary number of states approved the Fifteenth Amendment.

STRUGGLE IN THE SOUTH

Between 1868 and 1870, all of the former rebel states held constitutional conventions and carried out free elections, open for the first time to freedmen. Some 700,000 new black voters were added to the electoral rolls, and 150,000 southern whites were disenfranchised for having held federal or state office before 1861 and having violated their oath to uphold the Constitution of the United States. Everywhere but in Virginia, the new governments were under Republican control. These were the so-called "carpetbagger" regimes of "Black Reconstruction." Both labels are misleading.

"Carpetbagger" was the invidious term applied by southern white conservatives to northerners who migrated south following the war in search of wealth and power, allegedly men with only enough possessions to fit in a carpetbag. In fact, those who came were from no single social group, and many brought with them funds the war-torn southern economy badly needed. The number of Yankee newcomers was vastly exaggerated by political opponents who argued that no southern white could possibly cooperate politically with blacks. The 1870 Census found a total of less than 50,000 northern-born persons living in the ex-Confederate states—a mere .6 percent of the population. And many of them had undoubtedly come before the war. In 1850, almost 85,000 northerners lived in the South, and it is highly unlikely that all of them had died or moved away by 1870. Fewer than 50,000 true carpetbaggers, probably many fewer, resided among the more than eight million people of the region. It is true that newly arrived Yankees assumed posts of political leadership far out of proportion to their numbers. They constituted approximately 60 percent of the Congressmen sent to Washington from the reconstructed states. But the political success of this infinitesimal fraction of the population depended on their ability to persuade others to vote for them.

Many who did, of course, were blacks, who joyfully seized the opportunity to participate in politics despite white efforts to intimidate and coerce them into staying away from the polls. The extent of black political dominance in these years has often been exaggerated. Whites were a majority of the voters in five of the ten elections to select delegates for constitutional conventions in the reconstructed states, and were nowhere outnumbered by much. A majority of delegates elected were white in eight out of the ten contests, and in a ninth—Louisiana—an equal number came from each race. The willingness of blacks to transcend racial loyalties and give their votes to whites they felt they could trust was even more evident in subsequent elections of state and local officials. During the entire era, blacks were in a majority in the legislature of only one state, and then in the lower house alone. No black governors were chosen, and only two senators.

This is not to suggest that able black politicians did not develop. The number and quality of the black leaders who emerged during Reconstruction was impressive, given the lives the vast majority of them had lived as slaves and the prohibitions that the small free black community of the South had to endure. Not surprisingly, few former field hands became politically prominent at the state level. Most of those who rose to prominence were literate, and had been free before the war or had been skilled craftsmen as slaves. At the grassroots level, however—which has been little studied—there is evidence that some ordinary agricultural laborers were quite active in mobilizing their neighborhoods on election day.

Scalawags

Blacks formed only about a third of the southern population, and the number of northern whites who came south during Reconstruction, we have seen, was much too small to make a majority capable of governing. The new Republican governments, it follows, must have had the backing of at least a significant minority of southern whites. The whites who supported the Republicans, at least for a time, were denounced by their opponents as "scalawags," traitors to the cause of white supremacy. They were the critical swing vote, whose eventual disaffection allowed opponents of Reconstruction—the "Redeemers"—to carry the day.

Some of the scalawags were oldtime planters of Whig persuasion, who had been lukewarm about secession and believed that with paternalistic skill they might be able to manipulate the black vote for their own ends. Some were rising businessmen from outside the planter class, who found the business-oriented economic policies of the Republican party attractive. The most important source of scalawag support, however, were the poor whites from marginal farming areas.

Many small farmers living on relatively infertile soil outside the large plantation areas of the Black Belt had long been resentful of planter domination. Although potential class conflict had generally remained submerged in the antebellum South, it had surfaced on the eve of the war, in the crucial elections on the question of secession. Almost three-fourths of the plantation areas voted in favor of withdrawal. In counties with few or no slaves, however, the pattern was reversed: Almost two-thirds of them opposed provoking a war to defend an institution in which they had no stake. Such places—in mountain areas from West Virginia into northern Georgia, Alabama, and Mississippi, in particular—were centers of Unionist disaffection from the Confederacy during the war and of Republican strength after it. Few of the poor whites there relished association with blacks— most had strong prejudices—but significant numbers were willing for a time to join an electoral coalition that included the freedmen, a coalition of the poor against the master class. The scalawags, said one opponent, were "the party paying no taxes, riding poor horses, wearing dirty shirts, and having no use for soap." It was a biased but broadly accurate generalization about the social base of the movement.

Accomplishments of Reconstruction Governments

The reconstructed governments were relatively short-lived. The most enduring, in Florida, Louisiana, and South Carolina, fell in less than a decade. Most survived hardly half that time before being overturned by white "Redeemers." In that brief time, the governments accomplished a good deal. The new constitutions they drew up were considerably more democratic than the ones they replaced. They reduced the number of crimes punishable by death, enlarged the rights of women, and established fairer apportionments of seats in the legislature.

Opponents of reconstruction regimes denounced them for profligate spending and rampant corruption. Corruption there was, although not notably more than in other states or after "Redemption." State debts increased sharply, but largely to finance the physical redevelopment of a war-torn region and to develop what the South had always lacked—a public school system. In the old South, slaves received no schooling and ordinary white children precious little. The reconstructed governments, assisted by a flood of volunteer Yankee school mistresses who came south to enlist in the crusade, made valiant efforts to develop a comprehensive common school system. (It was racially segregated everywhere but in New Or-

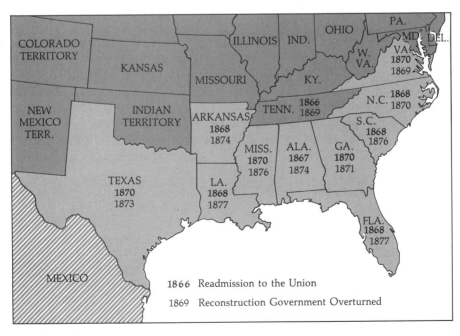

MAP 16-1
The Reconstruction Governments

leans.) In South Carolina in 1868 only 12 percent of school-age white children and 8 percent of the blacks were enrolled. By 1875 the figures had risen to 50 percent for whites and 41 percent for blacks. In Florida the number of pupils in public schools tripled between 1869 and 1873. At the close of Reconstruction, the southern educational system still lagged far behind that of the rest of the nation, but a giant stride forward had been taken.

In a variety of other ways the Republican governments acted to protect the interests of those who were less well-to-do, white as well as black. They put an end to debt imprisonment, and repealed laws favoring landlords over tenants. They reduced high poll taxes and increased levies on landed property. They provided salaries for public officials, so that someone other than a wealthy planter could afford to serve.

Collapse

The radical phase of Reconstruction lasted only an average of four and a half years; by November of 1876, only three southern states were still under Republican rule, and those fell within the next few months as the last federal troops were withdrawn. The Redeemers employed two strategies to topple them. They whipped up racial fears to win back the scalawag vote, persuading many that having a government in all white hands was more important than having a government responsive to the needs of the masses of common people. At the same time, they discouraged blacks from turning out to vote, by measures ranging from economic coercion and social ostracism to whipping, torture, and murder.

Throughout the South, the Ku Klux Klan, militia organizations with names like the White League and the Red Shirts, and local "rifle clubs" murdered blacks on the road on election day. On the eve of the elections that redeemed Mississippi in 1875, the Democratic press adopted the forthright slogan: "Carry the election peaceably if we can, forcibly if we must." Accurate statistics are not available, but the number of blacks murdered in that campaign in one state almost certainly numbered in the hundreds. Six heavily black Mississippi counties that produced more than 14,000 Republican votes in 1873 returned a mere 723 in 1876. The lesson of the "Mississippi Plan" was not lost on white conservatives in other unredeemed states; similar savagery produced equally devastating results.

The first instances of large-scale antiblack violence brought forceful federal action. Congress passed a series of measures that provided machinery to enforce the Fourteenth and Fifteenth Amendments. In October of 1871, President Grant proclaimed that nine South Carolina counties in the grip of KKK violence were in a state of rebellion again, and put them under martial law. After that, however, the North's determination to uphold the civil liberties of Republican voters in the South flagged. In 1872, Congress declared a general amnesty for ex-Confederates, allowing them to re-enter public life. The federal courts that were supposed to bring terrorists to justice were pathetically understaffed, and Congress refused to appropriate funds to expand them. A Democrat committed to ending all federal intervention in the South nearly won the Presidency in 1872, and in 1874 the House of Representatives fell to the Democrats. "The whole public," said President Grant, "is tired of these outbreaks in the South." Radical leaders like Stevens and Sumner died or retired from politics, to be replaced by younger men more concerned with issues of economic policy than with events south of the Mason–Dixon line. The final surrender came after the 1876 elections, the outcome of which hinged on the returns from the last three unredeemed states—Louisiana, Florida, and South Carolina. A congressional commission awarded the electoral votes of those states to the Republican Rutherford B. Hayes, in exchange for his pledge that he would withdraw all federal troops from the South, appoint a southern white to his cabinet, and support the construction of a southern transcontinental railroad.

The Rise of Sharecropping

While blacks were being forced out of politics, they were also falling into a new form of economic dependency—the sharecropping system. The failure to give land to the freedmen meant that they would be forced to work for those who did own it—by and large, the old planter group. The common impression that the Civil War meant the death of the planter class is quite false. Although they lost the ownership of their slaves, they usually held onto their land, and not infrequently expanded their holdings. The richest 10 percent of landowners in one Alabama cotton county in 1860 owned 55 percent of the landed wealth; by 1870 the figure was up to 63 percent. Without the capital to establish farms of their own, former slaves had to turn to the master class for employment.

They were, however, able to resist the planters' efforts to recreate the plantation system. Despite the spur of the Black Codes (until those were repealed by the reconstructed governments) and pressure from Freedmen's Bureau officials, most freedmen flatly refused to work in the fields in gangs under the supervision of an overseer. Even though some planters offered high wages for gang labor, they found few takers—it was too reminiscent of slavery. Blacks would work only if granted a degree of independence and autonomy. The sharecropping system that developed was, as an Alabama paper put it, "an unwilling concession" to the freedman's desire to be a proprietor. The essence of the concession was to decentralize the plantation, dividing it into many separate small plots farmed by individual black families. A striking symbol of their hunger to be free of supervision was the way that freedmen sometimes hitched a team of mules to their old slave cabins and dragged them off to the acres assigned them. They would live out of sight of "the big house," and would refuse to let their wives and young children toil in the fields.

Although these were great gains from the freedmen's point of view, their independence was sorely limited in one critical respect: They were not ordinary renters who could grow whatever crop they pleased and had a prospect of substantial profits if the harvest was good and crop prices high. Slavery had left them no capital, and they needed credit—funds for tools, seed, farm animals, and food until harvest time. Under the sharecropping system, these were supplied by the landlord (or sometimes a country merchant) who determined what was to be grown, and took half of the crop at harvest time as his share in return for having

A TYPICAL SHARECROPPING AGREEMENT, 1886

This contract made and entered into between A.T. Mial of one part and Fenner Powell of the other part both of the County of Wake and State of North Carolina—

Witnesseth—That the Said Fenner Powell hath barganed and agreed with the Said Mial to work as a cropper for the year 1886 on Said Mial's land on the land now occupied by Said Powell on the west Side of Poplar Creek and a point on the east Side of Said Creek and both South and North of the Mial road, leading to Raleigh, That the Said Fenner Powell agrees to work faithfully and dilligently without any unnecessary loss of time, to do all manner of work on said farm as may be directed by Said Mial, And to be respectful in manners and deportment to Said Mial. And the Said Mial agrees on his part to furnish mule and feed for the same and all plantation tools and Seed to plant the crop free of charge, and to give the Said Powell One half of all crops raised and housed by Said Powell on Said land except the cotton seed. The Said Mial agrees to advance as provisions to Said Powell fifty pound of bacon and two sacks of meal pr month and occationally Some flour to be paid out of his the Said Powell's part of the crop or from any other advance that may be made to Said Powell by Said Mial. As witness our hands and seals this the 16th day of January A.D. 1886.

Witness   A.T. Mial (*signed*) (Seal)

W.S. Mial (*signed*)   Fenner (*his mark*) Powell (Seal)

supplied the land, a cabin, tools, and seed. In fact, he often took the other half of the crop as well for having provided the food and clothing needed by the cropper's family. The tenant had to accept a "crop lien" agreement that gave landlords and merchants first claim on the crop. Once the Redeemers came to power, they repealed Republican legislation that protected debtors, and passed new laws slanted to favor creditors. Towering interest rates, higher prices for goods bought on credit (the "two-price system"), and sometimes outright cheating that could not be detected by an illiterate customer usually produced debts that matched or exceeded the income from the sale of the tenant's share of the crop. Moving away to escape the unpaid debt was fruitless, for other landlords would not enter into a sharecropping arrangement with a new tenant without checking with the previous landlord.

Only an extraordinarily diligent minority of blacks could save enough under this system to purchase land of their own. In Georgia in 1880, for example, the black half of the population owned less then 2 percent of the taxed land. The

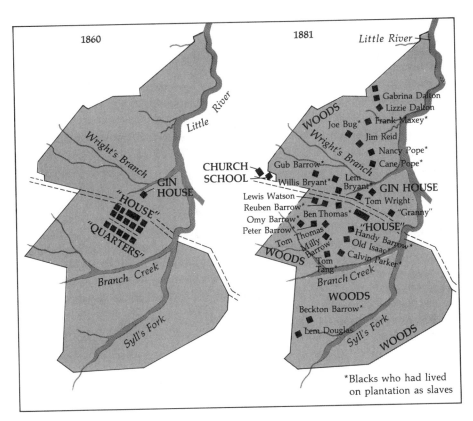

MAP 16–2
A Georgia Plantation, 1860 and 1881

overwhelming majority of blacks were chained in poverty. Some economic historians argue that 15 years after the war the average sharecropper had a *lower* standard of living than the average slave in the 1850s. A more sanguine analysis estimates that freedom gave blacks 29 percent more income, for considerably less arduous labor. Even in the most optimistic appraisal, the economic results of emancipation in the United States were deeply flawed. It left blacks the most impoverished element of the population in by far the most impoverished region of the country.

The Effects of Reconstruction

Reconstruction left its mark upon America. The Thirteenth, Fourteenth, and Fifteenth Amendments, which were in effect the final terms of peace between North and South, were the only major alterations in the U.S. Constitution during the entire century. The thrust toward equal rights they represented was soon blunted by judicial interpretation in an altered political climate, but they remained on the books and in the following century would become powerful levers for social change. The freedmen, although finally stripped of many of the rights they enjoyed temporarily and reduced to a condition of semiservitude in communities devoted to white supremacy, had tasted freedom and had gained confidence in their ability to govern themselves if given the chance. The schools established by the reconstruction regimes survived, although expenditures—particularly for black schools—were sharply cut by the Redeemers when they seized power. In 1879, one southern state spent $1.60 per pupil on white schools and only $.52 per black student. The tide of change, however, was not reversed entirely. At the time of emancipation, hardly 1 black in 20 could read and write; by 1890 it was 9 in 20, by 1910 almost 14 in 20.

The Reconstruction experiment might have effected still more far-reaching and enduring changes in American life. Three fundamental circumstances, however, set the limits beyond which experimentation could not go. First, too few Americans understood the sociology of freedom well enough to grasp that regimes whose continued existence depended so heavily on the votes of a propertyless black proletariat could not long survive without external support. Americans' faith in the fairness of the race along the "dusty and rugged highway of competition," and a general blindness to the realities of economic coercion led them to reject any scheme that would alter existing property relations on behalf of the freedmen. The effort to make dramatic changes of a purely political character was bound to fail.

Second, the dominant American suspicion of strong central government and attachment to the federal system made it necessary to conceive of Reconstruction as a temporary emergency effort. To engineer a deeper change in southern society would have required strong external pressure for decades rather than years. A few radicals called for a long-term occupation of the South on those grounds, but to most that seemed vindictive and unconstitutional.

Finally, the depth of racial prejudice in the North limited the moral energy that might have gone into the struggle for black rights, and gave southern whites reason to denounce northern hypocrisy. To appease fears that fleeing slaves would flock into the North during the war, the Union army had carried out a "containment policy" to keep them in the South. The same determination to discourage large-scale northward migration of southern blacks manifested itself at many points during Reconstruction. After one Congressman suggested placing freedmen in jobs in northern industrial areas, even Charles Sumner of Massachusetts, the most liberal state in the Union on racial matters, denounced the scheme as "utterly untenable." When another key northern senator assured his nervous constituents that the objective of Reconstruction was to give freedmen "liberty and rights" in the South so that "they will stay there and never come into a cold climate to die," solicitude for the health of potential black migrants was not his primary motive. It would be cynical but not altogether inaccurate to say that Reconstruction was the North's attempt to keep southern blacks where they were by pressuring southern whites to treat them more decently than the relatively few blacks of the North were treated. The racism that underlay the thinking of most northerners surfaced more and more as the reconstructed regimes began to founder. Instead of blaming their collapse on the violence of the Redeemer crusade, the feebleness of preventive federal intervention, or the inability of landless blacks to resist economic coercion, northerners advanced a quite different explanation, that conveniently exempted the nation from further responsibility. A New York Republican newspaper, once in the vanguard of the struggle, announced in 1877 that blacks "had been given ample opportunity to develop their own latent capacities," and had succeeded only in proving that "as a race they are idle, ignorant and vicious." This was the self-serving lesson the masses of white Americans, North and South, seemed to have learned from the Reconstruction experiment.

SUGGESTED READINGS

For compact overviews, see John Hope Franklin, *Reconstruction After the Civil War* (1961), Kenneth M. Stampp, *The Era of Reconstruction* (1965), and Rembert Patrick, *The Reconstruction of the Nation* (1967). On the political struggles within the North over Reconstruction policies, LaWanda and John Cox, *Politics, Principles, and Prejudice, 1865–1866* (1963), W.R. Brock, *An American Crisis: Congress and Reconstruction, 1865–1867* (1963), Eric L. McKitrick, *Andrew Johnson and Reconstruction* (1960), David Donald, *The Politics of Reconstruction* (1965); Michael Les Benedict, *A Compromise of Principle: Congressional Republicans and Reconstruction, 1863–1869* (1974), and Martin Mantell, *Johnson, Grant and the Politics of Reconstruction* (1973) present contrasting views. Michael Benedict, *The Impeachment and Trial of Andrew Johnson* (1973) and Hans L. Trefousse, *The Impeachment of a President* (1975) are stimulating recent treatments. Constitutional issues are skillfully dissected in Stanley Kutler, *Judicial Power and Reconstruction Politics* (1968) and Harold Hyman, *A More Perfect Union* (1973). Michael Perman, *Revolution without Compromise: The South and Reconstruction, 1865–68* focuses on Southern white resistance to change.

The fullest and richest account of the economic situation of blacks in the South is Roger L. Ransom and Richard Sutch, *One Kind of Freedom: The Economic Consequences of Emancipation* (1978). A more optimistic economic analysis is offered in Robert Higgs, *Competition and Coercion: Blacks in the American Economy, 1865–1914* (1977). Further insight into the social and economic adjustment of blacks may be gained from Willie Lee Rose, *Rehearsal for Reconstruction* (1964), William S. McFeely, *Yankee Stepfather: General O. O. Howard and the Freedmen* (1968), Peter Kolchin, *First Freedom* (1972), Louis S. Gerteis, *From Contraband to Freedman* (1973), and Edward Magdol, *A Right to the Land* (1977). Jonathan M. Weiner, *Social Origins of the New South: Alabama, 1860–1885* (1978) reveals the staying power of the planter class. Thomas Holt, *Black Over White* (1978) is an excellent study of South Carolina. Albion W. Tourgee, *A Fool's Errand* (1879) is an illuminating novel by a carpet-bagger who served as a judge in the Reconstruction government in North Carolina.

The campaign of violence that helped to bring the Reconstruction governments down is analyzed in Allen W. Trelease, *White Terror* (1971). The political bargaining that led to final withdrawal of federal troops is exposed in C. Vann Woodward, *Reunion and Reaction* (1956).

Index

U.S. Naval War College, 501
United States Steel Co., 401, 526, 654
U.S. vs. Darby, 627
U.S.S.R., *see* Russia
Universal Negro Improvement Association, 607
University Settlement, 514
Utah, 309, 314, 441
Utica, NY, 217

Van Buren, Martin, 286, 308
Vandenburg, Arthur, 678, 700
Vanderbilt, Cornelius, 402
Van Rensselaer family, 160
Vanzetti, Bartolomeo, 554–55
Vardaman, James K., 597
Vassar College, 588, 614
Veblen, Thorstein, 445
Venezeula, 503, 531
Venice, 5
Vermont, 93, 167, 270, 276, 654
Versailles Treaty, 552–54, 639, 668
Vesey, Denmark, 245, 291
Veteran's Administration, 703
Vice-admirality courts, 130, 132
Vicksburg, Battle of, 343, 348, 362
Vietcong, *see* National Liberation Front
Vietnam War, 153, 334, 712–13, 725–27, 731–36, 738–40
Villard, Oswald Garrison, 598
Vincennes, IN, 202
Virgin Islands, 501, 540
Virginia, in Antebellum period, 183, 191, 193, 245, 248, 252, 281, 325–26; since the Civil War, 335, 337, 371, 497; as a colony, 16–35, 43, 50–51, 53, 66–69, 79, 86–87, 91–95, 98–99, 108, 112–13, 117–18, 121; in Revolutionary era, 131, 140, 152, 159–60, 162, 165–66, 174–75
Virginia Company, 18, 20, 23, 26–28, 30, 43, 45, 114
Virginia Resolutions, 190, 290
Volcker, Paul, 747
Voting Rights Act, 730, 756, 759

Wade, Benjamin, 337
Wade–Davis Bill, 352
Wagner Act, *see* National Labor Relations Act
Walker, Francis A., 418
Wallace, George, 736
Walloons, 82
Waltham, MA, 209, 211, 216
War Industries Board, 549
War Labor Board, 549
War of 1812, 182, 197–202, 211, 252, 278, 282, 311
War on Poverty, 730–31

Warren, Earl, 690, 714
Washington, 304, 441, 626
Washington Booker T., 595–98, 607
Washington, D.C., 183, 199, 261, 336–37, 340, 355, 451, 584, 639
Washington, George, 94; administration of, 180–88; criticisms of Articles, 171, 175; as military leader, 143, 150–54; on slavery, 77, 161–62
Washington Naval Conference, 666–67
Watergate, 369, 738–39, 741–42
Waters, Ethel, 607
Watertown, MA, 49
Watson, Tom, 457
Watts Riot, 734
Wealth Against Commonwealth, 400
Wealth Tax Act, 650
Weaver, James B., 490
Webster, Daniel, 286, 309, 312
Webster, Noah, 221
Weems, Parson, 228
Weld, Theodore Dwight, 297, 299
Wellesley College, 614
Wells, David A., 385
Welsh, 84, 216, 476
Westchester County, NY, 118
Westerly, RI, 141
Western Union, 391
West Indies, 53, 67, 69–71, 75–76, 78, 84, 110, 112, 130, 154, 157, 168, 187, 296, 607
Westinghouse, George, 566
Westminster, 123
West Roxbury, MA, 425
West Virginia, 325, 372, 456, 584
Weyler, General, 504
Whig Party, 276, 280, 286–89, 294, 305, 308, 310–17, 372, 485
Whiskey Rebellion, 184, 191
White, E.B., 588
White, William Allen, 524
Whitefield, George, 101–102
White League, 374
Whiteman, Paul, 607
White Plains, NY, 153
Whitestown, NY, 217
Whitman, Walt, 348, 399
Whitney, Eli, 209, 210, 217, 233, 234
Why Is There No Socialism in America?, 473
Wilkie, Wendell, 678–79
Willard, Francis, 624
William and Mary College, 47
William of Orange, King of England, 115
Williams, Keith Shaw, 151
Williams, Roger, 54–55, 98, 100
Wills, Gary, 722
Wilmot Proviso, 308, 310
Wilson, Charles E., 713
Wilson, Woodrow, 180, 512, 529; domestic policies of, 534–38, 548–51, 557–58, 624; foreign policies of, 540–48, 551–54

B 4
C 5
D 6
E 7
F 8
G 9
H 0
I 1
J 2